T0210955

Communications in Computer and Information Science 1072

Commenced Publication in 2007
Founding and Former Series Editors:
Phoebe Chen, Alfredo Cuzzocrea, Xiaoyong Du, Orhun Kara, Ting Liu,
Krishna M. Sivalingam, Dominik Ślęzak, Takashi Washio, Xiaokang Yang,
and Junsong Yuan

More information about this series at http://www.springer.com/series/7899

An Zeng · Dan Pan · Tianyong Hao ·
Daoqiang Zhang · Yiyu Shi ·
Xiaowei Song (Eds.)

Human Brain and Artificial Intelligence

First International Workshop, HBAI 2019
Held in Conjunction with IJCAI 2019
Macao, China, August 12, 2019
Revised Selected Papers

 Springer

Editors
An Zeng
Guangdong University of Technology
Guangzhou, China

Tianyong Hao
South China Normal University
Guangzhou, China

Yiyu Shi
University of Notre Dame
South Bend, IN, USA

Dan Pan
Guangdong Construction Polytechnic
Guangzhou, China

Daoqiang Zhang
Nanjing University of Aeronautics
and Astronautics
Nanjing, China

Xiaowei Song
Simon Fraser University
Vancouver, BC, Canada

ISSN 1865-0929 ISSN 1865-0937 (electronic)
Communications in Computer and Information Science
ISBN 978-981-15-1397-8 ISBN 978-981-15-1398-5 (eBook)
https://doi.org/10.1007/978-981-15-1398-5

This Springer imprint is published by the registered company Springer Nature Singapore Pte Ltd.
The registered company address is: 152 Beach Road, #21-01/04 Gateway East, Singapore 189721, Singapore

Preface

Human brain research and artificial intelligence (AI) are two everlasting and interrelated hot topics.

The aim of human brain research is to achieve a comprehensive basic understanding in the field of human brain function that serves as a foundation for future translational research and the development of effective therapies for various neurological diseases, while at the same time leading to insights in the information processing function of the brain, which could be utilized in new methods and technologies for information processing and even a paradigm change in brain-inspired AI. AI aims to aid as a supplement to human intelligence and help resolve the rapid increase and complexity of challenges human beings are facing.

Human brain research provides opportunities for developing novel AI methods. Some of the grand challenges in human brain research include global mental health and neuroscience, brain wellness and aging, cognitive development, brain energetics in health and diseases, neuroimaging, models of disorders, as well as applications in neuroinformatics, brain computer/machine interfaces, etc. But, more specifically, how can human brain research raise new fundamental questions or insights in AI?

AI holds a tremendous repertoire of algorithms and methods that constitute the core of different topics of computational brain science. AI approaches can revolutionize the new age of brain informatics and computational brain science with discoveries in human brain-related health, diseases, social behavior, neuroscience, brain connectivity, brain intelligence paradigms, cognitive information, etc. However, in detail, how can AI techniques contribute to human brain research, and in particular address the cognitive, physiological, biological, physical, ecological, and social perspectives of brain research?

The aim of HBAI is to bring together active researchers and practitioners at the frontier of AI and human brain research for presentation of original research results, as well as for the exchange and dissemination of innovative and practical development experiences on computational brain science, brain-inspired AI, and their applications. This workshop is very meaningful and helpful for the developments of AI and human brain research.

Held in conjunction with the 28th International Joint Conference on Artificial Intelligence (IJCAI 2019), the First International Workshop on Human Brain and Artificial Intelligence (IJCAI-HBAI 2019) took place in Macao, China, on August 12, 2019. More than 60 authors and attendees came from all over the world. This workshop has been proactive in coming to grips with important changes taking place with in the intersectional domain between AI and brain science.

The IJCAI-HBAI 2019 workshop solicited high-quality papers from North America, Europe, Asia, and Africa. There was also a great keynote talk given by Pheng Ann Heng from the Chinese University of Hong Kong, Hong Kong, China. The main scientific program of the workshop comprised 24 papers selected out of 62 reviewed submissions, and the papers were assessed based on originality, significance, technical merit, and clarity of the presentation in a single-blind review process, which corresponds to an acceptance rate of 38.7%. Three to five reviewers were assigned to a paper to ensure the quality of the proceedings. The proceedings were published by Springer in the *Communications in Computer and Information Science* (CCIS) series, as volume 1072.

As workshop chairs, we would like to express our gratitude to everybody who was involved in the organization of IJCAI-HBAI 2019. Even though this was the first edition of the IJCAI-HBAI workshop, IJCAI-HBAI 2019 had an exciting program with a number of features, ranging from a keynote talk to technical sessions. This would not have been possible without the generous dedication and engagement of the Program Committee members and additional reviewers in reviewing the workshop submissions, of our keynote and oral speakers in giving outstanding talks at the conference, and of organizers, volunteers, and audience members in their hard work and/or active participation. IJCAI-HBAI 2019 could not have taken place without the day-to-day operation and execution from the Workshop Program Committee and Local Arrangements Committee of IJCAI 2019 and generous help from sponsors. We would especially like to express our sincere appreciation to our kind sponsors, including IJCAI organization (https://www.ijcai.org), Springer Nature (https://www.springernature.com), Springer CCIS (https://www.springer.com/series/7899), Guangdong University of Technology (http://www.gdut.edu.cn), and Guangdong Society of Biomedical Engineering, the Branch of Medical Robotics and Artificial Intelligence (http://m-edrai.org/).

Special thanks go to Guobin Chen, Yin Huang, and Zheng Gao for their great assistance and support with the workshop's official website (http://www.ijcai-hbai.org) and the EasyChair submission system. We are grateful to Springer CCIS for their trust and for publishing the proceedings of IJCAI-HBAI 2019. We thank Springer, especially Anil Chandy, Celine Lanlan Chang, and Nick Wei Zhu, for their help in coordinating the publication of this special volume in an emerging and interdisciplinary research field.

August 2019   An Zeng
Dan Pan
Tianyong Hao
Daoqiang Zhang
Yiyu Shi
Xiaowei Song

Organization

General Chairs

An Zeng   Guangdong University of Technology, China
Dan Pan   Guangdong Construction Polytechnic, China
Tianyong Hao   South China Normal University, China
Daoqiang Zhang   Nanjing University of Aeronautics and Astronautics, China
Yiyu Shi   University of Norte Dame, USA
Xiaowei Song   Simon Fraser University, Canada

Program Committee

Dejing Dou   University of Oregon, USA
Tianyong Hao   South China Normal University, China
Bing Li   Technical university of Munich, Germany
Wenyin Liu   Guangdong University of Technology, China
Zhi Lu   A*Star, Singapore
Dong Ni   Shenzhen University, China
Dan Pan   Guangdong Construction Polytechnic, China
Xiang Ren   University of Southern California, USA
Yiyu Shi   University of Norte Dame, USA
Xiaowei Song   Simon Fraser University, Canada
Jiantao Sun   Microsoft, USA
Yizhou Sun   University of California, Los Angeles, USA
Hao Wang   Norwegian University of Science and Technology, Norway
Jinhui Wang   South China Normal University, China
Shan Wang   University of Macau, Macau, China
Yalin Wang   Arizona State University, USA
Haoran Xie   The Education University of Hong Kong, Hong Kong, China
Jun Yan   Yidu Cloud Technology Inc., China
Rongqian Yang   South China University of Technology, China
Guoxian Yu   Southwest University, China
An Zeng   Guangdong University of Technology, China
Daoqiang Zhang   Nanjing University of Aeronautics and Astronautics, China
Yong Zhang   Weber State University, USA
Yuanting Zhang   City University of Hong Kong, Hong Kong, China
Xingming Zhao   Fudan University, China

Additional Reviewers

Ruichu Cai
Bing Li
Fuchun Liu
Qianli Ma
Wei Yang
Zhengguo Yang
Weiwen Zhang

Contents

Brain-Inspired Artificial Intelligence and Its Applications

Computational Brain Science and Its Applications

EEGNAS: Neural Architecture Search for Electroencephalography Data Analysis and Decoding

Elad Rapaport[1(✉)], Oren Shriki[2], and Rami Puzis[1]

[1] Software and Information Systems Engineering,
Ben-Gurion University of the Negev, Beersheba, Israel
eladr@post.bgu.ac.il
[2] Cognitive and Brain Sciences, Ben-Gurion University of the Negev,
Beersheba, Israel

Abstract. EEG, Electroencephalography, is the acquisition and decoding of electric brain signals. The data acquired from EEG scans can be put to use in many fields, including seizure prediction, treatment of mental illness, brain-computer interfaces (BCIs) and more. Recent advances in deep learning (DL) in fields of image classification and natural language processing have motivated researchers to apply DL for classification of EEG signals as well. One major caveat in DL is the amount of human effort and expertise required for the development of efficient and effective neural network architectures. Neural architecture search algorithms are used to automatically find *good enough* neural network architectures for a problem and dataset at hand. In this research, we employ genetic algorithms for optimizing neural network architectures for multiple tasks related to EEG processing while addressing two unique challenges related to EEG: (1) small amounts of labeled EEG data per subject, and (2) high diversity of EEG signal patterns across subjects. Neural network architectures produced during this study successfully compete with state of the art architectures published in the literature. Particularly successful are architectures optimized for all (human) subjects, with evolution and training performed on a mixed dataset including all subjects' data.

Keywords: Neural architecture search · EEG · Time series

1 Introduction

Brain research is a highly developing field in recent years. New technologies allow the acquisition of high-dimensional brain activity and consequently, novel data science techniques are required for the analysis and manipulation of these complex datasets. EEG is a method for monitoring electrical activity in the brain by placing electrodes on the scalp and measuring the electrical current. By use of machine learning, we can interpret these signals in various forms.

© Springer Nature Singapore Pte Ltd. 2019
A. Zeng et al. (Eds.): HBAI 2019, CCIS 1072, pp. 3–20, 2019.
https://doi.org/10.1007/978-981-15-1398-5_1

EEG has many practical uses today including epileptic seizure prediction [16], improving cognitive performance [31], the ability to control a computer interface via imagined movement [21], and measuring cognitive load [2]. Compared to other brain imaging techniques, EEG recording is fairly cheap, which makes it popular and relevant for these tasks.

Following the surge in DL research in areas such as image processing and text analysis, DL EEG methods are becoming popular as well [25,28]. Particularly, several studies have been conducted on the effectiveness of convolutional neural networks (CNNs) for EEG signal classification and decoding. Development of efficient and effective DL architectures requires a significant amount of human effort and appropriate expertise both in DL and in the subject domain (EEG in our case). Automated neural architecture search (NAS) alleviates this, sometimes hard to get, requirement and eases the development of good enough neural network models for a given problem and dataset. NAS has been proven to yield competitive results in various studies, focusing mainly on image and text processing [14,23]. However, to the best of our knowledge, the advances of NAS have not yet been utilized in the field of EEG processing.

Analysis of EEG signals is especially challenging because: (1) It contains high levels of noise and many "artifacts" such as distortions caused by eye blinks, muscle movement, heartbeats, sweat and more [3]. (2) EEG data is very subject dependent. EEG data of two subjects performing the same activity can be inherently different. In this study, we implement and customize NAS, in a way that will enable reaching EEG classification models that are robust to noise, while utilizing cross-subject data to maximize performance.

We employ genetic algorithms (GAs) as the means for NAS. GAs are randomized heuristic search algorithms designed for nondifferentiable optimization problems. They are inspired by the natural breeding and selection process [26]. Our first contribution is the proposed NAS algorithm, which generates CNN architectures from scratch and can reach state of the art performance in various EEG classification tasks. This will make DL more accessible to EEG researchers and practitioners that do not possess the required DL expertise, and maybe even lead to better performing neural network (NN) architectures that have not been explored by EEG researchers to date.

Our second contribution is the analysis of the evolution of NN architectures over time, which helps better understand the NAS process. Our main insights from this analysis are:

– Generalization ability in EEG classification is key to good architectures. Combining several human subjects' data in one experiment yields better results than experiments conducted on each subject in isolation, despite the high variability of EEG data between subjects.
– Reusing trained weights between generations of the genetic NAS algorithm is helpful for training and yields better performing architectures.
– Analysis of the distribution of layer types during the evolution of NN architectures suggests the algorithm's tendency toward more complex architectures with a high affinity toward convolutional and pooling layers.

2   Related Work

2.1   Deep Learning EEG Classification Methods

DL, and particularly CNNs have been getting much attention in the past few years and brought notable success to fields such as computer vision [8], natural language processing [15] and time series forecasting [9]. EEG data are not the "classic" input for CNNs. This is because they are unique for every human subject and are not easy to attain. The result is small, high noise datasets which prove a challenge for DL models. Despite this, recent advances in DL, after tweaking and optimization, have been useful for EEG decoding, bringing DL to the forefront of EEG research [10,25,27]. Several architecture types have been used for EEG classification including CNNs and recurrent neural networks (RNNs), while CNNs are most widely used.

Motor imagery (MI) is the controlling of a computer interface via imagined movement. Schirrmeister et al. tested several design and training choices for CNNs across different MI datasets against traditional methods [25]. They developed several CNNs for EEG classification while incorporating recent advancements in DL. A cropping training strategy was used by creating overlapping time windows from EEG recordings, which resulted in a multiplicative increase in available data. EEGNet [10] is a group of CNN architectures, developed for performing classification on different EEG datasets. A key feature in these architectures is depthwise separable convolutions, that minimize parameter usage by learning separate convolution kernels for each channel in the previous layer.

Oh et al. [19] utilized CNN for the automated detection of Parkinson's disease from EEG signal data. The use of a 13-layer CNN allowed the use of minimal pre-processing of the data (epoching and bandpass filtering), while reducing the need for traditional EEG feature extraction techniques.

An additional recent study was performed by Chambon et al., using CNNs, to classify patients' sleep stages using EEG recordings [5]. A multimodal architecture was created for the simultaneous processing of EEG, EOG and EMG data. The temporal context was utilized via the aggregation of adjacent sequences in time, for better classification of the sleep stages.

A common property of the CNN architecture designs in the aforementioned studies is a spatial filtering convolutional layer, which detects prominent features by combining the data from different electrodes. This procedure mimics the spatial feature extracting methods used in traditional EEG analysis methods, such as Common Spatial Filtering [1]. Most CNN EEG methods operate on almost raw EEG data (with minimal pre-processing, such as bandpass filtering), while feature extraction and selection methods are learned by the network.

Although the CNN architectures above are effective on various training data, they are hard-coded and this required much human effort of parameter tuning. Additionally, We hypothesize that a specific CNN architecture might not deliver sufficient performance for all EEG classification tasks. For this we create a CNN architecture search procedure yielding task-specific architectures, with less human effort involved. To test the robustness of the architectures mentioned above we compare their performance on several datasets against the CNN architectures derived from our NAS algorithm.

Volker et al. studied CNN architecture robustness by successfully applying transfer learning for EEG data across trials in the same (human) subject, across subjects and across experimental paradigms [28]. In our study, we make use of cross-subject data by feeding data from multiple subjects into a genetic algorithm to find a CNN architecture with maximum average classification performance for all human subjects.

RNNs have been utilized in several studies to classify and analyze EEG data. Subhrajit et al. created a RNN architecture to classify abnormal EEG recordings, based on the TUH Abnormal EEG Corpus [12], while setting new benchmarks for accuracy and showing applicability on a non-EEG time series dataset as well. Despite this, we focus on CNN-based classification and analysis for their relative power which has been proved, and for simplicity's sake.

2.2 Evolutionary NAS Algorithms

The use of evolutionary algorithms for optimizing neural networks is known as Neuro-Evolution (NE). In traditional NE approaches [17,30], only the weight space of a single network topology was searched to find optimal weight values. In later approaches, evolution was applied to the network topology search as well.

Real et al. developed an evolutionary algorithm using mutation operators to evolve NN architectures in a fairly unrestricted search space [23]. This method is able to find competitive NN architectures for the CIFAR-10 and CIFAR-100 [7] image classification datasets, though this comes at a vast computational cost. At each training stage, two models are compared, the worse model is killed and the better model is copied. The copy is then mutated with a random operation, and put back in the model pool. This algorithm is highly distributable across several machines. Mostly mutation was used to generate new models in this genetic algorithm, and not crossover (the recombination of two models into one). As opposed to the above method, our algorithm initializes a population of random architectures and not necessarily simple ones. Moreover, we utilize crossover as an inherent part of our GA.

In a follow-up study by Real et al., the best performing architecture from a random sample in each training step was mutated to generate an offspring, and the oldest model (instead of the worst-performing one) was killed [22]. This yielded a broader search, by avoiding local optima caused by relatively good models at the beginning of the search. To reduce the computational complexity of the previous method, the search space was reduced to the optimization of cell structures instead of full NN architectures, which are combined in a predefined manner to produce the final architecture.

Miikkulainen et al. introduced large scale use of the combination of two models by crossover in a method called DeepNEAT [14]. During evolution, historical markings were used to determine how every pair of networks can be aligned and combined. Additionally, They expanded the feasible search space in a method called CoDeepNEAT. In this method, two populations were evolved separately, a population of modules and a population of blueprints, and a final NN architecture was constructed by combining modules using the blueprint specification. Our method relates to DeepNEAT, in that it utilizes crossover to combine two unrelated architectures, but as opposed to DeepNEAT, offsprings are generated by aligning two networks in a predefined manner and recombining randomly.

3   Methods

We employ a GA to evolve a population of CNN architectures. This method was chosen over newer evolutionary algorithms such as particle swarm optimization [29], where multiple agents are used to explore the search space of CNN architectures, or for its simplicity and robustness. As opposed to other methods, with a GA there is no need for a CNN encoding method that allows computation of the distance between different architectures and a direct encoding can be used.

The input to each neural networks is one-dimensional EEG data samples with multiple channels corresponding to the readings of the EEG electrodes. Algorithm 1 summarizes the general approach we employ for searching through the space of CNN architectures. Below we define the basic building blocks of the GA with EEGNAS.

- **Population** - Defines the group of current candidate CNN architectures. This group's size stays constant over the algorithm's generations. The population is instantiated in line 1 of Algorithm 1.
- **Generation** - The genetic algorithm is composed of generations. Each generation contains a population of architectures. Stronger architectures have a higher chance of surviving to the next generation and producing offsprings.
- **Chromosome** - A certain candidate neural network architecture, being a series of 10 layers at most.
- **Selection** - In each generation, certain architectures are removed with probability $rank/population\_size$, with $rank$ based upon their performance relative to the other models. This can be seen in lines 6,7 of Algorithm 1.
- **Crossover** - The recombination of two NN architectures to create a new one. The new architecture is created by selecting an index i and concatenating the first i layers of the first network with the next $network\_length - i$ layers from the second network, as shown in Fig. 1. In Algorithm 1 this occurs in the "Breed" function in line 11.
- **Mutation** - A morph operation in a single neural architecture, by selecting a single layer and replacing it with a new random layer, with random parameters (such as kernel sizes for convolution and pooling layers). Mutation occurs only after the crossover stage in the newly created models. In Algorithm 1 this occurs in the "Breed" function in line 11.

The crossover, mutations, and random initialization used in the GA allow for exploration of the CNN search space, while the evolutionary process of keeping the better architectures with a higher probability allows for exploitation of

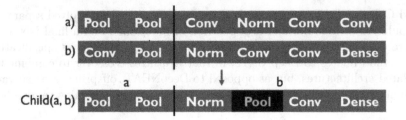

Fig. 1. The crossover process. A cut point is selected at random, half the layers of the child are taken from one parent and the other half from the second parent. Mutation can be activated as well, and this will replace a certain layer of the child randomly (highlighted in the example).

achieved progress. The algorithm is generational, meaning that a new generation of models can be trained and evaluated only once the previous generation is completed. We run the algorithm for a predetermined number of generations.

3.1 Neural Network Construction and Training

In our GA, each CNN architecture contains at most 10 layers, with layers being either the identity function, ELU activation function [6], batch normalization, dropout, convolution or max-pooling. Dropout probability was set to 0.5, and kernel sizes of max-pooling and convolution layers were shuffled at random for each new layer created. The possible range for the number of filters in convolution layers is [1–50], for kernel size in convolution layers is [1–20], for kernel size in pooling layers is [1–3], and for stride in pooling layers is [1–3]. During the GA, each network was trained for a maximum of 80 epochs with a negative log-likelihood loss function, and early stopping by the objective function on the validation set. After the GA, the best performing architecture was selected and trained for a maximum of 800 epochs to produce the final test measurement.

As a result of crossover or random creation, illegal architectures may be instantiated. An example of such an illegal architecture is a convolutional layer with a kernel size larger than its input. If this happens during the random initial architecture instantiation, the bad architecture is discarded and a new one is created instead. If this happens as a result of crossover and mutation a fixing strategy is applied. In convolutional layers, if the kernel size is larger than the layer's input, the kernel's size is reduced to that of the layer's input. In Max-pooling layers, the kernel's size and stride are reduced repetitively until a legal operation is obtained.

3.2 Per-subject, Cross-subject, and Mixed Data Evolution Paradigms

We tested per-subject, cross-subject and mixed data configurations of the GA. In the per-subject configuration, the GA runs for each subject in isolation, so the architecture search is based only on the training and validation data of that subject. In the cross-subject configuration, the GA is configured to maximize the average performance while retraining each neural network in a generation on each one of the subjects separately. In the mixed data configuration evolution and training is performed on a mixed dataset containing all subjects' data. In all configurations, a clear distinction was made between train, validation and test sets, with the test set being used only for the final evaluation. The performance calculation for each method is in the "SortByFitness" function in line 3 of Algorithm 1.

The last configuration yielded the best results, which can be explained by the fact that each trained neural network received more input data, and thus was able to generalize better. In cross-subject and per-subject, the overall number of train instances is the same and, therefore, the evolution complexity is equal. In mixed data, the evolution complexity is lower, due to fewer NN training rounds overall in the experiment (even though each NN is trained on more data) as seen in Table 2.

3.3 Weight Inheritance

Weight inheritance is the act of passing trained weights of CNN architectures from one generation to the next. Same-model inheritance is when the weights of a surviving architecture are passed from one generation to the next, causing the training to continue where it was halted. Crossover weight inheritance is when a child model receives half of its weights from the first parent and half from the second. This creates networks which don't train from scratch but receive weights from two sources that don't necessarily comply. For cross-subject training, same-model weight inheritance creates the effect of training the same CNN *model* (architecture + weights) on several subjects. This is done when a surviving architecture in a new generation receives the weights from training on a *specific* random subject from a previous generation. Thus, the same *model* over many generations can be trained on many different subjects. Weight inheritance is explained graphically in Fig. 2.

3.4 Dynamic Mutation Rate

After the creation of a new architecture by crossover, a certain layer at a random index can be swapped by a new random layer, with a certain probability. This probability is called the mutation rate, which can be controlled dynamically. This is done to control the number of unique architectures in the population, and thus promote diversity in the GA. When this is activated, for each generation where the number of unique architectures is less than $0.7 * population\ size$, the mutation rate is doubled. When the number of unique architectures returns to a normal state (above $0.7 * population\ size$), the mutation rate is reset to the original value. The number of unique architectures in the population is measured at the start of each generation, before line 3 in Algorithm 1.

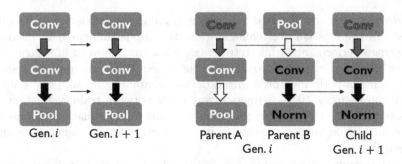

Fig. 2. Weight inheritance. Shown on the left is same-model weight inheritance between generations i and $i+1$. On the right is crossover weight inheritance, with weights from both parents in the previous generation being imported to a new network.

3.5 Objective Functions

GA and CNN training can be configured to optimize several objective functions. We set a specific objective for each dataset (accuracy, AUC, kappa or F1). Using an objective function, a GA can sort architectures by their fitness (line 3 in Algorithm 1), and thus promote stronger and inhibit weaker ones. In CNN training an objective function is used in the early stopping procedure. After each epoch, the validation set is evaluated on the objective function, and if its score didn't rise for a predefined number of epochs, training stops.

In per-subject experiments, the objective function is evaluated only on one subject's data, and in cross-subject, the average performance on all subjects' data is taken into account.

4   Experiments and Results

4.1 Datasets

BCI Competition IV 2a Dataset [4]: A 4 class MI experiment, including 9 human subjects. Each subject in each trial was given a visual cue indicating whether to imagine movement in the left hand, right hand, feet or tongue. The brain waves recorded in each trial are considered a training example. The data were recorded with an EEG headset containing 22 electrodes at 250 Hz. The train set contains 288 trials per subject, and the test set is of equal size. The goal is to classify correctly the classes in the unlabeled test set.

High Gamma Dataset [25]: A four-class motor imagery experiment. Contains 14 subjects and 880 trials per subject.

Kaggle Inria BCI Challenge [13]: Contains data from 26 subjects performing a P300 spelling task. In this task, an array of flashing letters on a screen, at different frequencies, was presented to the subject. The subject was required to spell a word by focusing on a specific letter, one by one. This attention evoked a

---

Algorithm 1. GENETIC NAS

Input: *num_generations, population_size, training_data*
Output: best found CNN architecture
1 *population* := new array of *population_size* models
2 **for** *generation* in *num_generations* **do**
3   *sorted_population* := SortByFitness(*population, training_data*)// `measure`
      `objective function on validation set`
4   **if** *generation* = *num_generations* **then**
5   **return** *sorted_population[0]*// `return best performing model in`
         `final generation`
6   **for** *i* := *0* to *length(sorted_population)* **do**
7   delete *sorted_population[i]* with probability *i/length(sorted_population)*
      // `selection - remove worst performing architectures`
8   *children* := empty list
9   **while** *length(sorted_population)* + *length(children)* < *population_size* **do**
10   *i,j* := different random numbers between 0 and *length(sorted_population)*
11   *new_model* := Breed(*sorted_population[i], sorted_population[j]*)
12   *children*.add(*new_model*)
      // `crossover + mutation`
13   *sorted_population*.AddAll(*children*)

---

response called P300, which can be discerned by a classification algorithm. The goal of the Kaggle task was to identify classification errors in the experiment, given the subject's brain waves. Since the subject's data are mixed, only mixed data evaluation was performed. EEG data were recorded using 56 electrodes at 600 Hz. Kaggle URL - https://www.kaggle.com/c/inria-bci-challenge.

BCI Competition IV 2b Dataset [11]: A two-class MI experiment with 9 human subjects. Subjects were requested to imagine left/right-hand movement. EEG data were recorded with 3 electrodes at 250 Hz.

Opportunity Activity Recognition Challenge Dataset [24]: A non-EEG dataset, comprising of data from several human subjects performing different physical activities. These activities were monitored by several sensors, whether body-worn or ambient. The goal is to classify the activity performed given the sensor data. For this mixed dataset, only mixed data evaluation was performed as well.

All experimental results, except Table 1 refer to the BCI Competition IV 2a dataset and show results of *partial* training in the GA. Full training results of the top-performing architectures appear in Table 1.

4.2   Baselines and Tools

We compare our results to several hand-designed EEG CNN architectures from previous studies [10, 25]. The CNN training procedure is based on the open source "braindecode" BCI toolbox [25]. EEG data loading and pre-processing are based on "braindecode" and on "moabb", an additional open source BCI toolbox [18]. Pre-processing includes bandpass filtering and standardization of the data, as well as splitting the data into epochs. Pre-processing for the "Opportunity" dataset is based on code from [20].

4.3   Evolution Paradigms and Weight Inheritance

We ran 9 different experiment configurations by testing mixed data, cross-subject and per-subject evolution paradigms with either of 3 weight inheritance settings: same-model + crossover weight inheritance, only crossover weight inheritance, and no weight inheritance. Figure 3 shows that mixed data and cross-subject outperform per-subject in terms of accuracy. It is assumed the exposure of the GA to all subjects' data increased the generalization ability of the generated architectures. Furthermore, the utilization of both types of weight inheritance, in all three experiment configurations resulted in accuracy gains. In cross-subject and mixed data, the use of weight inheritance introduces transfer learning to the algorithm, as new networks are created in each generation with pre-trained weights learned from different subjects' data.

For average training time, in the per-subject case, it decreases when using both types of weight inheritance, and even more so when using only same-model weight inheritance. Same-model weight inheritance allows the networks to converge faster, but crossover weight inheritance introduces interference, by mixing the weights of two models. Similar behavior can be observed for mixed data, where each network is trained on the whole dataset every run. In mixed data, both types of weight inheritance have a similar effect on run-time. This can be explained by the large variance of the data which allows tolerance for the action of a child network inheriting weights from two different parents. In cross-subject, weight inheritance *increases* run-time, because weights are inherited *between* subjects. This introduces additional interference, which hurts training time overall.

Top performance is gained when both types of weight inheritance are utilized, showing that both types are beneficial. Our findings generally coincide with [23], where weight inheritance is found to improve run time and accuracy.

4.4   Layer Distribution

Shown in Fig. 4 are distributions of different layer types as the GA progresses. Dropout layer numbers decrease dramatically over time and we assumed this is due to the ineffectiveness of dropout in the random initial networks. To test this, we ran the GA for 100 generations and injected dropout layers midway through the experiment, by turning every layer into dropout with a 20% chance. We see that dropout quantity decreases at a higher rate than before and accuracy improves at a higher rate. This can be explained by: (1) Despite the injection, architectures at generation 50 are of proven quality after evolution in the GA and good performance can be achieved quicker. (2) The injection introduces

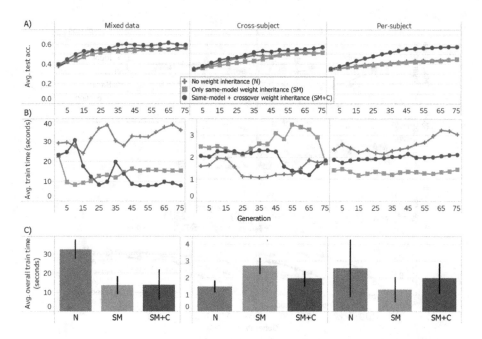

Fig. 3. Results of mixed data, cross-subject and per-subject experiments, with 3 different weight inheritance configurations. Row A shows average test accuracy by generation, row B shows average network train time per generation and row C shows average network train time per experiment. Training times for the mixed data configuration are shown on a different scale because the amount of data in these experiments is 9 times larger (as the number of subjects in the experiment). The differences for all values in the row C (per experiment type) are statistically significant with $p-value < 0.001$, except the difference between SM and SM+C for Mixed data. Final training accuracies for (SM+C, SM, N): per-subject - (0.93, 0.87, 0.84), cross-subject - (0.93, 0.95, 0.96), mixed data - (0.77, 0.82, 0.77)

a "shock" effect, thus allowing escape from local optima, as seen in [23]. If our assumption were true we would expect dropout layer numbers, after the injection, not to decrease dramatically again. Moreover, we would expect a higher accuracy increase rate to result in a lower dropout layer number decrease rate, as higher accuracy means more developed networks. In light of this, we conclude that the decrease in the number of dropout layers cannot be attributed to the poor performance of the initial random architectures. Identity layer numbers decrease as well, which means that that deep networks of up to 10 layers attain better performance than shallow ones and under these circumstances, complex networks are preferable to simple ones. This can be seen with the highest clarity in the mixed data experiment, where identity layer numbers are lowest. In this configuration, the NNs received the most training data per single run and thus the most complex networks overall were created. Training time was not part of the GA fitness function so it made no impact on these results.

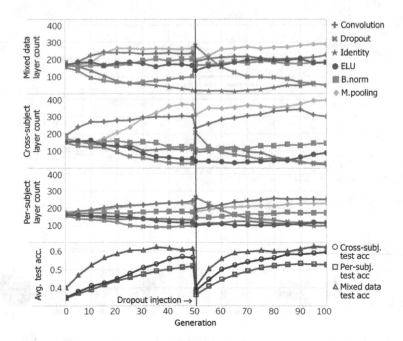

Fig. 4. Distribution of layer types over the GA's generation, with a manual injection of dropout layers at generation 50. Comparison of mixed data, cross-subject, and per-subject. M.pooling = max-pooling, B.norm = batch normalization

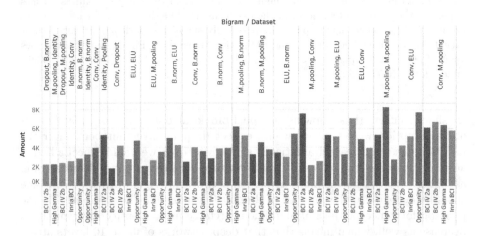

Fig. 5. Sum of layer bigram quantities in the architectures generated in the GA. The top 10 bigrams per each dataset are shown, while the rest fall under the "other" category (not shown). If a dataset does not show in a bigram column this means it was not one of the top 10 for this dataset. "Other" bigrams count for BCI IV 2a, BCI IV 2b, High Gamma, Inria BCI, and Opportunity are 27147, 25725, 20626, 29661, 26473. Results are for the "mixed data" configuration.

In Fig. 5, a count of the different bigrams of layers (two successive layer types in the CNN architectures) is shown. A clear affinity for the convolution-max pooling bigram is seen for almost all datasets, as common in state-of-the-art architectures, providing additional validation of the method. For the High Gamma dataset, there are high numbers of the max pooling - max pooling bigram, suggesting that larger pooling filters were required for this large dataset.

4.5   Dynamic Mutation Rate

To evaluate the effectiveness of dynamic mutation rate, it was either used or not used, and the initial mutation rate was set to 0.5 or 0.1. These settings were evaluated for per-subject, cross-subject and mixed data configurations, with results in Fig. 6. For per-subject, a static mutation rate of 0.1 outperforms other configurations. This means that diversifying the population with higher mutation rates (statically or dynamically) worsened performance. We hypothesize this is due to little data being involved in training (only the data of a single subject), causing an early specialization of all architectures, with most attempts to deviate from the specialization failing. For mixed data, we see a high performance with little mutation as well, but the networks here are more robust to mutations. This can be explained by the diverse training data which each network is trained on. In cross-subject, we observe a similar performance for all configurations, except worse performance with dynamic 0.5. In this scenario, each network is still trained with little data, but evolution is guided by the average performance on all subjects. Thus, a tolerance for high mutation is observed. Despite this, the highest mutation setting of dynamic, 0.5 still delivers poor performance as opposed to mixed data. Overall, the best performance is gained using a minimal amount of mutations.

4.6   Other Datasets

Shown in Table 1 are the results of EEGNAS with mixed data, cross-subject and per-subject configurations against four hand-designed CNN architectures from recent studies and one non-DL method called Filter Bank Common Spatial Pattern [1]. The last method combines several classic machine learning techniques such as feature and classifier selection while finding the optimal configuration for several EEG data. Optimized EEGNAS configurations for each dataset allowed performance on-par with the competition, and occasionally outperforming it.

4.7   Training and Architecture Search Times

Training time was recorded for all 3 experimental configurations: per-subject, cross-subject and mixed data. The average training time per network ranged from 0.45 s to 50.57 s, while the total NAS time ranged from 8.44 to 184.37 h (depending on the experiment). Table 2 shows the training time summary for the different experiments. Overall we can see that although it might take hours,

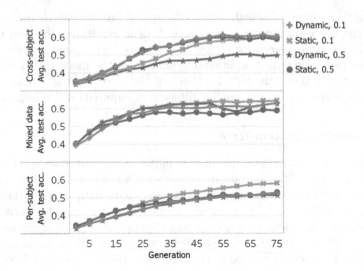

Fig. 6. Average test accuracy compared across 12 different settings of mutation rate and per/cross-subject/mixed data.

Table 1. Comparison between EEGNAS and hand designed CNN architectures. Dynamic mutation rate, starting at 0.1, was used for all datasets. EEGNAS results for the mixed data configuration in BCI IV 2a, BCI IV 2b and Inria BCI show the average and standard deviation of 5 GA runs. All other EEGNAS results represent a single GA run. Per-subject is irrelevant for Inria BCI and Opportunity (mixed datasets). Implementation of [5] includes only the CNN architecture, without the mentioned multimodal or multivariate approach, because shorter length data are used and no EOG/EMG data is available

	BCI IV 2a(acc.)	BCI IV 2b(kappa)	Inria BCI(AUC)	High Gamma(acc.)	Opportunity(F1)
EEGNAS Cross-subject	0.711	0.478	NA	0.89	NA
EEGNAS Per-subject	0.597	0.345	NA	0.88	NA
EEGNAS Mixed Data	**0.759**($\pm$0.03) min-0.71, max-0.79	0.508($\pm$0.02) min-0.49, max-0.54	**0.673**($\pm$0.015) min-0.65, max-0.69	0.92	**0.878**
DeepConvNet [25]	0.719*(c) 0.72**(c)	0.599*(c) 0.533**(c)	NA	0.925*(c) 0.887**	NA
ShallowConvNet [25]	0.737*(c) 0.656**(c)	0.629*(c) 0.529**(c)	0.609**	0.893*(c) 0.886**	0.837**
EEGnet [10]	0.69*	0.466**	0.65**	0.823**	0.856**
FBCSP [1]	0.68*	0.599*	NA	0.912*	NA
CNN by Oh et al. [19]	0.376**	0.216**	0.5**	NA	NA
CNN by Chambon et al. [5]	0.422**	NA	NA	0.88**	NA

* - as reported in [25], ** - self-run, (c) - cropped training strategy (see [25].), NA - could not run the experiment for technical reasons

or even days to find the optimal neural network for a given dataset, this replaces many human hours spent on trial and error with different CNN configurations. The experiments were run on an Intel Core i7-6900K CPU @ 3.20GHz machine with 132GB RAM, utilizing a single Nvidia Titan X GPU with 12GB RAM.

Table 2. Training and Architecture Search Times. "Train Time" regards the average training time of a single NN architecture. "Total Train Time" is *Train Time* · *#Networks Trained*, regarding the total time spent on NN training. "Exp Time" regards the total run time, including all pre and post processing.

Configuration	Dataset	# Epochs	Train time (s)	# Networks trained	Total train time (h)	Exp. time (h)
Cross-subject	BCI IV 2a	17.5	3.44	67500	64.5	77
Cross-subject	BCI IV 2b	10	0.95	67500	17.8	63
Cross-subject	High Gamma	10.5	4.88	105000	142	162
Per-subject	BCI IV 2a	7.1	0.83	67500	15.5	31
Per-subject	BCI IV 2b	4.3	0.45	67500	8.5	54
Per-subject	High Gamma	4	2.05	105000	59	83
Mixed data	BCI IV 2a	7.47	15.46	7500	32.2	36.2
Mixed data	BCI IV 2b	4.7	3.48	7500	7.25	8.44
Mixed data	High Gamma	7.75	21.85	7500	45.52	50.48
Mixed data	Inria BCI	11.57	16.46	7500	34.29	38.5
Mixed data	Opportunity	8.54	50.57	7500	105.35	184.37

4.8 Hyper-parameter Tuning and Ensembling

After hyper-parameter tuning and ensembling of CNNs, some of the above results were improved on. Using a maximum length of 30 layers instead of 10, and ensembling the top-5 models created in the last generation of the GA by taking the average prediction of all models, yielded **0.814** test accuracy for a single run of EEGNAS mixed data on the BCI IV 2a dataset.

4.9 Code

All code used in this study can be found in our git repository: https://bitbucket. org/eladrapaport/eegnas.

5 Conclusions

In this work we presented an EEG targeted NAS method, yielding results on par with hand designed CNNs, on several datasets. By the application of mutation and crossover on populations of randomly generated CNN architectures, we were able to construct successful EEG classifying CNNs. We also demonstrated the competence of EEGNAS on the non-EEG "Opportunity" dataset, to show the applicability on other time series data types.

We found that the GA can benefit from cross-subject data, even though EEG data tend to be very subject-specific. Mixed data and cross-subject training improved the generalization ability of the generated architectures and yielded more robust CNN architectures. Weight inheritance further improved our algorithm, bringing regularization by crossover weight inheritance, and reducing training time by same-model weight inheritance. Analysis of the distribution of layer types over the generations of the GA led us to conclude that architectures with high complexity are preferred, in networks of up to 10 layers.

As expected of NAS, our method was able to adapt to several datasets by generating unique CNN architectures for each problem. We utilized different objective functions (accuracy, kappa, F1, AUC) for regulating the NN training and for guiding the evolution process, thus promoting success for each individual dataset and goal.

We introduced a basic evolution scheme which can be further optimized. A direction for future work is the generation of more complex CNN architectures, including skip connections and more types of layers. The GA can be enhanced, by the use of distributed methods such as those used in [23] to improve the algorithm's efficiency. Furthermore, additional analyses of the architectures output from EEGNAS and examination of the time-frequency features of the EEG data, which affect the CNNs' output, can be made. The applicability of this method should be tested on more types of multivariate time series data as well.

Acknowledgments. This research was supported by the Israeli Ministry of Defense.

References

1. Ang, K.K., Chin, Z.Y., Zhang, H., Guan, C.: Filter bank common spatial pattern (FBCSP) in brain-computer interface. In: IEEE International Joint Conference on Neural Networks, IJCNN 2008, (IEEE World Congress on Computational Intelligence), pp. 2390–2397. IEEE (2008)
2. Antonenko, P., Paas, F., Grabner, R., Van Gog, T.: Using electroencephalography to measure cognitive load. Educ. Psychol. Rev. **22**(4), 425–438 (2010)
3. Britton, J.W., et al.: Electroencephalography (EEG): an introductory text and atlas of normal and abnormal findings in adults, children, and infants. American Epilepsy Society, Chicago (2016)
4. Brunner, C., Leeb, R., Müller-Putz, G., Schlögl, A., Pfurtscheller, G.: BCI Competition 2008-Graz Data Set A (2008)
5. Chambon, S., Galtier, M.N., Arnal, P.J., Wainrib, G., Gramfort, A.: A deep learning architecture for temporal sleep stage classification using multivariate and multimodal time series. IEEE Trans. Neural Syst. Rehabil. Eng. **26**(4), 758–769 (2018)
6. Clevert, D.A., Unterthiner, T., Hochreiter, S.: Fast and accurate deep network learning by exponential linear units (ELUs). arXiv preprint arXiv:1511.07289 (2015)
7. Krizhevsky, A., Hinton, G.: Learning multiple layers of features from tiny images. Technical report. Citeseer (2009)

8. Krizhevsky, A., Sutskever, I., Hinton, G.E.: ImageNet classification with deep convolutional neural networks. In: Advances in Neural Information Processing Systems, pp. 1097–1105 (2012)
9. Längkvist, M., Karlsson, L., Loutfi, A.: A review of unsupervised feature learning and deep learning for time-series modeling. Pattern Recogn. Lett. **42**, 11–24 (2014)
10. Lawhern, V.J., Solon, A.J., Waytowich, N.R., Gordon, S.M., Hung, C.P., Lance, B.J.: EEGNet: a compact convolutional network for EEG-based brain-computer interfaces. arXiv preprint arXiv:1611.08024 (2016)
11. Leeb, R., Brunner, C., Müller-Putz, G., Schlögl, A., Pfurtscheller, G.: BCI Competition 2008-Graz Data Set B. Graz University of Technology, Austria (2008)
12. Lopez, S., Suarez, G., Jungreis, D., Obeid, I., Picone, J.: Automated identification of abnormal adult EEGs. In: 2015 IEEE Signal Processing in Medicine and Biology Symposium (SPMB), pp. 1–5. IEEE (2015)
13. Margaux, P., Emmanuel, M., Sébastien, D., Olivier, B., Jérémie, M.: Objective and subjective evaluation of online error correction during p300-based spelling. Adv. Hum.-Comput. Interact. **2012**, 4 (2012)
14. Miikkulainen, R., et al.: Evolving deep neural networks. In: Artificial Intelligence in the Age of Neural Networks and Brain Computing, pp. 293–312. Elsevier (2019)
15. Mikolov, T., Chen, K., Corrado, G., Dean, J.: Efficient estimation of word representations in vector space. arXiv preprint arXiv:1301.3781 (2013)
16. Mirowski, P., Madhavan, D., LeCun, Y., Kuzniecky, R.: Classification of patterns of eeg synchronization for seizure prediction. Clin. Neurophysiol. **120**(11), 1927–1940 (2009)
17. Montana, D.J., Davis, L.: Training feedforward neural networks using genetic algorithms. In: IJCAI, vol. 89, pp. 762–767 (1989)
18. NeuroTechX: Neurotechx/moabb, February 2019. https://github.com/NeuroTechX/moabb
19. Oh, S.L., et al.: A deep learning approach for Parkinson's disease diagnosis from EEG signals. Neural Comput. Appl. 1–7 (2018)
20. Ordóñez, F., Roggen, D.: Deep convolutional and lstm recurrent neural networks for multimodal wearable activity recognition. Sensors **16**(1), 115 (2016)
21. Pfurtscheller, G., Neuper, C.: Motor imagery and direct brain-computer communication. Proc. IEEE **89**(7), 1123–1134 (2001)
22. Real, E., Aggarwal, A., Huang, Y., Le, Q.V.: Regularized evolution for image classifier architecture search. arXiv preprint arXiv:1802.01548 (2018)
23. Real, E., et al.: Large-scale evolution of image classifiers. arXiv preprint arXiv:1703.01041 (2017)
24. Roggen, D., et al.: Collecting complex activity datasets in highly rich networked sensor environments. In: 2010 Seventh International Conference on Networked Sensing Systems (INSS), pp. 233–240. IEEE (2010)
25. Schirrmeister, R.T., et al.: Deep learning with convolutional neural networks for eeg decoding and visualization. Hum. Brain Mapp. **38**(11), 5391–5420 (2017)
26. Srinivas, M., Patnaik, L.M.: Genetic algorithms: a survey. Computer **27**(6), 17–26 (1994)
27. Tang, Z., Li, C., Sun, S.: Single-trial EEG classification of motor imagery using deep convolutional neural networks. Optik-Int. J. Light Electron Opt. **130**, 11–18 (2017)
28. Völker, M., Schirrmeister, R.T., Fiederer, L.D., Burgard, W., Ball, T.: Deep transfer learning for error decoding from non-invasive EEG. In: 2018 6th International Conference on Brain-Computer Interface (BCI), pp. 1–6. IEEE (2018)

29. Wang, B., Sun, Y., Xue, B., Zhang, M.: Evolving deep convolutional neural networks by variable-length particle swarm optimization for image classification. In: 2018 IEEE Congress on Evolutionary Computation (CEC), pp. 1–8. IEEE (2018)
30. Whitley, D., et al.: Genetic algorithms and neural networks. Genetic Algorithms Eng. Comput. Sci. **3**, 203–216 (1995)
31. Zoefel, B., Huster, R.J., Herrmann, C.S.: Neurofeedback training of the upper alpha frequency band in EEG improves cognitive performance. Neuroimage **54**(2), 1427–1431 (2011)

Multi-task Dictionary Learning Based on Convolutional Neural Networks for Longitudinal Clinical Score Predictions in Alzheimer's Disease

Qunxi Dong[1(✉)], Jie Zhang[1], Qingyang Li[1], Pau M. Thompson[2], Richard J. Caselli[3], Jieping Ye[4], Yalin Wang[1], and for the Alzheimer's Disease Neuroimaging Initiative

[1] School of Computing, Informatics, and Decision Systems Engineering, Arizona State University, Tempe, AZ, USA
qdong17@asu.edu

[2] Imaging Genetics Center, Institute for Neuroimaging and Informatics, University of Southern California, Los Angeles, CA, USA

[3] Department of Neurology, Mayo Clinic Arizona, Scottsdale, AZ, USA

[4] Department of Computational Medicine and Bioinformatics, University of Michigan, Ann Arbor, MI, USA

Abstract. Computer-aided diagnosis (CAD) systems for medical images are seen as effective tools to improve the efficiency of diagnosis and prognosis of Alzheimer's disease (AD). The current state-of-the-art models for many images analyzing tasks are based on Convolutional Neural Networks (CNN). However, the lack of training data is a common challenge in applying CNN to the diagnosis of AD and its prodromal stages. Another challenge for CAD applications is the controversy between the requiring of longitudinal cortical structural information for higher diagnosis/prognosis accuracy and the computing ability for processing varied imaging features. To address these two challenges, we propose a novel computer-aided AD diagnosis system CNN-Stochastic Coordinate Coding (MSCC) which integrates CNN with transfer learning strategy, a novel MSCC algorithm and our effective AD-related biomarkers–multivariate morphometry statistics (MMS). We applied the novel CNN-MSCC system on the Alzheimer's Disease Neuroimaging Initiative (ADNI) dataset to predict future cognitive clinical measures with baseline Hippocampal/Ventricle MMS features and cortical thickness. The experimental results showed that CNN-MSCC achieved superior results. The proposed system may aid in expediting the diagnosis of

Q. Dong and J. Zhang—Authors contributed equally.

Acknowledgments: Data used in preparation of this article were obtained from the Alzheimer's Disease Neuroimaging Initiative (ADNI) database (adni.loni.usc.edu). As such, the investigators within the ADNI contributed to the design and implementation of ADNI and/or provided data but did not participate in analysis or writing of this report. A complete listing of ADNI investigators can be found at: http://adni.loni.usc.edu/wp-content/uploads/how_to_apply/ADNI_Acknowledgement_List.pdf.

A. Zeng et al. (Eds.): HBAI 2019, CCIS 1072, pp. 21–35, 2019.
https://doi.org/10.1007/978-981-15-1398-5_2

AD progress, facilitating earlier clinical intervention, and resulting in improved clinical outcomes.

Keywords: Computer-aided diagnosis · Multi-task dictionary learning · Convolutional Neural Networks (CNN) · Transfer learning · Alzheimer's Disease

1   Introduction

AD and its early stage, Mild Cognitive Impairment (MCI), are becoming the most prevalent neurodegenerative brain diseases in elderly people worldwide [1]. Mini Mental State Examination (MMSE) and Alzheimer's Disease Assessment Scale cognitive subscale (ADAS-Cog) are well-known AD assessment scales [2, 3]. Clinicians and researchers have used them to evaluate currently individual cognitive decline led by AD factors. It is valuable to predict future cognitive progression for an early intervention or prevention.

Brain changes due to AD occur even before amnestic symptoms appearing [4], AD Studies on magnetic resonance (MR) images have shown that objective brain structure measures, such as hippocampal, ventricle structures and cortical thickness, could identify significant cortical structural deformations related with AD pathology [5,6] even before observing obviously lower MMSE/ADAS-Cog scores [7–9]. Our previous studies proposed a novel 3D surface measure, multivariate morphometry statistics (MMS), consisting of multivariate tensor-based morphometry (mTBM) and radial distance (distances from the medial core to each surface point) and demonstrated that MMS of ventricles and hippocampi are potential preclinical AD imaging biomarkers [10,11]. Our previous work [12,13] applied cortical thickness measures to predict future clinical scores related with AD symptoms. Seldom existing CAD systems considered the inherent correlations among the above effective brain structure measures that may be useful for robust and accurate predictions of MMSE/ADAS-Cog scales. So this work expect to develop a CAD system using these three structure measures to predict future MMSE/ADAS-Cog scales, and then by referring the scale trends, the clinicians can provide early intervention or prevention to slow or even stop the degenerate trends.

Deep learning models [14,15] are capable of learning the hierarchical structure of features extracted from real-world images. Convolutional Neural Networks (CNNs) are a class of multi-layer, fully trainable models that are able to capture highly nonlinear mappings between inputs and outputs [16]. Recently, CNNs have been successfully applied to the domain of brain imaging analysis, including image classification [17], segmentation [18], and autistic diagnosis [19]. But there is still little CNNs studies on AD diagnosis, a key challenge is a lack of training data. Transfer learning (TF) can help feature learning in the data-scarce target domain by transferring knowledge from similar data-rich source domain, it is potential to address this challenge [15,20].

After using CNNs with TF, we confront another challenge that is high dimensional feature maps derived from small number of individual MR images in AD research domain. To address this so called *large p, small n* problem, dictionary learning was proposed to use a small number of basis vectors termed dictionary to represent high dimensional features effectively and concisely [21–23]. However, most existing studies on dictionary learning focus on the prediction of target on a single brain structure measure [24,25]. In general, a joint analysis of tasks from multiple cortical measures is expected to improve the performance but remains a challenging problem.

Recently, Multi-Task Learning (MTL) has been successfully used on regression under the different cortical structure measures [26]. Further, there have been studies to combine TF and MTL together to solve the issue of small sample size. Zhang et al. integrated CNN, transfer learning and MTL for biological image analysis [27]. These studies indicated that integrating abnormal features among different cortical structures performed better than using single type of structural measures. Based on MTL, we made a multi-task Stochastic Coordinate Coding (MSCC) algorithm to partition the dictionaries into the common and individual parts and more suitable for the situation of individual features of varied structural measures. And we proposed a CAD system CNN-MSCC which utilized TF strategy to get one initial CNN model pre-trained from millions of images in ImageNet dataset [28,29], employed MSCC to refine and fuse features from varied structural measures, and performed the Lasso [30] to predict future MMSE/ADAS-Cog scales representing AD progression. The proposed algorithm CNN-MSCC aims to resolve the CNN application challenges of the limited sample size, high dimension feature maps refining and multiple sources of features integrations.

Our main contributions can be summarized as follows:

- We employ transfer learning and CNN to explore whether the transfer learning property of CNN can be enhanced to generate features from geometry meshes of biological images since the current bottleneck for CNNs to be applied to many biological problems is the limited amount of available labeled training data. We pre-train the deep neural network on the ImageNet data and transfer the knowledge of natural images to generate the neuroimaging features for the real world application.
- We considered the variance of subjects from different cortical structure measures and proposed a novel unsupervised dictionary learning method, termed Multi-task Stochastic Coordinate Coding (MSCC), learning the different tasks simultaneously and utilizing shared and individual dictionary to encode both consistent and varied imaging features. To the best of our knowledge, it is the first deep model to integrate multi-task learning with dictionary learning research for brain imaging analysis.
- We tested CNN-MSCC on three baseline brain structure measures to better predict the future clinical cognitive scores. Specifically, we used multiple baseline structure measures as multiple tasks input to predict three future time

points clinical scores. Our new approach is able to boost the performance of diagnoses ranging from cognitively unimpaired to AD.

2   Multi-task Dictionary Learning Based Convolutional Neural Networks

Our first goal here is to explore whether this transfer learning framework of CNN can be generalized to biological image studies. Specifically, we pre-train the CNN model using ImageNet data [28], containing millions of labeled natural images with thousands of categories to obtain initial parameters and subsequently generate the features on the longitudinal data for each task. In the experiments, we apply Alexnet [17], which contains 7 layers, including convolutional layers with fixed filter sizes and different numbers of feature maps. We employ rectified non-linearity, max-pooling on each layer in our CNN model. We pretrain the CNN model on the ImageNet dataset, then remove the last fully-connected layer (this layer's outputs are the 1000 class scores for a different task like ImageNet). Finally, we treat the rest of the CNN as a fixed feature extractor for the publicly available Alzheimer's Disease Neuroimaging Initiative (ADNI) database [31].

We further propose to use multi-task learning strategy to boost the future clinical score regression accuracy. The entire pipeline of our method is illustrated in Fig. 1. To be specific, we train the deep CNN model on the Imagenet dataset firstly. Then we employ the pretrained network as a feature extractor for the ADNI dataset from multiple baseline structure measures. The AlexNet has a seven layer structure deep neural network. As a result, we generate seven-deep output features for each structure measure. We further employ MSCC to conduct the multi-task learning simultaneously, generating the sparse features and dictionaries from the deep features of different structure measures. In MSCC, we utilize shared and individual dictionaries to encode both consistent and varied imaging features along multiple structure measures. In the end, we employ the sparse codes generated from MSCC to perform the Lasso [30] and predict the future AD progression. MSCC is one kind of online learning methods and the advantage of online learning method is to solve the cases that the size of the input data might be too large (sample size up to 2867562 in this work) to fit into memory or the input data comes in a form of a stream.

3   Multi-task Stochastic Coordinate Coding

3.1   Dictionary Learning

Given a finite training set of signals $X = (x_1, ..., x_n)$ where $X \in \mathbb{R}^{p \times n}$. Each x_i is an image patch and $x_i \in \mathbb{R}^p$. Dictionary learning aims to learn a dictionary D where $D \in \mathbb{R}^{p \times l}$ and a sparse code matrix Z, $Z \in \mathbb{R}^{l \times n}$. The original signals X is modeled by a sparse linear combination of D and Z as $X \approx DZ$. Given one image patch x_i, we can formulate the following optimization problem:

$$\min_{D \in \Psi, z_i \in \mathbb{R}^l} f(D, z_i) = \frac{1}{2}||x_i - Dz_i||_2^2 + \lambda||z_i||_1, \tag{1}$$

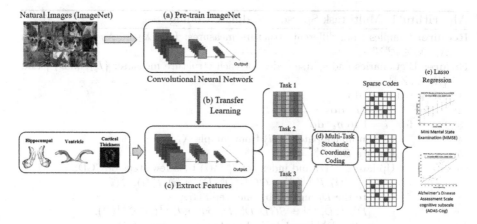

Fig. 1. The streamline of our proposed framework. We pre-train the deep CNN model on the Imagenet dataset and use the pre-trained model as a feature extractor for the ADNI dataset. We employ the extracted features from three cortical structure measures to conduct the multi-task dictionary learning for AD progression prediction, generating the sparse features for different structure measures. Finally, we use Lasso regression on the learnt features to predict future MMSE and ADAS-Cog scores.

where $\Psi = \{D \in \mathbb{R}^{p \times l} : \forall j \in 1, ..., l, \|D_j\|_2 \leq 1\}$, D_j denotes the jth column of D. λ is the positive regularization parameter. z_i is the learnt sparse codes for x_i and $Z = (z_1, ..., z_n)$.

The optimization of Eq. 1 can be decomposed into an alternative learning process in the Online Dictionary Learning methods (ODL) [22]. Given each image patch x_i, ODL keeps the D fixed and learn z_i, then keep z_i fixed and learn D. The learning process runs κ (a fixed constant) iterations until there are no more changes on D and Z.

3.2 The Proposed Algorithm

Given features from T different tasks: $\{X_1, X_2, ..., X_T\}$, our objective is to learn a set of sparse codes $\{Z_1, Z_2, ..., Z_T\}$ for each task where $X_t \in \mathbb{R}^{p_t \times n}$, $Z_t \in \mathbb{R}^{l_t \times n}$ and $t \in \{1, ..., T\}$. p_t is the image patch number of X_t (i.e. cortical measure), n is the number of subjects for X_t and l_t is the dimension of each sparse code in Z_t. When employing the ODL to learn the sparse codes Z_t by X_t individually, we obtain a set of dictionary $\{D_1, ..., D_T\}$ but there is no correlationship between learnt dictionaries. Another solution is to construct the features $\{X_1, ..., X_T\}$ into one matrix X to obtain the dictionary D. However, if there is no latent common information shared by the same subject with different cortical structure measures, only one dictionary D is not enough to show the variation among features from different structure measures. Such fact is supposed to be easily revealed in the variance of dictionary atoms and the sparsity of their corresponding sparse code matrices. To address this challenge, we integrate the idea of multi-task learning into the online dictionary learning method. We propose a

---

Algorithm 1. Multi-task Sparse Coordinate Coding

Require: Samples from different structure measures: $\{X_1, X_2, ...X_T\}$ and for each
$\quad X_t, X_t \in \mathbb{R}^{p \times n_t}$
Ensure: Dictionaries and sparse codes for each structure measure: $\{D_1, ..., D_T\}$ and
$\quad \{Z_1, ..., Z_T\}$
1: **for** $k = 1$ to κ **do**
2: $\quad$ **for** $t = 1$ to T **do**
3: $\quad\quad$ **for** $i = 1$ to n_t **do**
4: $\quad\quad\quad$ Get an image patch $x_t(i)$ from sample X_t.
5: $\quad\quad\quad$ Update $\hat{D}_t^k$: $\hat{D}_t^k = \Phi$.
6: $\quad\quad\quad$ Update $z_t^{k+1}(i)$ and index set $I_t^{k+1}(i)$ by a few steps of CCD:
7: $\quad\quad\quad\quad$ $[z_t^{k+1}(i), I_t^{k+1}(i)] = CCD(\hat{D}_t^k, \bar{D}_t^k, x_t(i), I_t^k(i), z_t^k(i))$.
8: $\quad\quad\quad$ Update the $\hat{D}_t$ and $\bar{D}_t$ by one step SGD:
9: $\quad\quad\quad\quad$ $[\hat{D}_t^{k+1}, \bar{D}_t^{k+1}] = SGD(\hat{D}_t^k, \bar{D}_t^k, x_t(i), I_t^{k+1}(i), z_t^{k+1}(i))$.
10: $\quad\quad\quad$ Normalize $\hat{D}_t^{k+1}$ and $\bar{D}_t^{k+1}$ based on the index set $I_t^{k+1}(i)$.
11: $\quad\quad\quad$ Update the shared dictionary Φ: $\Phi = \hat{D}_t^{k+1}$.
12: $\quad\quad$ **end for**
13: $\quad$ **end for**
14: **end for**

---

novel dictionary learning algorithm, termed as *Multi-task Stochastic Coordinate Coding* (MSCC), to learn the sparse codes of subjects from different structure measures. In this work each task corresponds one special structure measure.

For the subjects' feature matrix X_t of a particular task, MSCC learns a dictionary D_t and sparse codes Z_t. D_t is composed of two parts: $D_t = [\hat{D}_t, \bar{D}_t]$ where $\hat{D}_t \in \mathbb{R}^{p_t \times \hat{l}}$, $\bar{D}_t \in \mathbb{R}^{p_t \times \bar{l}_t}$ and $\hat{l} + \bar{l}_t = l_t$. $\hat{D}_t$ is the same among all the learnt dictionaries $\{D_1, ..., D_T\}$ while $\bar{D}_t$ is different from each other and only learnt from the corresponding subjects' feature matrix X_t. Therefore, objective function of MSCC can be reformulated as follows:

$$\min_{\left(\substack{D_1, \cdots, D_T, \\ Z_1, \cdots, Z_T}\right)} \sum_{t=1}^{T} \tfrac{1}{2} \|X_t - [\hat{D}_t, \bar{D}_t] Z_t\|_F^2 + \lambda \sum_{t=1}^{T} \|Z_t\|_1 :$$

$$\text{subject to } \hat{D}_1 = \cdots = \hat{D}_T \text{ and } D_t \in \Psi_t \quad (2)$$

where $\Psi_t = \{D_t \in \mathbb{R}^{p \times l_t} : \forall j \in 1, ..., l_t, \|[D_t]_j\|_2 \le 1\}$ and $[D_t]_j$ is the jth column of D_t.

Figure 2 illustrates the framework of MSCC with features of ADNI from three different tasks (i.e. cortical structure measures), which represents as X_1, X_2 and X_3, respectively. Through the multi-task learning process of MSCC, we obtain the dictionary and sparse codes for features from each task t: D_t and Z_t. In MSCC, a dictionary D_t is composed by a shared part $\hat{D}_t$ and an individual part $\bar{D}_t$, $\hat{D}_1 = \hat{D}_2 = \hat{D}_3$. For the individual part of dictionaries, MSCC learns a different $\bar{D}_t$ only from the corresponding feature matrix X_t. We vary the number of columns $\bar{l}_t$ in $\bar{D}_t$ to introduce the variant in the learnt sparse codes Z_t. As a result, the dimensions of learnt sparse codes matrix Z_t are different from each other.

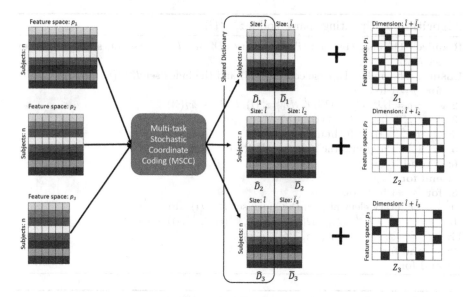

Fig. 2. Illustration of the learning process of MSCC.

The initialization of dictionaries in MSCC is critical to the entire learning process. We propose a random patch method to initialize the dictionaries from different tasks. The main idea of the random patch method is to randomly select l image patches from n subjects $\{x_1, x_2, ..., x_n\}$ to construct D where $D \in \mathbb{R}^{p \times l}$. It is a similar way to perform the random patch approach in MSCC. In MSCC, the way we initialize $\hat{D}_t$ is to randomly select $\hat{l}$ subjects' feature from features' matrices across different tasks $\{X_1, \cdots, X_T\}$ to construct it. For the individual part of each dictionary, we randomly select $\bar{l}$ subjects' feature from the corresponding matrix X_t to construct $\bar{D}_t$. After initializing dictionary D_t for each task, we set all the sparse code Z_t to be zero at the beginning. The key steps of MSCC are summarized in Algorithm 1.

In Algorithm 1, k denotes the epoch number where $k \in [1, \kappa]$. Φ represent the shared part of each dictionary D_t which is initialized by the random patch method. For each subject's feature $x_t(i)$ extracted from X_t, we learn the ith sparse code $z_t^{k+1}(i)$ from Z_t by several steps of Cyclic Coordinate Descent (CCD) [32]. Then we use learnt sparse codes $z_t^{k+1}(i)$ to update the dictionary $\hat{D}_t^{k+1}$ and $\bar{D}_t^{k+1}$ by one step Stochastic Gradient Descent (SGD) [33]. Since $z_t^{k+1}(i)$ is very sparse, we use the index set $I_t^{k+1}(i)$ to record the location of non-zero entries in $z_t^{k+1}(i)$ to accelerate the update of sparse codes and dictionaries. Φ is updated in the end of kth iteration to ensure $\hat{D}_t^{k+1}$ is the same among all the dictionaries.

The learning process of sparse code $z_t^{k+1}(i)$ is shown in Algorithm 2. At first, we generate the non-zero index set I_t^{k+1} by one step of CCD to record the nonzero entry of $z_t^{k+1}(i)$. Then we perform S steps CCD to update the sparse codes only on the non-zero entries of $z_t^{k+1}(i)$, accelerating the learning process

---

Algorithm 2. Updating sparse codes $z_t^{k+1}(i)$

Require: The image patch $x_t(i)$, dictionaries $\hat{D}_t^k$ and $\bar{D}_t^k$, sparse codes $z_t^k(i)$ and index set $I_t^k(i)$

Ensure: The updated sparse code $z_t^{k+1}(i)$ and the index set $I_t^{k+1}(i)$.

1: **for** $j = 1$ to l_t **do**
2:      $g = [\hat{D}_t^k, \bar{D}_t^k]_j^T (\Omega([\hat{D}_t^k, \bar{D}_t^k], z_t^k(i), I_t^k(i)) - x_t(i))$
3:      $z_t^{k+1}(i)_j = \Gamma_\lambda(z_t^k(i)_j - g)$
4:      **if** $z_t^{k+1}(i)_j \neq 0$ **then**
5:          Put j into the index set $I_t^{k+1}(i)$.
6:      **end if**
7: **end for**
8: **for** $s = 1$ to S **do**
9:      **for** every element μ in the index set $I_t^{k+1}(i)$ **do**
10:        $g = [\hat{D}_t^k, \bar{D}_t^k]_\mu^T (\Omega([\hat{D}_t^k, \bar{D}_t^k], z_t^{k+1}(i), I_t^{k+1}(i)) - x_t(i))$
11:        $z_t^{k+1}(i)_\mu = \Gamma_\lambda((z_t^{k+1}(i)_\mu - g)$
12:      **end for**
13: **end for**

Algorithm 3. Updating dictionaries $\hat{D}_t^{k+1}$ and $\bar{D}_t^{k+1}$

Require: The image patch $x_t(i)$, dictionaries $\hat{D}_t^k$ and $\bar{D}_t^k$, sparse codes $z_t^{k+1}(i)$ and index set $I_t^{k+1}(i)$.

Ensure: The updated dictionaries $\hat{D}_t^{k+1}$ and $\bar{D}_t^{k+1}$.

1: Update the Hessian matrix H_t^{k+1}: $H_t^{k+1} = H_t^k + z_t^{k+1}(i)z_t^{k+1}(i)^T$.
2: $R = \Omega([\hat{D}_t^k, \bar{D}_t^k], z_t^{k+1}(i), I_t^{k+1}(i)) - x_t(i)$.
3: **for** $j = 1$ to p **do**
4:      **for** every element μ in the index set $I_t^{k+1}(i)$ **do**
5:        $[\hat{D}_t^{k+1}, \bar{D}_t^{k+1}]_{j,\mu} = [\hat{D}_t^k, \bar{D}_t^k]_{j,\mu} - \frac{1}{H_t^{k+1}(\mu,\mu)} z_t^{k+1}(i)_\mu R_j$.
6:      **end for**
7: **end for**

---

significantly. Ω is a sparse matrix multiplication function that has three input parameters. Take $\Omega(A, b, I)$ as an example, A denotes a matrix, b is a vector and I is an index set that records the locations of non-zero entries in b. The return value of function Ω is defined as: $\Omega(A, b, I) = Ab$. When multiplying A and b, we only manipulate the non-zero entries of b and corresponding columns of A based on the index set I, speeding up the calculation by utilizing the sparsity of b. Γ is the soft thresholding shrinkage function [34] and the definition of Γ is given by: $\Gamma_\varphi(x) = sign(x)(|x| - \varphi)$.

The procedure of updating dictionaries is shown in Algorithm 3. We perform one step SGD to update the dictionaries: $\hat{D}_t^{k+1}$ and $\bar{D}_t^{k+1}$. The learning rate is set to be an approximation of the inverse of the Hessian matrix H_t^{k+1}, which is updated by the sparse codes $z_t^{k+1}(i)$ in kth iteration. For the μth column of dictionary, we set the learning rate as the inverse of the diagonal element of the Hessian matrix, which is $1/H_t^{k+1}(\mu, \mu)$. Since $D_t \in \Psi_t$ in Eq. (2), it is necessary to normalize the dictionaries $\hat{D}_t^{k+1}$ and $\bar{D}_t^{k+1}$ after updating them. We can perform the normalization on the corresponding columns of non-zero entries from $z_t^{k+1}(i)$ because the dictionaries updating only occurs on these columns. Utilizing the non-zero information from $I_t^{k+1}(i)$ can accelerate the whole learning process.

4   Experiments

AD and its early stage, Mild Cognitive Impairment (MCI), are becoming the most prevalent neurodegenerative brain diseases in elderly people worldwide [1]. To this end, there have been a lot of studies [5,7,11,35] on investigating the underlying biological or neurological mechanisms and also discovering biomarkers for early diagnosis of AD and MCI. Data for testing the performances of our proposed framework were obtained from the ADNI database (adni.loni.usc.edu). [36], which has been considered as the benchmark database for performance evaluation of various methods for AD diagnosis. The ADNI was launched in 2003 as a public-private partnership, led by Principal Investigator Michael W. Weiner, MD. The primary goal of ADNI is to test whether biological markers such as serial MRI and positron emission tomography (PET), combined with clinical and neuropsychological assessment can measure the progression of MCI and early AD. The structural MR images were acquired from 1.5 T scanners. The raw MR images and MMSE/ADAS-Cog scales were downloaded from the public ADNI website (www.loni.ucla.edu/ADNI). The information about subjects criteria are in www.adni-info.org. In the experimental dataset, there are 837 baseline subjects between 68–82 years of age.

4.1   Image Patches of Three Cortical Structure Measures

We utilized three baseline structural measures of brain, which are hippocampal multivariate morphometry statistics (MMS), lateral ventricle MMS and cortical thickness. For the hippocampal surface features, we used FIRST software [37] and marching cube method [38] to automatically segment and reconstructed hippocampal surfaces for each brain MR image. Then, we registered and computed hippocampal MMS [39]. For each subject, we obtained a 120,000 dimensional features of the hippocampal surfaces and we used a 50×50 window to obtained a collection of image patches, then we get 220968 baseline hippocampal image patches.

For the ventricular surface features we did the following. First, we segmented images of the lateral ventricles to build the ventricular structure surface models using a level-set based topology preserving method [40]. Then we computed surface registrations using the canonical holomorphic one-form segmentation method [41]. Finally, MMS [39] were computed and obtained as a 308,247 dimensional features of the ventricular surfaces for each subject. The cortical thickness was computed by FreeSurfer [42] which deforms the white surface to pial surface and measures deforming distance as the cortical thickness. The spherical parameter surface and weighted spherical harmonic representation [43] are used to register pial surfaces across subjects, which means each subjects have the same dimension (161,800) cortical thickness. After preprocessing the data with the 50×50 patch window size, we have 2867562, 1504926 image patches for ventricle and cortical thickness measures, respectively.

4.2 CNN-MSCC Modeling and Evaluation

We build a prediction model on these multiple task geometry surface features from 837 baseline subjects of AD, MCI and cognitively unimpaired (CU) categories, we expect to predict future MMSE/ADAS-Cog scales (from 6th month to 24th month). In this study, we took Alexnet structure [17] as the initial CNN model, which contains 7 layers, including convolutional layers with fixed filter sizes and different numbers of feature maps and the architecture of our CNN is shown in Table 1. We pretrained the CNN model on the ImageNet dataset [28], containing millions of labeled natural images with thousands of categories then removed the last fully-connected layer (this layer's outputs are the 1000 class scores for a different task like ImageNet). Finally, the rest of the CNN was transferred and used to extract feature maps from MMS image patches of special cortices and cortical thickness [36].

We implemented our CNN model using the Caffe toolbox [44]. The network was trained on a Intel (R) Xeon (R) 48-core machine, with 2.50 GHZ processors, 256 GB of globally addressable memory and a single Nvidia GeForce GTX TITAN black GPU. In the experimental setting of MSCC, the sparsity $\lambda = 0.1$. Also, we selected 10 epochs with a batch size of 1 in Algorithm 1 and 3 iterations of CCD in Algorithm 2 (P is set to be 1 and S is set to be 3) in all the experiments. After we get the MSCC features, we used Max-Pooling for further dimension reduction. Therefore, the feature dimension of each subject is a 1×2000 vector. To predict future clinical scores, we used Lasso regression following CNN-MSCC. For the parameter selection, 5-fold cross validation is used to select model parameters in the training data (between 10^{-3} and 10^{3}).

In order to evaluate CNN-MSCC model, we randomly split the data (image patches and their corresponding MMSE/ADAS-Cog scores) into training and testing sets using an 8:2 ratio and used 10-fold cross validation to avoid data bias. Lastly, we evaluated the overall regression performance of our proposed system using normalized mean square error (nMSE), weighted correlation coefficient (wR) and root mean square error (rMSE) for task-specific regression performance measures [45]. The three measures are defined as follows:

$$nMSE(Y, \hat{Y}) = \frac{\sum_{i=1}^{t} \|Y_i - \hat{Y}_i\|_2^2 / \sigma(Y_i)}{\sum_{i=1}^{t} n_i},$$

$$wR(Y, \hat{Y}) = \frac{\sum_{i=1}^{t} Corr(Y_i, \hat{Y}_i) n_i}{\sum_{i=1}^{t} n_i},$$

$$rMSE(y, \hat{y}) = \sqrt{\frac{\|y - \hat{y}\|_2^2}{n}}.$$

For nMSE and wR, Y_i is the ground truth of target of task i and $\hat{Y}_i$ is the corresponding predicted value, $\sigma(Y_i)$ is the Standard deviation of Y_i, $Corr$ is

Table 1. The architecture of CNN used in this work.

Deep layer	Function	# of neurons
1	Convolutional layer	253440
2	Pooling layer	186624
3	Convolutional layer	64896
4	Convolutional layer	64896
5	Convolutional layer Pooling layer	43264 9216
6	Fully connected layer	4096
7	Fully connected layer	4096

the correlation coefficient between two vectors and n_i is the number of subjects of task i. For rMSE, y is the ground truth of target at a single task and $\hat{y}$ is the corresponding prediction by a prediction model. The smaller nMSE and rMSE, as well as the bigger wR mean the better results. nMSE and wR are used to evaluate the overall performances of the proposed system across three times points, rMSE is used to evaluate CNN-MSCC performance of each time point. We reported the mean and standard deviation based on 40 iterations of experiments on different splits of data.

4.3   Performance Analysis

After We constructed CNN-MSCC model with the image patches from the combined three kinds of features, we used Lasso to individually predict 6-month (M06), 12-month (M12) and 24-month (M24) MMSE and ADAS-cog scores with 8:2 ratio on training and testing data sets. The prediction results are reported in Fig. 3(a) and (b). Figure 3(a) shows the overall nMSE and wR measures of CNN-MSCC to predict MMSE and ADAS-Cog scores across three time points (M06, M12 and M24), for MMSE and ADAS-Cog score predictions, CNN-MSCC achieves nMSE of 0.274 ± 0.051 and 0.762 ± 0.012 respectively, it also achieves wR of 0.751 ± 0.083 and 0.862 ± 0.045, respectively.

Figure 3(b) shows the rMSE measures for MMSE and ADAS-Cog scores at M06, M12 and M24, respectively, for MMSE and ADAS-Cog scores at M06, CNN-MSCC achieves rMSE of 2.198 ± 0.062 and 4.322 ± 0.269, for MMSE and ADAS-Cog scores at M12, the proposed method achieves rMSE of 2.211 ± 0.459 and 4.930 ± 0.912, for MMSE and ADAS-Cog scores at M24, we achieves rMSE of 2.290 ± 0.601 and 5.521 ± 0.816. We can observe that the rMSE of predicting M06, M12 and M24 scores of MMSE and ADAS-Cog are stable across all three time points. Especially there is an obvious improvement of the proposed CNN-MSCC for later time points (12, 24-month). This may be due to the data sparseness in later time points, as the proposed sparsity-inducing models are expected to achieve better prediction performance.

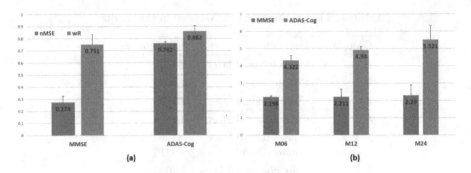

Fig. 3. MMSE and ADAS-Cog prediction performances in terms of nMSE and wR (a) and in terms of rMSE (b) using proposed CNN-MSCC model.

Zhou et al. proposed similar multi-task learning models to predict future MMSE and ADAS-Cog scores related with AD progression using baseline MRI features, MRI data were from 648 subjects of ADNI dataset, 5 categories of MRI features were used, they were cortical thickness, volumes or surface measures [45]. The nMSE, wR and rMSE results estimated from our proposed system are very comparable to the best results reported in [45]. There are three main reasons about the outperformances of the proposed multi-task model: advanced cortical structure measure MMS was introduced, this effective biomarker had been well studied in our previous work and outperformed volume measure [10,11]; since deep model is good at modeling the complex cortical structure in the medical imaging field [46], pretrained CNN was used to generate hierarchical structure features from high-dimension MMS and cortical thickness measures; we developed a novel unsupervised learning method MSCC to improve the computing ability for processing hierarchical structure features multi-tasks.

5   Conclusions and Future Work

In this work, we proposed a deep learning model, CNN-MSCC, to model multiple cortical structure features, for predicting future MMSE/ADAS-Cog scores. The proposed model is validated by extensive experimental studies and shown to be more efficient than similar studies. In future work, we will optimize our method and investigate its capability on brain multimodality imaging datasets.

Acknowledgement. Algorithm development and image analysis for this study was funded, in part, by the National Institute on Aging (RF1AG051710 to QD, JZ, PMT, JY and YW, R01EB025-032 to YW, R01HL128818 to QD and YW, R01AG031581 and P30AG19610 to RJC, U54EB020403 to PMT and YW), the National Science Foundation (IIS-1421165 to JZ and YW), and Arizona Alzheimer's Consortium (JZ, RJC and YW). We gratefully acknowledge the support of NVIDIA Corporation with the donation of the Tesla K40 GPU used for this research.

Data collection and sharing for this project was funded by the ADNI (National Institutes of Health Grant U01 AG024904) and DOD ADNI (Department of Defense award number W81XWH-12-2-0012). ADNI is funded by the National Institute on Aging, the National Institute of Biomedical Imaging and Bioengineering, and through generous contributions from the following: AbbVie, Alzheimer's Association; Alzheimer's Drug Discovery Foundation; Araclon Biotech; BioClinica, Inc.; Biogen; Bristol-Myers Squibb Company; CereSpir, Inc.; Cogstate; Eisai Inc.; Elan Pharmaceuticals, Inc.; Eli Lilly and Company; EuroImmun; F. Hoffmann-La Roche Ltd and its affiliated company Genentech, Inc.; Fujirebio; GE Healthcare; IXICO Ltd.; Janssen Alzheimer Immunotherapy Research & Development, LLC.; Johnson & Johnson Pharmaceutical Research & Development LLC.; Lumosity; Lundbeck; Merck & Co., Inc.; Meso Scale Diagnostics, LLC.; NeuroRx Research; Neurotrack Technologies; Novartis Pharmaceuticals Corporation; Pfizer Inc.; Piramal Imaging; Servier; Takeda Pharmaceutical Company; and Transition Therapeutics. The Canadian Institutes of Health Research is providing funds to support ADNI clinical sites in Canada. Private sector contributions are facilitated by the Foundation for the National Institutes of Health (www.fnih.org). The grantee organization is the Northern California Institute for Research and Education, and the study is coordinated by the Alzheimer's Therapeutic Research Institute at the University of Southern California. ADNI data are disseminated by the Laboratory for Neuro Imaging at the University of Southern California.

References

1. Brookmeyer, R., Johnson, E., Ziegler-Graham, K., Michael Arrighi, H.: Forecasting the global burden of Alzheimer's disease. Alzheimer's Dementia **3**(3), 186–191 (2007)
2. Folstein, M.E.: A practical method for grading the cognitive state of patients for the children. J. Psychiatr res **12**, 189–198 (1975)
3. Rosen, W.G., Mohs, R.C., Davis, K.L.: A new rating scale for Alzheimer's disease. Am. J. Psychiatry (1984)
4. Buckner, R.L.: Memory and executive function in aging and AD: multiple factors that cause decline and reserve factors that compensate. Neuron **44**(1), 195–208 (2004)
5. Thompson, P.M., et al.: Mapping hippocampal and ventricular change in Alzheimer disease. Neuroimage **22**(4), 1754–1766 (2004)
6. Chung, M.K., Robbins, S., Evans, A.C.: Unified statistical approach to cortical thickness analysis. In: Christensen, G.E., Sonka, M. (eds.) IPMI 2005. LNCS, vol. 3565, pp. 627–638. Springer, Heidelberg (2005). https://doi.org/10.1007/11505730_52
7. Frisoni, G.B., Fox, N.C., Jack Jr., C.R., Scheltens, P., Thompson, P.M.: The clinical use of structural MRI in Alzheimer disease. Nat. Rev. Neurol. **6**(2), 67 (2010)
8. Cacciaglia, R., et al.: Effects of APOE-ε4 allele load on brain morphology in a cohort of middle-aged healthy individuals with enriched genetic risk for Alzheimer's disease. Alzheimer's Dementia **14**(7), 902–912 (2018)
9. Operto, G., et al.: White matter microstructure is altered in cognitively normal middle-aged APOE-ε4 homozygotes. Alzheimer's Res. Ther. **10**(1), 48 (2018)
10. Dong, Q., et al.: Applying surface-based hippocampal morphometry to study APOE-E4 allele dose effects in cognitively unimpaired subjects. NeuroImage Clin. **22**, 101744 (2019)

11. Shi, J., et al.: Studying ventricular abnormalities in mild cognitive impairment with hyperbolic Ricci flow and tensor-based morphometry. NeuroImage **104**, 1–20 (2015)

12. Fan, Y., Wang, G., Lepore, N., Wang, Y.: A tetrahedron-based heat flux signature for cortical thickness morphometry analysis. In: Frangi, A.F., Schnabel, J.A., Davatzikos, C., Alberola-López, C., Fichtinger, G. (eds.) MICCAI 2018. LNCS, vol. 11072, pp. 420–428. Springer, Cham (2018). https://doi.org/10.1007/978-3-030-00931-1_48

13. Zhang, J., et al.: Multi-task sparse screening for predicting future clinical scores using longitudinal cortical thickness measures. In: 2018 IEEE 15th International Symposium on Biomedical Imaging (ISBI 2018), pp. 1406–1410. IEEE (2018)

14. Razavian, A.S., Azizpour, H., Sullivan, J., Carlsson, S.: CNN features off-the-shelf: an astounding baseline for recognition. In: Proceedings of the IEEE Conference on Computer Vision and Pattern Recognition Workshops, pp. 806–813 (2014)

15. Zhang, J.: Deep transfer learning via restricted Boltzmann machine for document classification. In: 2011 10th International Conference on Machine Learning and Applications and Workshops (ICMLA), vol. 1, pp. 323–326. IEEE (2011)

16. LeCun, Y., Bottou, L., Bengio, Y., Haffner, P.: Gradient-based learning applied to document recognition. Proc. IEEE **86**(11), 2278–2324 (1998)

17. Krizhevsky, A., Sutskever, I., Hinton, G.E.: ImageNet classification with deep convolutional neural networks. In: Advances in Neural Information Processing Systems, pp. 1097–1105 (2012)

18. Turaga, S.C., et al.: Convolutional networks can learn to generate affinity graphs for image segmentation. Neural Comput. **22**(2), 511–538 (2010)

19. Hazlett, H.C., et al.: Early brain development in infants at high risk for autism spectrum disorder. Nature **542**(7641), 348 (2017)

20. Pan, S.J., Yang, Q.: A survey on transfer learning. IEEE Trans. Knowl. Data Eng. **22**(10), 1345–1359 (2010)

21. Donoho, D.L., Elad, M.: Optimally sparse representation in general (nonorthogonal) dictionaries via L1 minimization. Proc. Natl. Acad. Sci. **100**(5), 2197–2202 (2003)

22. Mairal, J., Bach, F., Ponce, J., Sapiro, G.: Online dictionary learning for sparse coding. In: Proceedings of the 26th Annual International Conference on Machine Learning, ICML 2009, pp. 689–696. ACM, New York (2009)

23. Lin, B., et al.: Stochastic coordinate coding and its application for drosophila gene expression pattern annotation. arXiv preprint arXiv:1407.8147 (2014)

24. Zhang, J., et al.: Hyperbolic space sparse coding with its application on prediction of Alzheimer's disease in mild cognitive impairment. In: Ourselin, S., Joskowicz, L., Sabuncu, M.R., Unal, G., Wells, W. (eds.) MICCAI 2016. LNCS, vol. 9900, pp. 326–334. Springer, Cham (2016). https://doi.org/10.1007/978-3-319-46720-7_38

25. Zhang, J., et al.: Applying sparse coding to surface multivariate tensor-based morphometry to predict future cognitive decline. In: 2016 IEEE 13th International Symposium on Biomedical Imaging (ISBI), pp. 646–650. IEEE (2016)

26. Zhang, D., Shen, D., Initiative, A.D.N., et al.: Multi-modal multi-task learning for joint prediction of multiple regression and classification variables in Alzheimer's disease. NeuroImage **59**(2), 895–907 (2012)

27. Zhang, W., et al.: Deep model based transfer and multi-task learning for biological image analysis. In: Proceedings of the 21th ACM SIGKDD International Conference on Knowledge Discovery and Data Mining, pp. 1475–1484. ACM (2015)

28. Deng, J., Dong, W., Socher, R., Li, L.-J., Li, K., Fei-Fei, L.: ImageNet: a large-scale hierarchical image database. In: IEEE Conference on Computer Vision and Pattern Recognition, CVPR 2009, pp. 248–255. IEEE (2009)

29. Kermany, D.S., et al.: Identifying medical diagnoses and treatable diseases by image-based deep learning. Cell **172**(5), 1122–1131 (2018)

30. Tibshirani, R.: Regression shrinkage and selection via the lasso. J. R. Stat. Soc. Ser. B (Methodol.) 267–288 (1996)

31. Weiner, M.W., et al.: The Alzheimer's disease neuroimaging initiative: a review of papers published since its inception. Alzheimer's Dementia **9**(5), e111–e194 (2013)

32. Canutescu, A.A., Dunbrack, R.L.: Cyclic coordinate descent: a robotics algorithm for protein loop closure. Protein Sci. **12**(5), 963–972 (2003)

33. Zhang, T.: Solving large scale linear prediction problems using stochastic gradient descent algorithms. In: Proceedings of the Twenty-First International Conference on Machine Learning, p. 116. ACM (2004)

34. Combettes, P.L., Wajs, V.R.: Signal recovery by proximal forward-backward splitting. Multiscale Model. Simul. **4**(4), 1168–1200 (2005)

35. Duchesne, S., Caroli, A., Geroldi, C., Louis Collins, D., Frisoni, G.B.: Relating one-year cognitive change in mild cognitive impairment to baseline MRI features. NeuroImage **47**(4), 1363–1370 (2009)

36. Jack Jr., C.R., et al.: The Alzheimer's disease neuroimaging initiative (ADNI): MRI methods. J. Magn. Reson. Imaging: Official J. Int. Soc. Magn. Reson. Med. **27**(4), 685–691 (2008)

37. Patenaude, B., Smith, S.M., Kennedy, D.N., Jenkinson, M.: A Bayesian model of shape and appearance for subcortical brain segmentation. Neuroimage **56**(3), 907–922 (2011)

38. Lorensen, W.E., Cline, H.E.: Marching cubes: a high resolution 3D surface construction algorithm. In: Proceedings of the 14th Annual Conference on Computer Graphics and Interactive Techniques, SIGGRAPH 1987, pp. 163–169. ACM, New York (1987)

39. Wang, Y., et al.: Surface-based TBM boosts power to detect disease effects on the brain: an n = 804 ADNI study. Neuroimage **56**(4), 1993–2010 (2011)

40. Han, X., Chenyang, X., Prince, J.L.: A topology preserving level set method for geometric deformable models. IEEE Trans. Pattern Anal. Mach. Intell. **25**(6), 755–768 (2003)

41. Wang, Y., Chan, T.F., Toga, A.W., Thompson, P.M.: Multivariate tensor-based brain anatomical surface morphometry via holomorphic one-forms. In: Yang, G.-Z., Hawkes, D., Rueckert, D., Noble, A., Taylor, C. (eds.) MICCAI 2009. LNCS, vol. 5761, pp. 337–344. Springer, Heidelberg (2009). https://doi.org/10.1007/978-3-642-04268-3_42

42. Fischl, B.: Freesurfer. Neuroimage **62**(2), 774–781 (2012)

43. Chung, M.K., Dalton, K.M., Davidson, R.J.: Tensor-based cortical surface morphometry via weighted spherical harmonic representation. IEEE Trans. Med. Imaging **27**(8), 1143–1151 (2008)

44. Jia, Y., et al.: Caffe: convolutional architecture for fast feature embedding. arXiv preprint arXiv:1408.5093 (2014)

45. Zhou, J., Liu, J., Narayan, V.A., Ye, J.: Modeling disease progression via multi-task learning. Neuroimage **78**, 233–248 (2013)

46. Suzuki, K.: Overview of deep learning in medical imaging. Radiol. Phys. Technol. **10**(3), 257–273 (2017)

A Robust Automated Pipeline for Localizing SEEG Electrode Contacts

Zefan Lin[1], Guofu Wang[2], Jiaru Cheng[1], Yaoxin Lin[2], Jianping Liu[3], Jiayin Lin[1], Guomin Luan[4], and Jie Luo[1(✉)] (iD)

[1] School of Biomedical Engineering, Key Laboratory of Sensing Technology and Biomedical Instrument of Guangdong Province, Guangdong Provincial Engineering and Technology Center of Advanced and Portable Medical Devices, Sun Yat-Sen University, Guangzhou 510006, China
luoj26@mail.sysu.edu.cn

[2] Department of Functional Neurosurgery, The First People's Hospital of Foshan, Foshan 528000, China

[3] Department of Radiology, The First People's Hospital of Foshan, Foshan 528000, China

[4] Department of Functional Neurosurgery, Sanbo Brain Hospital Capital Medical University, Beijing 100000, China

Abstract. Stereo-electroencephalography (SEEG) provides a powerful tool for preoperative evaluation of patients with drug-refractory epilepsy, and can supply more quantified and systematic information for epilepsy surgeons. Precise localization of the electrode contacts is fundamental for the clinical evaluation based on SEEG. The difficulties of segmentation of the electrode contacts include handling the metal artifacts in post-implantation CT images, separating electrodes close to each other, and identifying the contacts belong to the same electrode. Here, we developed a pipeline for automatic segmenting the SEEG electrode contacts from post-implantation CT volume data. The pipeline mainly includes morphological closing determination (MCD), threshold-reduction region growing (TRRG), electrode enter point repair (EEPR) based on electrode geometric information, such as directions, angles, and distances, interconnected electrodes determination and separation (IEDS), and craniocerebral interference removing (CCIR). The robustness and generality of our algorithm was validated on 12 subjects (135 electrodes, 1812 contacts). Compared to the manual segmentation (240 contacts), automatic localization was more precise and 9 times faster. Moreover, the sensitivity was as high as $99.55\% \pm 0.60\%$, while the positive predictive value reached $95.25\% \pm 1.38\%$. In addition, our algorithm successfully separated 14 sets of interconnected electrodes, verifying the stability of accurately segmenting close electrodes. To provide more useful information about electrode contacts, we fused post-implantation CT images with pre-implantation MRI T1 images, and provided the structural and functional brain region of each contact using AAL atlas and Brainnetome parcellation. We also developed a friendly MATLAB-based graphical user interface (GUI) in which the pipeline was implemented.

Keywords: Epilepsy · SEEG · Electrode contacts · Automatic localization

© Springer Nature Singapore Pte Ltd. 2019
A. Zeng et al. (Eds.): HBAI 2019, CCIS 1072, pp. 36–51, 2019.
https://doi.org/10.1007/978-981-15-1398-5_3

1 Introduction

For preoperative evaluation of epilepsy, the development trend [1] is using stereo-electroencephalography (SEEG) to more accurately locate the cortical or subcortical epileptogenic zone. In the past decade, SEEG has gradually evolved into the gold standard for preoperative evaluation of patients with medically intractable epilepsy. Epileptic lesions can even be directly destroyed through minimally invasive method of thermocoagulation [2] with the SEEG electrodes to cure some patients. In addition, more and more attention has been paid to the innovative idea that epilepsy is a brain network disease in recent years [3]. The analysis of SEEG signal provides more quantified and systematic information for surgeons. For example, time-frequency analysis have been used to calculate epilepsy index (EI) [4] for different electrode contacts to quantify the probability of a brain region to be an epileptic lesion, which is essential for thermocoagulation therapy and surgical resection. Using SEEG electrode contacts for brain network analysis can better describe the temporal patterns and spatial propagations [5, 6] of epileptic activities. Precise localization of the electrode contacts is a significant prerequisite for the clinical evaluation based on SEEG. However, since the number of contacts could be more than 100 for a regular patient, manual marking is time-consuming and labor-intensive. Moreover, when the CT artifacts are strong, the gray level of the guide wire between the contacts is close to that of the contacts, which makes the boundary of different contacts merged together and difficult to be visually recognized, resulting in a great error of manual segmentation. Therefore, there is an urgent need for developing an efficient and accurate automatic localization tool of SEEG electrode contacts to assist clinical practice.

Several groups have proposed computer-assisted localization algorithms of SEEG electrode contacts. Wang et al. [7] used clustering algorithm to realize semi-automatic contact segmentation, and tracked the depth electrode by fitting quadratic curve. To provide fully-automatic identification of SEEG electrodes, Meesters et al. [8] estimated the electrode direction according to bolt direction on the skull, but the robustness of their algorithm should be further verified. Actually, there are many difficulties to overcome to implement a robust fully-automatic segmentation algorithm. For example, several electrodes may be so close to each other (called close electrodes) that the contacts on them are prone to be incorrectly recognized as on the same electrode. In this case, the close contacts from other electrode could be considered as a kind of interference during contact recognition and clustering. Arnulfo et al. [9] proposed an algorithm which was robust to close electrodes. They used the priori locations of the entry point and target point during electrode planning. But the real locations of the electrodes might be deviated from those in planning. In addition, some electrodes appeared to be curved rather than straight during surgical implantation. In order to accurately localize the contacts of the bent electrode, Granados et al. [10] proposed a contact search algorithm based on the direction of the bolt with distance and angle constraints. However, none of the above studies considered strong CT artifact condition. Because when the metal artifacts are weak, it could only blur the voxels of electrode contacts, keeping the contrast between contacts and guide wire great enough to disconnect each contact. On this occasion, the voxels of contacts are convergent

(Fig. 1a) [9]. But if the artifacts are strong, the gray levels of the contacts and the guide wire are so close that the contacts are connected with each other (Fig. 1b), which would bring a lot of difficulties in segmenting the contacts with their morphological features. One more problem with the previous work was that they did not focus on performing detailed classification of the non-contact components with relatively high gray levels (i.e., interferences), hence the robustness has not been fully demonstrated. We would put much effort on this issue. Due to no consideration of the strong CT artifacts and no detailed description of removing different interferences in previous studies, we are unable to provide specific comparison results with existing related work.

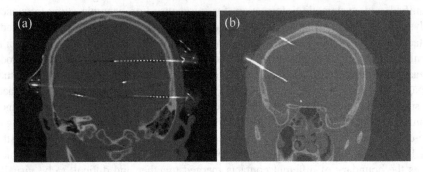

Fig. 1. Examples of post-implantation images at different CT artifact levels. (a) Convergent contacts under weak CT artifacts; (b) Connected contacts due to strong CT artifacts.

Our main contribution is a robust and generalizable localization method that can automatically segment and cluster SEEG electrode contacts, which will be elaborated in Sects. 2–4. Our algorithm has high anti-interference ability, and can precisely recognize the close contacts from different electrodes and accurately segment the connected contacts due to strong CT artifacts. Moreover, the robustness and generality of the pipeline were verified and evaluated on 12 subjects (135 electrodes, 1812 contacts) in Sect. 5. We also developed a friendly MATLAB-based graphical user interface (GUI) in which the pipeline was implemented (Sect. 6), providing a convenient way for neurosurgeons to view the contacts and their site information (such as RAS coordinates, AAL brain region, etc.). The software is available at https://github.com/BrainNetworks/ContactSegmentation.

2   Understanding and Pre-processing of the Data

Our data were obtained from the Department of Functional Neurology, the First People's Hospital of Foshan. The pre-implantation structural MRI images were generated by a 3T scanner with in-plane isotropic resolution of 0.42–0.55 mm (TR = 7–8 ms; TE = 2.8–3.3 ms; TI = 450 ms; FOV = 24*24). After implantation, CT scans were acquired with in-plane isotropic resolution of 0.38–0.52 mm (FOV = 512*512). Each SEEG Depth electrode (Alcis, France, or HKHS Healthcare, China) contains 5–

18 contacts with a central distance of 3.5 mm between two adjacent contacts, all of which are arranged at equal distances on the electrode. Each contact is a platinum-iridium cylinder with a diameter of 0.8 mm and a length of 2 mm, as shown in Fig. 2. Since the contacts are small in size, the sub-millimeter resolution of CT is required to ensure that each contact contains enough CT voxels. There were totally 1812 contacts on 135 electrodes from 12 drug-resistant patients (3 males, 9 females, mean age 19.1 years, range 3–35). Our goal is to automatically segment these electrode contacts from CT images, and cluster the contacts on the same electrode. Two references used to evaluate the accuracy of our work were: (i) the surgeons' manual localization of the convergent contacts; and (ii) the manually visual evaluation of the automatic localized contacts.

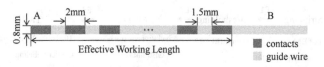

Fig. 2. Specification of SEEG electrode contact. "A" denotes the terminal deep in the brain, whereas "B" is the part intersected with the skull, forming the enter point of the electrode.

Data Preprocessing

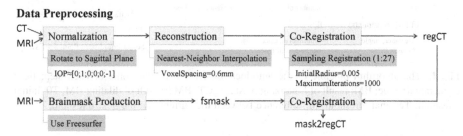

Fig. 3. The algorithm pipeline of the pre-processing procedure. IOP: a "field" in the header of DICOM (Digital Imaging and Communications in Medicine) format, denoting the image orientation of patients. For example, [0; 1; 0; 0; 0; −1] means the scans are aligned to Sagittal plane; regCT: registered CT volumes after co-registration; fsmask: a brain mask obtained from Freesurfer suite with MRI volume data; mask2regCT: the registered brain mask.

The pre-processing of the data consists of two steps (Fig. 3): first, co-registering CTs and MRIs to get registered CT images (regCT); second, obtaining an MRI brain mask (fsmask) with Freesurfer (http://freesurfer.net/), and registering fsmask onto regCT to get a CT brain mask (mask2regCT) for the stripping of extracranial tissue. The boundary of mask2regCT is an accurate estimate of the brain boundary, which is very important for eliminating extracranial interference. In addition, the voxel spacing of both regCT and mask2regCT in the three dimensions was resampled to 0.6 mm.

3   Auto-localization of the SEEG Electrode Contacts

After implantation, the terminal A of the electrode was deepest in the brain, while the point B was around the skull (Fig. 1). We call the intersection of the skull and the guide wire around point B the Electrode Enter Point (EEP). The main idea of automatic contact location algorithm is to connect all voxels of contacts belonging to the same electrode at first, and then segment each contact on the electrode according to the contacts' geometry. The pipeline of the auto-localization can be divided into eight steps (Fig. 4):

Auto-Segmentation of Contacts

mask2regCT

		E1		E2		E3	
	EcT Stripping	→	Thresholding	→	MCD	→	TRRG

regCT

Dilation of BM	T0=max(E1)*0.7	ball structure (r =3~10)	T0~Te, th=2, Te=max(E1)*0.01
rectangle structure (20×20)		Constraints	Outlier Labeling
BM2.*regCT		distance between centres, number of pixels	constraint on the centre-axis distance

E4		E5		E6		E7	
→	EEPR	→	IEDS	→	CCIR	→	Contacts Modeling

Reverse TRRG	IED	Constraints	BM.*E6 →E8
PCA	number of bolts	orientation, distance	Artifacts Reduction →E9
EEPAJ (constraints)	IES		PCA
orientation, angle, distance, PCA	minimum distance, centre-axis distance		Select Equidistant Points →$Csub_i$

Fig. 4. The algorithm pipeline of the auto-localization. E1–E9: outcome of each step; EcT: extracranial tissue; BM: result of binarizing mask2regCT; BM2: result of dilating BM; T0: initial threshold; Te: final threshold; th: difference between the current and the next threshold.

1. Extracranial tissue stripping. The brain mask (mask2regCT) obtained in the pre-processing procedure did not contain the skull, but the EEP on the skull was a part of the electrode, which provided useful information about the electrodes, such as the direction and position of the electrodes. It should not be stripped initially. We dilated the binary mask (BM) of mask2regCT to obtain BM2, which contain the skull. And then, extracranial tissue (EcT) was stripped by dot-multiplying BM2 and regCT. This step eliminated extracranial interference, and the outcome volume of this step was called E1.

2. Threshold processing. The threshold used to extract electrode was T0 (i.e., 0.7 times the maximum gray value of voxels in E1). The result of threshold processing is E2, which was a binary volume (Fig. 5). It could be seen that most of the contacts could be extracted by threshold processing when the CT artifacts were weak (Fig. 5a), but a lot of contacts were neglected due to strong CT artifacts (Fig. 5b). To make our description clearer, we categorized the connected components in the binary volume into three kinds (Fig. 6): (1) Intracranial Connected components (ICC), all of whose voxels were in the brain; (2) Cranial Connected Components (CCC), all of whose

voxels located on the skull; (3) CranioCerebral Connected Components (CCCC), part of whose voxels located on the skull, whereas the others in the brain. Both of CCC and CCCC were Non-Intracranial Connected Components (NICC). Both of ICC and CCC were Non-Cranial Connected Components (NCCC).

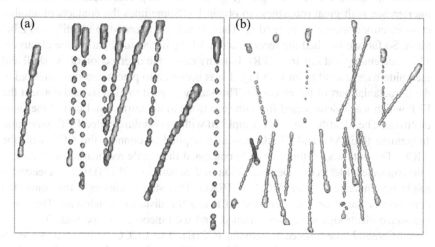

Fig. 5. The outcome of threshold processing (E2). (a) A case under the weak CT artifact condition; (b) a case under the strong CT artifact condition.

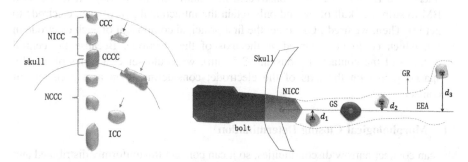

Fig. 6. Three categories of con-nected components in E2 after threshold processing. ICC: Intracra-nial Connected Components; CCC: Cranial Connected Components; CCCC: CranioCerebral Connected Components. ICC and CCCC are collectively referred to as NCCC, while CCC and CCCC are both NCCC. The three connected com-ponents indicated by arrows are interferences (i.e., they are not parts of an electrode).

Fig. 7. The principle of the abnormal point marking procedure. The connected component that is not belonged to the electrode but is included in the grown region is called an abnormal point, which is identified by the distance between the component and the electrode axis. The black ICC is GS (growing seed), and the two gray dotted lines depicted the boundary of the grown region (GR). The red line is an estimate of the electrode axis determined by connecting the center of the NICC and the GS. In this case, three ICCs are included in GR. The 2 blue ones are ICCs on the same electrode, while the yellow one is the ICC on another close electrode. (Color figure online)

3. Morphological closing determination (MCD). This step was used to connect the contacts in weak CT artifact cases (Fig. 5a) by morphological closing (MC). The outcome of this step was E3.
4. Threshold-reduction region growing (TRRG). TRRG was used to connect the contacts in strong CT artifact cases (Fig. 5b). This step could remove intracranial interference with great robustness to obtain E4. Sometimes the contacts of another close electrode were also merged in. Therefore, it was needed to identify and label them. So far, we finished the reconstruction of the intracranial part of the electrode.
5. Electrode enter point repair (EEPR). In many cases, the intersection of the skull and the guide wire around point B in Fig. 1 was broken into pieces and disconnected to the intracranial part of the electrode. This step was used to identify and connect the EEP which was disconnected from one electrode to the intracranial part of the same electrode. The identification was completed with a procedure called EEP Ascription Judgement (EEPAJ), and TRRG was also applied to connect the CCC with the NICC. The outcome of this step (E5) contained the whole reconstructed electrode.
6. Interconnected Electrodes Determination and Separation (IEDS). Close electrodes might be connected during MCD or TRRG. This step re-clustered the connected components based on the identified EEP and the distance constraints. The interconnected electrodes were disassembled, and the outcome volume was E6.
7. CranioCerebral Interference Removing (CCIR). The CCCC which was not electrode was craniocerebral interference (CCI). CCI was the interference leftover to be removed in this step. The product of this step was E7.
8. Contact modeling. The electrodes in E7 may be "obese" because of TRRG. We intersected E7 with E2 to reconstructed the "slim" electrode (E8). Next, we used BM to strip the skull of E8 and only retain the intracranial part of each electrode to get E9. Then, we used PCA to get the first principal component of each electrode in E9, which could be regarded as the axis of the electrode. Because the central distance of the contacts is constant (3.5 mm), we could select a series of equally spaced points on the axis of the electrode, considering them as the centers of contacts.

3.1 Morphological Closing Determination

MC can connect narrow discontinuities, so it can connect the uniformly distributed and convergent contacts (Fig. 5a) efficiently. However, after the threshold processing, many of the contacts might be lost because the gray values of them were lower than the threshold value due to strong CT artifacts (Fig. 5b). In this case, the gap between the adjacent ICCs from the same electrode might be too wide to be morphologically closed. Therefore, we use MCD to determine which ICCs in E2 should be morphologically closed. The method was as follows:

1. MC was applied to E2 to get E2closed, and its connected components were labeled as $E2C_i, i = 1, 2, \ldots, N$. Connected components $C_{ij}, j = 1, 2, \ldots, M$ were obtained by intersecting $E2C_i$ with E2.
2. If the contacts were convergent, the volumes of $C_{ij}, j = 1, 2, \ldots, M$ were from the same electrode and similar with each other, and the distance between each two

adjacent C_{ij} should be close. These were different in the strong artifact case. Accordingly, we established geometric constraints, i.e., the standard deviation of the volumes of C_{ij} and the distances between the adjacent C_{ij}. If the difference was small, the metal artifacts of E2 were considered weak, and MC was suitable for E2. The result of performing MC on E2 was E3. Otherwise, E3 = E2.

3.2   Threshold-Reduction Region Growing

TRRG is implemented iteratively in three-dimensional space. Each ICC in E3 was used as Growing Seed (GS). If any of the voxels in the 26 neighborhoods of the GS boundary possessed a gray value larger than the threshold T, the voxel was set to "1". Therefore, the GS was grown until there was no voxels in the neighborhood with gray value larger than T, and that was the end of the iteration in the TRRG. Threshold reduction meant that the threshold T was lowered in each iteration by 2, with T0-2 the initial value and Te (i.e., 0.1 times the maximum gray value of voxels in E1) the final value. The growth termination condition was that the ICC connecting to an NICC in E3 or the threshold value was reduced to Te. If the metal artifacts of CT were strong, the gray values of voxels between the guide wire and the contacts were close but higher than those of the surrounding brain tissues. Therefore, if GS was the ICC located on the electrode, the voxels of the guide wire and the lost contacts would be included in the TRRG process step by step, and the intracranial part of the electrode would be reconstructed as the GS grew. The TRRG result (GR) of each GS was added to E3, yielding E4. On the other hand, if GS was an intracranial interference, it usually could not grow and connect to an NICC. Therefore, the intracranial interferences would be removed.

TRRG usually tended to connect ICCs on the same electrode. These ICCs needed not growing for the sake of computation efficiency. However, TRRG could also absorb the ICC of another close electrode (the yellow ICC in Fig. 7). If we didn't identify this ICC, the most dangerous result was that the close electrode would not be reconstructed at all if it only had one ICC (Fig. 5b) after threshold processing (step 3 of the pipeline). Therefore, we needed to mark this type of ICCs and still perform TRRG on them. This process was called abnormal point marking. The method was as following: a line was determined through the center of the NICC and the GS, and this line was regarded as an estimate of the electrode axis (EEA). Calculate the distances from the center of the ICCs to the EEA (e.g., d_1, d_2, d_3), called the center-axis distance (CAD). We believed that the CAD must small enough (say, <2 voxels) for the ICCs on the same electrode; otherwise, it was more likely that the ICC was an abnormal point.

3.3   Electrode Enter Point Repair

After TRRG, the ICC of each electrode in E3 was connected to the corresponding CCCC of the same electrode. EEPR was the process of connecting the CCC of the electrode to the CCCC. In this step, the TRRG could be applied to one of the CCC, but the growing would be affected by the skull interference. For the sake of distinction, TRRG in EEPR was called reverse TRRG. The threshold used in reverse TRRG was the same as that of TRRG. Since the intensities of the skull voxels was larger than those of the brain, the reverse TRRG sometimes reconstructed the skull instead of the EEP. Therefore, we proposed EEPAJ to remove the skull interference.

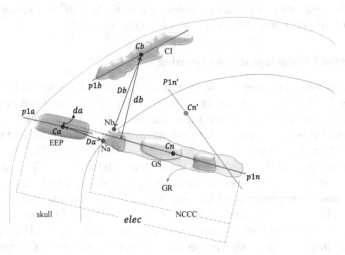

Fig. 8. Illustration of the constraints used in the EEPAJ procedure. Perform PCA on NCCC, EEP, and CI to obtain the first principal components $p1n$, $p1a$, and $p1b$, respectively. With Cn as the origin, we establish the PCA coordinate space of the NCCC. Then, we project the voxels on the EEP onto the PCA space of the NCCC, and the directional constraint is that the coordinates of all the EEP voxels in the first main direction should be uniformly larger or smaller than those of all the NCCC voxels. The angular constraint is that the angle formed by the first main axis of the CCC (e.g., $p1a$ or $p1b$) and $p1n$ should be small. The distance constraint is that the minimum distance (Da or Db) from voxels in the NCCC to the center of a CCC (e.g., Ca or Cb) should be small.

The implementation of EEPAJ was based on constraints such as direction, angle, and distance (Fig. 8). Let one of the electrodes *elec* in E4 broke into two parts after TRRG: an NCCC and an EEP. There was an interfering CCC around it called CI. The centers of NCCC, EEP, and CI were denoted with Cn, Ca, and Cb, respectively. In order to accurately identify the EEP and connect it to the NCCC, without interfered by CI, we established the following constraints:

1. Directional constraints. If the directions of both NCCC and CCC aligned with the radial axis of the implanted electrode, and the projections of NCCC and EEP on the radial axis did not overlap with each other, then, this CCC should be an EEP, not a CI. We applied principle component analysis (PCA) to extract the first main directions of the NCCC, which was an estimate of the electrode axis. Then, we projected the voxels in the CCC onto the PCA space of the NCCC. If the coordinates of all the CCC voxels in the first main direction were uniformly larger or smaller than those of all the NCCC voxels, then the NCCC and the CCC should not be overlapped.

2. Angular constraints. When the percent variability explained by the first principal component was large, the shape of the CCC was close to a line. In this case, if the angle formed by the first main axis of the CCC and that of the NCCC was small, then the NCCC and the CCC should be on the same axis, and the CCC was likely to be an EEP.

3. Distance constraints. The distance between an NCCC and an EEP should be relatively small, since the EEP was broken on the skull, whose thickness was small. Therefore, we could calculate the distance from all voxels of NCCC to the center of a CCC (denoted by Ca in Fig. 8) and found a voxel (Na) with the minimum distance (Da). If Da was small (say, <40), the CCC was likely to be an EEP. In addition, we could double check if the CCC was an EEP by the distance between Ca and the first main axis ($p1n$) of the NCCC, which should be also small.

The CCC that could grow to an NCCC in E4 was considered to be an EPP, or if a CCC meet the EEPAJ constraints, we considered this CCC to be an EEP and connected the center of this CCC to that of the NCCC. The CCCs could not be EEPs were considered as CIs, and the voxels of CIs were set to "0". The outcome of EEPR was E5.

3.4 Interconnected Electrodes Determination and Separation

The close electrodes might be connected during MCD or TRRG. Therefore, we needed to find the interconnected electrodes in E5 and separate them. This step was called IEDS. There was only one EEP for each electrode, but if a connected component in E5 ($E5C_i$) was formed of several interconnected electrodes, it would possessed more than one EEP. We counted the number of EEPs (Ni) of each $E5C_i$ based on some features of the bolts on the skull, such as the extracranial guide wire. If Ni>1, we considered the i-th connected component as a group of interconnected electrodes and performed interconnected electrodes separation. The separation was implemented based on a distance-based re-clustering strategy. Suppose we had a connected component composed of two interconnected electrodes (e_1 and e_2), the EEPs for the two electrodes were EEP_1 and EEP_2, respectively (Fig. 9). The separation process consist of the following 2 steps:

1. Search of anchor ICC. During interconnected electrodes separation, the ICCs in the connected component should be re-clustered to different groups based on the EEPs. For each EEP, the nearest ICC belonging to the same electrode was considered as the anchor ICC used to link other ICCs (e.g., ICC1 should be an anchor ICC, which is denoted with anchor1 in Fig. 9a). However, due to strong CT artifacts, the nearest ICC might be someone on the other electrode (Fig. 9a). Therefore, we checked the normalized intersection of the connected component ($E5C_i$) and the connection at both centers of each ICC and the EEP. The ICC with the largest intersection (e.g., $anchor_2$ in Fig. 9a) should be belonged to the electrode where the current EEP was located, and it was considered as the anchor ICC in this case.

2. ICC re-clustering. Since we had identified the anchor ICC of each electrode in, this step we re-clustered all the leftover ICCs iteratively into different groups. During the initial iteration, we connected the centers of the EEP and the anchor ICC of one

of the electrodes and defined the line as the estimated radial axis of the electrode. Then, we calculated the distances from the centers of the leftover ICCs to the estimated axis, and the ICC with the minimum distance was clustered into the group of current anchor ICC. During the new iteration, a new estimated axis would be obtained with the center of the anchor ICC replaced with that of all clustered ICCs. The more ICCs clustered into a group, the closer the estimated axis to the real electrode axis. All the leftover ICCs would be re-clustered as the iteration finished.

We connected all the ICCs belonging to the same electrode and their EEP, thus all the electrodes had been identified. The outcome of IEDS was E6.

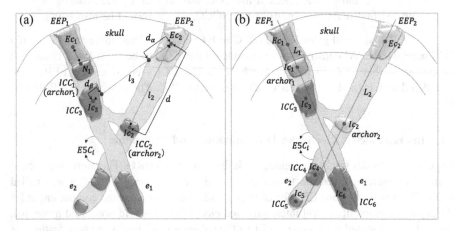

Fig. 9. The principle of the interconnect electrodes separation. (a) Search of the anchor ICC. The connected component $E5$ C_i includes two electrodes e_1 and e_2, and their EEPs (EEP_1 and EEP_2). The anchor ICC of e_1 is ICC_1, and that of e_2 is ICC_2. $Anchor_1$ could be easily found by its smallest distance to the center of EEP_1 (Ec_1), but the nearest ICC to EEP_2 is ICC_3 instead of ICC_2, which is the real anchor ICC of e_2. In this case, we connect each ICC to specific EEP, and calculate the normalized intersection of each connection and $E5$ C_i. For example, for ICC_2, the normalized intersection is d/l_2; for ICC_3, the normalized intersection is $(d_\alpha + d_\beta)/l_3$. Since $(d_\alpha + d_\beta)/l_3 < d/l_2 = 1$, ICC_2 should be $anchor_2$; (b) ICC re-clustering. Red lines are estimated electrode axis by connecting centers of each EEP and its anchor ICC. The leftover ICCs are re-clustered with their distances to different electrode axes. (Color figure online)

3.5   Craniocerebral Interference Removing

In the previous steps, we removed extracranial interference (in EcT stripping), intracranial interference (in TRRG) and cranial interference (in EEPR), and the last type of interference left in E6 to be removed was craniocerebral interference (CCI). Since the electrode we recognized was also a CCCC, all of the connected components in E6 were CCCCs (Fig. 10), and we could not tell which one was electrode. To identify electrodes, we divided the voxels of each CCCC into two parts: the intracranial part and the cranial part, and established the following constraints:

1. Axial directional constraints. Most of the electrodes pointed to the deep brain rather than the cerebral cortex. We extracted the axial direction by the first principle component of the CCCC. If the projections of the cranial voxels and the intracranial ones overlapped with each other to a large extent, this CCCC was likely to be a CCI; otherwise, it was likely to be an electrode.
2. Shape constraints. The shape of an electrode was linear. We examined the percent variability explained by the first principal components of these CCCCs. The larger percent variability explained, the more linear of the CCCC.
3. Length constraints. If the length of a CCCC was less than 18 mm, it was likely not an electrode, since the effective implantation length of the electrode is at least 18 mm. The length can be approximately calculated by the length of the projection of the CCCC on its first principal component.

After removing CCI, E7 was obtained. With E7, we could model the electrodes as well as the contacts based on the specifications, and then the three-dimensional coordinates of all the contacts could be obtained (Fig. 11).

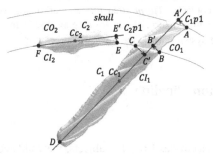
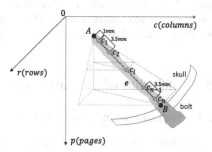

Fig. 10. The principle of CCIR. The voxels in a CCCC were divided into two parts: intracranial (yellow part, e.g., CO_1 of C_1 and CO_2 of C_2) and cranial part (blue part, e.g., CI_1 of C_1 and CI_2 of C_2). The red lines denoted the first principle components of the CCCCs. If the direction of a CCCC was towards the deep brain, only a small part of the projection of the intracranial voxels (e.g., $B'C'$) would be overlapped with that of the cranial voxels (e.g., $B'D$). Otherwise, the CCCC would be an interference. (Color figure online)

Fig. 11. The principle of contact modeling. The red line denoted the radial axis of the electrode, "A" denoted the depth terminal of the electrode, "B" denoted the enter point terminal, and the blue dots on the red line denoted the centers of contacts determined by electrode specifications. (Color figure online)

4 Determination of the Brain Areas Where Contacts Located

In Sect. 3, we described the procedure of obtaining the index coordinates of the electrode contacts in regCT. To provide more information for clinical use, we reported the brain areas where contacts located based on AAL and Brainnetome atlas (https://atlas.brainnetome.org). First, we obtained the RAS coordinates of the MRI images, and co-registered the MRI images with a canonical brain (avg152T1), obtaining the transformational matrix *Tform* and *M*. Then, we applied *Tform* and M^{-1} to the indexes of the contacts to obtain their MNI coordinates (Fig. 12). Finally, we provided the structural and functional brain area of each contact according to the AAL atlas and Brainnetome parcellation.

Determine the Brain Areas of Contacts

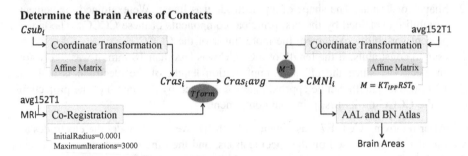

Fig. 12. Algorithm pipeline of determining the brain areas of contacts. $Csub_i$: index coordinates of the contacts in regCT; $Cras_i(Csub_iavg)$: RAS coordinates of the contacts in regCT (avg152T1); $CMNI_i$: MNI coordinates of the contacts; *Tform*: transformational matrix of registering the MRI images onto avg152T1; *M*: the affine matrix of transforming avg152T1 from native space to real world space (RAS coordinate system); M^{-1}: the inverse matrix of *M*.

5   Validation of the Auto-localization Pipeline

5.1   Robustness and Generality

Using data containing 1812 contacts on 135 electrodes from 12 subjects, we validated five of the eight steps (referred to Sect. 3) in the auto-localization pipeline: MCD, TRRG, EEPR, IEDS and CCIR. In these steps, we have established a variety of constraints based on geometric characteristics such as volume, direction, angle, distance, etc. to identify and deal with specific objects. For example, in TRRG, we needed to mark the abnormal ICCs so that they could be grown in the following steps. Whether these objects were correctly recognized was crucial to the validity of the pipeline. We compared the automatic recognition with manual one (Table 1), and found that the results of manual and automatic recognition were identical, which suggested that the algorithm was applicable to a relatively high extent.

Table 1. Comparison of manual and automatic recognition in 5 steps of the pipeline

Procedure	Objects	Manual (no.)	Automatic (no.)
MCD	Datasets whose contacts were convergent	2	2
TRRG	Abnormal ICCs should be marked	2	2
EEPR	EEPs should be repaired	87	87
IEDS	Connected component containing interconnected electrodes	14	14
CCIR	Electrodes identified	135	135

5.2 Accuracy

In a total of 135 electrodes (1812 contacts), we extracted all the electrodes and obtained 1896 contacts (1803 true contacts and 93 false contacts), and 9 contacts were missed. The false and missed contacts were mainly distributed around the electrode enter points (EEPs), bathing in cerebral spinal fluid, where the seizure focus was unlikely located in. The mean sensitivity over 12 subjects (Fig. 13) was 99.55% (s.d.: 0.6%), and the mean positive predictive value was 95.25% (s.d.: 1.38%).

We invited two neurosurgeons to perform manual markup of two subjects (240 contacts) with convergent contacts. The Euclidean distance between the RAS coordinates of manual markup and automatic localized contacts was calculated to quantify the difference. The mean difference over all the contacts was 1.055 mm (s.d.: 0.449 mm). The difference was small, and compared to manual markup (black dots in Fig. 14), the most automatic localized contacts (red dots) were closer to the center of the real contacts (translucent blue connected components), which demonstrated that our automatic contact localization algorithm possessed a high accuracy. In addition, the pipeline automatically localized 8.3 contacts per minute, which is 9 times faster than manual markup (0.9 contacts per minute).

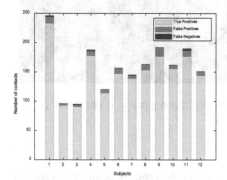

Fig. 13. The true positives, false positives, and false negatives of the 12 subjects.

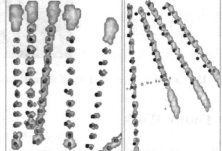

Fig. 14. Comparison of manual markup (black dots) and automatic localized contacts (red dots). (Color figure online)

6 Graphical User Interface

To provide a friendly user interface, we designed a MATLAB-based graphical user interface (GUI) for clinicians (Fig. 15). Our auto-localization pipeline was implemented into the GUI (code available at https://github.com/BrainNetworks/ContactSegmentation). The left part of the interface with a blue background was the Tool Panel, and the right side was a View Panel. The Tool Panel was divided into three modules: data import, image viewing, data processing including images resampling, coordinate transforming, multimodal registration, and contact information viewing. Formats of the import data could be dicom, nii. The RAS coordinates, MNI coordinates, AAL and Brainnetome (BN) brain region of each contact could be browsed. In addition, the information of all contacts could be exported to an Excel format file for clinicians to view and perform further analysis.

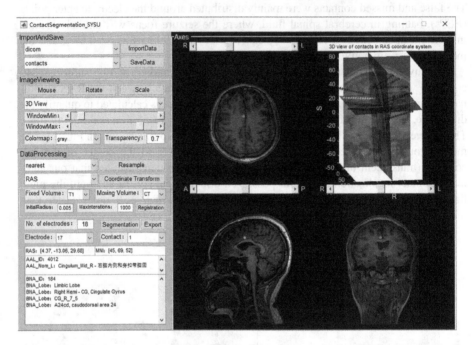

Fig. 15. Graphical user interface of the automated localization pipeline. (Color figure online)

7 Future Work

In the future, More data should be applied to improve the robustness and generality of our pipeline. For example, in our dataset, only mild bending electrodes were observed, which need not excess handling. But for moderate bending electrode, a little modification, introducing curve-fitting, in the electrode and contact modelling step could solve the problem. In addition, with accurate contact locations, more neuroinformatics analysis could be performed combining SEEG and multimodal brain images, providing a more profound understanding of epilepsy production and propagation, hence assisting clinical diagnosis and treatment.

8 Conclusion

In this study, we developed a fully automatic SEEG electrode contact localization pipeline considering strong CT artifacts and removing different types of interferences. The algorithm was of highly robustness, generality, and accuracy. A friendly GUI implemented the algorithm was provided for surgeons to conveniently browse the sites of different contacts in structural MRI volumes. Not only the automated pipeline speeds up the manual marking up of the contacts, but the GUI also provides the anatomical and functional brain region where each contact locates, which is a very useful information for epilepsy preoperative evaluation.

Acknowledgement. This research is supported by a Union Grant of the Guangdong Province and National Natural Science Foundation of China (No. U1801265) and a grant from National Nature Science Foundation of China (No. 61403430).

References

1. Bartolomei, F., et al.: Defining epileptogenic networks: contribution of SEEG and signal analysis. Epilepsia **58**(7), 1131–1147 (2017). https://doi.org/10.1111/epi.13791
2. Scholly, J., et al.: High-frequency oscillations and spikes running down after SEEG-guided thermocoagulations in the epileptogenic network of periventricular nodular heterotopia. Epilepsy Res. **150**, 27–31 (2019). https://doi.org/10.1016/j.eplepsyres.2018.12.006
3. Jehi, L.: Outcomes of epilepsy surgery for epileptic networks. Epilepsy Curr. **17**(3), 160–162 (2017). https://doi.org/10.5698/1535-7511.17.3.160
4. Bartolomei, F., Chauvel, P., Wendling, F.: Epileptogenicity of brain structures in human temporal lobe epilepsy: a quantified study from intracerebral EEG. Brain **131**(7), 1818–1830 (2008). https://doi.org/10.1093/brain/awn111
5. Proix, T., Bartolomei, F., Guye, M., Jirsa, V.K.: Individual brain structure and modelling predict seizure propagation. Brain **140**(3), 641–654 (2017). https://doi.org/10.1093/brain/awx004
6. Jirsa, V.K., et al.: The virtual epileptic patient: individualized whole-brain models of epilepsy spread. NeuroImage **145**, 377–388 (2017). https://doi.org/10.1016/j.neuroimage.2016.04.049
7. Qin, C., et al.: Automatic and precise localization and cortical labeling of subdural and depth intracranial electrodes. Front. Neuroinform. **11**, 1–10 (2017). https://doi.org/10.3389/fninf.2017.00010
8. Meesters, S., et al.: Automated identification of intracranial depth electrodes in computed tomography data. In: 2015 IEEE 12th International Symposium on Biomedical Imaging (ISBI), pp. 976–979. IEEE, New York (2015). https://doi.org/10.1109/ISBI.2015.7164034
9. Arnulfo, G., Narizzano, M., Cardinale, F., Fato, M.M., Palva, J.M.: Automatic segmentation of deep intracerebral electrodes in computed tomography scans. BMC Bioinform. **16**(99), 1–12 (2015). https://doi.org/10.1186/s12859-015-0511-6
10. Granados, A., et al.: Automatic segmentation of stereoelectroencephalography (SEEG) electrodes post-implantation considering bending. Int. J. Comput. Assist. Radiol. Surg. **13**(6), 935–946 (2018). https://doi.org/10.1007/s11548-018-1740-8

Early Diagnosis of Alzheimer's Disease Based on Deep Learning and GWAS

Dan Pan[1,2], Yin Huang[3], An Zeng[3,4(✉)], Longfei Jia[3], Xiaowei Song[5], and for Alzheimer's Disease Neuroimaging Initiative (ADNI)

[1] Guangdong Construction Polytechnic,
Guangzhou 510440, People's Republic of China
[2] Guangzhou Dazhi Networks Technology Co. Ltd.,
Guangzhou 510000, People's Republic of China
[3] Guangdong University of Technology,
Guangzhou 510006, People's Republic of China
zengan@gdut.edu.cn
[4] Guangdong Key Laboratory of Big Data Analysis and Processing,
Guangzhou 510006, People's Republic of China
[5] ImageTech Lab, Simon Fraser University, Vancouver V6B 5K3, Canada

Abstract. Alzheimer's disease (AD) is a typical irreversible neurodegenerative disease. At present, the pathogenesis of AD remains elusive and the effective treatment of AD is still a challenge for clinicians. Therefore, early diagnosis is of great importance for the development of new drugs to prevent the progression of AD. With the rapid advancement of neuroimaging technology and deep learning, more and more researchers have turned to deep learning to analyze the brain images for early diagnosis of AD. Plus, studies have demonstrated that it is very likely that the genetic makeup of an individual may influence his/her susceptibility to AD traits. Researchers have begun to identify the genetic biomarkers associated to AD and evaluate the effects of genes upon the changes in the structure and function of the brain of AD patients. In this study, an ensemble model of multi-slice classifiers based on convolutional neural network (CNN) was proposed to make an early diagnosis of AD and at the same time to identify the significant brain regions related to AD. The morphological data of these identified brain regions and the genotype were utilized to carry out genome-wide association studies (GWAS) to explore the potential genetic biomarkers of AD.

Keywords: Alzheimer's disease (AD) · Magnetic resonance imaging (MRI) · Convolutional neural network (CNN) · Genome-wide association study (GWAS)

Data used in preparation of this article were obtained from the Alzheimer's Disease Neuroimaging Initiative (ADNI) database (adni.loni.usc.edu). As such, the investigators within the ADNI contributed to the design and implementation of ADNI and/or provided data but did not participate in analysis or writing of this report. A complete listing of ADNI investigators can be found at: http://adni.loni.usc.edu/wp-content/uploads/how_to_apply/ADNI_Acknowledgement_List.pdf.

1   Introduction

Alzheimer's disease (AD) is a chronic neurodegenerative disease. It is clinically manifested as amnesia, loss of mobility and language ability, etc. [1] The World Alzheimer Report 2016 issued by Alzheimer's Disease International proposed that the number of AD patients worldwide would increase from 47 million to 132 million in 2050 [2]. The pathogenesis of AD remains elusive and the course of AD is irreversible. No drugs available can cure AD or completely stop the progression of AD. Therefore, early diagnosis of AD is of great significance for developing new drugs and measures to prevent further deterioration of the disease.

Mild cognitive impairment (MCI) is a state between AD and healthy controls (HC), which can be subdivided into MCI patients who will convert to AD (MCIc) and MCI patients who will not convert to AD (MCInc). Previous studies have demonstrated that MCI could be more likely to convert to AD [3]. At present, many researchers have attempted to deliver an early diagnosis of MCIc. How to accurately diagnose the current stage of disease has become the focus of early diagnosis of AD.

With the rapid advancement of neuroimaging technology, magnetic resonance imaging (MRI) has been widely applied in the diagnosis of AD. In recent years, deep learning has been successfully applied in multiple domains. It integrates low-level features to form more abstract high-level representations to discover the distributed feature representations of data [4]. Deep learning model include stacked autoencoder (SAE) [5], deep belief network (DBN) [6] and deep convolutional neural network (CNN) [7], etc. At present, an 8-layer CNN structure proposed in [8] was utilized to deliver differential diagnosis based on MR images, aiming to effectively improve the accuracy and stability of the model for early diagnosis of AD.

Imaging genomics is a research hotspot which emerges with the development of high-throughput sequencing technologies and multimodal neuroimaging techniques. The main purpose is to obtain effective associations between traits, e.g. multimodal imaging features, and genetics variants, such as single nucleotide polymorphisms (SNPs) [9]. Researches have suggested that it is very likely that the genetic makeup of an individual may influence his/her susceptibility to AD traits. Thus, the research on genetic biomarkers of AD is of clinical significance. Here, on the basis of the MR imaging and genotype data from the enrolled subjects, the certain loci and genes, which were considered as candidate genetic biomarkers of AD, were eventually identified with the help of deep learning and genome-wide association studies (GWAS).

2   Materials and Methods

2.1   Dataset and Pre-processing

ADNI Database. Data used in the preparation of this article were obtained from the Alzheimer's Disease Neuroimaging Initiative (ADNI) database (adni.loni.usc.edu). The ADNI was launched in 2003 as a public-private partnership, led by Principal Investigator Michael W. Weiner, MD. The primary goal of ADNI has been to test whether serial magnetic resonance imaging (MRI), positron emission tomography (PET), other biological markers, and clinical and neuropsychological assessment can be combined to measure the progression of mild cognitive impairment (MCI) and early Alzheimer's disease (AD).

In this study, the following steps were followed to discover the potential genetic biomarkers for early diagnosis of AD: (1) to determine the quantitative traits, including the brain regions involved in GWAS; (2) to select the subjects involved in the GWAS; (3) to obtain the phenotypic values (i.e. volumes) of the determined brain regions for the selected subjects; (4) to acquire the genotype data (i.e. SNPs) for the selected subjects; (5) to perform the quality control of genetic data; (6) to complete the GWA studies and generate the plots and tables.

Here, the early diagnosis of AD was further divided into three binary classification problems, i.e. AD vs. HC, MCIc vs. HC and MCIc vs. MCInc. An ensemble model of multi-slice classifiers based on CNN was proposed to make an early diagnosis of AD and at the same time to identify the significant brain regions related to AD. In each of binary classification problems, the five single-slice base classifiers with the best generalization results for each orientation (coronal, sagittal, or transverse) were selected using the verification set to yield a multi-slice classifier. Three multi-slice classifiers (i.e. coronal, sagittal, and transverse) constituted the ensemble model of multi-slice classifiers. The slices in the three orientations corresponding to the three multi-slice classifiers could form multiple intersection points in the MNI space. With the help of the Atlas, the brain regions with the most mapped slice intersection points in the three binary classification experiments were identified as those with the most contributions to the early diagnosis of AD. Subsequently, the morphological data of these identified brain regions and the genotype were utilized to carry out GWAS to explore the potential genetic biomarkers of AD.

MRI Data and Pre-processing. In this study, the MRI data was downloaded from ADNI database according to ImageID indicated in the appendix of [10], including 137 AD subjects, 76 MCIc subjects, 134 MCInc subjects and 162 HC (Health Control) subjects. Descriptions of the 509 subjects are shown in Table 1, including gender, age, weight, MMSE (Mini-Mental State Examination) score and CDR (Clinical Dementia Rating Scale) score, GDS (Geriatric Depression Scale) score. As the training and test set, the MRI data set was employed to train the single-slice base classifiers and to test the built ensemble model of multi-slice classifiers. In addition, the data set was utilized to generate phenotypic values for the quantitative traits (i.e. the volumes of the selected brain regions) as well.

Plus, the MR images of additional 100 AD subjects, 100 HC subjects, 39 MCIc subjects and 39 MCInc subjects were downloaded from ADNI database as the verification set because the experimental setting required the validation set to screen out the single-slice base classifiers with the excellent generalization capabilities and the corresponding 2D slices while the proposed ensemble

Table 1. Descriptions of the subjects in the training and test dataset.

Group	Male/female	Age	Weight	MMSE	CDR	GDS
AD (N = 137)	67/70	76.00 ± 7.28	70.90 ± 13.97	23.21 ± 2.00	0.75 ± 0.25	1.59 ± 1.32
MCIc (N = 76)	43/33	74.78 ± 7.31	72.71 ± 14.34	26.47 ± 1.84	0.50 ± 0.00	1.38 ± 1.14
MCInc (N = 134)	84/50	74.47 ± 7.20	76.22 ± 12.89	27.19 ± 1.71	0.50 ± 0.00	1.52 ± 1.37
HC (N = 162)	86/76	76.28 ± 5.36	73.77 ± 13.58	29.18 ± 0.96	0.00 ± 0.00	0.80 ± 1.08

model of multi-slice classifiers based on CNN was built in a data-driven way. Descriptions of the 278 subjects in the validation set are shown in Table 2.

Table 2. Descriptions of the subjects in the validation dataset.

Group	Male/female	Age	Weight	MMSE	CDR	GDS
AD (N = 100)	60/40	74.24 ± 7.82	76.04 ± 15.83	23.84 ± 2.08	0.82 ± 0.24	1.81 ± 1.56
MCIc (N = 39)	23/16	74.15 ± 7.10	73.59 ± 14.14	27.05 ± 1.59	0.50 ± 0.00	1.92 ± 1.35
MCInc (N = 39)	29/10	76.02 ± 7.00	78.35 ± 12.99	27.56 ± 1.83	0.50 ± 0.00	1.79 ± 1.45
HC (N = 100)	45/55	73.36 ± 5.70	76.16 ± 15.66	28.92 ± 1.25	0.00 ± 0.00	0.83 ± 1.34

Here, CAT12 toolkit was firstly utilized for MR image pre-processing, which included skull removal, registration to MNI standard space and image smoothing. The default values were employed as the parameters of pre-processing procedures while the CAT12 toolkit was used. After pre-processing, all MR images were $121 \times 145 \times 121$ in size and 1.5 mm in spatial resolution. And then, the gray scale values of each MRI were normalized to reduce the difference in the absolute values of image gray scale of different tissues while preserving the difference in the gray scale with diagnostic value, which enabled the CNN model to be more easily converged.

And then, 2D slices were utilized as the training data. Hence, 3D MR images were subject to slicing processing. For convenience of description, the vertical directions of the sagittal, coronal and transverse planes of 3D MR images were denoted as X-axis, Y-axis and Z-axis, and the coordinate ranges on the three axes were $[1, 121], [1, 145]$ and $[1, 121]$, respectively. Thus, each 3D image of a subject was re-sliced into three 2D image sets, each of the sagittal, coronal, or transverse orientation (with X, Y, and Z axes perpendicular to the sagittal, coronal, and transverse planes, respectively). A preprocessed 3D MRI image (of $121 \times 145 \times 121$) was thus re-sliced into 121 sagittal, 145 coronal, and 121 transverse 2D slices. The sizes of the sagittal, coronal, and transverse slices obtained through re-slicing were 145×121, 121×121, and 121×145, respectively. Each of the 2D slice was reformatted to 145×145 using edge padding and zero filling, so that the 2D slice is squared, while the center and the spatial resolution of the resized image remained unchanged. The overall pre-processing procedure is illustrated in Fig. 1.

Fig. 1. Pre-processing procedure.

Phenotype Data. The "Brainetome Atlas [11]" was imported into FreeSurfer [12] to automatically calculate the morphological parameters of the brain regions of 509 subjects on the basis of their MR images. The volume values of 246 brain regions of each subject could be obtained with FreeSurfer. Due to the errors occurring while processing the MR images of two subjects using FreeSurfer, for each of only 507 subjects, the volume values of 246 brain regions were eventually acquired to help prepare for phenotype data for GWA Studies on the basis of the 507 MR images.

2.2   Gene Data and Pre-processing

In this study, the genetic data in PLINK [13] format was also downloaded from ADNI database. In this downloaded dataset, 620,901 SNPs were collected from 757 subjects. The information about the subject and the gene were stored in three files with .bim, .fam and .bed suffixes, respectively.

For GWAS analysis, both genotype data and phenotype data of a subject should be available at the same time. Thus, a total of 458 subjects with both SNPs and morphological parameters were selected to complete the subsequent GWA Studies.

To limit the nuisances, such as missing data and population stratification, we did quality control of genetic data in this study. With the PLINK package, the following eight steps were done. (1) Screening subjects with the heterozygosity rate; (2) Screening subjects with the locus deletion rate; (3) Screening locus with the deletion rate of locus; (4) Filtering locus based on the Hardy-Weinberg equilibrium law; (5) Filtering locus based on linkage disequilibrium; (6) Screening subjects with individual independence; (7) Obtaining an eigenvector matrix with principal component analysis; (8) Correcting the population stratification by using the eigenvector matrix. And then, the acquired genetic data were used for the GWAS analysis.

2.3   Experiment

Imaging Datasets. Among the downloaded 787 MR images from the 787 subjects in the ADNI database, 509 and 278 MR images were used as the training and test set and as the validation set, respectively. Five-fold cross-validation method was adopted. The validation dataset was NOT involved in training the single-slice base classifiers or testing the built ensemble model of multi-slice classifiers, but was ONLY utilized to screen the trained base classifiers in order to prevent from the potential data leakage among three binary classification tasks. Here, the subjects were classified into four groups, i.e. AD, MCIc, MCInc and HC.

Data Augmentation. In order to acquire a CNN model with good generalization capability, a large number of images are usually required. If only the original slices were directly utilized to train the base classifiers of CNN, the amount of data was far from sufficient. Hence, the data augmentation (DA) was employed. New slices were generated from the original slices applying the following six operations: rotation, translation, gamma correction, random noise addition, scaling and random affine transformation. For example, in the binary classification experiment of MCIc vs. HC, for each slice from HC, ten new slices were generated with each of the six operations. Thus, the total number of slices from HC has multiplied by 61 times after DA.

Base Classifier. A base classifier is a model for learning the features from a single 2D slice, and its structure is the 8-layer CNN classifier described in [8], as demonstrated in Fig. 2.

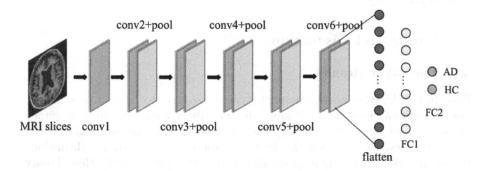

Fig. 2. Base classifier structure.

Genome-Wide Association Study (GWAS). Because each of MRI slices was individually employed to train a corresponding single-slice base classifier, such a specific arrangement enabled us to respectively select the slices with the largest contributions to the AD classification in each orientation (coronal, sagittal, or transverse) with the help of the validation set. These selected slices in the three orientations formed a slice grid in the MNI space, and accordingly, multiple intersection points. Since the intersection points were located in the slices with the largest contributions to the AD classification in the three orientations at the same time, there is no reason to doubt that an intersection point is able to act as a valid proxy for the ability of a brain region in which the point is located to classify AD. Thus, the number of those points could be used to rank the brain regions they are located in according to the contributions to classification of AD from each of these brain regions.

In this way, 125 points in the MNI space were determined by the top five sagittal, coronal, and transverse slices. And then, these 125 points were mapped onto brain regions using the Brainnetome Atlas. Thus, the ability of a brain region to help classify AD was assessed with the number of intersection points located in that region. The brain regions with the intersection points in three binary classification experiments were summarized and ranked altogether. Accordingly, ten brain regions with the most mapped intersection points served as the brain regions significantly associated with AD. The volume values of the 10 brain regions, which were screened out among those of 246 brain regions from 458 subjects, were acted as the phenotype to be analyzed in the subsequent GWA Studies.

After the phenotype and genotype data were converted to PLINK format files, we did the GWAS experiment using PLINK package. During GWAS experiment, when the phenotype to be analyzed was qualitative, Logistic regression model was mainly employed. When the phenotype to be analyzed was quantitative, linear regression model was primarily used. Since the volume of a brain region was quantitative, linear regression model was chosen for GWAS experiment in this study.

3   Results and Discussion

3.1   Phenotype Results

Prior to GWAS experiment, the phenotype to be analyzed should be acquired. For the built ensemble model of multi-slice classifiers, the classification accuracy on the test set in the three binary classification experiments were AD vs. HC 81%, MCIc vs. HC 79% and MCIc vs. MCInc 62%, respectively. Meanwhile, the brain regions with the mapped slice intersection points in the three binary classification experiments were summarized and ranked, as illustrated in Fig. 3 Here, the Y-axis denoted the brain region labels from Brainnetome Atlas, and the X-axis represented the total number of slice intersection points mapped into a brain region in the three binary classification experiments.

According to the statistical results in Fig. 3, the top 10 brain regions, i.e. R.rHipp, L.rHipp, R.mAmyg, L.A21r, L.A22r, L.A20cv, L.mAmyg, R.34, L.A37lv and R.lAmyg, were determined.

3.2   GWAS Results

The volumes of the top 10 brain regions utilized as the phenotype in the GWA Studies, and the 10 corresponding GWAS experiments were conducted. Linear regression model was adopted to perform correlation analysis on the genotype and phenotype data to obtain the significant correlation (P value) between each SNP and phenotype. Subsequently, Manhattan plots of the obtained P values for the association between SNPs and the volumes of the 10 brain regions were shown in Figs. 4, 5, 6, 7, 8, 9, 10, 11, 12 and 13, respectively.

SNPs with high correlation with the volumes of the ten brain regions were summarized from the 10 GWAS experiments, as demonstrated in Table 3. That

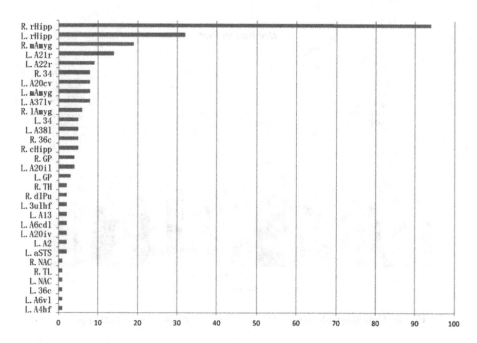

Fig. 3. The number of intersection points in each significant brain region.

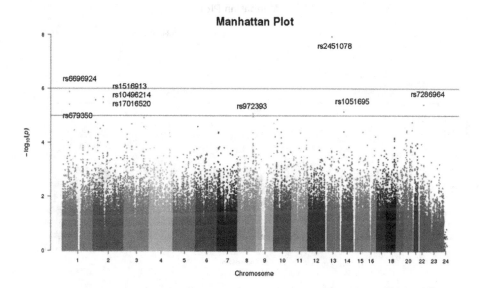

Fig. 4. Genome-wide association analysis results of region R.rHipp.

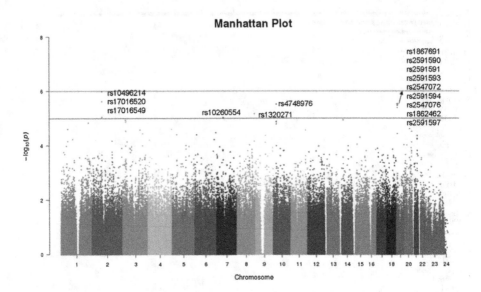

Fig. 5. Genome-wide association analysis results of region L.rHipp.

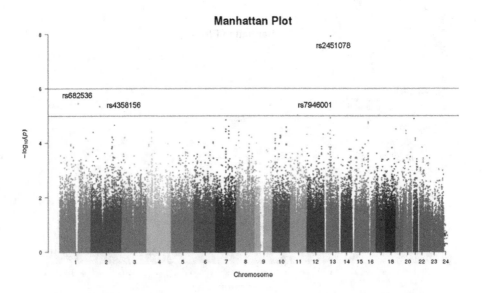

Fig. 6. Genome-wide association analysis results of region R.mAmyg.

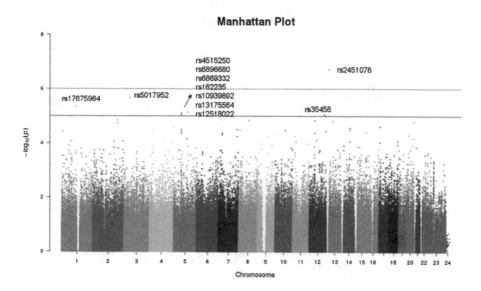

Fig. 7. Genome-wide association analysis results of region L.A21r.

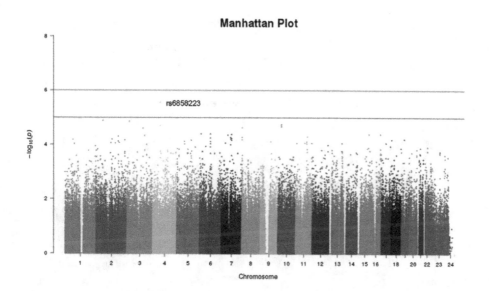

Fig. 8. Genome-wide association analysis results of region L.A22r.

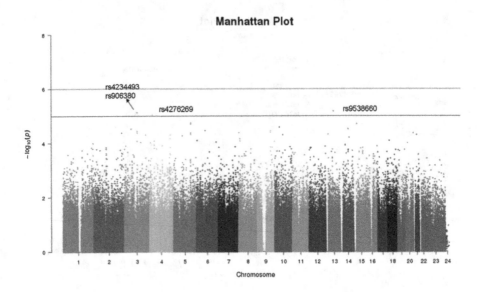

Fig. 9. Genome-wide association analysis results of region L.A20cv.

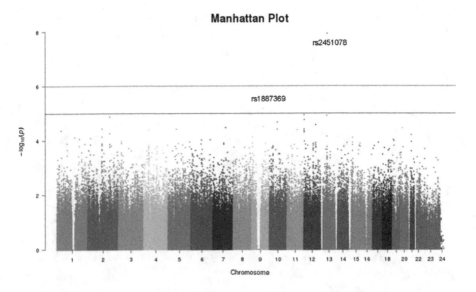

Fig. 10. Genome-wide association analysis results of region L.mAmyg.

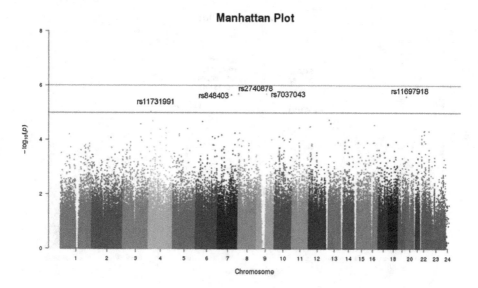

Fig. 11. Genome-wide association analysis results of region R.34.

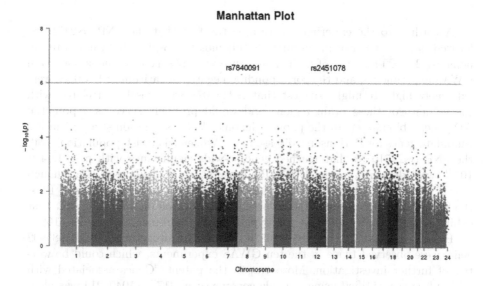

Fig. 12. Genome-wide association analysis results of region L.A37lv.

could help provide clues to pathogenesis of this complex brain disorder. Here, the negative logarithm of P value was used to determine the statistical significance of the associations between variants and traits. The genome wide significance p-value threshold of 1×10^{-5} was adopted.

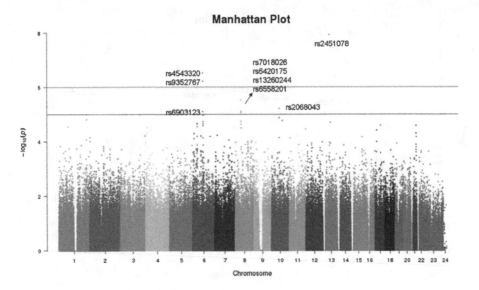

Fig. 13. Genome-wide association analysis results of region R.lAmyg.

According to the experimental results, the fact that the SNP (rs2451078) located in the gene transmembrane phosphoinositide 3-phosphatase and tensin homolog 2 (TPTE2) was of high significance were observed in the seven of ten GWAS experiments, and the corresponding negative logarithm of P values were extremely high. It might suggest that rs2451078 was closely correlated with the volumes of these brain regions and would probably serve as a potential AD genetic biomarker. In the paper "Genome-Wide association study identifies candidate genes for Parkinson's disease in an Ashkenazi Jewish population" [14], the SNP (rs2451078) that reached genome-wide significance with $p < 1.94 \times 10^{-10}$ was identified in the CIDR/Pankratz et al. 2009 dataset [15], though it was not replicated in the Ashkenazi Jewish [14] or a second dataset. Plus, the SNP (rs2451078) were found to be allegedly located on autosomes but that exhibited significantly different genotype frequencies in men and women [16].

Besides, rs10496214 and rs17016520, located in altogether LOC107985902 gene, were observed twice in the ten GWAS experiments, which could be worthy of further investigation. Moreover, in the patent "Genes associated with schizophrenia identified using a whole genome scan" [17], rs10496214 was identified as schizophrenia SNPs significantly associated and concordant in both collections, i.e. the Munich and Aberdeen Collections which consisted of 438 cases and 414 controls, and 440 cases and 453 controls, respectively. The SNP rs17016520 has not been studied so far.

In summary, rs2451078, rs10496214, rs17016520 as well as TPTE2 and LOC107985902 were identified as the potential genetic biomarkers of AD in this study, which could deserve further in-depth research and validation to offer certain insights for AD studies.

Table 3. The details of significant SNPs.

Brain region to be analyzed	Chromosome number	SNP	Negative log of P value	Gene where SNP is located
R.rHipp	1	rs6696924	5.409604053	C8A
R.rHipp	1	rs679350	5.886725308	C8A
R.rHipp	2	rs1516913	5.57741016	None
R.rHipp	2	rs10496214	5.692290077	LOC107985902
R.rHipp	2	rs17016520	5.492548939	LOC107985902
R.rHipp	8	rs972393	5.067526235	None
R.rHipp	13	rs2451078	22.68634365	TPTE2
R.rHipp	14	rs1051695	5.153848523	AKAP6
R.rHipp	22	rs7286964	5.40494491	PARVB
L.rHipp	2	rs10496214	5.984221244	LOC107985902
L.rHipp	2	rs17016520	5.615825861	LOC107985902
L.rHipp	2	rs17016549	5.043735497	LOC107985902
L.rHipp	7	rs10260554	5.02346662	None
L.rHipp	8	rs1320271	5.162916849	COL22A1
L.rHipp	10	rs4748976	5.516412703	None
L.rHipp	13	rs2451078	22.56129947	TPTE2
L.rHipp	19	rs1867691	5.502517463	MUC16
L.rHipp	19	rs2591590	5.462180905	MUC16
L.rHipp	19	rs2591591	5.479909672	MUC16
L.rHipp	19	rs2591593	5.518844129	MUC16
L.rHipp	19	rs2547072	5.529442515	MUC16
L.rHipp	19	rs2591594	5.529442515	MUC16
L.rHipp	19	rs2547076	5.529442515	MUC16
L.rHipp	19	rs1862462	5.386158178	MUC16
L.rHipp	19	rs2591597	5.529442515	MUC16
R.mAmyg	1	rs682536	5.455435903	PDE4DIP
R.mAmyg	2	rs4358156	5.34428545	ANTXR1
R.mAmyg	11	rs7946001	5.024017056	MS4A15
R.mAmyg	13	rs2451078	17.63152716	TPTE2
L.A21r	1	rs17675964	5.356744775	KCND3
L.A21r	3	rs5017952	5.675306086	LIMD1
L.A21r	5	rs4515250	5.03891128	DEPDC1B
L.A21r	5	rs6896680	5.105019709	DEPDC1B
L.A21r	5	rs6869332	5.070427821	ELOVL7
L.A21r	5	rs162235	5.114525697	NDUFAF2
L.A21r	5	rs10939892	5.097997109	None
L.A21r	5	rs13175564	5.097997109	None
L.A21r	5	rs12518022	5.137212902	EPB41L4A
L.A21r	12	rs35458	5.051293691	LOC102723639
L.A21r	13	rs2451078	6.721246399	TPTE2
L.A22r	4	rs6858223	5.555330769	ADGRL3
L.A20cv	3	rs4234493	5.128543826	None
L.A20cv	3	rs906380	5.136558171	None

(*continued*)

Table 3. (continued)

Brain region to be analyzed	Chromosome number	SNP	Negative log of P value	Gene where SNP is located
L.A20cv	4	rs4276269	5.04522701	PPARGC1A
L.A20cv	13	rs9538660	5.171791386	LOC105370228
L.mAmyg	9	rs1887369	5.178290003	LINC00484
L.mAmyg	13	rs2451078	15.28008894	TPTE2
R.34	4	rs11731991	5.032686082	KCNIP4
R.34	7	rs848403	5.653060537	None
R.34	8	rs2740878	5.691008971	CSMD1
R.34	9	rs7037043	5.680269506	RORB
R.34	20	rs11697918	5.594824454	ANGPT4
L.A37lv	8	rs7840091	6.328364403	None
L.A37lv	13	rs2451078	6.399353764	TPTE2
R.lAmyg	6	rs4543320	6.217814134	LINC01621
R.lAmyg	6	rs9352767	6.517555208	LINC01621
R.lAmyg	6	rs6903123	5.103253384	LINC01621
R.lAmyg	8	rs7018026	5.087193607	LOC105375814
R.lAmyg	8	rs6420175	5.525638024	None
R.lAmyg	8	rs13260244	5.066462098	None
R.lAmyg	8	rs6558201	5.121535655	LOC107986885
R.lAmyg	10	rs2068043	5.215953584	ANK3
R.lAmyg	13	rs2451078	16.8065971	TPTE2

4   Conclusion

First of all, in order to obtain the phenotype, a CNN-based ensemble model of multi-slice classifiers for early diagnosis of AD was proposed, which could be used for computer-aided diagnosis of diseases in clinical settings as well. In this investigation, the features of the model are as follows:

(1) In this model, six different operations were adopted to perform data augmentation on the original MRI slices, which significantly increased the number of training samples and made the sample size of two classes of images almost the same in the data sets used in a binary classification experiment after data augmentation.

(2) Conventionally, a specific slice from MR images was selected to build 2DCNN-based models for early diagnosis of AD according to prior experience, which highly depended on domain knowledge and had certain limitations. In this advocated model, selected multiple sagittal, coronal, and transverse slices were employed to train an ensemble model of multi-slice classifiers. Moreover, these slices did NOT need to be pre-specified on the basis of domain knowledge but were chosen in a data-driven way. After all, for the same brain region, the morphologies significantly varied from orientation to orientation. Combining the sagittal, coronal, and transverse slices together further improved the classification accuracy and stability.

(3) In comparison with that based on the three-dimensional images, the proposed ensemble model based on two-dimensional slices did NOT have high hardware requirements. In addition, each base classifier was independently trained, which considerably enhanced the training efficiency in a parallel mode.

Secondly, as a model for phenotype acquisition, the advocated model for early diagnosis of AD was good at pinpointing the brain regions significantly associated with AD. Here, an intersection point determined by the discriminable sagittal, coronal, and transverse slices acted as a valid proxy for the ability of a brain region in which the point was located to classify AD. Thus, the brain regions with most intersection points were considered as those mostly contributing to the early diagnosis of AD. In this way, the 10 brain regions with high correlation with AD were identified.

Finally, while the morphological data (i.e. volumes) of these 10 brain regions acted as phenotype in the GWA Studies, three loci including rs2451078, rs10496214 and rs17016520, as well as two genes of TPTE2 and LOC107985902 were identified, which might serve as potential genetic biomarkers of AD and offer some clues to subsequent AD research. Moreover, the SNPs rs2451078 and rs10496214 have been studied in research on other brain disorders, e.g. Parkinson disease and schizophrenia, while the SNP rs17016520 has not been investigated so far.

Acknowledgments. This study was supported by NSF of China (grant No. 61976058 and 61772143), NSF of Guangzhou city (grant No. 201601010034 and 201804010278), the Fund for Opening Project of Guangdong Key Laboratory of Big Data Analysis and Processing (grant No. 201801) and the Special Fund for Public Interest Research and Capacity Building Project of Guangdong province (grant No. 2015A030401107). Data collection and sharing for this project was funded by the Alzheimer's Disease Neuroimaging Initiative (ADNI) (National Institutes of Health Grant U01 AG024904) and DOD ADNI (Department of Defense award number W81XWH-12-2-0012). ADNI is funded by the National Institute on Aging, the National Institute of Biomedical Imaging and Bioengineering, and through generous contributions from the following: AbbVie, Alzheimer's Association; Alzheimer's Drug Discovery Foundation; Araclon Biotech; BioClinica, Inc.; Biogen; Bristol-Myers Squibb Company; CereSpir, Inc.; Cogstate; Eisai Inc.; Elan Pharmaceuticals, Inc.; Eli Lilly and Company; EuroImmun; F. Hoffmann-La Roche Ltd. and its affiliated company Genentech, Inc.; Fujirebio; GE Healthcare; IXICO Ltd.; Janssen Alzheimer Immunotherapy Research & Development, LLC.; Johnson & Johnson Pharmaceutical Research & Development LLC.; Lumosity; Lundbeck; Merck & Co., Inc.; Meso Scale Diagnostics, LLC.; NeuroRx Research; Neurotrack Technologies; Novartis Pharmaceuticals Corporation; Pfizer Inc.; Piramal Imaging; Servier; Takeda Pharmaceutical Company; and Transition Therapeutics. The Canadian Institutes of Health Research is providing funds to support ADNI clinical sites in Canada. Private sector contributions are facilitated by the Foundation for the National Institutes of Health (www.fnih.org). The grantee organization is the Northern California Institute for Research and Education, and the study is coordinated by the Alzheimer's Therapeutic Research Institute at the University of Southern California. ADNI data are disseminated by the Laboratory for Neuro Imaging at the University of Southern California.

References

1. Ulep, M.G., Saraon, S.K., McLea, S.: Alzheimer disease. J. Nurse Pract. **14**(3), 129–135 (2018)
2. Prince, M.J.: World Alzheimer Report 2015: The Global Impact of Dementia: An Aalysis of Prevalence, Incidence, Cost and Trends. Alzheimer's Disease International, London (2015)
3. Liu, S., Liu, S., Cai, W., Pujol, S., Kikinis, R., Feng, D.: Early diagnosis of Alzheimer's disease with deep learning. In: 2014 IEEE 11th International Symposium on Biomedical Imaging (ISBI), pp. 1015–1018. IEEE, Beijing, April 2014
4. Schmidhuber, J.: Deep learning in neural networks: an overview. Neural Netw. **61**, 85–117 (2015). https://doi.org/10.1016/j.neunet.2014.09.003
5. Vincent, P., Larochelle, H., Lajoie, I., Bengio, Y., Manzagol, P.A.: Stacked denoising autoencoders: learning useful representations in a deep network with a local denoising criterion. J. Mach. Learn. Res. **11**(Dec), 3371–3408 (2010)
6. Hinton, G.E.: Deep belief networks. Scholarpedia **4**(5), 5947 (2009)
7. LeCun Y.: LeNet-5, convolutional neural networks (2015). http://yann.lecun.com/exdb/lenet/
8. Wang, S.H., Phillips, P., Sui, Y., et al.: Classification of Alzheimer's disease based on eight-layer convolutional neural network with leaky rectified linear unit and max pooling. J. Med. Syst. **42**(5), 85 (2018)
9. Huang, H., Shen, L.I., Thompson, P.M., et al.: Imaging genomics. In: Pacific Symposium, vol. 23, p. 304 (2018)
10. Salvatore, C., Cerasa, A., Battista, P., et al.: Magnetic resonance imaging biomarkers for the early diagnosis of Alzheimer's disease: a machine learning approach. Front. Neurosci. **9**, 307 (2015)
11. Fan, L., et al.: The human brainnetome atlas: a new brain atlas based on connectional architecture. Cereb. Cortex **26**, 3508–3526 (2016)
12. Fischl, B.: FreeSurfer. Neuroimage **62**(2), 774–781 (2012)
13. Chang, C.C., Chow, C.C., Tellier, L.C.A.M., Vattikuti, S., Purcell, S.M., Lee, J.J.: Second generation PLINK: rising to the challenge of larger and richer datasets. GigaScience **4**, 7 (2015)
14. Liu, X., Cheng, R., Verbitsky, M., et al.: Genome-wide association study identifies candidate genes for Parkinson's disease in an Ashkenazi Jewish population. BMC Med. Genet. **12**(1), 104 (2011)
15. Pankratz, N., Wilk, J.B., Latourelle, J.C., et al.: Genomewide association study for susceptibility genes contributing to familial Parkinson disease. Hum. Genet. **124**(6), 593–605 (2009). https://doi.org/10.1007/s00439-008-0582-9
16. Galichon, P., Mesnard, L., Hertig, A., et al.: Unrecognized sequence homologies may confound genome-wide association studies. Nucleic Acids Res. **40**(11), 4774–4782 (2012)
17. Jean, P.S.: Genes associated with schizophrenia identified using a whole genome scan. U.S. Patent Application 11/970,611 (2008)

Trends and Features of Human Brain Research Using Artificial Intelligence Techniques: A Bibliometric Approach

Xieling Chen[1], Xinxin Zhang[2], Haoran Xie[1], Fu Lee Wang[3],
Jun Yan[4], and Tianyong Hao[5(✉)]

[1] Department of Mathematics and Information Technology,
The Education University of Hong Kong, Hong Kong SAR, China
shaylyn_chen@163.com, hxie@eduhk.hk
[2] Institute for Brain Research and Rehabilitation,
South China Normal University, Guangzhou, China
2017022860@m.scnu.edu.cn
[3] School of Science and Technology, The Open University of Hong Kong,
Hong Kong SAR, China
pwang@ouhk.edu.hk
[4] AI Lab, Yidu Cloud (Beijing) Technology Co., Ltd., Beijing, China
jun.yan@yiducloud.cn
[5] School of Computer Science, South China Normal University,
Guangzhou, China
haoty@m.scnu.edu.cn

Abstract. Artificial Intelligence (AI) plays an increasingly important role in advancing human brain research, given the continually growing number of academic research articles in the last decade. Meanwhile, human brain research can provide opportunities for the development of innovative AI techniques. Exploring and tracking patterns of the scientific articles of human brain research using AI can provide a comprehensive overview of the interdisciplinary field. Thus, this paper presents a bibliometric analysis to identify research status and development trend of the field between 2009 and 2018. Specifically, we analyze annual distributions of articles and their citations, identify prolific journals and affiliations, and visualize characteristics of scientific collaboration. Furthermore, research topics are analyzed and revealed. The obtained findings benefit scholars in the field, to understand the current status of research as well as monitoring scientific and technological activities.

Keywords: Human brain research · Artificial Intelligence · Bibliometric analysis · Scientific collaboration · Research hotspots

1 Introduction

Artificial Intelligence (AI) is a computer system utilizing approaches to manifest cognitive behavior to mimic human intelligence [1]. Usually, AI consists of a set of machine learning algorithms such as support vector machine, association rule mining,

© Springer Nature Singapore Pte Ltd. 2019
A. Zeng et al. (Eds.): HBAI 2019, CCIS 1072, pp. 69–83, 2019.
https://doi.org/10.1007/978-981-15-1398-5_5

convolutional neural networks and so on. At the dawn of information age, AI has developed dramatically as a result of the improvement of the processing capacity of computers and the accumulation of big data [2]. AI is receiving increasing attention and is being incorporated into a variety of fields, including human brain research.

Human brain research primarily aims to gain a comprehensive understanding of human brain functions, thus providing a foundation for the development of effective neurological diseases therapies and future translational research. The development of brain informatics and computational brain science can be advanced in the process of addressing different human brain topics and problems with the utilization of AI techniques. At the same time, novel AI methods can be developed based on findings of cognitive and brain science, such as the Long Short Term Memory model in deep learning.

In recent years, rapid progress has been made in the interdisciplinary field of AI and human brain research and has gradually become an active research field given the ever-increasing number of articles in academic communities. The research issues center on disease diagnosis, detection, and prediction, brain image segmentation, and classification, feature extraction, and selection, as well as pattern classification about Alzheimer's disease (AD), schizophrenia, and epilepsy. Research data are usually collected from the use of Electroencephalogram (EEG), functional Magnetic Resonance Imaging (fMRI), and positron emission tomography. Research methods about techniques such as machine learning, deep learning are commonly found. Brain-computer interface is also a study focus. Some representative works are as follows. Many related studies focus on the utilization of classification algorithms to solve human brain issues such as classification of patients with certain diseases and classification of brain images or brain tumors. For example, with the use of the AD Neuroimaging Initiative database, Cuingnet et al. [3] evaluated the performance of ten approaches for the classification of patients with AD. Gao et al. [4] explored the significance of using burgeoning deep learning techniques, especially the use of a convolutional neural network for the classification of CT brain images. A significant number of researches were conducted based on the use of EEG and fMRI. For example, by comparing seven classifiers with Fuzzy Sugeno Classifier for the detection of normal, pre-ictal, and ictal conditions from recorded epileptic EEG signals, Acharya et al. [5] highlighted the Fuzzy classifier with high accuracy up to 98.1%. Morabito et al. [6] proposed a novel technique of quantitative EEG for differentiating patients with early-stage Creutzfeldt-Jakob disease from other forms of rapidly progressive dementia using a deep learning method. Dosenbach et al. [7] proposed a support vector machine-based multivariate pattern analysis method to extract information from fMRI data for predicting individuals' brain maturity across development. By combing independent component analysis and hierarchical fusion of classifiers, Salimi-Khorshidi et al. [8] provided an automated solution for denoising fMRI data. Many studies were conducted focusing on AD. Zhang et al. [9] combined three modalities of biomarkers for discriminating between AD and healthy controls with the use of a kernel combination method. With the use of concepts from graph theory, Stam et al. [10] examined changes in the large-scale structure of resting-state brain networks in patients with AD compared with non-demented controls.

The amount of published articles about human brain research using AI techniques available in the bibliography is huge. It is of great significance to thoroughly explore the research states and development structure. Bibliometric analytical technique is an effective approach to quantitatively analyze academic articles using mathematical and statistical methods, and has been widely performed in a variety of disciplines [11–20] for describing the distribution patterns of articles within a given topic, field, and an affiliation [21]. These works have provided strong evidence that bibliometric is a powerful and effective approach for analyzing research articles. Word frequency analysis, as a common way of content analysis, has also been widely applied for exploring the core content and research topic of research articles. Research hotspots of a given area can be quantitatively and visually examined.

Currently, articles related to the interdisciplinary field of AI and human brain research have not been comprehensively reviewed from a quantitative perspective. To fill this gap and help advance the field, this study applies bibliometric analysis to provide insights into research topics and their evolution. It can also help identify research gaps and determine consensus findings for scholars to take advantage of. The specific goals of this study include: (1) uncovering trends and features of the research articles in the field during the period 2009–2018; (2) outlining scientific contributions at levels of affiliation and journal; (3) revealing scientific collaborations; and (4) identifying emergent research topics through keywords analysis.

2 Data and Methods

2.1 Data

Before data retrieval, one critical step was to obtain appropriate keywords related to AI and brain research separately. With refer to the work of Hassan et al. [22], the following strategy was used, in which AI was taken for instance. Step 1: Domain experts were invited to provide a list of seed keywords related to AI, e.g., machine learning, text analytics, natural language processing, image recognition, and intelligent system. Step 2: The seed keywords were used to form a retrieval query to obtain articles with keywords in the title, abstracts, and author defined keywords matched against the seed keywords. Step 3: Co-occurred author defined keywords of the retrieved articles that are of highly cited were presented to domain experts. The experts selected relevant keywords and added them to the initial seed keywords to form a final keywords list for AI. We then followed the same strategy to obtain a keyword list for human brain research.

Using the two final keyword lists, we conducted data retrieval in ISI Web of Science from Science Citation Index Expanded (SCI-EXPANDED) and Social Sciences Citation Index (SSCI) databases. "TS" (Topics), referring to title, abstract or keywords of an article, was selected as a search field. We conducted the search on March 27, 2019. A total of 30,316 articles published during the period 2009–2018 with full bibliographic information as well as their annual citations were collected.

Filtering work with referring to the work of Du et al. [23], was carried out by domain experts from AI and human brain research fields to ensure the close relevance of data to the research topic. Take AI as an instance, two domain experts piloted filtering by evaluating 300 articles, and the inter-rater reliability turned out to be 95%.

Then they together filtered the rest of the articles. Similar filtering process was employed from the perspective of human brain research. Finally, 6,317 articles related to both AI and human brain research were identified for further analysis.

2.2 Methods

To analyze the impact and influence of the articles, the two measures of citation count and Hirsch index (H index) were introduced. As a quantitative indicator, citation count is popular and powerful for reflecting relative impact and influence that an article has on the academic communities. Thus, citation count was used as an analytical tool for impact evaluation via the H index in this field. As defined by Hirsch and Buela-Casal [24], H index has the meaning that H of one's total articles has at least H citations each, indicating both the quantity and quality of one's work. Impact factor (IF), the five-year impact factor (5-year IF), JCR quartile in category (Q), SCImago Journal Rank (SJR), Impact Per Publication (IPP), and Source Normalized Impact per Paper (SNIP) were also utilized as measures for journals.

Social network analysis is widely used for visualizing and analyzing the relations among a variety of nodes in bibliometric related studies, such as academic collaborations among affiliations or countries/regions. The D3 JavaScript force directed network graph created using an R package named *networkD3* was utilized to conduct the collaboration analysis and visualization, based on collaboration data in the same published articles. The size of nodes and weight of edges were proportional to article counts and the times the affiliations, or countries/regions have published together, respectively. The nodes were colored based on the modularity class, i.e., countries/regions or continents to affiliations or countries/regions, respectively. In this study, articles that originated from England, Scotland, Northern Ireland, and Wales were grouped as the United Kingdom (UK), while publication articles from Hong Kong, Macau, and Taiwan were independently counted.

We also applied the nonparametric Mann-Kendall test [25] to evaluate whether increasing or decreasing trends were existing in the high frequently used keywords with a null hypothesis of no trend. We first calculated the proportion of each keyword in the whole article collection to estimate the relative popularity of the keyword in the research field. $P_k = \theta_k/D$ denoted the proportion of the k_{th} keyword in the collection, where θ_k was the number of article containing the k_{th} keyword while D was the article count in the whole collection. Then we calculated the proportion of the k_{th} keyword in year t as $P_{k,t} = \theta_{k,t}/D_t$ for temporal trend analysis, where $\theta_{k,t}$ was the number of article containing the k_{th} keyword in year t and D_t was the article count in year t.

3 Results

3.1 Trends Analysis of Article and Citation Counts

The annual distributions of article and citation counts were depicted in Fig. 1. Polynomial regression analysis was applied to fit the development trends of articles and citation counts (described as y and z) with *year* as the independent variable x. The fitting results were also displayed in the figure, that was, two polynomial regression curves with the R^2 and P values.

Clearly, for both article count and citation count, an upward trend was clearly observed from the actual development curves (solid orange line for article counts and solid blue line for citation counts). Two coefficients of determination for the two curves, i.e., 98.66% and 99.53%, suggested that the regression models fitted the development trends of article and citation counts well. This reflected a growing enthusiasm and increasing interest in the research field in academia.

By examining the increasing rate, it was interesting to find that the curve representing citation counts had a steeper slope than that of article counts. This indicated that the citation counts increased at a faster rate than the article count over the past ten years. With the regression formulas, the predictive values for future years can be calculated. In short, the increasing trend for both article and citation counts reflected that the research field of the human brain using AI techniques enjoyed an increasing influence and effect over time.

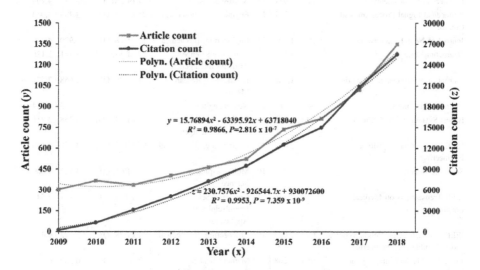

Fig. 1. Trend analysis of article and citation counts

3.2   Journal Analysis

Table 1 showed the top 20 prolific journals in the research field. They all together contributed to 34.15% of the total studied articles. The top five journals included *Neuroimage, PLoS ONE, Frontiers in Human Neuroscience, Human Brain Mapping,* and *Frontiers in Neuroscience. Neuroimage* had a highest H index as 59, showing the high-quality citation and quantity of its articles in the research.

From Table 2, we found that *Neuroimage* showed excellent performance in highly cited articles with 4, 35, and 75 articles reaching a citation up to 300, 100, and 50, respectively. It should also be noted that *IEEE Transactions on Biomedical Engineering*, *IEEE Transactions on Medical Imaging*, and *Journal of Neuroscience* also had relatively more articles with high citations although with a rather lower position in terms of article count.

The comparison of the top 10 prolific journals by SJR, IPP, SNIP, and IF indexes was further presented in Fig. 2. *Neuroimage* had the highest values for all the four indexes. *Human Brain Mapping* ranked at 2nd except for the SNIP index.

Table 1. Top prolific journals with their article counts, citation counts, H index and so on.

Journals	AC	CC	H	JCR category	Rank	IF	5-y IF
Neuroimage	356	13,059	59	Neuroimaging	1 of 14, Q1	5.426	7.079
PLoS ONE	263	3,977	32	Multidisciplinary Sciences	15 of 64, Q1	2.766	3.352
Frontiers in Human Neuroscience	117	1,081	18	Psychology	21 of 78, Q2	2.871	4.022
Human Brain Mapping	114	2,382	28	Neuroimaging	2 of 14, Q1	4.927	5.431
Frontiers in Neuroscience	111	951	18	Neurosciences	77 of 261, Q2	3.877	4.294
Biomedical Signal Processing and Control	99	1,267	19	Engineering, Biomedical	25 of 78, Q2	2.783	3.063
Journal of Neural Engineering	99	1,480	23	Engineering, Biomedical	12 of 78, Q1	3.920	4.220
Neurocomputing	97	1,503	23	Computer Science, Artificial Intelligence	27 of 132, Q1	3.241	3.126
Journal of Neuroscience Methods	95	1,738	22	Biochemical Research Methods	31 of 79, Q2	2.668	2.571
Neuroimage-Clinical	94	888	16	Neuroimaging	3 of 14, Q1	3.869	4.814
Expert Systems with Applications	92	2,268	26	Computer Science, Artificial Intelligence	20 of 132, Q1	3.768	3.711
IEEE Transactions on Biomedical Engineering	88	2,417	24	Engineering, Biomedical	9 of 78, Q1	4.288	4.140
Scientific Reports	85	459	10	Multidisciplinary Sciences	12 of 64, Q1	4.122	4.609
IEEE Transactions on Medical Imaging	74	2,446	24	Computer Science, Interdisciplinary Applications	3 of 105, Q1	6.131	5.546
IEEE Transactions on Neural Systems and Rehabilitation Engineering	69	1,074	19	Engineering, Biomedical	11 of 78, Q1	3.972	4.404
Journal of Medical Imaging and Health Informatics	65	208	7	Mathematical & Computational Biology	57 of 59, Q4	0.549	0.533
Clinical Neurophysiology	62	1,393	18	Clinical Neurology	53 of 197, Q2	3.614	3.638
International Journal of Imaging Systems and Technology	62	437	10	Engineering, Electrical & Electronic	164 of 260, Q3	1.423	1.344
Computer Methods and Programs in Biomedicine	58	745	15	Computer Science, Interdisciplinary Applications	34 of 105, Q2	2.674	2.840
Journal of Neuroscience	57	2,214	27	Neurosciences	30 of 261, Q1	5.971	6.518

Abbreviations: AC: article count; CC: citation count; H: H index; IF: impact factor and JCR quartile in category for the year 2017; 5-y IF: five-year impact factor. JCR category, Rank: with regard to the category with the highest Q value.

Table 2. Research performance of highly cited articles during specific time periods for the top prolific journals

Journals	>=300	>=100	>=50	2009–2013 AC	2009–2013 CC	2014–2018 AC	2014–2018 CC
Neuroimage	4	35	75	149	2,925	207	10,134
PLoS ONE	0	5	17	84	509	179	3,468
Frontiers in Human Neuroscience	0	0	5	21	108	96	973
Human Brain Mapping	0	3	10	32	460	82	1,922
Frontiers in Neuroscience	0	1	3	19	59	92	892
Biomedical Signal Processing and Control	0	1	4	18	85	81	1,182
Journal of Neural Engineering	0	0	5	26	199	73	1,281
Neurocomputing	0	1	6	27	138	70	1,365
Journal of Neuroscience Methods	0	3	10	32	282	63	1,456
Neuroimage-Clinical	0	0	4	10	2	84	886
Expert Systems with Applications	0	4	9	42	328	50	1,940
IEEE Transactions on Biomedical Engineering	0	6	17	41	398	47	2,019
Scientific Reports	0	0	3	0	0	85	459
IEEE Transactions on Medical Imaging	0	7	15	30	467	44	1,979
IEEE Transactions on Neural Systems and Rehabilitation Engineering	0	1	6	15	177	54	897
Journal of Medical Imaging and Health Informatics	0	0	1	8	2	57	206
Clinical Neurophysiology	0	2	7	28	363	34	1,030
International Journal of Imaging Systems and Technology	0	0	3	15	37	47	400
Computer Methods and Programs in Biomedicine	0	0	3	13	56	45	689
Journal of Neuroscience	0	5	16	24	505	33	1,709

Abbreviations: AC: article count; CC: citation count; >=300, >=100, >=50: count of articles with more than 300, 100, and 50 citations, respectively.

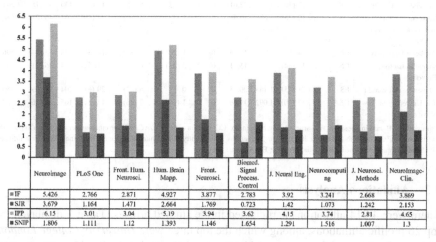

	Neuroimage	PLoS One	Front. Hum. Neurosci.	Hum. Brain Mapp.	Front. Neurosci.	Biomed. Signal Process. Control	J. Neural Eng.	Neurocomputing	J. Neurosci. Methods	Neuroimage-Clin.
IF	5.426	2.766	2.871	4.927	3.877	2.783	3.92	3.241	2.668	3.869
SJR	3.679	1.164	1.471	2.664	1.769	0.723	1.42	1.073	1.242	2.153
IPP	6.15	3.01	3.04	5.19	3.94	3.62	4.15	3.74	2.81	4.65
SNIP	1.806	1.111	1.12	1.393	1.146	1.654	1.291	1.516	1.007	1.3

Fig. 2. The comparison of IF, SJR, IPP, and SNIP for the top 10 most prolific journals

Table 3. Top prolific affiliations in the research field.

Affiliations	CY	2009–2018							2009–2013		2014–2018	
		AC	H (R)	CC	CC/AC	>=300	>=100 (R)	>=50 (R)	AC (R)	CC	AC (R)	CC
University College London	UK	132	34 (2)	3,550	26.89	0	8 (3)	24 (1)	49 (2)	822	83 (2)	2,728
Chinese Academy of Sciences	CN	113	15 (40)	981	8.68	0	1 (70)	4 (55)	19 (19)	69	94 (1)	912
University of Pennsylvania	USA	111	30 (3)	2,750	24.77	0	6 (7)	12 (10)	39 (3)	578	72 (5)	2,172
Harvard University	USA	104	35 (1)	4,534	43.60	1	9 (1)	23 (2)	55 (1)	923	49 (16)	3,611
University of North Carolina at Chapel Hill	USA	96	25 (6)	2,988	31.13	1	9 (1)	15 (4)	21 (12)	391	75 (4)	2,597
King's College London	UK	90	27 (4)	2,665	29.61	0	7 (5)	14 (5)	38 (4)	638	52 (15)	2,027
Korea University	KR	85	19 (20)	1,252	14.73	0	1 (70)	6 (33)	7 (109)	17	78 (3)	1,235
University of Toronto	CA	85	22 (13)	1,449	17.05	0	3 (23)	7 (26)	28 (7)	242	57 (10)	1,207
Indian Institutes of Technology	IN	84	23 (10)	1,738	20.69	0	2 (34)	11 (11)	17 (23)	58	67 (6)	1,680
McGill University	CA	80	19 (20)	1,541	19.26	0	4 (17)	8 (19)	21 (12)	326	59 (7)	1,215
University of California, Los Angeles	USA	79	21 (15)	1,505	19.05	0	2 (34)	7 (26)	30 (5)	386	49 (16)	1,119
Stanford University	USA	78	26 (5)	2,363	30.29	0	5 (11)	16 (3)	20 (15)	371	58 (8)	1,992
University of Oxford	UK	78	23 (10)	2,639	33.83	2	6 (7)	14 (5)	23 (11)	364	55 (11)	2,275
Imperial College London	UK	76	25 (6)	2,552	33.58	1	8 (3)	14 (5)	18 (21)	249	58 (8)	2,303
University of California, San Diego	USA	75	25 (6)	2,324	30.99	1	4 (17)	13 (8)	20 (15)	468	55 (11)	1,856
Johns Hopkins University	USA	73	18 (25)	1,348	18.47	1	2 (34)	4 (55)	20 (15)	171	53 (13)	1,177
Columbia University	USA	70	23 (10)	1,460	20.86	0	1 (70)	8 (19)	17 (23)	79	53 (13)	1,381
National Institutes of Health	USA	65	22 (13)	1,840	28.31	0	7 (5)	11 (11)	20 (15)	342	45 (23)	1,498
Istituto Di Ricovero e Cura a Carattere Scientifico	IT	62	17 (30)	983	15.85	0	2 (34)	5 (45)	15 (31)	159	47 (19)	824
University of Pittsburgh	USA	61	21 (15)	1,374	22.52	0	3 (23)	6 (33)	24 (8)	244	37 (30)	1,130
University of Cambridge	UK	59	17 (30)	1,334	22.61	0	3 (23)	5 (45)	11 (61)	130	48 (18)	1,204
University of Electronic Science and Technology of China	CN	58	12 (76)	620	10.69	0	1 (70)	4 (55)	12 (49)	64	46 (21)	556
Southeast University	CN	57	14 (51)	754	13.23	0	1 (70)	3 (82)	14 (36)	58	43 (24)	696
Shanghai Jiaotong University	CN	57	13 (64)	907	15.91	0	3 (23)	6 (33)	11 (61)	74	46 (21)	833
University of Granada	ES	57	21 (15)	1,154	20.25	0	0	6 (33)	29 (6)	204	28 (59)	950
The University of New Mexico	USA	57	17 (30)	1,092	19.16	0	1 (70)	7 (26)	15 (31)	105	42 (26)	987

Abbreviations: R: ranking position; AC: article count; H: H index; CC: citation count; CC/AC: average citations per article; >=300, >=100, >=50: counts of articles with more than 300, 100, or 50 citations. CY: country (UK: United Kingdom; CN: China; USA: United States; KR: South Korea; CA: Canada; IN: India; IT: Italy; ES: Spain).

3.3 Affiliations Analysis

There were 4,214 affiliations participated in the studied articles. Table 3 displayed the top 26 prolific affiliations, among which the top three were *University College London*, *Chinese Academy of Sciences*, and *University of Pennsylvania*. For H index perspective, *Harvard University* was ranked in the first position although with a relatively smaller article count as 104. It was worth noting that as for *Chinese Academy of*

Sciences, it had a relatively lower position for article count during period 2009–2013, ranked at 19th. However, during the period 2014–2018, it had the highest article count as 94, reflecting its fast and flourishing development in the research field in recent five years. The situation for *Harvard University* was quite different. It had the most articles published during the first period, while during the second period, it was only ranked at 16th with 49 articles. However, it was worth mentioning that the average citations per article (CC/TC) for *Harvard University* was the highest among the listed affiliations in the table, indicating its high research influence.

3.4 Scientific Collaboration Analysis

Scientific collaborations in the level of the country/region and affiliation were reported and visualized. The collaborations among countries/regions were shown as Fig. 3 with 86 nodes and 665 links. Most countries involved were from Asia and Europe. The USA donated as the largest node in blue color was located in the center of the collaboration network, and had the most collaborations with others. The USA and China had the most collaborations (297 articles), followed by USA-UK (132 articles), and USA-Germany (128 articles). The scientific collaborations among affiliations with article

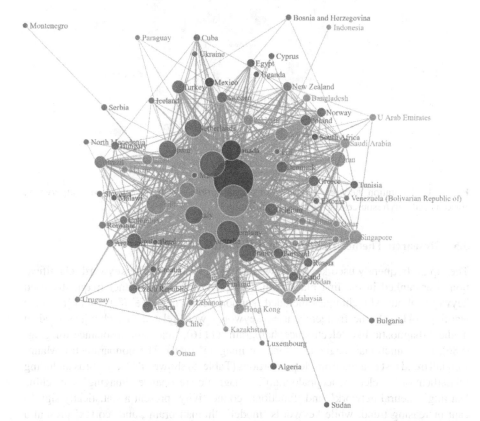

Fig. 3. Collaboration network among countries/regions, accessed via http://www.zhukun.org/haoty/resources.asp?id=HBAI_country

count equaling to or more than 40 were displayed as Fig. 4 with 52 nodes and 465 links. Most of the affiliations (46.15%) were originated from the USA. *The University of North Carolina at Chapel Hill* and *Korea University* had the most collaborations (56 articles), followed by *Harvard University-Massachusetts General Hospital*, and *University of College London-Kings College London*. By accessing the dynamic networks, and simply clicking on the nodes with regard to any country/region as well as affiliation, one can explore the specific collaborative relations.

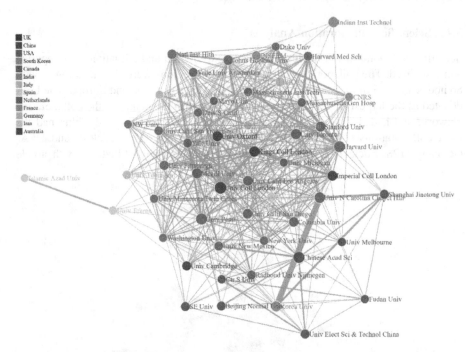

Fig. 4. Collaboration network of affiliations with articles >=40, accessed via http://www. zhukun.org/haoty/resources.asp?id=HBAI_affiliation

3.5 Research Themes Discovery and Evolution Analysis

The top 20 frequently used keywords were shown in Table 4. The keyword 'classification' was ranked in the first place with a frequency of 1,362. Other frequently used keywords about AI techniques included 'support vector machine' (803), and 'machine learning' (416). Some frequently used keywords were related to techniques used in medical diagnostic like 'electroencephalogram' (1116), 'magnetic resonance imaging' (886), and 'functional magnetic resonance imaging' (660). The nonparametric Mann-Kendall trend test of annual article proportions (Table 5) showed that keywords including 'classification', 'electroencephalogram', 'magnetic resonance imaging', 'machine learning', 'neural network', and 'functional connectivity' present a statistically significant increasing trend, while keywords 'model', 'human brain', and 'cortex' present a statistically significant decreasing trend, both at the two-sided $p = 0.05$ level.

Table 4. Top 20 frequently used keywords

Keywords	2009–2018		2009–2010		2011–2012		2013–2014		2015–2016		2017–2018	
	AC	%	AC (R)	%	AC (R)	%	AC (R)	%	AC (R)	%	AC (R)	%
Classification	1,362	21.56	105 (1)	15.67	137 (1)	18.49	202 (1)	20.47	344 (1)	22.19	574 (1)	24.23
Electroencephalogram	1,116	17.67	94 (2)	14.03	118 (2)	15.92	163 (2)	16.51	300 (2)	19.35	441 (2)	18.62
Magnetic resonance imaging	886	14.03	77 (4)	11.49	88 (5)	11.88	153 (4)	15.50	219 (4)	14.13	349 (3)	14.73
Brain computer interface	852	13.49	74 (5)	11.04	88 (5)	11.88	154 (3)	15.60	231 (3)	14.90	305 (4)	12.87
Support vector machine	803	12.71	59 (9)	8.81	89 (4)	12.01	146 (5)	14.79	213 (5)	13.74	296 (6)	12.49
Alzheimer disease	736	11.65	64 (7)	9.55	92 (3)	12.42	136 (6)	13.78	175 (7)	11.29	269 (7)	11.36
Brain	707	11.19	74 (5)	11.04	74 (7)	9.99	99 (7)	10.03	161 (8)	10.39	299 (5)	12.62
Functional magnetic resonance imaging	660	10.45	80 (3)	11.94	72 (8)	9.72	96 (8)	9.73	176 (6)	11.35	236 (8)	9.96
Model	431	6.82	61 (8)	9.10	51 (9)	6.88	80 (9)	8.11	97 (13)	6.26	142 (14)	5.99
Algorithm	418	6.62	37 (14)	5.52	36 (18)	4.86	66 (12)	6.69	124 (9)	8.00	155 (10)	6.54
Machine learning	416	6.59	16 (54)	2.39	23 (37)	3.10	43 (19)	4.36	104 (10)	6.71	230 (9)	9.71
System	411	6.51	40 (12)	5.97	44 (11)	5.94	72 (11)	7.29	101 (11)	6.52	154 (11)	6.50
Segmentation	403	6.38	33 (17)	4.93	40 (15)	5.40	75 (10)	7.60	101 (11)	6.52	154 (11)	6.50
Neural network	374	5.92	33 (17)	4.93	44 (11)	5.94	53 (15)	5.37	97 (13)	6.26	147 (13)	6.21
mild cognitive impairment	352	5.57	26 (23)	3.88	42 (14)	5.67	58 (13)	5.88	88 (15)	5.68	138 (16)	5.83
Human brain	313	4.95	43 (11)	6.42	45 (10)	6.07	55 (14)	5.57	81 (18)	5.23	89 (36)	3.76
Cortex	306	4.84	44 (10)	6.57	43 (13)	5.80	39 (29)	3.95	69 (22)	4.45	111 (23)	4.69
Signal	299	4.73	22 (32)	3.28	26 (31)	3.51	33 (35)	3.34	88 (15)	5.68	130 (18)	5.49
Functional connectivity	295	4.67	13 (66)	1.94	13 (74)	1.75	41 (22)	4.15	88 (15)	5.68	140 (15)	5.91
Independent component analysis	290	4.59	22 (32)	3.28	28 (24)	3.78	47 (16)	4.76	80 (19)	5.16	113 (22)	4.77

Abbreviations: R: ranking position; AC: article count; %: proportion.

Table 5. The Mann-Kendall trend test for the top 20 frequently used keywords

Keywords	Mann-Kendall trend test			
	Z	p-value	S	Trend
Classification	3.7566	0.0002	43	↑↑↑↑
Electroencephalogram	1.9677	0.0491	1.9677	↑↑
Magnetic resonance imaging	1.9677	0.0491	23	↑↑
Brain computer interface	1.4311	0.1524	17	↑
Support vector machine	0.53666	0.5915	7	↑
Alzheimer disease	0	1	1	-
Brain	1.2522	0.2105	15	↑
Functional magnetic resonance imaging	−0.35777	0.7205	−5	↓
Model	−2.5044	0.0123	−29	↓↓
Algorithm	1.61	0.1074	19	↑
Machine learning	3.3988	0.0007	39	↑↑↑↑
System	0.35777	0.7205	5	↑
Segmentation	0.89443	0.3711	11	↑
Neural network	2.5044	0.0123	29	↑↑

(continued)

Table 5. (*continued*)

Keywords	Mann-Kendall trend test			
	Z	p-value	S	Trend
Mild cognitive impairment	1.4311	0.1524	17	↑
Human brain	−2.8622	0.0042	−33	↓↓↓
Cortex	−1.9677	0.0491	−23	↓↓
Signal	1.7889	0.0736	21	↑
Functional connectivity	2.8622	0.0042	33	↑↑↑
Independent component analysis	1.0733	1.0733	13	↑

Abbreviations: Z: Z statistics; S: Kendall score (S > 0 means increasing trend; S < 0 means decreasing trend); *p: significance level; -: no significant change of trend; ↑(↓): increasing (decreasing) trend but not significant ($p > 0.05$); ↑↑(↓↓), ↑↑↑(↓↓↓), ↑↑↑↑(↓↓↓↓): significantly increasing (decreasing) trend ($p < 0.05$, $p < 0.01$, and $p < 0.001$, respectively).

4   Discussion

The trend analysis of articles and citations in relation to human brain research using AI techniques demonstrated a fast and flourishing development of the interdisciplinary research field, especially since 2014. The journal analysis recognized a list of journals that were most likely to publish articles within the scope of the studied interdisciplinary research field. The studied articles were diversely distributed but still centered on JCR categories such as *Neuroimaging, Neurosciences, Engineering, Biomedical, Computer Science, Artificial Intelligence,* and so on.

University College London and *Chinese Academy of* Sciences were the top two prolific affiliations. Especially, the *Chinese Academy of Sciences* had the highest article count as 94 during 2014–2018, reflecting a very fast and flourishing development. However, from the article influence perspective (e.g., H index and CC/AC index), it still has to pay more attention to improve research quality and influence. Several prolific affiliations (e.g., *University College London, King's College London*) playing a prominent role in the interdisciplinary research were from the UK. Collaborations among countries/regions and affiliations were quite close from the social network analysis, with interior and trans-regional research collaborations going hand in hand.

Keyword analysis depicted major keywords in the articles published over five time periods in the past decade, i.e., 2009–2010, 2011–2012, 2013–2014, 2015–2016, and 2017–2018. There were several recurring keywords throughout the last decade. Firstly, the term 'classification' was the top one frequently used keyword in articles across the five periods, indicating that most studies centered on the use of classification methods in human brain research. For example, classification is widely used in studies on brain diseases such as Alzheimer's disease [26], seizure [27], and autism spectrum disorder [28], as well as brain tumor [29]. Secondly, the term 'electroencephalogram' was always the second frequently used keyword in articles throughout the studies periods, reflecting the importance of electroencephalogram technique in interdisciplinary research. Especially, a great number of studies collected research data from the use of such techniques for medical diagnostic with magnetic resonance imaging and functional magnetic resonance imaging as well. Thirdly, many studies targeted brain computer interface with a focus primarily on transforming the brain activity of different mental tasks into a control signal. Fourthly, in addition to classification, other specific AI techniques such as 'support vector machine' had consistently been the research focus of research. Some relatively broad terms such as 'model', 'algorithm', and 'system' also constantly appeared. Fifthly, many related studies focused on 'alzheimer disease', which was listed within the top 6 most frequently used keywords. Other brain-related diseases such as 'schizophrenia' and 'epilepsy' were less focused compared with 'alzheimer disease'. Last, regarding the center role of the interdisciplinary research, without doubt, the keyword 'brain' had a constant ranking position in the list, while 'human brain' had a relatively lower position.

The trend analysis of top frequently used keywords emphasized the significantly increasing trend of research on 'classification', 'electroencephalogram', 'magnetic resonance imaging', 'machine learning', 'neural network', and 'functional connectivity'. These can serve as scientific direction for current and future research.

5 Conclusion

This study was the first to present a bibliometric based comprehensive overview of the academic articles about human brain research using AI techniques during the last decade. Analyzing techniques included statistical analysis, keywords analysis, and social network analysis. Trends and features of the interdisciplinary research field were explored in terms of trends of articles, citations, prolific journals, affiliations, scientific collaborations, as well as the discovery of research topic. It should be acknowledged that the findings were based on one database, WoS. Further investigations by extending to more databases such as PubMed can also be considered. These findings are useful for better understanding the research status and development trends of the research. For scholars in the field, the study can help optimize research topic decision and identify potential collaborators for conducting scientific collaborations.

Acknowledgements. This work was supported by National Natural Science Foundation of China (No. 61772146).

References

1. Lee, E.J., Kim, Y.H., Kim, N., Kang, D.W.: Deep into the brain: artificial intelligence in stroke imaging. J. Stroke **19**(3), 277 (2017)
2. Lu, H., Li, Y., Chen, M., Kim, H., Serikawa, S.: Brain intelligence: go beyond artificial intelligence. Mob. Netw. Appl. **23**(2), 368–375 (2018)
3. Cuingnet, R., Gerardin, E., Tessieras, J., Auzias, G., Lehéricy, S., Habert, M.O., et al.: Automatic classification of patients with Alzheimer's disease from structural MRI: a comparison of ten methods using the ADNI database. Neuroimage **56**(2), 766–781 (2011)
4. Gao, X.W., Hui, R., Tian, Z.: Classification of CT brain images based on deep learning networks. Comput. Methods Programs Biomed. **138**, 49–56 (2017)

5. Acharya, U.R., Molinari, F., Sree, S.V., Chattopadhyay, S., Ng, K.H., Suri, J.S.: Automated diagnosis of epileptic EEG using entropies. Biomed. Signal Process. Control **7**(4), 401–408 (2012)
6. Morabito, F.C., Campolo, M., Mammone, N., Versaci, M., Franceschetti, S., Tagliavini, F., et al.: Deep learning representation from electroencephalography of early-stage Creutzfeldt-Jakob disease and features for differentiation from rapidly progressive dementia. Int. J. Neural Syst. **27**(02), 1650039 (2017)
7. Dosenbach, N.U., Nardos, B., Cohen, A.L., Fair, D.A., Power, J.D., Church, J.A., et al.: Prediction of individual brain maturity using fMRI. Science **329**(5997), 1358–1361 (2010)
8. Salimi-Khorshidi, G., Douaud, G., Beckmann, C.F., Glasser, M.F., Griffanti, L., Smith, S. M.: Automatic denoising of functional MRI data: combining independent component analysis and hierarchical fusion of classifiers. Neuroimage **90**, 449–468 (2014)
9. Zhang, D., Wang, Y., Zhou, L., Yuan, H., Shen, D.: Alzheimer's disease neuroimaging initiative: multimodal classification of Alzheimer's disease and mild cognitive impairment. Neuroimage **55**(3), 856–867 (2011)
10. Stam, C.J., et al.: Graph theoretical analysis of magnetoencephalographic functional connectivity in Alzheimer's disease. Brain **132**(1), 213–224 (2008)
11. Chen, X., Weng, H., Hao, T.: A data-driven approach for discovering the recent research status of diabetes in China. In: Siuly, S., et al. (eds.) HIS 2017. LNCS, vol. 10594, pp. 89–101. Springer, Cham (2017). https://doi.org/10.1007/978-3-319-69182-4_10
12. Chen, X., Chen, B., Zhang, C., Hao, T.: Discovering the recent research in natural language processing field based on a statistical approach. In: Huang, T.-C., Lau, R., Huang, Y.-M., Spaniol, M., Yuen, C.-H. (eds.) SETE 2017. LNCS, vol. 10676, pp. 507–517. Springer, Cham (2017). https://doi.org/10.1007/978-3-319-71084-6_60
13. Hao, T., Chen, X., Li, G., Yan, J.: A bibliometric analysis of text mining in medical research. Soft. Comput. **22**(23), 7875–7892 (2018)
14. Chen, X., Liu, Z., Wei, L., Yan, J., Hao, T., Ding, R.: A comparative quantitative study of utilizing artificial intelligence on electronic health records in the USA and China during 2008–2017. BMC Med. Inform. Decis. Mak. **18**(5), 117 (2018)
15. Chen, X., Ding, R., Xu, K., Wang, S., Hao, T., Zhou, Y.: A bibliometric review of natural language processing empowered mobile computing. Wirel. Commun. Mob. Comput. (2018)
16. Chen, X., Xie, H., Wang, F.L., Liu, Z., Xu, J., Hao, T.: A bibliometric analysis of natural language processing in medical research. BMC Med. Inform. Decis. Mak. **18**(1), 14 (2018)
17. Chen, X., Hao, J., Chen, J., Hua, S., Hao, T.: A bibliometric analysis of the research status of the technology enhanced language learning. In: Hao, T., Chen, W., Xie, H., Nadee, W., Lau, R. (eds.) SETE 2018. LNCS, vol. 11284, pp. 169–179. Springer, Cham (2018). https://doi.org/10.1007/978-3-030-03580-8_18
18. Song, Y., Chen, X., Hao, T., Liu, Z., Lan, Z.: Exploring two decades of research on classroom dialogue by using bibliometric analysis. Comput. Educ. **137**, 12–31 (2019)
19. Chen, X., Lun, Y., Yan, J., Hao, T., Weng, H.: Discovering thematic change and evolution of utilizing social media for healthcare research. BMC Med. Inform. Decis. Mak. **19**(2), 50 (2019)
20. Chen, X., Wang, S., Tang, Y., Hao, T.: A bibliometric analysis of event detection in social media. Online Inf. Rev. **43**(1), 29–52 (2019)
21. Peng, B., Guo, D., Qiao, H., Yang, Q., Zhang, B., Hayat, T., et al.: Bibliometric and visualized analysis of China's coal research 2000–2015. J. Clean. Prod. **197**, 1177–1189 (2018)
22. Hassan, S.U., Haddawy, P., Zhu, J.: A bibliometric study of the world's research activity in sustainable development and its sub-areas using scientific literature. Scientometrics **99**(2), 549–579 (2014)

23. Du, H.S., Ke, X., Chu, S.K., Chan, L.T.: A bibliometric analysis of emergency management using information systems (2000–2016). Online Inf. Rev. **41**(4), 454–470 (2017)
24. Hirsch, J.E., Buela-Casal, G.: The meaning of the H-index. Int. J. Clin. Health Psychol. **14**(2), 161–164 (2014)
25. Mann, H.B.: Nonparametric tests against trend. Econ.: J. Econ. Soc. **13**, 245–259 (1945)
26. Simoes, R., van Walsum, A.M.V.C., Slump, C.H.: Classification and localization of early-stage Alzheimer's disease in magnetic resonance images using a patch-based classifier ensemble. Neuroradiology **56**(9), 709–721 (2014)
27. Fu, K., Qu, J., Chai, Y., Dong, Y.: Classification of seizure based on the time-frequency image of EEG signals using HHT and SVM. Biomed. Signal Process. Control **13**, 15–22 (2014)
28. Jamal, W., Das, S., Oprescu, I.A., Maharatna, K., Apicella, F., Sicca, F.: Classification of autism spectrum disorder using supervised learning of brain connectivity measures extracted from synchrostates. J. Neural Eng. **11**(4), 046019 (2014)
29. Jayachandran, A., Sundararaj, G.K.: Abnormality segmentation and classification of multi-class brain tumor in MR images using fuzzy logic-based hybrid kernel SVM. Int. J. Fuzzy Syst. **17**(3), 434–443 (2015)

Investigating Lexical and Semantic Cognition by Using Neural Network to Encode and Decode Brain Imaging

Lu Cao[1] and Yue Zhang[2(✉)]

[1] Singapore University of Technology and Design, Singapore, Singapore
lu_cao@mymail.sutd.edu.sg
[2] West Lake University, Hangzhou, China
yue.zhang@wias.org.cn

Abstract. The question of how the human brain represents conceptual knowledge has received significant attention in many scientific fields. Over the last decade, there has been increasing interest in the use of deep learning methods for analyzing functional magnetic resonance imaging (fMRI) data. In this paper, we report a series of experiments with neural networks for fMRI encoding and decoding. Results show that by using neural networks, both encoding and decoding accuracies are improved compared to a linear model on the same input. To evaluate the contextual information influences in cognitive modeling, we also extend the stimuli dataset from single noun to description sentences. The experiments indicate the impact of context information varies from person to person. To illustrate the strong correlation between linguistic and visual representations in the human brain, we extend the stimuli from a single word to images which were not present to the participant during fMRI data collection.

Keywords: Semantics · fMRI · Cognitive

1 Introduction

How a simple concept is represented and organized by the human brain has been of long research interest [9, 15, 19]. The rising of brain imaging have now made it feasible to look at the neural representation of such concepts within the brain. In particular, the functional magnetic resonance imaging (fMRI) is a technique that allows for the visualization of activated brain regions. Neurons consume more oxygen as they become active. fMRI locates the activated neuron by measuring the blood-oxygen-level-dependent (BOLD) contrast. It has become an essential tool for analyzing the neural correlates of brain activity in recent decades [22, 30, 31, 33, 37, 38, 42].

Many fMRI studies identify correlations between brain activity and a task the participant performs during the scan. To this end, most current understanding has been achieved by analyzing fMRI data from the viewpoint of encoding

© Springer Nature Singapore Pte Ltd. 2019
A. Zeng et al. (Eds.): HBAI 2019, CCIS 1072, pp. 84–100, 2019.
https://doi.org/10.1007/978-981-15-1398-5_6

and decoding [32]. Here encoding refers to predict brain activity by using stimuli (Fig. 1) and decoding refers to predict stimuli by using brain activity. When analyzing data from the encoding perspective, researchers aim to understand how activity in the brain varies when there is concurrent variation in the real world. Neuroscientists have shown that distinct patterns of fMRI activity are associated with the different stimulus, such as viewing semantic categories of pictures, including tools, animals, and buildings, reading an article which describes a concrete or abstract concepts. When analyzing data from the decoding perspective, researchers attempt to determine how much can be learned about the word. Generally speaking, decoding brain imaging is to tell what participant is thinking during the scan.

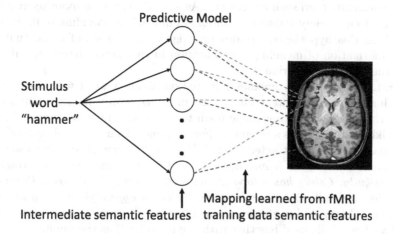

Fig. 1. Predict fMRI from word stimuli

In NLP, the idea that a word's context gives its meaning dominates the approach of word representation. Consequently, a word can be represented as a high-dimensional real-valued distributional semantic vector, where the similarity among vectors reflects the similarity of contexts. These representations of linguistic meaning capture the human judgments in various tasks (*e.g.*, word analogy, word similarity judgment, and word categorization). To test whether such word representations are also neurally plausible, some studies have attempted to learn mappings between semantic vectors and brain activation patterns. If such mapping can be learned and a model can be used to predict brain activation to a new stimulus, the model can reflect some aspects of meaning representation in the human brain.

[31] first introduced the task of taking a semantic representation of a single noun and predicting the brain imaging elicited by that noun. Subsequent research [13] has attempted to fulfill this task by using various word embeddings. Most of the above work uses linear models, assuming that the concept representations are a linear combination in the human brain. For example, the word "celery" is

the linear combination of concept "eat", "taste", "fill", etc. However, intuitively, the human brain is complex, which apart from the linear combination, should also capture non-linear functions. This hypothesis can be verified if a non-linear model can give high accuracy compared to a linear model when fitting the same noun representation to the brain imaging output. In this paper, we apply neural networks to capture complex knowledge representations and compare the performances with a linear model. Results show that by using neural networks, both encoding and decoding accuracies are improved compared to a linear model on the same input. This conforms our hypothesis that a non-linear function better simulates brain activation, which is also intuitive. In addition, rather than end-to-end mapping, associative thinking is also commonly believed as being involved in human cognition. For example, image thinking can be involved when giving a stimulus word such as "celery". As a result, it can be more accurate if a model is given a celery image as additional input when providing brain images. To address this hypothesis, we also investigate the impact of contextual and visual information of meaning representation in the human brain. Specifically, we do the following experiments:

First, human brain combines information about a word with its context. To evaluate how the context affects the meaning representation in mind, we extend the dataset [31] from single noun to some descriptive sentences. To this end, Wikipedia is used as a reference. For example, given the word "celery", the additional description extracted from Wikipedia, "*Celery (Apium graveolens) is a marshland plant in the family Apiaceae that has been cultivated as a vegetable since antiquity. Celery has a long fibrous stalk tapering into leaves. Depending on location and cultivar, either its stalks, leaves, or hypocotyl are eaten and used in cooking. Celery seed is also used as a spice and its extracts have been used in herbal medicine.*", is used together with the noun itself as the input.

Second, a growing body of evidence shows that visually embodied object representations elicited when participants are reading and contemplating object words [4,25,31]. More generally speaking, reading words evokes visual simulation, and viewing images evokes semantic representations [5,43]. The brain region of conceptual representations of linguistic is linked to visual perception. To illustrate this, we retrieve images from ImageNet [10] and using image features build the brain encoding and decoding models. Results show that out of 8 participants, the brain activation of most can be better predicted by adding visual inputs to the word, which strongly demonstrates that image associative thinking exist in human perceptron of noun semantics. Interestingly, the brain activation of 4 participants can also be better predicted by using the descriptive sentence as additional input information, which shows that some people can do analytically thinking when understanding a noun concept.

We investigate the cross-lingual brain encoding and decoding. The fMRI data are collected from English native speakers. We want to explore the brain semantic representation difference among different language speakers. To this end, we use Chinese word embeddings [45] to encode and decode brain imaging.

Surprisingly, the accuracy is close to using English word embeddings. This result suggests that semantic representations can be irrelevant to the language itself.

Finally, although languages and cultures vary, perceptron of common concepts can be universal across people.

In summary, we use neural network models to investigate aspects of meaning representation in the human brain, showing that they better reflect cognitive functions compared with linear models used in prior research. We additionally find that image and descriptive sentences can help better predict fMRI as additional inputs to the noun stimuli, which reflects that associative thinking is likely involved in the semantic understanding process. Interestingly, cross-lingual embedding inputs can give similar results for predicting fMRI images, which shows that there can be cross-lingual common ground in semantic representations of words.

2 Related Work

In word embeddings, there are two main methods map words from vocabulary to vectors of the real numbers. The first is one-hot encoding, in which each word is represented as a vocabulary size vector of zeros except one position of one (e.g., apple = [1, 0, 0 ... 0], fruit = [0, 0, 1, ..., 0]). The limitation of the one-hot representation is it fails to capture the relationship between words because the words are perpendicular in one-hot encoding. The other method to represent a word is distributed representation, in which word is mapped to a vector space of continues real number. [29] first efficiently trained the word embedding on Google News Corpus. The word to vector [29] is trained by language modeling by using skip-gram or continues bag of words (CBOW) algorithm. The CBOW is learning to maximize the probability of the target word by looking at the context while the skip-gram is to predict the context. Similarly, the GloVe [35] is trained on aggregated global word-word co-occurrence statistics from a corpus. The intuition underlying the model is ratios of word-word co-occurrence probabilities have the potential for encoding some form of meaning. There are many other versions word embeddings e.g., [6,12,21,24,39,45], released by different institutions. The main advantage of the distributed word representation mentioned above is that it captures the context of a word. By distributed representation, word-word relation can be reflected, for example, the cosine similarity of word vector *apple* and *fruit* is close compare to *apple* and *car*.

The brain encoding task was first introduced by [31], the task is to learn a mapping between word embedding and the human brain imaging. To this end, [31] created 25-dimension word vector trained on [7] and learned a mapping by using the linear model. In addition to using 25 semantic features [31], [20] incorporate the relatedness measures based on WordNet. [11] choose a set of verbs for semantic features. [13] use five semantic attributes directly related to sensory-motor experience-sound, color, visual motion, shape, and manipulation. The relevance of these attributes to each word is rating by the human.

On the decoding side, studies have shown that it is possible to accurately decode a participant's mental content for words [2,14,34,36], text snippets [17, 47], or sentences [3,28,46].

3 Methods

We build a linear model and a non-linear model for all our experiments. For the former, we follow [31] and use linear regression as the main method. For the latter, a standard multi-layer neural network is used.

For the encoding task, the inputs of the model are semantic features such as a single word and the model is required to predict the corresponding fMRI activation. [31] created 25 dimension distributed embeddings based on the co-occurrence statistics for each stimulus. Each word vector gives the normalized co-occurrence frequency of the stimulus noun with each of 25 verbs (*i.e.*, see, say, taste, wear, open, run, neared, eat, hear, drive, ride, touch, break, enter, move, listen, approach, fill, clean, lift, rub, smell, fear, push, manipulate). In this regard, a word is encoded into 25 semantic features. In addition to the 25 distributed features, we use the GloVe word vectors [35] as distributed semantic features. Compared with Mitchell's word vector [31]; GloVe [35] has flexible dimensions. With higher dimensions, the word can preserve rich semantic features.

The predicted value of y_t a voxel t in brain for the word w can be written as

$$y_t = \sum_{i=1}^{n} c_{ti} f_i(w),$$ (1)

where $f_i(w)$ is the $i^t h$ semantic feature of w, n is the dimension of semantic feature and c_{ti} is learn-able parameter. A multi-layer neural networks can be written as

$$y_t = \sum_{i=1}^{M} c_{ti} h_i + c_{i_0}$$ (2)

$$h_i = max(0, \sum_{j=1}^{N} c_{ji} x_j + c_{j_0}),$$ (3)

where y_t is the predicted value at voxel t, M is the number of hidden unit in a layer and h_i is the value of the $i^t h$ hidden unit for word w. c_{ti} is the learned coefficient that specifies the degree to which the ith semantic feature activates a voxel.

For the decoding task, the inputs are the fMRI images and outputs are predicted semantic representations. The same algorithms are used.

3.1 Training Objective

To train a multiple regression classifier, if the number of training examples is larger than the semantic feature dimension, a unique solution exists. Otherwise, a solution can be obtained by introducing a regularization term. To train a neural network, we employ the standard back-propagating [44] algorithm, which minimizes the mean square loss between the real fMRI and predicted one.

Following [31], we train and evaluate separate computational models for each of the nine participants by using a cross-validation approach. The model was trained repeatedly by a leave-two-out procedure, in which the model was trained using 58 of the 60 stimuli. The process iterates 1770 times. At test two, each trained model predicts the fMRI for two "left-out" words and then match predicted fMIR to their corresponding left-out ones. Given a trained model, the two left-out words w_1, w_2 and their fMRI images i_1, i_2, the model predicts the fMRI p_1, p_2 for w_1, w_2, respectively. It then decide which is the better match ($i_1 = p_1$, $i_2 = p_2$) or ($i_1 = p_2$, $i_2 = p_1$) by computing the cosine similarity. The match score S is calculated as

$$S(p_1 = i_1, p_2 = i_2) = cosine(p_1, i_1) \\ + cosine(p_2, i_2). \tag{4}$$

Similarly, the match score for the decoder is the sum of cosine similarity between actual and predicted word vectors.

3.2 Incorporating Contextual Information in Encoding

We extend the dataset by retrieving an article for each noun manually from Wikipedia. Each noun is assigned 3 to 6 sentences which describe the properties of the word. For example, to describe the proprieties of the chisel, we retrieve the article: *'A chisel is a tool with a characteristically shaped cutting edge (such that wood chisels have lent part of their name to a particular grind) of blade on its end, for carving or cutting a hard material such as wood, stone, or metal by hand, struck with a mallet, or mechanical power. The handle and blade of some types of chisel are made of metal or of wood with a sharp edge in it. Chiselling use involves forcing the blade into some material to cut it. The driving force may be applied by pushing by hand, or by using a mallet or hammer. In industrial use, a hydraulic ram or falling weight ('trip hammer') may be used to drive a chisel into the material. A gouge (one type of chisel) serves to carve small pieces from the material, particularly in woodworking, wood-turning and sculpture. Gouges most frequently produce concave surfaces. A gouge typically has a 'U'-shaped cross-section'*. To preserve contextual information, we apply convolution neural networks (CNNs) to each article. The CNNs involves a filter $W \in R^h$, which is applied to a window of h words to produce new features [23]. For example, a feature s_i is produced from a window of words $x_{i:i+h-1}$ by

$$s_i = f(w \cdot x_{i:i+h-1} + b), \tag{5}$$

where $f(\cdot)$ is a non-linear function and b is the bias term. Then substitute s_i into Eq. 3 as x_j.

Since word embeddings are trained based on words that co-occur with one another in a given corpus, they already encodes the context to some extent, why do we use the article to encode/decode fMRI again? The answer can be the article describes the word exclusively, provides detail and precision information, which contributes the high-quality features for subsequent brain imaging encoding and decoding. Besides, a word can be different meaning in multiple contexts, *e.g.*, the word "monster" in describing a computer or a person. Using articles for encoding and decoding can eliminate ambiguity.

3.3 Image and Text Correlation

Conceptual representations of linguistic and visual perception are linked together in the human brain [5,43]. The word comprehensiveness first involves activation of shallow language-based conceptual representation and then complemented by deeper simulation of visual properties of the concept [26]. The latter can play a much more critical role.

Based on the above argument, we assume that the image augmented model should be able to encode and decode the brain activation elicited by a word. To this end, we retrieve 300 to 1500 images for each noun from ImageNet [10], one of the largest image databases, except 'hand', 'foot', 'arm', 'leg' and 'eye'. The ImageNet [10] does not include these human body words. We retrieve these images from Google [18] and [1].

Deep Residual Network (ResNet) [16] is widely used in image recognition. It is a deep neural network with many convolution layers stack together. With more convolution layers, the network can extract rich image features. In our implementation, we use ResNet to produce the image feature map. Concretely, we extract each feature of each image and then average all features of the same word. For example, an image feature map $Fmap_i$ of image x_i is produced by

$$Fmap_i = resnet(x_i), \tag{6}$$

where $resnet$ is the function that produces the feature map and $Fmap_i$ is a 2048 dimensional real value vector. Suppose there are N images of the word 'airplane', we produce the image feature map $Fairplane$ of 'airplane' by

$$F_{airplane} = \frac{\sum_{i=1}^{N} Fmap_i}{N}, \tag{7}$$

then substitute $F_{airplane}$ into Eq. 3 as x_j to train the neural network.

3.4 Cross-Lingual Embeddings

Is the semantic representation identical or various from different language speakers? The question can be answered by decode the brain imaging collected from different language speakers when shown the same word stimuli. With the word embedding, we give a simple alternative to answer this question. Since the word embedding captures semantic reasons while producing the text, if we can encode and decode the English native speakers' brain imaging using word embedding from a different language with high accuracy, we gain evidence there is the common ground of semantic representation.

We choose Chinese word embeddings [45] in our work, which consists 200-dimension vector representations which are pre-trained on large-scale high-quality data. These vectors, capturing semantic meanings for Chinese words and phrases, can be widely applied in many downstream Chinese processing tasks.

4 Experiments

We use the fMRI data from [31], which were collected from nine healthy, college-age participants. The stimuli are line drawings and nouns labels of 60 concrete objects from 12 semantic categories as Table 1. During data collection, the 60 word-picture pairs were presented to each participant six times with randomly permuting. To create a representative fMRI for each stimulus, we compute the mean fRMI response over its six scans. The mean of all 60 representative images is then subtracted from each image.

Table 1. The 60 noun and categories

Categories	Words
Man-made	Key, telephone, watch, bell, refrigerator
Building	Igloo, apartment, barn, house, church
Build part	Door, closet, arch, chimney, window
Tool	Hammer, screwdriver, chisel, saw, pliers
Furniture	Chair, dresser, desk, bed, table
Animal	Bear, cat, horse, dog, cow
Kitchen	Bottle, glass, spoon, cup, knife
Vehicle	Truck, bicycle, car, train, airplane
Insect	Fly, bee, ant, butterfly, beetle
Vegetable	Carrot, corn, tomato, lettuce, celery
Body part	Foot, eye, arm, leg, hand
Clothing	Dress, coat, skirt, pants, shirt

4.1 Experimental Settings

We design four experiments to evaluate our models:

- In Experiment 1, we re-implemented the linear model with Micheal's word vector [31] and GloVe [35].
- In Experiment 2, we use multiple layer feed-forward neural networks to predict fMRI activation.

- In Experiment 3, we incorporate the context into the model.
- In Experiment 4, we implement the linear and non-linear models to decode fMRI and analyze the results, respectively. Also, we also use the image feature as input to predict the fMRI activation.

4.2 Voxel Selected

The fMRI data is 3D image consists of voxels (volumetric pixels) covering millions of brain neurons. It comes from the machine as stacked 2D slices. The number of voxels is enormous, usually greater than 50000, it makes impossible to fit a standard linear model [41] because the number of observations are usually far less than the voxels. To deal with this problem, a simple way is to use a subset of the whole brain voxels. Depend on the specific task; there are many algorithms to choose a subset of the voxels, in our work, we follow [31]'s method to pick the 500 most stable voxels. During the training process, each voxel was assigned a "stability score" by using the data from 6 scan sessions of the 58 training stimuli. The 500 most stable voxels ranked highest by this stability score were used in the experiments.

4.3 Visualization of fMRI

t-SNE [27] is a supervised dimensionality reduction tool for visualization high-dimensional data into two-dimensional space using stochastic neighbor embedding.

The fMRI data is high dimensional, to help understand the properties of the data, we use t-SNE [27] to reduce the fMRI dimension to 2D and visualize them as Fig. 2.

The dataset [31] consists of 360 brain imaging (fMRI) of 12 categories as Table 1. In left side of the Fig. 2, each point represents an reduced dimension fMRI data. We assign different colors to each category and the label is the center of the category. Ideally, the points in Fig. 2 can be clustered to 12 categories and the distance between groups should be large. In our visualization, the groups are not ideally separable, but we still can find some valuable information from it. For example, the group of furniture, building, build-part, vehicle are close and the group of kitchen, vegetable, tool are close. This is accord to common sense since the vegetables and tools usually appear in a kitchen, and furniture, building, build-part, vehicle regularly appear in the same scenario. When we talk about the kitchen, it is very natural to think of tools such as cutlery and foods such as vegetables. When we talk about the apartment, it is more likely to think about furniture, vehicle, building, and building part. The right side of the Fig. 2 are images we retrieved from [8,40], as we can see, vegetables and knife appear in kitchen while furniture, building, build-part, vehicle appear together. But it is less likely think of car when talking about the kitchen. The visualization of the fMRI data gives us a preliminary conclusion that associative thinking is neurally plausible and can be reflected by fMRI categorization.

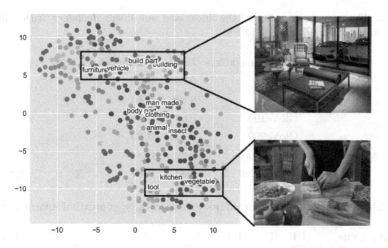

Fig. 2. Visualization of fMRI

Table 2. The average accuracy of the linear and non-linear *encoders* with different word vectors for participant P1 to P9

Word embeddings	Linear	Non-linear
[31]	**0.79**	0.77
GloVe50	0.69	**0.77**
GloVe100	0.74	**0.80**
GloVe200	0.74	**0.76**
GloVe300	0.77	**0.78**
Tencent200	0.75	**0.81**

4.4 Encoding

The linear model's results of Experiment 1 are shown in the left column of Table 2. From the results, we observe that with linear regression, Mitchell's 25-dimensional word vector [31] achieves the best prediction results, better than GloVe vectors [35]. The high dimensional GloVe embedding [35] preserves rich semantic information compared with the low dimensional vectors, but the result does not accord with intuition. There can be two main reasons. First, Mitchell's 25-dimensional word vector [31] is based on the most significant hand chosen semantic features which include the most common properties of a noun. For example, the word "celery" is represented as $celery = 0.837 \times eat + 0.346 \times taste + 0.315 \times fill + ... + 0 \times move$, where the concept "eat" contributes a 0.837 weight to celery, while to concept "move" contributes a 0 to celery. This conforms to common sense because celery is edible. GloVe [35], on the other hand, contains distributed semantic features, which can be irrelevant. The second reason is that linear regression is too simple to capture complex representations. Even if the

Table 3. The average accuracy of the linear and non-linear **decoders** with different word vectors for participant P1 to P9

Word embeddings	Linear	Non-linear
[31]	0.75	**0.76**
GloVe50	0.81	**0.84**
GloVe100	0.84	**0.86**
GloVe200	0.82	**0.85**
GloVe300	0.82	**0.84**
Tencent200	0.84	**0.87**

Table 4. The accuracy of **encoders** with or without contextual information

Participants	P1	P2	P3	P4	P5	P6	P7	P8	P9	AVG
Without context	0.88	0.71	**0.79**	0.87	0.76	**0.74**	0.72	**0.70**	0.81	0.78
With context	**0.90**	**0.77**	0.77	**0.88**	0.76	0.68	**0.78**	0.64	0.81	0.78

GloVe [35] preserves rich semantic information, where may not combine for the task. Hence a linear model may not be the best choice to learn the mapping between the human brain and the semantic representations. Instead, we need more expressive models to cope with the complexity.

The non-linear model results of Experiment 2 are shown in right column of Table 2. We observe that one hidden-layer neural network outweighs linear model on all GloVe [35] variants. The results support the view that the concept representation is not linearly combined in the human brain.

4.5   Decoding

We implement linear and non-linear decoders in Experiment 4. The results are summarized in Table 3. We observe that both linear and non-linear models can decode fMRI. The non-linear model outweighs the linear model on all word vectors. Both models have significant improvements by using GloVe [35]. This result implies that the human brain encodes semantic representation in a complicated function and a proper semantic space is essential to brain decoding.

The decoding is an illustration of *zero-shot learning* [34] of the human brain as the decoder can predict novel classes that were omitted from a training set with an accuracy much higher than chance. After training on a semantic feature space, the decoder can leverage a semantic knowledge base that encodes both training and test set features.

4.6   Impact of Hidden Layers

To evaluate the impact of network depth, we tested neural networks with one to five hidden layers and summarized the results as Fig. 3, from which we observe

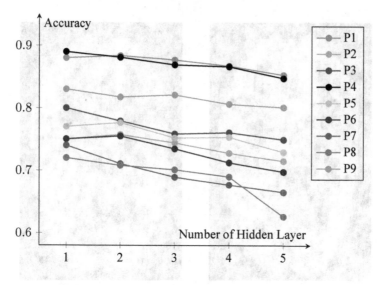

Fig. 3. The impact of number of hidden layers

that as the hidden layer increases, the accuracy decreases across all participants. Generally, the model can fit complex data with more hidden layers. We expect that the model could learn complex concepts from the semantic representations, but the result is the opposite. The reason can be over-fitting.

4.7 Impact of Contextual Information

In Experiment 3, we incorporate contextual information into the non-linear model. The results are summarized in Table 4. We observe that the impact of the contextual information varies from person to person. Compared to Experiment 2, the accuracy of participant P1, P2, P4, P7 increase, while that of P3 and P6 decrease. This result suggests that humans can understand the same concept from different perspectives. Through learning the mapping between large corpus-based semantic vectors and brain imaging, we may find out how the human brain associates one concept or thought to another.

4.8 Similarities Between Predicted and Actual Images

Figure 4 are the observed and predicted fMRI of the word "hand" after training uses 58 nouns. The left image is the observed fMRI, and the right one is the predicted. Although the predicted fMRI is not perfect, it captures main components of the ground truth. The yellow and green area near the top is the fusiform gyri. In neuroscience, the functionality of the fusiform gyrus has been linked to recognition (*e.g.*, processing of color information, face and body recognition, word recognition, within-category identification).

To provide more insight into the non-linear model. Figure 5 depicts for participant P1 the cosine similarity between each predicted images and real images.

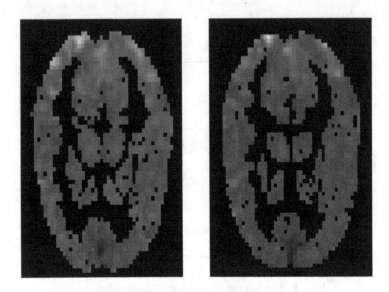

Fig. 4. Observed and predicted fMRI images for "hand"

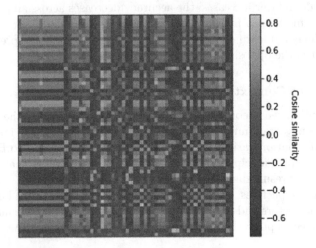

Fig. 5. Cosine similarity between actual and predicated images. The mean of the diagonal is **0.3371**, wheres the mean of entire matrix is **0.0720**. This indicates that the predicted image is similar to the real image than others in general.

Table 5. The accuracy of *encoders* with word embedding and images

Participants	P1	P2	P3	P4	P5	P6	P7	P8	P9	AVG
GloVe300	0.88	0.71	0.82	0.83	**0.80**	0.76	0.69	**0.67**	0.77	0.77
Images	**0.93**	**0.79**	0.82	**0.89**	0.78	**0.79**	**0.81**	0.66	**0.81**	**0.81**

4.9 Use Image Features to Encode Brain Imaging

We use the ResNet [16] extracted image features to predict the fMRI activation. Figure 6 is a part of celery images used in experiments. The result is obtained by using the linear regression model and is summarized in Table 5. Six out of nine participants' accuracy is improved, and average 4% increase across all participants.

The result supports the view that word comprehension involves both linguistic and visual processes in the human brain [26]. We use ResNet [16] to extract each image's feature as Eq. 6. The single image feature map contains noise, which leads to the model fail to encode the brain imaging. We extract multiple image features and average them on each dimension as Eq. 7. By means of sum up and average on all feature maps, the salient features of the celery are kept such as color, shape, texture, contour, etc., and the noises are suppressed.

Fig. 6. A part of celery images used in experiments

4.10 Cross-Lingual Analysis

The results of cross-lingual encoding and decoding are summarized in last line of Tables 2 and 3. Intuitively, the difference of semantic representation among different language speakers' brain exists and can be reflected by using cross-lingual brain imaging encoding and decoding. However, the experimental result is the opposite. The result of encoding and decoding of English native speakers' brain imaging by using Chinese word embedding [45] are very close. Even though we cannot conclude the semantic representation is human-wide identical for sure, which needs more biological experiments, the result still suggests the brain semantic representation among different language speakers is highly correlated.

This finding brings many possibilities to incorporate the brain imaging data into NLP models (*e.g.*, leverage brain imaging to supervise the machine translation models).

5 Conclusion

We use a machine learning approach in understanding human cognition process of word semantics, finding that non-linear models with distributed semantic vectors give better accuracies compared to linear models with hand-chosen distributional vectors. This reflects that word embeddings are a good representation of lexical semantics and that human cognition involves non-linear activities, which is highly intuitive. We additionally investigated associative thinking by using additional image and descriptive sentence inputs to the non-linear model for predicting fMRI, finding that both are useful, with the former being more effective. Finally, we found that cross-lingual word representations can be equally useful in predicting brain images of English speakers, which shows that there can be strong cross-lingual associations in word vectors. The dataset in this work is relatively small, and the stimuli are all nouns, which limits our work in a small part of brain understanding. We will extend our work to a sizeable semantic space, which covers most of the human concepts in future work.

References

1. Afifi, M.: 11k hands: gender recognition and biometric identification using a large dataset of hand images (2017)
2. Anderson, A.J., Kiela, D., Clark, S., Poesio, M.: Visually grounded and textual semantic models differentially decode brain activity associated with concrete and abstract nouns. Trans. Assoc. Comput. Linguist. **5**, 17–30 (2017)
3. Anderson, A.J., et al.: Predicting neural activity patterns associated with sentences using a neurobiologically motivated model of semantic representation. Cerebral Cortex **27**(9), 4379–4395 (2017)
4. Anderson, A.J., Bruni, E., Lopopolo, A., Poesio, M., Baroni, M.: Reading visually embodied meaning from the brain: visually grounded computational models decode visual-object mental imagery induced by written text. NeuroImage **120**, 309–322 (2015)
5. Binder, J.R., Desai, R.H.: The neurobiology of semantic memory. Trends Cogn. Sci. **15**(11), 527–536 (2011). 22001867[pmid]
6. Bojanowski, P., Grave, E., Joulin, A., Mikolov, T.: Enriching word vectors with subword information. Trans. Assoc. Comput. Linguist. **5**, 135–146 (2017)
7. Brants, T., Franz, A., Linguistic Data Consortium: Web 1t 5-gram version 1 (2006)
8. ColourBox: Colourbox (2019)
9. Cox, D.D., Savoy, R.L.: Functional magnetic resonance imaging (fMRI) "brain reading": detecting and classifying distributed patterns of fMRI activity in human visual cortex. NeuroImage **19**(2), 261–270 (2003)

10. Deng, J., Dong, W., Socher, R., Li, L.J., Li, K., Fei-fei, L.: Imagenet: a large-scale hierarchical image database. In: CVPR (2009)
11. Devereux, B., Kelly, C., Korhonen, A.: Using fMRI activation to conceptual stimuli to evaluate methods for extracting conceptual representations from corpora. In: Proceedings of First Workshop On Computational Neurolinguistics, NAACL HLT pp. 70–78 (2010)
12. Devlin, J., Chang, M.W., Lee, K., Toutanova, K.: Bert: Pre-training of deep bidirectional transformers for language understanding. arXiv preprint arXiv:1810.04805 (2018)
13. Fernandino, L., Humphries, C.J., Seidenberg, M., Gross, W., Conant, L., Binder, J.R.: Predicting brain activation patterns associated with individual lexical concepts based on five sensory-motor attributes. Neuropsychologia **76**, 17–26 (2015)
14. Handjaras, G., et al.: How concepts are encoded in the human brain: a modality independent, category-based cortical organization of semantic knowledge. NeuroImage **135**, 232–242 (2016)
15. Haxby, J.V., Gobbini, M.I., Furey, M.L., Ishai, A., Schouten, J.L., Pietrini, P.: Distributed and overlapping representations of faces and objects in ventral temporal cortex. Science **293**(5539), 2425–2430 (2001)
16. He, K., Zhang, X., Ren, S., Sun, J.: Deep residual learning for image recognition. In: 2016 IEEE Conference on Computer Vision and Pattern Recognition (CVPR), pp. 770–778 (2016)
17. Huth, A.G., de Heer, W.A., Griffiths, T.L., Theunissen, F.E., Gallant, J.L.: Natural speech reveals the semantic maps that tile human cerebral cortex. Nature **532**, 453 (2016)
18. Images, G.: Google images (1998). https://images.google.com
19. Ishai, A., Ungerleider, L.G., Martin, A., Schouten, J.L., Haxby, J.V.: Distributed representation of objects in the human ventral visual pathway. Proc. Natl. Acad. Sci. U.S.A. **96**(16), 9379–9384 (1999). 10430951[pmid]
20. Jelodar, A.B., Alizadeh, M., Khadivi, S.: Wordnet based features for predicting brain activity associated with meanings of nouns. In: Proceedings of the NAACL HLT 2010 First Workshop on Computational Neurolinguistics, CN 2010, pp. 18–26. Association for Computational Linguistics, Stroudsburg (2010)
21. Joulin, A., Grave, E., Bojanowski, P., Mikolov, T.: Bag of tricks for efficient text classification (2016)
22. Just, M.A., Cherkassky, V.L., Aryal, S., Mitchell, T.M.: A neurosemantic theory of concrete noun representation based on the underlying brain codes. PLoS ONE **5**(1), e8622 (2010)
23. Kim, Y.: Convolutional neural networks for sentence classification. In: Proceedings of the 2014 Conference on Empirical Methods in Natural Language Processing, EMNLP 2014, 25–29 October 2014, Doha, Qatar, A meeting of SIGDAT, a Special Interest Group of the ACL, pp. 1746–1751 (2014)
24. Kiros, R., et al.: Skip-thought vectors. In: Cortes, C., Lawrence, N.D., Lee, D.D., Sugiyama, M., Garnett, R. (eds.) Advances in Neural Information Processing Systems 28, pp. 3294–3302. Curran Associates, Inc. (2015). http://papers.nips.cc/paper/5950-skip-thought-vectors.pdf
25. Kriegeskorte, N., Mur, M., Bandettini, P.: Representational similarity analysis - connecting the branches of systems neuroscience. Front. Syst. Neurosci. **2**, 4 (2008)
26. Louwerse, M., Hutchinson, S.: Neurological evidence linguistic processes precede perceptual simulation in conceptual processing. Front. Psychol. **3** (2012). https://doi.org/10.3389/fpsyg.2012.00385

27. van der Maaten, L., Hinton, G.: Visualizing data using t-SNE. J. Mach. Learn. Res. **9**, 2579–2605 (2008)
28. Matsuo, E., Kobayashi, I., Nishimoto, S., Nishida, S., Asoh, H.: Describing semantic representations of brain activity evoked by visual stimuli (2018)
29. Mikolov, T., Chen, K., Corrado, G.S., Dean, J.: Efficient estimation of word representations in vector space. CoRR abs/1301.3781 (2013)
30. Mitchell, T.M., et al.: Learning to decode cognitive states from brain images. Mach. Learn. **57**(1–2), 145–175 (2004)
31. Mitchell, T.M., et al.: Predicting human brain activity associated with the meanings of nouns. Science **320**(5880), 1191–1195 (2008)
32. Naselaris, T., Kay, K., Nishimoto, S., Gallant, J.: Encoding and decoding in fMRI. NeuroImage **56**, 400–410 (2011)
33. Norman, K.A., Polyn, S.M., Detre, G.J., Haxby, J.V.: Beyond mind-reading: multivoxel pattern analysis of fMRI data. Trends Cogn. Sci. **10**(9), 424–430 (2006)
34. Palatucci, M., Pomerleau, D., Hinton, G.E., Mitchell, T.M.: Zero-shot learning with semantic output codes. In: Bengio, Y., Schuurmans, D., Lafferty, J.D., Williams, C.K.I., Culotta, A. (eds.) Advances in Neural Information Processing Systems 22, pp. 1410–1418. Curran Associates, Inc. (2009)
35. Pennington, J., Socher, R., Manning, C.D.: Glove: global vectors for word representation. In: Empirical Methods in Natural Language Processing (EMNLP), pp. 1532–1543 (2014)
36. Pereira, F., Botvinick, M., Detre, G.: Using Wikipedia to learn semantic feature representations of concrete concepts in neuroimaging experiments. Artif. Intell. **194**, 240–252 (2013)
37. Pereira, F., Detre, G., Botvinick, M.: Generating text from functional brain images. Front. Hum. Neurosci. **5**, 72 (2011)
38. Pereira, F., Mitchell, T.M., Botvinick, M.: Machine learning classifiers and fMRI: a tutorial overview. NeuroImage **45**(1 Suppl), S199–209 (2009)
39. Peters, M.E., et al.: Deep contextualized word representations. In: Proceedings of NAACL (2018)
40. pinterest: pinterest (2019)
41. Poldrack, R.A., Mumford, J.A., Nichols, T.E.: Handbook of Functional MRI Data Analysis. Cambridge University Press, Cambridge (2011). https://doi.org/10.1017/CBO9780511895029
42. Polyn, S.M., Natu, V.S., Cohen, J.D., Norman, K.A.: Category-specific cortical activity precedes retrieval during memory search. Science **310**(5756), 1963–1966 (2005)
43. Pulvermüller, F.: How neurons make meaning: brain mechanisms for embodied and abstract-symbolic semantics. Trends Cogn. Sci. **17**(9), 458–470 (2013)
44. Rumelhart, D.E., Hinton, G.E., Williams, R.J.: Learning representations by back-propagating errors. Nature **323**, 533 (1986)
45. Song, Y., Shi, S., Li, J., Zhang, H.: Directional skip-gram: explicitly distinguishing left and right context for word embeddings. In: Proceedings of the 2018 Conference of the North American Chapter of the Association for Computational Linguistics: Human Language Technologies, Volume 2 (Short Papers) (2018)
46. Wang, J., Cherkassky, V.L., Just, M.A.: Predicting the brain activation pattern associated with the propositional content of a sentence: modeling neural representations of events and states. Hum. Brain Mapping **38**(10), 4865–4881 (2017)
47. Wehbe, L., Murphy, B., Talukdar, P., Fyshe, A., Ramdas, A., Mitchell, T.: Simultaneously uncovering the patterns of brain regions involved in different story reading subprocesses. PLoS One **9**(11), e112575 (2014). 25426840[pmid]

Applying Attention Mechanism and Deep Neural Network for Medical Object Segmentation and Classification in X-Ray Fluoroscopy Images

Yong Zhang[1], Jun Yan[2], Haitao Huang[3(✉)], and Christopher Yencha[1]

[1] Weber State University, Ogden, UT 84408, USA
[2] Yidu Cloud Technology Co. Ltd., Beijing, China
[3] The People's Hospital of Liaoning Province, Shenyang, China
huanghaitao1216@hotmail.com

Abstract. We study how to apply attention mechanism and deep neural network for real-time segmentation and classification of balloon objects from X-ray fluoroscopy images during percutaneous balloon compression (PBC) surgical procedures. Fast and accurate identification of balloon shape and its relative location to the Meckel's cave can be of significant benefit to the success of the PBC procedure. In this work, we combine the most successful region-based convolutional neural network pipeline with attention mechanism to address these challenges.

Keywords: Percutaneous balloon compression · Attention mechanism · Deep learning · Convolutional neural network

1 Background

1.1 Percutaneous Balloon Compression

There are more than 4.3 million people in the United States afflicted by nerve generated facial pains. At the extreme end of this spectrum of disorders, classic trigeminal neuralgia (TN), commonly referred to as the most painful affliction known to medical science, strikes erratically with sharp shocks of pain [1]. Of all of the pain conditions that chronic pain patients experience, there are arguably none worse than the pain of TN. Often called the "suicide disease", TN is linked to higher rates of suicidal ideation in patients with severe migraines, as well as depression, anxiety, and sleep disorders [2, 3]. According to the National Institute of Neurological Disorders and Stroke (NINDS), it is reported that 150,000 people are diagnosed with trigeminal neuralgia every year in the US. While the disorder can occur at any age, it is most common in people over the age of 50 [4]. TN is an extremely painful disorder which can be difficult to diagnose and treat. Although described as early as the first century by Greek and Roman physicians, TN and related facial nerve pain remains a poorly understood and often misdiagnosed disease with no permanent cure [1, 5].

© Springer Nature Singapore Pte Ltd. 2019
A. Zeng et al. (Eds.): HBAI 2019, CCIS 1072, pp. 101–110, 2019.
https://doi.org/10.1007/978-981-15-1398-5_7

The most common surgical treatment options for TN include Microvascular Decompression (MVD), Gamma Knife Surgery (GKS), and Percutaneous Balloon Compression (PBC) [6–8]. GKS is a "destructive procedure" that relies on partially or totally damaging the trigeminal nerve in order to relieve symptoms. The surgery is also associated with longer time between treatment and pain improvement, lower rates of long-term pain relief, postoperative numbness, and motor dysfunction. MVD is unique in that it is a nondestructive, but invasive, surgical intervention that preserves the trigeminal nerve and the surrounding neurovascular structures, which leads to rapid and long-lasting pain relief. While MVD is nondestructive, it is the only surgical treatment for TN that requires a craniotomy; potential adverse effects include facial nerve dysfunction and hearing loss [6].

As one of the minimally invasive options, PBC is an effective and relatively safe treatment option suitable for patients with comorbidity, TN refractory to medical treatment, or when open surgery is an unsuitable option. Research study [9] shows that after PBC, 90% of patients were completely pain free without medication for TN. In patients without multiple sclerosis who had not been previously treated surgically, the initial success rate was 91% and the median time to recurrence was 48 months. A good compression, indicated by the shape of the balloon, its location relative to the Meckel's cave, and how it touches the trigeminal nerve, is crucial to achieve good pain relief [10–12]. The PBC procedure is performed under the guidance of intraoperative lateral radiograph. In spite of this aid, it could still be very challenging for surgeons to decide on proper locations and shapes of the balloon due to anatomical variations and limited visualizations. With the help of advances in image segmentation and classification, prior knowledge can be learned from previous successful PBC cases to properly model the balloons. Furthermore, locations and shapes of the balloons can be detected constantly during the procedure to help the surgeon decide where to position the balloon and when to stop its inflation.

1.2 Image Segmentation and Classification Algorithms

Image segmentation refers to the process of separating regions of interest from background in digital images. Image classification refers to the semantic understanding of the contents in digital images. Automated image segmentation is the foundation of image content understanding, object recognition, and feature analysis. Image segmentation algorithms can be roughly divided into three categories: image feature based segmentation, clustering based segmentation, and deep learning based segmentation. Image feature-based algorithms [13–16] utilize low level image features for segmentation, such as pixel/voxel intensity values, edges of objects, and gradient orientations. Clustering based algorithms [17–19] leverage the observation that similar appearing regions or elements tend to cluster in feature spaces.

In recent years, artificial intelligence-based algorithms, especially deep learning techniques, have been widely used in image classification, segmentation, semantic image understanding, and computer vision fields. In 2012, Krizhevsky et al. [20] apply deep convolutional neural network (CNN) in ImageNet classification and yield breakthrough results. Since then, CNN has become widely adopted in image segmentation and is now the most successful technique in the field. In 2014, based on

Krizhevsky et al.'s work, Girschick et al. [21] propose to use Regions with CNNs (R-CNN) for object detection and semantic segmentation in images. They apply selective search [22] to detect recommended regions of interest (also called region proposals) at different scales. These recommended regions are then input to an improved AlexNet [20] to classify potential objects in the regions. The last step of R-CNN is to apply a linear regression model to predict the boundaries of the objects. In 2015, Girschick et al. improve and speed up R-CNN algorithm in [23] by applying single-stage training to all network layers and ROI max pooling. In [24], Ren et al. further improve the efficiency of R-CNN by utilizing convolutional feature maps for region proposal generation to replace the time-consuming selective search. Their algorithm, called Faster R-CNN, is able to achieve real-time object detection by combining a deep fully convolutional network with region proposal network. He et al. [25] extend the Faster R-CNN by adding a branch in the CNN framework for segmenting objects to the existing branch for bounding box generation. They accurately align the ROI in the feature map with the one in the original image using bilinear interpolation. Such fine-tuning makes it possible for the proposed algorithm, Mask R-CNN, to produce high quality segmentation in the images.

Attention architecture [26], originally introduced for natural language processing, has been recently applied in various image processing tasks [27, 28]. By focusing on the most relevant parts in the image, attention mechanism has the potential to improve segmentation accuracy and performance.

In this work, we combine attention mechanism with the deep convolutional neural network in the task of balloon segmentation and classification in X-ray fluoroscopy images. Our goal is to provide real-time, accurate tracking and classification of balloon objects to provide valuable complimentary information for surgeons during PBC procedures. Our experiments show that the proposed framework is able to achieve high accuracy for segmentation and classification tasks for images of various qualities without human interaction.

This work is organized as follows. Section 2 describes our method. Section 3 shows the experimental results. Finally, Sect. 4 concludes our work.

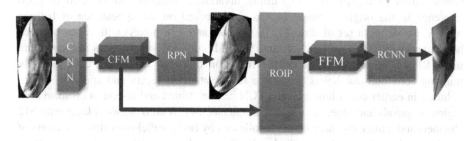

Fig. 1. Our unified deep CNN architecture. CFM: convolutional feature map; RPN: regional proposal network; ROIP: region of interest max pooling; FFM: fixed-size feature map; RCNN: regions with CNNs

2 Method

Our convolutional neural network is based on the Fast R-CNN [23] architecture, as shown in Fig. 1. An input X-ray fluoroscopy image is passed through a CNN initialized with the pre-trained ImageNet model [29]. Using a pre-trained model has the benefit of providing a meaningful starting point given that features trained in the very large ImageNet database [30] can be related and are useful for our task. The resulting convolutional feature map (CFM) is then fed into a region proposal network (RPN) to find a number of region proposals which may contain balloon objects. The feature map and region proposals are further down-sized by region of interests max pooling (ROIP) to fixed-sized feature vectors. The purpose of applying ROIP is to downsize the convolutional feature map suitable for feeding the R-CNN network while keeping those features that would correspond to the balloon objects. In the last step, the R-CNN network classifies and segments the balloon object detected in the region proposals. Further details are discussed in the following subsections.

2.1 CNN Architecture

We use ResNet-101 as the CNN architecture for feature extraction. By using skip/shortcut residual connections and batch normalization, a residual network (ResNet) [31] solves the problem of vanishing or exploding gradients, making it possible to efficiently train a very deep neural network and, thus, improve model accuracy. ResNet-101 is 101 layers deep with each ResNet block being 3 layers deep.

2.2 Region Proposal Network (RPN)

RPN is used to find regions that may contain balloon objects. Region proposals are represented as rectangular bounding boxes in the image. Anchors, specified by its central coordinates, width, and height, are used throughout the image to predict potential regions containing balloon objects. A set of anchors of different sizes and height/width ratios is created for each point in the convolutional feature maps (without consideration of depth). Due to shifting invariance, anchors can be used as good reference to the original image. In this work, based on the appearance of balloon objects, we define a set of sizes (8, 16, 32, 64, and 128 pixels) with ratios between height and width of boxes (0.5, 1, and 1.5). All combinations of sizes and ratios are used. RPN is implemented using the fully-convolutional network (FCN) [32]. By utilizing convolutional layers to replace fully connected layers and applying deconvolution in earlier convolution layers, FCN can be trained end-to-end to estimate both region proposals and objectness scores simultaneously. A convolutional layer with 512 channels and a three-by-three kernel is followed by two parallel convolutional layers of one-by-one kernel size. One is called a classification layer, which outputs an objectness estimation of each anchor. The other is called a regression layer, which outputs estimations of bounding box adjustments. In this work, we only pick the anchors most likely to contain the balloon objects and refine their bounding box sizes and locations.

2.3   ROI Pooling

After RPN outputs the foreground/background classification and the bounding box adjustment, the next step is to classify the balloon object in the regions of interest. The region proposals may have different sizes, while classifiers usually require a fixed input size. We adopt ROI Pooling to handle this case: the CFM is cropped using each region proposal, and then resized to a fixed $H \times W$ feature map using max pooling with a two-by-two kernel. Bilinear interpolation can be used to further improve the alignment of feature maps with original images [25]. We also adopt the feature pyramid network (FPN) [33] at this step. Standard feature extraction usually focuses on top-level features for object detection. FPN improves standard feature extraction by adding a second pyramid that takes high level features from the first pyramid and passes them down to lower layers. By doing so, it allows features at every level to include both lower (with weak semantic but strong spatial) and higher level (with strong semantic but spatial coarser) features. In this work, we adopt the FPN in the ROI Pooling step, as shown in Fig. 2, to improve balloon object detection at different scales.

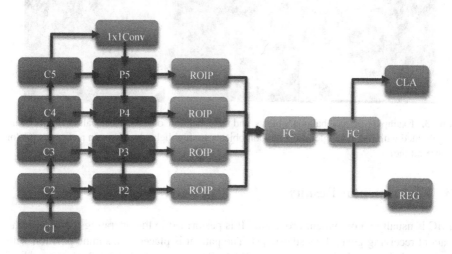

Fig. 2. FPN for ROIP: FC: fully connected layer; CLA: classification; REG: bounding box regression

2.4   R-CNN

A standard R-CNN framework can be used to classify the balloon objects, which can be helpful for the surgeon to decide on proper location and inflation of balloons during the surgical procedure. This step is very similar to the conventional CNN classification pipeline. That is, two fully connected (FC) layers of size 4096 with ReLU activation are applied to the fixed size feature map after ROI Pooling. One FC layer is for classification and the other is for tuning the bounding boxes (see Fig. 2).

2.5 Attention Mechanism

The shape of the balloon, its location relative to the Meckel's cave, and how it touches the trigeminal nerve are the critical factors in determining the success of PBC procedures. In X-ray fluoroscopy images, due to imaging artifacts and anatomical deformity, fake balloon objects could be detected. Figure 3 shows some examples in which real balloon objects are highlighted within red rectangles and fake objects within green rectangles. In addition, the location of the balloon relative to the Meckel's cave provides critical information to the surgeon during the PBC procedure. To improve model accuracy and provide relative location information, we incorporate SENets [34] into the CNN pipeline by adding SE blocks to each residual connection and rescaling the residuals before summation. In this way, the framework learns to adjust weights for features such that effective features in the feature map are emphasized.

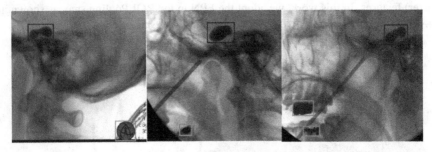

Fig. 3. Examples of real balloon objects and fake balloon objects. Real balloon objects are highlighted with red rectangles; fake balloon objects are highlighted with green rectangles (Color figure online)

3   Experimental Results

PBC is usually an outpatient procedure. It is performed in the operating room, with the patient receiving general anesthesia [1]. The patient is placed in a supine position with an extended neck. Using intermittent X-ray fluoroscopy and the Härtel approach, a cannula is inserted slightly above 1 cm from the orifice lateral angle via the thin wall at the blunt edge into the foramen ovale (FO). A 4 Fr embolectomy catheter is introduced through the cannula and, beyond its tip, into Meckel's cave. Using a non-iodine contrast medium approximately 0.5 to 1.0 ml, the balloon is inflated until it deforms into a pear shape (as seen on lateral X-ray fluoroscopy such as those shown in Fig. 4). Typically, when the filled balloon displayed by lateral X-ray fluoroscopy is seen as a pear-like or dumbbell-like shape [35], the puncture is considered a success (see Fig. 4 for an example). The balloon is kept inflated for at least 1 min, and then deflated and withdrawn together with the cannula. The patient is then taken out of general anesthesia [9].

In this work, we categorize balloon objects into four different classes. Since there are no standard medical terms for these categories, we call them Class-PD, Class-OS, Class-NM, and Class-BM, based on the balloon shapes and their relative locations to the Meckel's cave, as shown in Table 1. Class-PD is considered a success and the compression can be held for 1 to 3 min to finish the surgical operation. The other three classes provide suggestions to the surgeon to either adjust the catheter location or the balloon volume before the compression can be held for the trigeminal nerve.

Table 1. Balloon categorization based on their shapes and relative locations to the Meckel's cave

Class name	Balloon shapes	Balloon locations	Suggestions for surgical operations
Class-PD	Pear-like or dumbbell-like	Inside Meckel's cave	Puncture is successful, balloon volume is ideal
Class-OS	Any other shape	Inside Meckel's cave	Puncture is successful, balloon volume is inadequate
Class-NM	Any shape	Not yet reached Meckel's cave	Puncture is not successful, catheter needs to go further
Class-BM	Any shape	Beyond Meckel's cave	Puncture is not successful, catheter has gone too deep and could be dangerous

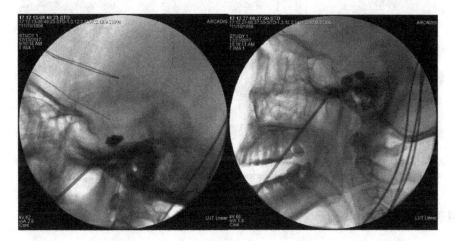

Fig. 4. Examples of lateral X-ray fluoroscopy images of filled balloon object seen during the PBC surgical procedure, showing pear-like shape (left) and dumbbell-like shape (right)

Out dataset includes X-ray fluoroscopy images of size 1024-by-1024 from 77 patients evenly distributed amongst the four classes. All images are manually labeled by domain experts for balloon object segmentation and classification. We generate an augmented image data set by applying random resizing, rotation, shifting, and flipping to increase the number of images to 800 while still keeping the shape and relative location unchanged. 80% of the images are used for training the CNN based on the pre-trained ImageNet model. 20% of the images are used for testing. Segmentation and classification are fully automated without any manual initialization or interaction. No image pre-processing steps, such as contrast adjustment, de-nosing, or histogram enhancement are used in this work. Figure 5 shows some of the segmentation results. We use Intersection over Union (IoU), also referred to as the Jaccard index, to evaluate segmentation performance. IoU measures the number of pixels common between the ground truth mask and the segmentation mask, divided by the total number of pixels present across both masks. Our experimental results show that the mean IoU over all testing images is 0.89 and the classification accuracy is 91%.

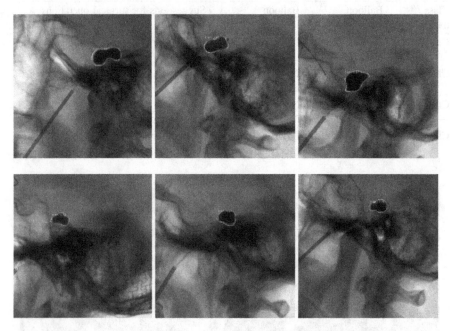

Fig. 5. Segmentation results of balloon objects in X-ray fluoroscopy images. Green regions: ground truth from domain experts; red regions: segmentation results. (Color figure online)

4 Conclusions

In this work, we present our unified deep convolutional neural network for balloon object segmentation and classification in X-ray fluoroscopy images. Accurate segmentation and proper classification of the balloon objects exhibited from the X-ray fluoroscopy can be useful to help surgeons during the PBC surgical procedure. The framework incorporates region-based CNN with attention mechanism to address challenges seen in such medical image processing tasks. R-CNN pipeline has the potential for real-time object detection by utilizing parameter sharing, RPN, and ROI pooling. Attention mechanism improves segmentation and classification performance by emphasizing effective features calculated from the CNN pipeline. The proposed framework has the potential to be used in a real-time setting to help guide PBC surgical procedures.

References

1. Facial Pain Association: FPA Patient Guide: Understanding trigeminal neuralgia and other forms of neuropathic face pain (2019)
2. Adams, H., et al.: Harvey Cushing's case series of trigeminal neuralgia at the Johns Hopkins Hospital: a surgeon's quest to advance the treatment of the 'suicide disease'. Acta Neurochir. **153**(5), 1043–1050 (2011)
3. Prasad, S., Galetta, S.: Trigeminal neuralgia: historical notes and current concepts. Neurologist **15**(2), 87–94 (2009)
4. NINDS, Trigeminal Neuralgia Fact Sheet. National Institute of Neurological Disorders and Stroke (2015)
5. Bendtsen, L., et al.: EAN guideline on trigeminal neuralgia. Eur. J. Neurol. **26**, 831–849 (2019)
6. Velagala, J., Mendelson, Z.S., Liu, J.K.: Pain-free outcomes after surgical intervention for trigeminal neuralgia: a comparison of gamma knife and microvascular decompression. Neurosurgery **62**(suppl 1), 228 (2015)
7. Zakrzewska, J.M., Akram, H.: Neurosurgical interventions for the treatment of classical trigeminal neuralgia. Cochrane Database Syst. Rev. **9**, CD007312 (2011)
8. Bhargava, D., et al.: TM2-4 Long Term Outcome of Percutaneous Balloon Compression for Trigeminal Neuralgia. BMJ Publishing Group Ltd., London (2019)
9. Asplund, P.: Percutaneous Balloon Compression for the Treatment of Trigeminal Neuralgia, Umeå universitet (2019)
10. Aydoseli, A., et al.: Neuronavigation-assisted percutaneous balloon compression for the treatment of trigeminal neuralgia: the technique and short-term clinical results. Br. J. Neurosurgery **29**, 1–7 (2015)
11. Georgiopoulos, M., et al.: Minimizing technical failure of percutaneous balloon compression for trigeminal neuralgia using neuronavigation. ISRN Neurol. **2014**, 630418 (2014)
12. Trojnik, T., Šmigoc, T.: Percutaneous trigeminal ganglion balloon compression rhizotomy: experience in 27 patients. Sci. World J. **2012**, 328936 (2012)
13. Vala, H.J., Baxi, A.: A review on Otsu image segmentation algorithm. Int. J. Adv. Res. Comput. Eng. Technol. (IJARCET) **2**(2), 387–389 (2013)
14. Wani, M.A., Batchelor, B.G.: Edge-region-based segmentation of range images. IEEE Trans. Pattern Anal. Mach. Intell. **3**, 314–319 (1994)
15. Senthilkumaran, N., Rajesh, R.: Edge detection techniques for image segmentation-a survey of soft computing approaches. Int. J. Recent Trends Eng. **1**(2), 250 (2009)
16. Li, C.: Distance regularized level set evolution and its application to image segmentation. IEEE Trans. Image Process. **19**(12), 3243–3254 (2010)
17. Coleman, G.B., Andrews, H.C.: Image segmentation by clustering. Proc. IEEE **67**(5), 773–785 (1979)
18. Sulaiman, S.N., Isa, N.A.M.: Adaptive fuzzy-K-means clustering algorithm for image segmentation. IEEE Trans. Consumer Electron. **56**(4), 2661–2668 (2010)
19. Chuang, K.-S., et al.: Fuzzy c-means clustering with spatial information for image segmentation. Comput. Med. Imaging Graph. **30**(1), 9–15 (2006)
20. Krizhevsky, A., Sutskever, I., Hinton, G.E.: Imagenet classification with deep convolutional neural networks. In Advances in Neural Information Processing Systems (2012)
21. Girshick, R., et al.: Rich feature hierarchies for accurate object detection and semantic segmentation. In: Proceedings of the IEEE Conference on Computer Vision and Pattern Recognition (2014)

22. Uijlings, J.R.: Selective search for object recognition. Int. J. Comput. Vis. **104**(2), 154–171 (2013)
23. Girshick, R.: Fast R-CNN. In: Proceedings of the IEEE International Conference on Computer Vision (2015)
24. Ren, S., et al.: Faster R-CNN: towards real-time object detection with region proposal networks. In: Advances in Neural Information Processing Systems (2015)
25. He, K., et al.: Mask R-CNN. In: Proceedings of the IEEE International Conference on Computer Vision (2017)
26. Bahdanau, D., Cho, K., Bengio, Y.: Neural machine translation by jointly learning to align and translate. In: International Conference on Learning Representations, San Diego, CA (2015)
27. Jiang, H., et al.: AHCNet: an application of attention mechanism and hybrid connection for liver tumor segmentation in CT volumes. IEEE Access **7**, 24898–24909 (2019)
28. Wang, W., et al.: Learning unsupervised video object segmentation through visual attention. In: CVPR (2019)
29. Simon, M., Rodner, E., Denzler, J.: Imagenet pre-trained models with batch normalization. arXiv preprint arXiv:1612.01452 (2016)
30. Deng, J., et al.: Imagenet: a large-scale hierarchical image database. In: 2009 IEEE Conference on Computer Vision and Pattern Recognition. IEEE (2009)
31. He, K., et al.: Deep residual learning for image recognition. In: Proceedings of the IEEE Conference on Computer Vision and Pattern Recognition (2016)
32. Long, J., Shelhamer, E., Darrell, T.: Fully convolutional networks for semantic segmentation. In: Proceedings of the IEEE Conference on Computer Vision and Pattern Recognition (2015)
33. Lin, T.-Y., et al.: Feature pyramid networks for object detection. In: Proceedings of the IEEE Conference on Computer Vision and Pattern Recognition (2017)
34. Hu, J., Shen, L., Sun, G.: Squeeze-and-excitation networks. In: Proceedings of the IEEE Conference on Computer Vision and Pattern Recognition (2018)
35. Abdennebi, B., Guenane, L.: Technical considerations and outcome assessment in retrogasserian balloon compression for treatment of trigeminal neuralgia. Series of 901 patients. Surg. Neurol. Int. **5**, 118 (2014)

Effect of Age on Postural Balance and Control: Graph Based Connectivity Analysis on Brain Network

Oishee Mazumder[1]($\boxtimes$), Kingshuk Chakravarty[1], Debatri Chatterjee[1],
Soumya Jyoti Banerjee[2], and Aniruddha Sinha[1]

[1] Embedded Systems and Robotics, TCS Research and Innovation, Kolkata, India
{oishee.mazumder,kingshuk.chakravarty,
debatri.chatterjee,aniruddha.s}@tcs.com
[2] Innovation Group, Scienaptic Systems, Bangalore, India
soumyajyoti.291@gmail.com

Abstract. Human brain undergoes various level of morphological changes with aging, volumetric atrophy of certain region being most common. Healthy aging is accompanied with deficits in motor and cognitive functions. Age-related atrophy of the motor cortical regions usually correlates with motor disabilities like postural imbalance, gait and coordination deficits etc. In this paper, we try to understand the changes in brain reorganization that occurs in normal healthy aging, specifically in regions involved in postural control. A brain network model has been developed implementing graph theory approach, using Diffusion Tensor Imaging (DTI) data for structural analysis, and resting-state functional MRI (fMRI) data for functional analysis, acquired from Nathan Kline Institute (NKI)-Rockland database. The data set have been divided in 'young' and 'old' group, based on age of individuals. Different conventional graph metrics have been evaluated for whole brain network as well as for specific regions like basal ganglia circuit, thalamus and brain stem in both structural and functional domain to analyze effect of aging. Results indicate network specific changes in cortico-basal ganglia region. Age related decreasing trend in graph metric parameters like local efficiency, modularity and clustering coefficient and an increasing trend for path length in both functional and structural connectivity analysis have been noticed. The insights from this study can be useful to identify healthy aging characteristics versus pathological changes.

Keywords: Aging · Basal ganglia · Functional connectivity · Postural stability · Structural connectivity

1 Introduction

Around 8.5% of total world population are aged above 65 and this rate is increasing in an unprecedented rate. According to Aging world report [1], this figure

S. J. Banerjee—This work was done during his association with TCS Research and Innovation.

© Springer Nature Singapore Pte Ltd. 2019
A. Zeng et al. (Eds.): HBAI 2019, CCIS 1072, pp. 111–120, 2019.
https://doi.org/10.1007/978-981-15-1398-5_8

is projected to reach to nearly 17% of the world's population by 2050. With advanced age, there are changes in brain morphology, cognition and a general decline in sensorimotor control and functioning. With progression of age, motor control areas of brain like prefrontal cortex and basal ganglia networks exhibits an enhanced involvement [2]. Human brain changes both functionally and structurally with aging, evident from diffusion imaging and functional Magnetic Resonance Imaging (fMRI). Understanding how brain changes between childhood to adulthood is important to identify healthy aging characteristics, thereby identifying deviations in structural and functional properties, as evident in different neuro-psychiatric disorders [3].

Cognition and associated memory loss and postural stability are the two major areas of concern with aging. Various studies have been conducted till date to study age-related differences in neural control of movement, but it is still a gray area with limited understanding [4]. Motor performance impairments with aging are likely due to changes in peripheral structures such as sensory receptors, musculo skeletal structure, peripheral nerves, etc, as well as central nervous system changes, specially at the cortico basal ganglia circuit. Studies have shown that alterations in the basal ganglia loops during normal aging likely contributes to age-related decline of motor control [5].

General research methodology to analyze structural and functional changes related to aging uses region-specific analyses, using a variety of approaches such as machine learning and seed-based functional connectivity analyses on certain brain region [6]. Region specific analysis are biased toward identifying local changes and consequently ignore the wider global neural changes that take place in aging [7]. Graph theoretic analysis provides insights in to brain network in a manner not offered by other connectivity approaches [8]. Brain networks falls under the category of 'small world network' are generally of two types: structural, representing white matter tract integrity in the brain and functional, which represents interaction between brain regions [9]. Graph theoretic analysis allows network characterization by defining set of interactions (edges) between large numbers of areas (nodes). Graph-theory based network analysis enables understanding of dynamic interactions between different brain regions. Graph metrics such as local efficiency, global efficiency, modularity, centrality and strength measures are often used to characterize brain network properties for group comparison [10].

In this paper, we try to understand the aspects of brain reorganization that are critical in normal aging, specifically in regions associated with postural control. We have developed a brain network model using graph theory methods applied to the resting-state functional MRI (fMRI) data and DTI data acquired from NKI Rockland data set. Two specific age groups, naming 'young' and 'geriatric' or 'old' were created for analyzing brain network specific changes, both in structural and functional domain to understand trend of healthy aging. Graph network parameters like modularity, global and local efficiency, path length, etc. were analyzed to understand the trend in functional and structural domain with aging. We aim to find structural and functional network parameters of whole brain for the two specific age groups and also analyze network specific changes in cortico-basal ganglia region, which is associated with motor movements, postural and gait related functions. Understanding network metrics for healthy aging brain can later be used to differentiate bio-markers for healthy aging and pathology induced changes. Key contributions of this paper are:

- Graph network analysis on structural and function connectivity matrix (CM) for two groups: adolescent (young) brain (age 6 to 19 years) and geriatric (old) brain (age 60 to 85 years).
- Graph network analysis of basal ganglia circuit, thalamus and brain stem region to understand age related variation in mobility control regions of brain.

2 Methodology

2.1 Network Creation

Open data ecosystem for neuro-science applications has been very popular globally. The Nathan S.Kline Institute for Psychiatric Research (NKI) has developed an open data system to investigate lifespan changes study. The NKI-Rockland is a large-scale data base comprised of neuro imaging and genetic data along with neuro-cognitive, physiologic, behavioral and psychiatric measurements [11]. NKI-Rockland phase I data set includes resting stage fMRI data of 250 individuals spanning from childhood to late adulthood (4–89 years old). Functional Connectivity Matrix (CM) of NKI-Rockland phase I data set have been downloaded from UCLA Multimodal Connectivity Database [12]. Along with fMRI data, UCLA database also hosts the structural connectivity matrix from DTI data of NKI population.

From the NKI Phase I data set, two age groups have been selected: Group I consisting of 22 individuals, with age range between 6 to 19 years (14 Male, 8 Female). This group is designated as young or adolescent group. Second group consists of 22 subjects with age range varying from 60 to 85 years (10 Male, 12 Female), designated as the old or geriatric group. All the subjects were healthy individuals. Data set of both age groups includes structural and functional connectivity matrix. The connectivity matrix is computed on 188 nodes of brain region, using the 'Craddock 200' atlas [13].

2.2 Structural and Functional Connectivity Parameters

The structural and functional connectivity matrix represents weighted undirected graphs. Connectivity matrix were processed to remove all the negative correlation values and network sparsity was selected based on correlation strength. Sparsity is equivalent to thresholding a network and is usually used to eliminate noisy or unreliable connections. There are several methods [14] to select optimum sparsity value. In this paper, sparsity has been selected as the value, which has the largest possible threshold allowing all nodes in the network to be connected at least to another node in the network [15]. Sparsity value of

0.2, i.e, top 20% of the correlations (Pearson r-values) were considered and a new connectivity matrix was generated for evaluation. The new CM was used to generate binary networks, setting all non-zero values to 1. Binarization is a common step in functional graphs in order to preserve only the strongest connections and treat them equivalently. All the graph theoretic features were calculated on the binarized connectivity matrix.

A graph G is defined as G(V, E), where, V is the vertex and E is the edge set, N ($N = |V|$) is the number of nodes and M ($M = |E|$) is the number of edges. Seven Graph theoretical metrics were calculated on G, formed by taking structural and functional CM as adjacency matrix. All computations were done using Brain connectivity Toolbox [16]. The metrics were: Characteristic Path length, Modularity, Clustering Coefficient, Global Efficiency, Local Efficiency, Between Centrality and Small worldness.

Characteristic path length (CPL) measures the average path length in a network, where the path length is defined as the minimum number of edges to be traversed to get from one node to another.

Clustering coefficient (CC) defines connectivity of a node with all other nodes in neighborhood. It is a measure of number of neighboring nodes of a given node that are also connected to each other, in proportion to the maximum number of connections in the network. Clustering coefficient Ci of a node i is defined as:

$$C_i = \frac{2T}{d_i(d_i - 1)} \qquad (1)$$

Where, T denotes the number of existing connections among the neighbors of i and d_i represents the degree of node 'i'.

Small Worldness (SW) is calculated as a ratio of local clustering (C_p) and characteristic path length (L_p) of a node relative to the same ratio in a randomized network. Mathematically represented as:

$$\sigma = \frac{\gamma}{\lambda} > 1; \gamma = \frac{C_p}{C_{prand}} > 1; \lambda = \frac{L_p}{L_{prand}} \approx 1; \qquad (2)$$

C_{prand} and L_{prand} are the mean clustering coefficient and characteristic path length of the matched random networks. 'SW' represents the balance between network differentiation and network integration.

Efficiency is a biologically relevant metric to describe brain networks from the perspective of information flow [17]. Global efficiency and local efficiency measure the ability of a network to transmit information at the global and local level. For the graph G(V, E), the global efficiency is defined as:

$$E_{glob}(G) = \frac{1}{N(N-1)} \sum_{i \in G j \in G, i \neq j} \frac{1}{d_{ij}} \qquad (3)$$

where, d_{ij} is the shortest path length between node i and node j in G. The local efficiency of G is measured as:

$$E_{loc}(G) = \frac{1}{N} \sum_{i \in G} E_{glob}(G_i) \qquad (4)$$

Where $E_{glob}(Gi)$ is the global efficiency of G_i, which is the sub-graph composed of the neighbors of node i.

Modules refer to a set of nodes with denser links among them but sparser links with the rest of the network [18]. Modularity (Q value) represent the difference in proportion of within-module edges in the network from within-module edges calculated from a similar random network. 'Louvalin method of community detection' [19] has been used to calculate modularity as following:

$$Q = \frac{1}{2m} \sum_{ij} [A_{ij} - \frac{K_i K_j}{2m}] \delta(c_i, c_j) \tag{5}$$

A_{ij} represents the edge weight between nodes i and j ; K_i and K_j are the sum of the weights of the edges attached to nodes i and j, respectively; m is the sum of all of the edge weights in the graph; c_i, c_j are the communities of the nodes; and δ is a simple delta function. Detection and characterization of modular structure in the brain system can help in identify groups of structurally or functionally associated components that perform specific biological functions.

Betweeness centrality measures how often the shortest path goes through a given node. The betweeness centrality captures the influence that one node has over the flow of information between all other nodes in the network and can be calculated as:

$$B_i = \sum_{m \neq i \neq n \in G} \frac{\sigma_{mn}(i)}{\sigma_{mn}} \tag{6}$$

where, σ_{mn} is the total number of shortest paths from node m to node n and $\sigma_{mn}(i)$ is the number of shortest paths from node m to node n that pass through node i.

2.3   Postural Stability Controlling Regions

Postural control under any type of movement is initiated by sequential activation of neurons in the brain stem and spinal cord. Cerebellum, cerebral cortex and brain stem are the main regions controlling posture, gait and balance. Basal ganglia network also contributes actively in the control and modulation of movements through its gamma-aminobutyric acid (GABA)-ergic projections to the cerebral cortex and brainstem [20, 21].

Anatomically, Basal ganglia refers to nuclei embedded deep in the brain hemispheres, differentiated in regions named striatum, caudate-putamen and globus pallidus. In the atlas used for deriving CM, basal ganglia regions are represented by multiple nodes, parceled around the area of putamen, caudate and pallidum. To understand the age related effect, we have selected nine specific brain regions, which are: Left and right Thalamus, Left and right putamen, caudate, pallidum and brain stem. These areas roughly covers the postural stability controlling regions.

Table 1. Descriptive statistics (mean and Standard Deviation) of features and group comparison using one tailed Mann-Whitney U test

Functional feature	Adolescent	Geriatric	p value
Path length	3.8567 ± 0.9762	4.0768 ± 1.2136	0.045*
Clustering coefficient	0.1841 ± 0.035	0.1585 ± 0.033	0.015*
Modularity	0.1976 ± 0.0618	0.1656 ± 0.0196	0.006*
Global efficiency	0.0404 ± 0.0672	0.0410 ± 0.0327	0.134
Local efficiency	0.2113 ± 0.0347	0.163 ± 0.0354	0.03*
Between centrality	56.183 ± 46.05	43.31 ± 30.98	0.134
Small worldness	0.0584 ± 0.0169	0.0403 ± 0.0183	0.32
Structural feature	Adolescent	Geriatric	p value
Path length	4.20 ± 0.672	4.34 ± 0.831	0.12
Clustering coefficient	0.1656 ± 0.0197	0.156 ± 0.0201	0.21
Modularity	0.4659 ± 0.0688	0.4049 ± 0.0320	0.04*
Global efficiency	0.0672 ± 0.0052	0.0610 ± 0.0073	0.216
Local efficiency	0.1954 ± 0.0208	0.1831 ± 0.0201	0.025*
Between centrality	139.83 ± 28.32	134.78 ± 38.32	0.051
Small worldness	0.0503 ± 0.0496	0.0387 ± 0.0054	0.09

* : p value < 0.05

Table 2. Descriptive statistics of metric 'Clustering Coefficient' for specific nodes involves in postural control using one tailed Mann-Whitney U test

Region names	Functional			Structural		
	Adolescent	Geriatric	p value	Adolescent	Geriatric	p value
Brain stem	0.201 ± 0.135	0.182 ± 0.134	0.320	0.230 ± 0.130	0.201 ± 0.054	0.119
Left putamen	0.125 ± 0.040	0.203 ± 0.053	0.041*	0.263 ± 0.120	0.296 ± 0.160	0.038*
Left caudate	0.042 ± 0.021	0.218 ± 0.076	0.022*	0.159 ± 0.020	0.164 ± 0.08	0.210
Left pallidum	0.090 ± 0.050	0.249 ± 0.080	0.015*	0.166 ± 0.040	0.190 ± 0.030	0.430
Left thalamus	0.230 ± 0.120	0.129 ± 0.080	0.530	0.274 ± 0.160	0.187 ± 0.110	0.040*
Right putamen	0.051 ± 0.040	0.229 ± 0.080	0.031*	0.156 ± 0.020	0.279 ± 0.040	0.581
Right caudate	0.159 ± 0.076	0.265 ± 0.12	0.53	0.148 ± 0.08	0.206 ± 0.04	0.62
Right pallidum	0.143 ± 0.120	0.196 ± 0.070	0.600	0.147 ± 0.060	0.297 ± 0.050	0.650
Right thalamus	0.215 ± 0.030	0.186 ± 0.080	0.530	0.155 ± 0.081	0.121 ± 0.040	0.020*

* : p value < 0.05

3   Result and Discussion

Analysis of graph metric on functional and structural CM across the subjects revealed certain differentiating trend between the 'young (adolescent)' group and the 'old (geriatric)' group. As tabulated in Table 1, Characteristic path length increases with age and the effect is evident on both functional and structural analysis. Clustering coefficient (CC) decreases with age, effect being evident only on functional CM and not in structural CM. Modularity value (Q) decreases

Table 3. Descriptive statistics of metric 'Efficiency' for specific nodes involves in postural control using one tailed Mann-Whitney U test

Region names	Functional			Structural		
	Adolescent	Geriatric	p value	Adolescent	Geriatric	p value
Brain stem	0.271 ± 0.180	0.210 ± 0.120	0.120	0.271 ± 0.142	0.250 ± 0.014	0.110
Left putamen	0.167 ± 0.110	0.253 ± 0.031	0.039*	0.271 ± 0.043	0.331 ± 0.120	0.280
Left caudate	0.061 ± 0.036	0.297 ± 0.051	0.042*	0.192 ± 0.034	0.207 ± 0.030	0.130
Left pallidum	0.090 ± 0.061	0.157 ± 0.121	0.013*	0.186 ± 0.040	0.190 ± 0.030	0.530
Left thalamus	0.296 ± 0.132	0.153 ± 0.112	0.230	0.310 ± 0.061	0.229 ± 0.216	0.310
Right putamen	0.058 ± 0.021	0.032 ± 0.181	0.420	0.179 ± 0.012	0.302 ± 0.014	0.210
Right caudate	0.231 ± 0.005	0.325 ± 0.059	0.430	0.201 ± 0.038	0.226 ± 0.140	0.290
Right pallidum	0.193 ± 0.298	0.161 ± 0.070	0.160	0.147 ± 0.073	0.341 ± 0.130	0.410
Right thalamus	0.236 ± 0.080	0.210 ± 0.080	0.360	0.186 ± 0.093	0.141 ± 0.049	0.260

* : p value < 0.05

Table 4. Descriptive statistics of metric 'Centrality' for specific nodes involves in postural control using one tailed Mann-Whitney U test

Region names	Functional			Structural		
	Adolescent	Geriatric	p value	Adolescent	Geriatric	p value
Brain stem	264.22 ± 63.30	221.32 ± 45.13	0.540	271.76 ± 61.78	252 ± 44.76	0.510
Left putamen	317.35 ± 53.23	387.91 ± 31.65	0.041*	58.23 ± 14.56	65.87 ± 12.98	0.220
Left caudate	132.56 ± 24.87	187.76 ± 42.15	0.032*	221.34 ± 3.34	20.23 ± 5.78	0.430
Left pallidum	45.87 ± 11.23	71.54 ± 14.34	0.043*	125.76 ±12.56	121.76 ± 32.87	0.610
Left thalamus	364.54 ± 41.7	329.65 ± 39.43	0.730	134.34 ± 24.76	54.87 ± 7.83	0.030*
Right putamen	48.18 ± 12.65	73.21 ± 4.67	0.223	29.56 ± 6.7	31.78 ± 5.76	0.350
Right caudate	156.76 ± 23.43	189.88 ±31.81	0.560	47.98 ± 13.25	56.89 ± 4.77	0.460
Right pallidum	68.43 ± 13.45	161.56 ± 25.76	0.460	33.51 ± 7.93	25.98 ± 4.98	0.610
Right thalamus	157.98 ± 12.54	121.87 ± 14.54	0.053	185.55 ± 9.43	132.65 ± 9.81	0.040*

* : p value < 0.05

with age in both functional and structural CM. Decrease in modularity indicates lower functional distinction across whole brain network with aging. Local efficiency shows a decreasing trend with age change but global efficiency almost remains similar and this trend is true for both functional and structural CM. Between centrality and small worldness shows slight decrease in their trend for both functional and structural CM but their value is not statistically significant (p value by Mann Whitney U test >0.05). In general variation of graph metric with age is much pronounced in functional CM analysis rather than structural. Decreasing trend in modularity and local efficiency is prominent and is statistically significant in both analysis. Local efficiency is a measure of local information processing. Degradation in cognitive performance with age is correlated with decreased local efficiency [22]. Our observations regarding the trend of graph metrics with age variation is consistent with some prior works [23].

For detecting change of postural control region with age, node specific graph metrics were calculated for the nine specific nodes under consideration. Metric under study were Clustering coefficient (CC), local efficiency and Between Centrality. Tables 2, 3 and 4 shows the variation in graph metrics (mean and standard deviation) for the nine specific nodes in functional and structural CM. Brain stem and thalamus region follows the trend of whole brain; metrics shows decreasing trend with age. Brain stem is one of the most functionally and structurally unaltered region in brain. Areas of Basal ganglia (putamen, caudate and pallidum), in both hemispheres shows a reverse trend with age. In the whole brain analysis (Table 1), efficiency and clustering coefficient decreased with age, but region specific analysis indicates that these regions have a reverse trend; activity in these regions are more pronounced with aging. These might be a neural compensation scheme to prevail postural stability.

Nodes representing basal ganglia region shows statistical significance in functional connectivity for all three metric under consideration. Significance in structural connectivity was not found consistent. Also, in our analysis, only the left nodes of Putamen, Caudate and Pallidum were seen to be statistically significant. In structural connectivity, node representing thalamus (both left and right) was statistically significant between young and old group for Clustering coefficient and Centrality metric. Similar trends have been reported in longitudinal studies, which reflects fast volumetric reduction rates in regions of Basal ganglia [24]. Volumetric reduction might be compensated by an increased functional connectivity, as inferred from the results. Similar to whole brain network features, functional metric shows more variation than their structural counterparts.

4   Conclusion

In this paper, we have tried to understand age related variation in graph metrics for whole brain as well as areas associated with postural control. Structural and functional network parameters has been analyzed on a group of 22 young brain (age 6 to 19 years) and 22 old brain (age 60 to 85 years). Results indicates a decreasing trend in graph metric parameter like local efficiency, modularity and clustering coefficient and an increasing trend for path length in both functional and structural connectivity analysis. Results also indicates network specific changes in cortico-basal ganglia region, which is associated with motor movements, postural and gait related functions. Regions associated with basal ganglia shows a reverse trend with respect to whole brain analysis with advancement of age. This might be a compensation mechanism to reduce the effect of volumetric atrophy of these regions. Extensive analysis of graph metric parameter for a larger subject pool may reveal more information for identifying structural and functional changes of healthy aging. Understanding network metrics for healthy aging brain can be used to differentiate pathology induced changes from healthy aging changes in geriatric patients.

References

1. http://www.un.org/en/sections/issues-depth/ageing/
2. Fjell, A., Walhovd, K.: Structural brain changes in aging: courses, causes and cognitive consequences. Rev. Neurosci. **21**, 187–221 (2010)

3. Peters, R.: Ageing and the brain. Postgrad. Med. J. **82**, 84–88 (2006)
4. Seidler, R., et al.: Motor control and aging: links to age-related brain structural, functional, and biochemical effects. Neurosci. Biobehav. Rev. **34**(5), 721–733 (2010)
5. Hoffstaedter, F., Grefkes, C., Roski, C., Caspers, S., Zilles, K., Eickhoff, S.B.: Age-related decrease of functional connectivity additional to gray matter atrophy in a network for movement initiation. Brain Struct. Funct. **220**(2), 999–1012 (2015)
6. Sala-Llonch, R., Bartrés-Faz, D., Junqué, C.: Reorganization of brain networks in aging: a review of functional connectivity studies. Front. Psychol. **6**, 663 (2015). https://doi.org/10.3389/fpsyg.2015.00663
7. Andrews-Hanna, J., et al.: Disruption of large-scale brain systems in advanced aging. Neuron **56**(5), 924–935 (2007)
8. Wang, J., Zuo, X., He, Y.: Graph-based network analysis of resting-state functional MRI. Syst. Neurosci. **4**, 16 (2010)
9. Betzel, R., et al.: The modular organization of human anatomical brain networks: accounting for the cost of wiring. Netw. Neurosci. **1**(1), 42–68 (2017)
10. Bullmore, E., Sporns, O.: Complex brain networks: graph theoretical analysis of structural and functional systems. Nature Rev. Neurosci. **10**, 186–198 (2009)
11. Nooner, K., Colcombe, S.J., Tobe, R.H.: The NKI-rockland sample: a model for accelerating the pace of discovery science in psychiatry. Frontiers Neurosci. **6**, 152 (2012)
12. Brown, J., Jeff, R.: The UCLA multimodal connectivity database: a web-based platform for brain connectivity matrix sharing and analysis. Frontiers Neurosci. **6**, 28 (2012)
13. Craddock, R., James, G., Holtzheimer, P., Hum, M.S.: A whole brain fMRI atlas generated via spatially constrained spectral clustering. J. Brain Mapp. **33**(8), 1914–28 (2011)
14. Bassett, D.S., Lindenberg, A.M., Achard, S., Duke, T., Bullmore, E.: Adaptive reconfiguration of fractal small-world human brain functional networks. PNAS **103**(51), 19518–19523 (2006)
15. Singh, P., Sreenivasan, S., Szymanski, B.K., Korniss, G.: Threshold-limited spreading in social networks with multiple initiators. Sci. Rep. **3**, 23–30 (2013)
16. Rubinov, M., Sporns, O.: Complex network measures of brain connectivity: uses and interpretations. NeuroImage **52**, 1059–1069 (2010)
17. Achard, S., Bullmore, E.: Efficiency and cost of economical brain functional networks. PLoS Comput. Biol. **3**(2), e17 (2007)
18. Newman, M.: Modularity and community structure in networks. PNAS **103**(23), 8577–8582 (2006)
19. De Meo, P., Ferrara, E., Fiumara, G., Provetti, A.: Generalized Louvain method for community detection in large networks. In: 11th International Conference on Intelligent Systems Design and Applications, Cordoba, pp. 88–93 (2011). https://doi.org/10.1109/ISDA.2011.6121636
20. Yin, H.: Action, time and the basal ganglia. Phil. Trans. R. Soc. B **369**, 20120473 (2012)
21. Manza, P., et al.: The effects of age on resting state functional connectivity of the basal ganglia from young to middle adulthood. Neuroimage **107**, 311–322 (2015)
22. Geerligs, L., Renken, R., Saliasi, E., Maurits, N., Monicque, M., Lorist, A.: Brain-wide study of age-related changes in functional connectivity. Cereb. Cortex **25**, 1987–1999 (2015)

23. Song, J., et al.: Age-related reorganizational changes in modularity and functional connectivity of human brain networks. Brain Connectivity **4**(9), 672–679 (2014)
24. Raz, N., Rodrigue, K., Kennedy, K., Head, D., Gunning-Dixon, F., Acker, J.D.: Differential aging of the human striatum: longitudinal evidence. Am. J. Neourora-diology **24**(9), 1849–1856 (2003)

Intraoperative Accurate Automatic Modeling of Skull Defects with Neuronavigation System

Yangjie Xie[1] and Rongqian Yang[1,2(✉)]

[1] Department of Biomedical Engineering, South China University of Technology,
Guangzhou 510006, Guangdong, China
[2] Department of Therapeutic Radiology, Yale University,
New Haven 06520, USA
bmeyrq@foxmail.com

Abstract. Reconstruction and repair of skull defects is a very important step for the prognosis of patients in skull base surgery. However, different surgical approaches will cause different surgical defects for patients, and it is difficult to accurately reconstruct the three-dimensional (3D) structure of the skull defects for complicated structures approaches such as the trans-eyebrow approach. This study aims at proposing a method with surgical navigation system for accurately and instantly obtaining the structure of skull defect resulting from craniotomies, which is important for skull repairing. CT scanning is completed and the skull is segmented in the preoperative operation plan. After completing the craniotomy approach operation, the surgeon uses the surgical probe to trace along the edge of the skull defect while the navigation system records the three-dimensional coordinates of the probe tip in real time, and the direction of the main view direction is also recorded. With above information, the structure of defect skull can be reconstructed automatically according to the preoperative segmented skull information. The method using the preoperative image scanning data and intraoperative navigation data to get the structure of the defect skull is accurate and rapid.

Keywords: Skull base surgery · Skull defect reconstruction · Navigation system

1 Instruction

Surgical approach, lesion excision and skull base reconstruction are the main steps of the skull base neurosurgery. The lesion area in the brain is always complex, it is often adjacent to or invading important nerve vessels. In order to minimize the patient's trauma, it is necessary to choose an appropriate surgical approach to minimize the hurt caused by the surgical approach [4,14,17]. The quality of skull base reconstruction directly affects the prognosis of patients. Insufficient skull closure will result in common complications. Such as defects in skull, soft

© Springer Nature Singapore Pte Ltd. 2019
A. Zeng et al. (Eds.): HBAI 2019, CCIS 1072, pp. 121–129, 2019.
https://doi.org/10.1007/978-981-15-1398-5_9

tissue and dural might lead to postoperative cerebrospinal fluid (CSF) leakage, encephalocele, intracranial infection and extracranial infection [1,11,15]. Hence the accurate modeling of skull defect is a considerable and popular research topic in skull base surgery [6,7,16]. The structure of the defect skull is usually segmented by the surgeon manually, which may need to be modified during the surgery and might cause inaccurate reconstruction.

With the rapid development of technology in navigation surgery, the surgical navigation system has been commonly used as auxiliary equipment in clinical surgery, especially in neurosurgery which needs high accuracy. Surgical navigation system can help surgeons by visualizing the patient's anatomical structures in real time, which solves the problem that the visual field in the real operation space is restricted in traditional surgery situation. The system helps surgeons locate the lesion area accurately so as to improve the surgical accuracy and reduce intraoperative trauma [2,9,10,12,13]. Given the challenge mentioned above, we proposed a feasible method of modeling the 3D structure of skull defect accurately and rapidly during the surgery with the help of the navigation system. This method can automatic segment the structure of skull defect using the preoperative image scanning data and the intraoperative navigation data (the information of the edge of the skull defect and the main view direction). Here we report the workflow of our method and the results of experiments with model.

2 Method and Experiment

The experiment was performed with the surgical navigation system (see Fig. 1(a)), which includes an optical navigator, a workstation and a navigation interface. Surgical navigation system can visualize and locate the anatomy of the patient and surgical tool (see Fig. 1(b)) in image space to surgeons. The system can obtain the transformation relationship(the transformation matrix was recorded as T) between operation space and image space through space registration step. After the surgical probe is calibrated, the system can track the probe and get its location in image space in real time. The surgical probe and its calibration with calibration plate is shown in Fig. 1(b, c). With all above being done, the system can locate the craniotomy incision and the surgical probe and then show them in image space on the navigation interface. In this study, a model of human skull was used as experimental subject (see Fig. 1(d, e)).

2.1 Scanning and Preoperative Preparation

The skull model was thin-layer scanned by the CT scanner. Then the sequence of scanned medical images were read and reconstructed into 3D structure with image coordinate system. The coordinates of the skull points were recorded as K and would be used in the procedure of the automatic segmentation of the skull defect during the surgery. In the preoperation plan of the skull model experiment, the surgical approach was choosed to be lateral orbitotomy approach in order to simulate the orbital tumor resection of neurosurgery. The skull defect would

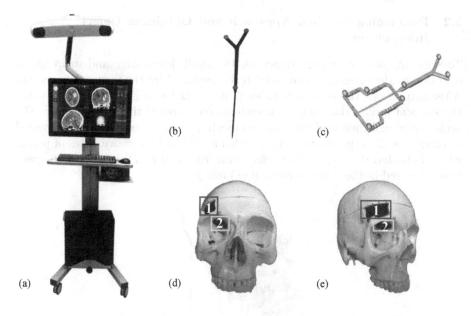

Fig. 1. The equipments and materials used in the method. (Color figure online)

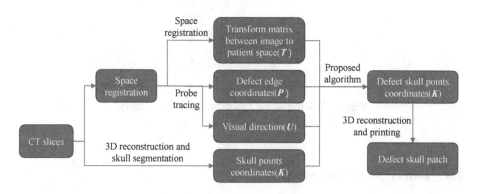

Fig. 2. The operation flow of the method.

appear in the orbit bone after the surgical approach during the surgery and then the method of automatically reconstrucing skull defect could be performed (see Fig. 1(d, e)). The defect outlined in red frame is caused by the surgical approach that removes the bone there, and it can be repaired directly using the removed bone. The defect outlined in yellow frame is caused by the tumor resection, the removed bone there is not a complete piece of bone so that it can't be used in the defect repair. Our purpose is to obtain the structure of defect outlined in yellow frame. The whole workflow of the proposed method is shown in Fig. 2.

2.2 Performing Surgical Approach and Obtaining Defect Information

To segment the skull defect structure, the skull defect edge and main visual direction of the operation were need to be recorded by the navigation system. After cutting out the skull defect, we draw along the edge of the defect using the surgical probe: the navigation system could record the coordinates of the probe tip in real time while the tip was moving along the edge. The main visual direction(the direction vector was recorded as U) and the coordinates of points which indicated the edge of the defect skull(recorded as P) in operation space would be used in the defect structure modeling step.

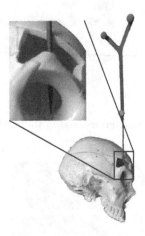

Fig. 3. Tracing along the defect edge in surgery.

2.3 Defect Structure Modeling

After obtaining the coordinates of the defect edge P and the main visual direction U in surgical space, the transformation matrix T between surgical space and image space, the structure of the defect can be automatically segmented from skull data K with the algorithm below:

(1) Calculating the corresponding coordinates of the defect edge in image space (Q) according to P and T. Calculating the main visual direction in image space (V) according to U and T:

$$Q = P \times T \tag{1}$$

$$V = U \times T \tag{2}$$

(2) Calculating the rotate matrix (R) that rotates V to be paralleled to the Z axis($\mathbf{z} = (0,0,1)$) of the image coordinate system, the calculation is done based on Rodrigo's formula (5):
the rotation angle θ:

$$\theta = \arccos\left(\frac{V \cdot z}{|V| |z|}\right) \tag{3}$$

the rotation axis k:

$$\mathbf{k} = \begin{pmatrix} k_x \\ k_y \\ k_z \end{pmatrix} = \frac{V \times z}{|V \times z|} \tag{4}$$

the rotation matrix R:

$$\mathbf{R} = \mathbf{E}\cos\theta + (1 - \cos\theta)\begin{pmatrix} k_x \\ k_y \\ k_z \end{pmatrix}(k_x, k_y, k_z) + \sin\theta\begin{pmatrix} 0 & -k_z & k_y \\ k_z & 0 & -k_x \\ -k_y & k_x & 0 \end{pmatrix} \tag{5}$$

(3) Rotating Q and K with the matrix R to get new pointsets $Q1$ and $K1$. This step is to make the main visual direction of $Q1$ is parallel to Z axis.
(4) Projecting pointsets $Q1$ and $K1$ on the XOY plane to get the 2D pointsets $Q2$ and $K2$;
(5) Calculating the outline (recorded as $Q2$-O) of $Q2$. Judging the every point of $K2$ which is inside this outline and keeping the point in pointset $K2$-I. Finding out all 3D points of pointset $K1$ that are corresponding to $K2$-I and keeping these points in pointset $K1$-I;
(6) Reconstructing pointset $K1$-I in to three dimension and finding out all the connected domains from it. The connected domain whose center is closest to the center of pointset $Q1$ is the defect structure and it will be saved in pointset Seg.

3   Results

As shown in Fig. 1, the defect of the head model is on the right orbit. The edge recorded by the navigation system and its position in the model is shown in Fig. 4(a). The blue points forming the skull of the head model are extracted from the CT slices according to the gray value of the skull part. The red points are the recorded coordinates of probe tip tracing along defect edge. The second step is to get the outsider outline of the defect edge: projecting the points of defect edge onto 2D plane along the recorded main visual direction to get the corresponding 2D points; triangulating these 2D points, these points and their triangular mesh relationship are shown in Fig. 4(b) in blue; starting with the leftmost point and searching for the boundary line so that the outermost edge points can be obtained, these boundary lines are shown in Fig. 4(b) in red. Then the 2D points of skull which are inside the boundary are found out, and their corresponding 3D points P are shown in Fig. 4(c) in green. The method we

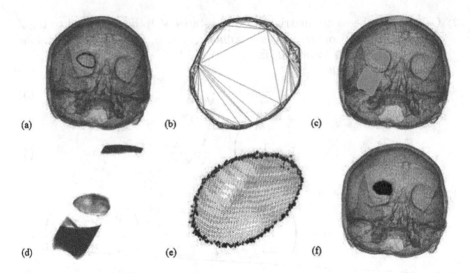

Fig. 4. The intermediate results of the automatic skull defects modeling. (Color figure online)

used to judge a point whether inside or outside an outline is called the ray casting method: draw horizontal ray l to the left from this point, and calculate the intersection times c between l and the edge boundary. If the value of c is odd, the point is considered to be inside the boundary; if it is even, then the point is outside the boundary. The skull defect was a part of the green pointset. Figure 4(d) shows the position relationship between pointset P and the recorded defect edge. To obtain the skull defect from pointset P, we find the minimum bounding box of P and binarize it: the value of points from P are 1, the value of the other points are 0. Then we can calculate the connected domains in the minimum bounding box, and the connected domain whose center is closest to the center of defect edge is the one we need. Figure 4(e) shows the defect edge in red and the skull defect in blue. The obtained defect and its position in skull is shown in Fig. 4(f).

To evaluate the method of modeling the skull defect, we rescanned the head model after the defect appeared. To compare the anastomosis of the defect and the calculated defect model, the skull of images scanned before defect appeared need to be matched with the skull of images scanned after defect appeared. This step makes the skull defect and the calculated defect model be in the same coordinate system. The evaluation method is calculating the closest distance between every points of recorded defect edge and the defective skull. Figure 5 shows five sets results of the average value of the boundary distance in two different defects. The mean value of distance between the automatic modeled defect edge and the real defect edge is 0.424 mm, which is allowed in clinical manufacturing of the skull defect patch.

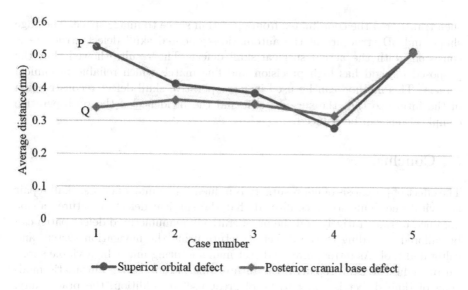

Fig. 5. The average distance of real defect edge and calculated defect model edge.

4   Discussion

Although the surgical technology has developed rapidly, CSF leaks and wound infection still occur occasionally, which are mainly results of the poor postoperative skull repair and improper reconstruction [3,7,8,15,16]. Most of the skull defect reconstruction is preoperative in previous researches, so that the pre-made defect patch might not match the surgical defect and need to be tailored according to the contour of surgical defect. The tailor process usually causes inaccuracy somewhat so that the intraoperative skull defect modeling is an important research content. Nevertheless, it was reported to be very challenging that modeling the skull defect directly during the surgery [5]. Because of the complex structure of the functional organization in the brain, the surgical approach is changed with the location of lesion so that the surgical defect varies in different surgeries. It's difficult to estimate the shape of the defect exactly before surgery. To our knowledge, the problem that how to segment the structure of the defect from the scanning image series automatically during the surgery hasn't previously been solved.

This study aimed at proposing an method that segment the skull defect structure automatic during surgery and accurate repair of skull defect. The defect structure was segmented from the reconstructed 3D structure patient's head, which guaranteed the model of defect is the exact same shape as the patient's defect. Our experiments verified the feasibility and good accuracy of the proposed segmenting method. In this study, the automatic modeling of skull defect method is based on the neuronavigation system. This system not only helps the surgeons visualize the anatomical structure of patient and location of the surgical tool, but also helped us get the coordinates of defect's edge in operation space and then transferred the coordinates from operation space to image space. The edge shape and 3D structure of the automatic segmented skull defect structure is consistent with the actual surgical skull defect. The results showed that the proposed method has high precision and fine match which reliable in clinical surgery. This method can be used in intraoperative skull defect reconstruction in the future so that the surgical cost and the incidence of the postoperative complications can be reduced.

5   Conclusions

The effect of prognosis of neurosurgery is influenced by many factors, skull repair is a vital one. This study confirmed that the surgical defect structure can be obtained intraoperatively and the preoperatively manufactured defect patch can be tailored according to the defect structure using the navigation system and calibrated tool. As intraoperative defect manufacturing might be a viable surgical procedure of skull repair in the future, this intraoperative automatic modeling of skull defect is going to be of great use. In addition, the practicality, robustness and efficiency of the method need to be verified through some clinical experiments. With the development of 3D printing technology in the future, the segmented skull defect structure could be manufactured quickly during the operation so that the patch could be acquired quickly and accurately during the operation for skull repair.

References

1. Badie, B., Preston, J.K., Hartig, G.K.: Use of titanium mesh for reconstruction of large anterior cranial base defects. J. Neurosurg. **93**(4), 711–714 (2000)
2. Cao, A., et al.: Laser range scanning for image-guided neurosurgery: investigation of image-to-physical space registrations. Med. Phys. **35**(4), 1593–1605 (2008)
3. Eseonu, C.I., et al.: Reduced CSF leak in complete calvarial reconstructions of microvascular decompression craniectomies using calcium phosphate cement. J. Neurosurg. **123**(6), 1476 (2015)
4. Essayed, W.I., Singh, H., Lapadula, G., Almodovar-Mercado, G.J., Anand, V.K., Schwartz, T.H.: Endoscopic endonasal approach to the ventral brainstem: anatomical feasibility and surgical limitations. J. Neurosurg. **78**(S 01), 1–8 (2017)
5. Essayed, W.I., et al.: 3D printing and intraoperative neuronavigation tailoring for skull base reconstruction after extended endoscopic endonasal surgery: proof of concept. J. Neurosurg. **79**(S 01), 1 (2018)
6. Harvey, R.J., Priscilla, P., Raymond, S., Zanation, A.M.: Endoscopic skull base reconstruction of large dural defects: a systematic review of published evidence. Laryngoscope **122**(2), 452–459 (2012)
7. Luginbuhl, A.J., Campbell, P.G., James, E., Marc, R.: Endoscopic repair of high-flow cranial base defects using a bilayer button. Laryngoscope **120**(5), 876–880 (2010)
8. Luigi Maria, C., et al.: Skull base reconstruction in the extended endoscopic transsphenoidal approach for suprasellar lesions. J. Neurosurg. **107**(4), 713–720 (2007)

9. Marmulla, R., Eggers, G.J.: Laser surface registration for lateral skull base surgery. Minim. Invasive Neurosurg. **48**(03), 181–185 (2005)

10. Nicolas, G., et al.: High-accuracy patient-to-image registration for the facilitation of image-guided robotic microsurgery on the head. IEEE Trans. Biomed. Eng. **60**(4), 960–968 (2013)

11. Raza, S.M., Banu, M.A., Donaldson, A., Patel, K.S., Anand, V.K., Schwartz, T.H.: Sensitivity and specificity of intrathecal fluorescein and white light excitation for detecting intraoperative cerebrospinal fluid leak in endoscopic skull base surgery: a prospective study. J. Neurosurg. **124**(3), 621 (2016)

12. Rüdiger, M., Stefan, H., Tim, L., Joachim, M.: Laser-scan-based navigation in cranio-maxillofacial surgery. J. Cranio-Maxillofac. Surg. **31**(5), 267–277 (2003)

13. Rüdiger, M., Tim, L., Joachim, M., Stefan, H.: Markerless laser registration in image-guided oral and maxillofacial surgery. J. Oral Maxillofac. Surg. Off. J. Am. Assoc. Oral Maxillofac. Surg. **62**(7), 845–851 (2004)

14. Sivashanmugam, D., Negm, H.M., Salomon, C., Anand, V.K., Schwartz, T.H.: Endonasal endoscopic transsphenoidal resection of tuberculum sella meningioma with anterior cerebral artery encasement. Cureus **7**(8), e311 (2015)

15. Sunil, M., Mark, W., Semaan, M.T., Megerian, C.A., Bambakidis, N.C.: Prevention of postoperative cerebrospinal fluid leaks with multilayered reconstruction using titanium mesh-hydroxyapatite cement cranioplasty after translabyrinthine resection of acoustic neuroma. J. Neurosurg. **119**(1), 113–120 (2013)

16. Victor, G.N., Anand, V.K., Schwartz, T.H.: Gasket seal closure for extended endonasal endoscopic skull base surgery: efficacy in a large case series. World Neurosurg. **80**(5), 563–568 (2013)

17. Zwagerman, N.T., et al.: Endoscopic transnasal skull base surgery: pushing the boundaries. J. Neurooncol. **130**(2), 319–330 (2016)

Brain-Inspired Artificial Intelligence and Its Applications

Task-Nonspecific and Modality-Nonspecific AI

Juyang Weng[1,2,3(✉)], Juan Castro-Garcia[1], Zejia Zheng[1], and Xiang Wu[1]

[1] Department of Computer Science, Michigan State University,
East Lansing, MI 48824, USA
{weng,castrog4,zhengzej,wuxiang1}@msu.edu
[2] Cognitive Science Program, Michigan State University,
East Lansing, MI 48824, USA
[3] Neuroscience Program, Michigan State University, East Lansing, MI 48824, USA

Abstract. It is widely accepted in Artificial Intelligence (AI) that different tasks require different learning methods. The same is true for different sensory modalities. However, auto-programming for general purposes seems to require a learning engine that is task-independent and modality-independent. We provided the Developmental Network (DN) as such an engine to all contestants of the AI Machine Learning Contest 2016 for learning three well-recognized bottleneck problems in AI—vision, audition, and natural languages. For vision, the network learned abstract visual concepts and their hierarchy with invariant properties and autonomous attention. For audition, sparse and dense actions jointly serve as auditory contexts. For natural languages, the network acquires two natural languages, English and French, conjunctively in a bilingual environment (i.e., patterns of text as inputs). All the three sensory modalities used the same DN learning engine, but each had a different body (sensors and effectors). The contestants independently verified the DN's base performance, and competed to add (hinted) autonomous attention for better performance. This seems to be the first task-independent and modality-independent learning engine, which was also verified by independent contestants. Much remains to be done in the learner-age related sophistication of learned tasks.

Keywords: Vision · Audition · Natural language understanding

1 Introduction

Visual cortex appears to take more than 50% of cortical areas in a human brain [2]. We will see here that other sensory modalities can be learned using the same set of developmental mechanisms but probably a different set of resource parameters (e.g., number of neurons). Of course, each modality results in very different learned circuits because the teaching signals are very different.

We first relate the new methods here with the major existing work in the literature and the *status quo* in the related research communities so that the reader can see what popular conventional thoughts we must overcome first.

© Springer Nature Singapore Pte Ltd. 2019
A. Zeng et al. (Eds.): HBAI 2019, CCIS 1072, pp. 133–150, 2019.
https://doi.org/10.1007/978-981-15-1398-5_10

The first departure was made by Cresceptron 1993 [30] that was the first deep learning network for 3-D worlds, but without any monolithic 3-D object model inside the network at all.

Neocognitron by Fukushima 1980 [3] was a handcrafted network that, although does not learn, classifies images each of which contains a single hand-written numeral (from 0 to 9). Inspired by Neocognitron, a deep-learning convolutional neural network called Cresceptron 1993 [30], 1997 [31] appears to be the first that used a deep convolutional network to learn for 3D. It detects, to recognizes, and segments 3-D objects from 2-D images each of which contains many other objects. Since Cresceptron, we have not seen many systems that do detection, recognition, and segmentation altogether. Instead, we have seen *many* systems that do only classification of 3-D objects from 2-D images without telling which is which (e.g., using a bag of features method).

Cresceptron 1993 is also the first network that dealt with 2-D images of 3-D objects *without* any monolithic 3-D object model inside the network—a major difference from then a popular method called aspect graphs that requires a monolithic 3-D object model. This was methodologically different from the earlier 2-D work of Fukushima 1980 [3] and more recent work of LeCun 1998 [14] and Hinton 2006 [8] that used deep convolutional networks to deal with handwritten characters because handwritten characters are intrinsically 2-D.

Although the first departure has been widely practiced as deep learning, the second departure is much more powerful.

The second departure is away from CNNs. Although deep CNNs with error back-propagation learning have become popular [11, 13, 19], the DN engine avoided the use any of the following popular techniques that are hallmarks of CNNs:

(1) *No convolution*: Convolution means every layer is sensory only, instead of sensorimotor in DN. In DN, sensorimotor representations enable learning abstraction with invariances without the leaky "strides" [31].

(2) *No master map* [24]: Using an attention window with different scales, Cresceptron extracts many image patches at different pixel locations and with different scales. First normalize the scale of the image patch to become a *master map* and then apply the network to the *master map*. Instead, a DN learns from an autonomous and recurrent sequence of attention without any master map. In Fig. 3, each attention fixation (e.g., global) provides cues (e.g., location, type, and scale) of the next attention fixation (e.g., local) and so on. Namely, learned dynamic attention skills avoid the intractable exponential complexity [25] of the hypothetical master map [18, 24]. Furthermore, such dynamic attention fixations are not only about pixel location and scale, but also about other concepts such as feature type, and any subset thereof.

(3) *No error back-propagation* for learning: (a) No error is available at the baby's muscle ends and (b) the gradient-based error back-propagation indiscriminately erases long-term memory from neurons that are not responsible for the current context. The optimal Hebbian learning enables a DN to

be "skull closed"—all hidden learning is fully "unsupervised" but external actions always self-supervise the network.

(4) *No max-pooling* first proposed and used by Cresceptron as confirmed by [19]: The function of max is still pixel-oriented, but each DN's hidden neuron is sensorimotor, not just sensory. The max-pooling leaves many "holes" in the network as explained in [31].

Why? E.g., Marvin Minsky criticized that neural networks are scruffy [15] and Michael Jordan complained that neural networks do not abstract well [4]. The departure by DN has addressed these criticisms: A DN abstracts well, mastering probably the most powerful logic (not scruffy) known to the human race— universal Turing machines.

In Where-What Network 1 (WWN-1) [10] emergent representations abstract using motor signals. Sensorimotor is not new in symbolic representations as we will see with Finite Automata (FA) in the remainder of the paper, but for emergent representation, WWN-1 seems to be the first. WWN-1 has been followed by WWN-2 through WWN-9, each of which added a new mechanism.

These sensorimotor-based competition-based emergent representations are fundamentally different from feedback control in classical control theories because classical control theories do not self-generate representations at all.

However, an animal brain is a physical and physiological entity that employs its internal mechanisms to develop itself through lifetime interactions with the external environments. Here "internal" and "external" refers to the skull: inside the skull means internal and outside the skull (include the extra-skull body) is external. The animal body works with the brain to move molecules into and out of the brain as construction elements and energy for metabolism and computation. A mystery of this brain entity—it auto-programs from the physical world for general purposes—has largely escaped research attention in physics, neurophysiology, and computer science, although each individual disciplines have made impressive progress, which has served as the basis of this work. For example, biological brains demonstrated impressive cross-modality plasticity [21,26] but the computational mechanisms for such plasticity are elusive.

Task-nonspecificity: The DN theory argues that each hidden neuron is sensorimotor, corresponding to a transition in the control of a Universal Turing Machine, which is equivalent to a Finite Automaton (FA) proved in [29]. This learning system is task-nonspecific [32]. Figure 2 contrasts the major differences between a DN and a traditional network. Each hidden neuron in DN measures not only its weight match with the sensory (bottom-up) input but also the weight match with the motor (top-down) input. The DN always uses muscle signals to *supervise* (self-supervised or teacher supervised) but the clustering inside the skull is always *unsupervised* because the skull must be closed throughout the life, not accessible to any teacher for supervision. This mixture of supervision and nonsupervision in a single system requires a new distinction of where a supervision is applied—muscles are supervisable but everything inside the skull is not.

This work argues that symbols and text pose great limitations that have not been exposed clearly in the literature. By symbols, we mean a set of handcrafted set Σ of finite number of symbols.

In an *ungrounded* network, the human programmer handcrafts a mapping $f : \Sigma \mapsto R^n$ which maps each symbol $\sigma \in \Sigma$ in a symbolic set Σ to a unique vector $\mathbf{x}$ in the vector space R^n of a static dimensionality n. This mapping converts relations in $\Sigma \times \Sigma$ between symbols (σ_1, σ_2) into vector-to-vector relations. Therefore, numerical techniques such as error back-propagation are used for minimization of approximation errors where neurons with weights become interpolators. This is effective if the vectors are sparse in the vector space R^n.

Computer vision systems using CNN are *grounded*. Namely, they deal with many images each of which is a vector $\mathbf{x}$ in the vector space $X = R^m$, where m can be considered the number of pixels in an image. However, many computer systems still assume the above handcrafted mapping $f : \Sigma \mapsto R^n$.

However, because the set Σ is static, the learner is not able to automatically learn and discover new concepts beyond the statically given set Σ.

Weng 2012 [28] treats natural intelligence and AI in a unified way. It went beyond pattern recognition based a static symbolic set so that a new kind of learning systems could accomplish the grand goals of task-nonspecificity [32].

Along this line, in this paper we address a very challenging problem that a biological brain faces: We do not require the human programmer to handcraft a set of symbols, neither for sensor nor for motor, as explained below.

1. Sensor: the learner directly receives sensory inputs (e.g., images) from a sensor (e.g., camera) where each image is represented by a vector. Each sensory vector $\mathbf{x} \in X$ corresponds to a natural image that contains a projection (i.e., patches) of many 3D objects, such as in a street scene.
2. Motor: Each motor vector is not "pure" like a "pure" vector that corresponds to a clean class label "human". Each motor vector $\mathbf{z} \in Z$ contains multiple subvectors each of which corresponds to the action of (e.g., saying) a certain concept, action, goal, intent, etc., in a way similar to, but not the same as, how images are projected from natural world.

Importantly, both the image vectors and the motor vectors are not pure, i.e., not monolithic. A major difference between a sensor and a motor is that a vector of the former is from the extra-body 3D world which the leaning agent can only partially change; but a vector from the latter is from the body of the learning agent which the learning agent can apply much change (e.g., actions) limited by its own body constraints.

We explain how such a learner automatically learns from the natural physical world, via real time sensory vectors $\mathbf{x} \in X$ and motor vectors $\mathbf{z} \in Z$, with or without human teachers in the environment. The DN generates hidden neurons with weight vectors $\mathbf{y} \in Y$ using optimal statistics. An emergent Universal Turing Machine (UTM) is learned so that the agent gradually learns how to Auto-Program for General Purposes (APFGP) in the natural world from infancy to adulthood. The programmer of the learning engine DN must enable the agent to learn skills from simple to complex, and early learned skills assist later learning of new skills.

None of the following sections should be skipped if one wants to gain a basic degree of understanding.

2   Sensorimotor Formulations, Not Axioms

Mathematics starts from a system of axioms, but gene-regulated development of biological brains seems to root in sensors and effectors. A developmental learning agent has a set of sensors $(S_1, S_2, ..., S_l)$ and a set of motors $(M_1, M_2, ..., M_m)$. It improves through lifetime, but may make errors while learn.

In the remainder of paper, we consider one sensor only and one motor only because the DN algorithm is the same. Similarly, we do not require that each motor (e.g., muscle) vector in each motor corresponds to a symbolic action or a class label. Instead, each motor provides only a motor vector $\mathbf{z}(t)$ at time t.

The above formulation leads to an interesting but important outcome: The DN algorithm is independent of the number of sensors and the number of motors. It is task-nonspecific and modality-nonspecific. By modality, we have sensory modality (vision, audition, touch, etc.). By motor modality, we have leg, mouth, arm, etc. For simplicity, we assume that each neuron has an initial sensory receptive field and an initial motor receptive field, both of which dynamically change.

2.1   Finite Automata: Symbolic

We start from the well-known Finite Automata (FA) since they are simple and powerful. Then, we will remove symbols.

Consider the "state" of a motor vector as a symbolic "state" of a Finite Automaton (FA). The transition function of an FA takes the current state $q \in Q$ and the current input $\sigma \in \Sigma$ and maps (q, σ) to the next state $q' \in Q$, but for convenience we write the pair of q and σ vertically as a column vector:

$$\begin{bmatrix} q \\ \sigma \end{bmatrix} \rightarrow \begin{bmatrix} q' \\ \sigma' \end{bmatrix}. \tag{1}$$

where σ' is the next input, or the predicted next input when the input is absent. This new representation of FA, q at top and σ at bottom, is useful for our discussion below about internal representation in the hidden area Y.

Why FA? In computer science, the Universal Turing Machines were widely recognized as a model for any general purpose digital computers (Von Neumann computers). However, Weng [29] recently proved that the control of any Turing Machine is an FA. Thus, learning any FA is sufficient for any Universal TM and sufficient for general purposes.

2.2 Emergent FA: Non-Symbolic

Below, we bridge a large gap between symbols and vectors. We enable DN to do abstraction that we handcraft symbols for, but without a human in the loop of handcrafting symbols.

We consider the "skull" to be the boundary of DN (brain). Inside the skull is "internal" and outside the skull is "external". Running at discrete times $t = 0, 1, 2, 3, ...$, the sensory area X of DN takes input patterns $\mathbf{x}$ and the muscles area Z of DN takes state pattern $\mathbf{z}$. State/action $\mathbf{z}$ is taught by the environment but very often self-supervised.

2.3 Many-to-Many Mapping: Without Symbols

Symbol-to-Vector: To deal with sensing from the real world, we must deal with sensory vectors in $X = R^n$ where R is the set of real numbers and n is the dimension of sensor, the motor vectors in $Z = R^m$ where m is the number of muscles (or the number of muscle neurons). DN extends the input space Σ to become a vector sensory space X, and the state space Q to a vector motor space Z:

$$\Sigma \equiv X; \quad Q \equiv Z \tag{2}$$

where $\equiv$ means each element in the set of symbols on one side corresponds to a unique vector in the set of vectors on the other side.

Many Vectors: However, one symbol may correspond to many possible vectors from a sensor of the real world. For example, many image patches of a cat at different image locations in a natural scene correspond to the same cat. Further, each image of a cluttered scene may contain multiple objects each represented by a different symbol in Σ. Therefore, we extend Eq. (2) to the following two expressions:

$$\Sigma \lhd X; \quad Q \lhd Z \tag{3}$$

where $\lhd$ represents many to many correspondences, but left-hand side is a much smaller symbolic set than the right-hand side vector set.

Similarly many actions $\mathbf{z} \in Z$ (e.g., pronounced sounds for "cat" with different accents) correspond to the same symbol in Q (e.g., as a symbol "cat"). Thus, $Q \lhd Z$. Similarly, $Z \rhd Q$ means Z is a much larger vector set than the right-hand side symbolic set, and they are related by a many-to-many correspondence.

Framewise Pattern Recognition: Suppose X is lower (more concrete) and Z is higher (more abstract). Then, establishing a bottom-up framewise mapping

$$\delta_f : X \mapsto Q \tag{4}$$

is a *spatial pattern recognition* problem.

Context-Based Pattern Recognition: A context-based pattern recognition problem is to construct a mapping:

$$\delta_c : Q \times X \mapsto Q. \tag{5}$$

Many time-varying video analysis and speech recognition problems, including many Markov models, belong to this framework. The major limitation of this framework is that Q is static, not emergent.

Emergent-Context Emergent-Input: DN, along with its embodiments Where-What Networks (WWN-1 to WWN-9 [10,22]), aim at the following framework, called ECEI framework. The ECEI framework extends the symbolic set Q to an emergent vector space Z, to fully learn an emergent finite automaton that realizes the mapping:

$$\delta_{ecei} : Z \times X \mapsto Z \tag{6}$$

or, if X is also predicted,

$$\delta_{ecei} : Z \times X \mapsto Z \times X. \tag{7}$$

This framework is not intimidating if we unfold the time, as time in a life.

Unfolding Time: We should treat X and Z external as they can be "supervised" by the physical environment as well as "self-supervised" by the network itself. We add the internal area Y to be hidden—cannot be directly supervised by external teachers. Furthermore, we should unfold the time t and allow the network to have three areas X, Y, and Z that learns incrementally through time $t = 0, 1, 2, ...$:

$$\begin{bmatrix} X(0) \\ Y(0) \\ Z(0) \end{bmatrix} \rightarrow \begin{bmatrix} X(1) \\ Y(1) \\ Z(1) \end{bmatrix} \rightarrow \begin{bmatrix} X(2) \\ Y(2) \\ Z(2) \end{bmatrix} \rightarrow ... \tag{8}$$

where $\rightarrow$ means neurons on the left links to the neurons on the right.

3   GENISAMA: Eight Properties

The acronym GENISAMA means eight properties:

Grounded: All patterns $\mathbf{z} \in Z$ and $\mathbf{x} \in X$ are from the external environment (i.e., the body and the extra-body world), not from any symbolic tape.

Emergent: All patterns $\mathbf{z} \in Z$ and $\mathbf{x} \in X$ emerge from activities (e.g., images). All vectors $\mathbf{y} \in Y$ emerge automatically from $\mathbf{z} \in Z$ and $\mathbf{x} \in X$.

Natural: All patterns $\mathbf{z} \in Z$ and $\mathbf{x} \in X$ are natural from real sensors and real effectors, without using any task-specific encoding.

Incremental: The machine incrementally updates at times $t = 1, 2, ...$ Namely DN uses $(\mathbf{z}(t), \mathbf{x}(t))$ for update the network and discard it before taking the next $(\mathbf{z}(t+1), \mathbf{x}(t+1))$. We avoid storing images for offline batch training (e.g., as in ImageNet) because the next image $\mathbf{x}(t+1)$ is unavailable without first generating and executing the agent action $\mathbf{z}(t)$ which typically alters the scene that determines $\mathbf{x}(t+1)$.

Skulled: As the skull closes the brain to the environment, everything inside the Y area (neurons and connections) are initialized at $t = 0$ and off limit to environment's direct manipulation after $t = 0$.

Attentive: In every cluttered sensory image $\mathbf{x} \in X$ only the attended parts correspond to the current attended symbol set s. New here is the attention to cluttered motor image $\mathbf{z} \in Z$ so that the attended parts correspond to the current state symbol q (e.g., firing muscle neurons in the mouth and arms). Two symbols correspond to a pattern (not necessarily connected, as in $s = \{\text{car2, pedestrian1}\}$). Note: The attention here for $\mathbf{x}$ is about the cluttered sensory world, consistent with the literature [17,18] but the attention in [5,6] is about the structured internal memory instead, different from the literature.

Motivated: Different neural transmitters have different effects to different neurons, e.g., resulting in (a) avoiding pains, seeking pleasures and speeding up learning of important events and (b) uncertainty- and novelty-based neuronal connections (synaptic maintenance for auto-wiring) and behaviors (e.g., curiosity).

Abstractive: Each learned concept (e.g., object type) in Z are abstracted from concrete examples in $\mathbf{z} \in Z$ and $\mathbf{x} \in X$, invariant to other concepts learned in Z (e.g., location, scale, and orientation). E.g., the type concept "dog" is invariant to "location" on the retina (dogs are dogs regardless where they are). Invariance is different from correlation: dog-type and dog-location are correlated (e.g., dogs are typically on ground).

4   Developmental Networks

The hidden Y area corresponds to the entire "brain". In the following, we assume the brain has a single area but it will emerge many areas and subareas.

The brain takes input from vector $(\mathbf{z}, \mathbf{x})$, not just sensory $\mathbf{x}$ but also motor $\mathbf{z}$, to produce an internal response vector $\mathbf{y}$ which represents the best match of $(\mathbf{z}, \mathbf{x})$ with one of many internally stored patterns of $(\mathbf{z}, \mathbf{x})$:

The winner-take-all learning rule, which is highly nonlinear and simulates parallel lateral inhibition in the internal (hidden) area Y of DN is sufficient to prove in [29] that a DN that has sufficient hidden neurons learns any Turing Machine (TM) perfectly, immediately, and error-free.

The n neurons in Y give a response vector $\mathbf{y} = (y_1, y_2, ...y_n)$ of n neurons in which only the best-matched neuron fires at value 1 and all other neurons do not fire giving value 0:

$$y_j = \begin{cases} 1 & \text{if } j = \underset{1 \leq i \leq n}{\operatorname{argmax}}\{f(\mathbf{t}_i, \mathbf{z}, \mathbf{b}_i, \mathbf{x})\} \\ 0 & \text{otherwise} \end{cases} \qquad j = 1, 2, ...n, \qquad (9)$$

where f is a function that measures the similarity between the top-down weight vector $\mathbf{t}_i$ and the top-down input vector $\mathbf{z}$ as well as the similarity between

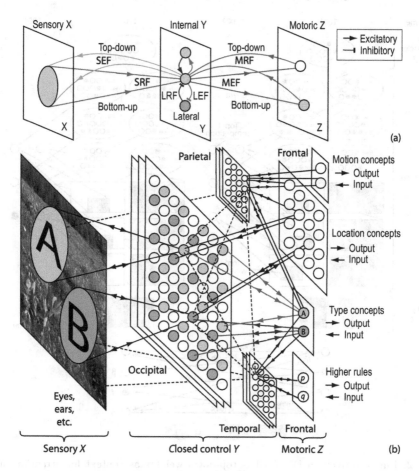

Fig. 1. Brain Y is modeled as the two-way bridge of the sensory X and the motor Z.

the bottom-up weight vector $\mathbf{b}_i$ and the bottom-up input vector $\mathbf{x}$. The value of similarity is the inner product of their length-normalized versions [29]. Corresponding to FA, both the top-down weight and the bottom-up weight must match well for f to give a high value as inner product.

The response vector $\mathbf{y}$ the hidden Y area of DN is then used by Z and X areas to predict the next $\mathbf{z}$ and $\mathbf{x}$ respectively in discrete time:

$$\begin{bmatrix} \mathbf{z} \\ \mathbf{x} \end{bmatrix} \rightarrow \mathbf{y} \rightarrow \begin{bmatrix} \mathbf{z}' \\ \mathbf{x}' \end{bmatrix} \tag{10}$$

where $\rightarrow$ denotes the update on the left side using the left side as input. The first $\rightarrow$ above is highly nonlinear because of the top-1 competition so that only one Y neuron fires (i.e., exactly one component in binary $\mathbf{y}$ is 1). The second $\rightarrow$ consists of simply links from the single firing Y neurons to all firing neurons on the right side.

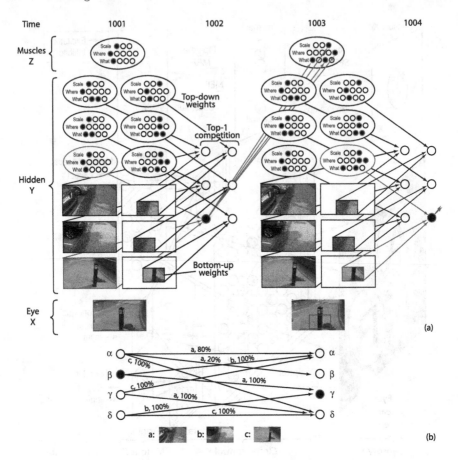

Fig. 2. Put intuitively, a DN (a) has top-down weights as context for attention but a traditional neural network in (b) does not. This DN incrementally learns a finite automaton that is the control of a Universal Turing Machine—amounting to auto-programming for general purposes.

The expression in Eq. (10), is extremely rich as illustrated in Fig. 1: Self-wiring within a Developmental Network (DN) as the control of GENISAMA TM, based on statistics of activities through "lifetime", without any central controller, Master Map, handcrafted features, and convolution.

Like the transition function of the FA in Eq. (1), each prediction of $\mathbf{z}'$ in Eq. (10) is called a *transition*, but now in real-valued vector, without any symbols. The same $\mathbf{y}$ can also be used to predict the binary (or real-valued) $\mathbf{x}' \in X$ in Eq. (10).

The above vector formalization is simple but very powerful in practice. Illustrated in Fig. 2(a), the pattern in Z can represent the binary pattern of any abstract concept—context, state, muscles, action, intent, object type, object group, object relation. However, as far as DN is concerned, they mean the same—a firing pattern of the Z area!

Namely, unified numerical processing-and-prediction in DN amounts to any abstract concepts above. In symbolic representations, it is a human to handcraft every abstract concept as a symbol; but DN does not have a human in the "skull". It simply learns, processes, and generates vectors. In the eyes of a human outside the "skull", the DN gets smarter and smarter.

Consider learning. Suppose human society together with mother nature as a teacher is a huge and complex Turing Machine (TM), including a Universal Turing Machine.(UTM) Because its control is an FA, represented by a huge FA transition table having r rows and c columns. At each time t, $t = 1, 2, ...$, only the winner Y neuron fires at response value 1 and incrementally updates its weight vector $(\mathbf{z}_i, \mathbf{x}_i)$ as the vector average of attended part of $(\mathbf{z}, \mathbf{x})$. This is called the incremental Hebbian learning rule. Then, the i-th Y neuron memorizes perfectly the i-th distinct input pair $(\mathbf{z}, \mathbf{x})$ observed in life, because the teacher TM has no errors. When the teacher has errors the DN is optimal in the sense of maximum likelihood, as proved in [29].

5   Basic Theorems

Weng 2015 [29] has proved: (1) The control of a TM is an FA. Thus, the emergent FA can learn a emergent UTM for APFGP. (2) The DN is always optimal in the sense of maximum likelihood conditioned on the number of neurons and the learning experience. When there are neurons in the hidden brain to be initialized, the learning is further error-free.

6   More Needed: Motivation

Motivation is very rich. It has two major aspects (a) and (b) in the current DN model. All reinforcement learning methods other than DN, as far as we know, are for symbolic methods (e.g., Q-learning [16,23]) and are in aspect (a) exclusively. DN uses concepts (e.g., important events) instead of the rigid time-discount in Q-learning to avoid the failure of far goals.

(a) Pain avoidance and pleasure seeking to speed up learning important events. Signals from pain (aversive) sensors release a special kind of neural transmitters (e.g., serotonin [1]) that diffuse into all neurons that suppress Z firing neurons but speed up the learning rates of the firing Y neurons. Signals from sweet (appetitive) sensors release a special kind of neural transmitters (e.g., dopamine [12]) that diffuse into all neurons that excite Z firing neurons but also speed up the learning rates of the firing Y neurons. Higher pains (e.g., loss of loved ones and jealousy) and higher pleasure (e.g., praises and respects) develop at later ages from lower pains and pleasures, respectively.

(b) Synaptic maintenance—grow and trim the spines of synapses [7, 27]—to segment object/event and motivate curiosity. Each synapse incrementally estimates the average error β between the pre-synaptic signal and the synaptic conductance (weight), represented by a kind of neural transmitter (e.g., acetylcholine [33]). See Fig. 1(b) for how a neuron can cut off their direct connections with Z to become early areas in the occipital lobe or their direct connections with the X areas to become latter areas inside the parietal and temporal lobes. However, we cannot guarantee that such "cut off" are 100% based on the statistics-based wiring theory here.

7 Experiments

The experimental results of DN include (1) vision that includes simultaneous recognition and detection and vision-guided navigation on MSU campus walkways, (2) Audition to learn phonemes with a cochlea, and (3) acquisition of English and French in an interacti bilingual environment.

7.1 Vision

The vision modality corresponds to learning vision from a "lifelong" retina sequence. The vision task is autonomous navigation on a university campus, where GPS signals are often missing, not accurate enough, and will lead to failures without a sufficient visual capability using a single video camera. As an option, the organizer provided an extensively explained hint along with the illustration in Fig. 3—how to add the attention mechanisms for vision without adding more hidden neurons. The audition and natural language tasks of the experiment do not have large "background" distractors like video, other than disjoint sensorimotor experiences that arise from auditory variations and natural noise.

Invariance: In order to reach location invariance and type invariance for all attended landmarks, our experiments used additional images that were automatically generated from the available sequence through a variety of image shifts (left, right, up, down), along with the correspondingly "shifted" actions. Only 2000 hidden neurons were allowed for the experiments.

The experiments implemented such attention mechanisms for the vision modality, having reduced the base error 26.4% for vision by 80.3%. Therefore, the attention appeared to be the primary reason for the drastic 80.3% improvement. Many methods, other than attention, tried by other laboratory using the same learning engine did not show any improvements probably because the base program is already optimal in the sense of maximum likelihood.

7.2 Audition

This modality corresponds to learning audition from a "lifelong" cochlear sequence. For the audition modality, each input image to X is the pattern that

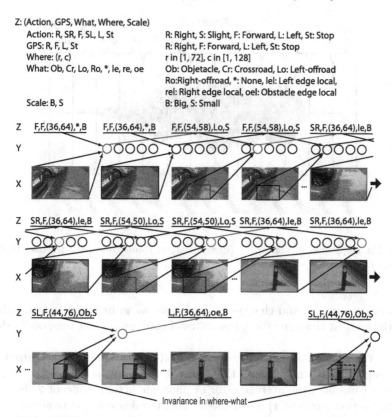

Fig. 3. How a task-nonspecific and modality-nonspecific engine learns. **Vision modality:** The sensory area X takes images. Concepts learned include where, what, scale and navigation actions, while learning an attention sequence global, local, global, local ... but any arbitrary attention sequence can be learned in a similar way. **Audition modality:** the X area takes a firing pattern of the simulated hair cells in the cochlea. **Natural language modality:** the X area takes a binary pattern representing a text (word or punctuation).

simulates the output from an array of hair cells in the cochlea. We model the cochlea in the following way. The cells in the base of the cochlea correspond to filters with a high pass band. The cells in the top correspond to filters with a low pass band. At the same height, cells have different phase shifts. Potentially, such a cochlear model could deal with music and other natural sound, more general than the popular Mel Frequency Cepstral Coefficients (MFCCs) that are mainly for human speech processing.

It is important to note that it is necessary for a developmental agent to learn from early baby babble. Therefore, real phonemes were recorded as auditory stimuli.

Take /u:/ as an example shown in Fig. 4. The state of concept 2 keeps as silence when inputs are silence frames. It becomes a "free" state when phoneme

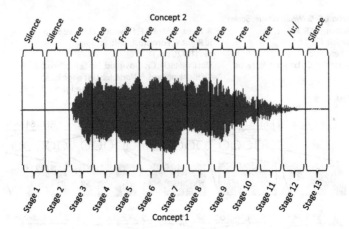

Fig. 4. The sequences of concept 1 (dense, bottom) and concept 2 (sparse, top) for phoneme /u:/.

frames are coming in, and changes to /u:/ state when first silence frame shows up at the end. At the same time, the states of concept 1 count temporally dense stages.

With the exact training sequence as input (re-substitution), the output was nearly perfect. With new inputs that are not the same as any of the training sequences (disjoint), the average error of phoneme action (concept 2) is 23% if the dense action (concept 1) is not used. Using the dense action (concept 1), the average error of phoneme action (concept 2) was reduced by 46% to 12%. Only 335 hidden neurons were allowed for learning 44 phonemes. The more hidden neurons are allowed, the smaller the expected average error.

7.3   Natural Languages

This modality corresponds to learning two natural languages from a "lifelong" word sequence. As far as we know, this seems to be the first work that deals with language acquisition in a bilingual environment, largely because the DN learns directly from emergent patterns, both in word input and in action input (supervision), instead of static symbols.

The input to X is a 12-bit binary pattern, each represents a word, which potentially can represent 2^{12} words using binary patterns. The system was taught 1,862 English and French sentences from [20], using 2,338 unique words (case sensitive). As an example of the sentences: English: "Christine used to wait for me every evening at the exit." French: "Christine m'attendait tours les soirs à la sortie."

The Z area was taught two concepts: language type (English, French, and language neutral, e.g., a number or name) represented by 3 neurons (top-1 firing), and the language-independent meanings as meaning states, as shown in Fig. 5. The latter is represented by 18 neurons (18-bit binary pattern), always top 5

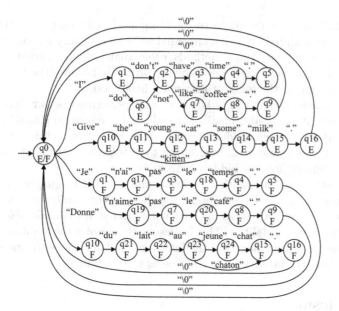

Fig. 5. The finite automaton for the English and French versions of some sentences. The DN learned a much larger finite automaton. Cross-language meanings of partial- and full-sentences are represented by the same state of meaning context q_i, $i = 0, 1, 2, ..., 24$. See, e.g., q_1, q_3, q_4, and q_5. But the language specific context is represented by another concept: language type.

neurons firing, capable of representing $C(18, 5) = 8,568$ possible combinations as states, but only $6,638$ actual meanings were recorded. Therefore, the Z area has $3 + 18 = 21$ neurons, potentially capable of representing a huge number 2^{21} binary patterns if all possible binary patterns are allowed.

Without adding noise to the input X, the recognition error is zero, provided that there is a sufficient number of Y neurons. We added Gaussian noise into the bits of X. Let α represent the relative power of the signal in the noisy signal. When α is 60%, the state recognition rate of DN is around 98%. When α is 90%, the DN has reached 0% error rate, again thanks to the power of DN internal interpolation that converts a huge discrete (symbolic) problem into a considerably smaller continuous (numeric) problem.

8   AI Machine Learning Contest 2016

AI Machine Learning (AIML) Contest was the first contest where the contests must use a task-nonspecific and modality-nonspecific machine learning engine. Provided with DN as such an learning engine and sensorimotor sequences, the contest teams are required to improve the performance of the base sequences.

The first place team and our in-house version implemented such attention mechanisms for the vision modality, having reduced the base error 26.4% for vision by 56.3% and 80.3%, respectively. Compared with other teams, the implementation of this hinted attention appeared to be the primary reason for the first place team to stand out. Many methods, other than attention, tried by the first place team did not show any improvements probably because the base program is already optimal in the sense of maximum likelihood.

The main reason that the in-house version performed better than the first place team is that it has additionally synaptic maintenance explained in the companion report where each hidden neuron automatically cuts off input lines that do not match the weight well, amounting to automatic cutting-off background pixels that "leaked" into all hidden neurons.

For the other two modalities, audition and natural languages, the lifelong average errors of the DN base engine supplied to the contestants were 11.5% and 4.9%, respectively. Contestants have not reported any considerable improvements for these two modalities. This is reasonable because the audition modality has only one human speaker, and the language modality has only one stream of text. Therefore, the attention-free DN seems to be optimal.

9   Conclusions

Since Weng et al. 2001 [32] proposed task-nonspecificity for autonomous mental development, the Developmental Network (DN) appears to be the first engine that has reached not only the goal of task-nonspecificity but also proved general-purpose in the sense of emergent universal Turing machines. Furthermore, the DN engine is also modality nonspecific in the sense that it can be applied to any sensor modality and effector modality. Using DN, emergent AI is no longer a black box, contrary to what is stated in [9]. These fundamentals have been proved mathematically and experimentally. However, much remains to be done. Full GENISAMA on a system has yet to be realized and many interesting open questions need to be answered.

References

1. Daw, N.D., Kakade, S., Dayan, P.: Opponent interactions between serotonin and dopamine. Neural Netw. **15**(4–6), 603–616 (2002)
2. Felleman, D.J., Van Essen, D.C.: Distributed hierarchical processing in the primate cerebral cortex. Cereb. Cortex **1**, 1–47 (1991)
3. Fukushima, K.: Neocognitron: a self-organizing neural network model for a mechanism of pattern recognition unaffected by shift in position. Biol. Cybern. **36**, 193–202 (1980)
4. Gomes, L.: Machine-learning maestro Michael Jordan on the delusions of big data and other huge engineering efforts. IEEE Spectrum (Online article posted 20 Oct 2014)
5. Graves, A., et al.: Hybrid computing using a neural network with dynamic external memory. Nature **538**, 471–476 (2016)
6. Graves, A., Wayne, G., Danihelka, I.: Neural Turing machines. Technical report, Google DeepMind, London, UK 10 December 2014. arXiv:1410.5401

7. Guo, Q., Wu, X., Weng, J.: Cross-domain and within-domain synaptic maintenance for autonomous development of visual areas. In: Proceedings of the Fifth Joint IEEE International Conference on Development and Learning and on Epigenetic Robotics, Providence, RI, pp. 1–6, 13–16 August 2015
8. Hinton, G.E., Osindero, S., Teh, Y.W.: A fast learning algorithm for deep belief nets. Neural Comput. **18**, 1527–1554 (2006)
9. Holm, E.A.: In defense of the black box. Science **364**(6435), 26–27 (2019)
10. Ji, Z., Weng, J., Prokhorov, D.: Where-what network 1: "Where" and "What" assist each other through top-down connections. In: Proceedings of IEEE International Conference on Development and Learning, Monterey, CA, pp. 61–66, 9–12 August 2008
11. Jordan, M.I., Mitchell, T.M.: Machine learning: trends, perspectives, and prospects. Science **349**, 255–260 (2015)
12. Kakade, S., Dayan, P.: Dopamine: generalization and bonuses. Neural Netw. **15**, 549–559 (2002)
13. LeCun, Y., Bengio, L., Hinton, G.: Deep learning. Nature **521**, 436–444 (2015)
14. LeCun, Y., Bottou, L., Bengio, Y., Haffner, P.: Gradient-based learning applied to document recognition. Proc. IEEE **86**(11), 2278–2324 (1998)
15. Minsky, M.: Logical versus analogical or symbolic versus connectionist or neat versus scruffy. AI Mag. **12**(2), 34–51 (1991)
16. Mnih, V., et al.: Human-level control through deep reinforcement learning. Nature **518**, 529–533 (2015)
17. Moran, J., Desimone, R.: Selective attention gates visual processing in the extrastrate cortex. Science **229**(4715), 782–784 (1985)
18. Olshausen, B.A., Anderson, C.H., Van Essen, D.C.: A neurobiological model of visual attention and invariant pattern recognition based on dynamic routing of information. J. Neurosci. **13**(11), 4700–4719 (1993)
19. Schmidhuber, J.: Deep learning in neural networks: an overview. Neural Netw. **61**, 85–117 (2015)
20. Scriven, R., Amiot-Cadey, G.: Collins: Collins French grammar. HarperCollins, Glasgow (2011)
21. Sharma, J., Angelucci, A., Sur, M.: Induction of visual orientation modules in auditory cortex. Nature **404**, 841–847 (2000)
22. Solgi, M., Weng, J.: WWN-8: incremental online stereo with shape-from-x using life-long big data from multiple modalities. In: Proceedings of INNS Conference on Big Data, San Francisco, CA, pp. 316–326, 8–10 August 2015
23. Sutton, R.S., Barto, A.: Reinforcement Learning. MIT Press, Cambridge (1998)
24. Treisman, A.M.: A feature-integration theory of attention. Cogn. Sci. **12**(1), 97–136 (1980)
25. Tsotsos, J.K.: A 'complexity level' analysis of immediate vision. Int. J. Comput. Vis. **1**(4), 303–320 (1988)
26. Voss, P.: Sensitive and critical periods in visual sensory deprivation. Front. Psychol. **4**, 664 (2013). https://doi.org/10.3389/fpsyg.2013.00664
27. Wang, Y., Wu, X., Weng, J.: Synapse maintenance in the where-what network. In: Proceedings of International Joint Conference on Neural Networks, San Jose, CA, pp. 2823–2829, 31 July–5 August 2011
28. Weng, J.: Natural and Artificial Intelligence: Introduction to Computational Brain-Mind. BMI Press, Okemos (2012)
29. Weng, J.: Brain as an emergent finite automaton: a theory and three theorems. Int. J. Intell. Sci. **5**(2), 112–131 (2015). Received Nov. 3, 2014 and accepted by Dec. 5, 2014

30. Weng, J., Ahuja, N., Huang, T.S.: Learning recognition and segmentation of 3-D objects from 2-D images. In: Proceedings of IEEE 4th International Conference Computer Vision, pp. 121–128, May 1993
31. Weng, J., Ahuja, N., Huang, T.S.: Learning recognition and segmentation using the Cresceptron. Int. J. Comput. Vis. **25**(2), 109–143 (1997)
32. Weng, J., et al.: Autonomous mental development by robots and animals. Science **291**(5504), 599–600 (2001)
33. Yu, A.J., Dayan, P.: Uncertainty, neuromodulation, and attention. Neuron **46**, 681–692 (2005)

Brain Research and Arbitrary Multiscale Quantum Uncertainty

Rodolfo A. Fiorini[✉] ⓘ

DEIB, Politecnico di Milano University, 20133 Milan, Milan, Italy
rodolfo.fiorini@polimi.it

Abstract. The fact that we can build devices that implement the same basic operations as those the nervous system uses leads to the inevitable conclusion that we should be able to build entire systems based on the network organizing principles used by the nervous system. Nevertheless, the human brain is at least a factor of 1 billion more efficient than our present digital technology, and a factor of 10 million more efficient than the best digital technology that we can imagine. The unavoidable conclusion is that we still have something fundamental to learn from the brain and neurobiology about new ways and much more effective forms of computation. To acquire new knowledge on multiscale system uncertainty management, three specific interpretations of the Heisenberg Uncertainty Principle are presented and discussed, even at macroscale level. To solve complex, arbitrary multiscale system problems, by advanced deep learning and deep thinking systems, we need a unified, integrated, convenient, and universal representation framework, by considering information not only on the statistical manifold of model states, but also on the combinatorical manifold of low-level discrete, directed energy generators. Understanding this deep layer of thought is vital to develop highly competitive, reliable and effective human-centered symbiotic autonomous systems.

Keywords: Knowledge representation · Neuroscience · Cognition and behavior · Machine learning · Modeling · Simulation · CICT · Deep learning

1 Introduction

In a different paper published elsewhere we already discussed the major intrinsic limitations of "Science 1.0" brain arbitrary multiscale (AMS) modeling and strategies to get better simulation results by "Science 2.0" approach [1]. Nevertheless, while there is ample evidence that both microscale and macroscale features are key factors of nervous system organization, our knowledge about how these different scales of organization interact is remarkably sparse. In fact, a major goal of computational neuroscience is to produce predictive mesoscale theories of biological computation that bridge the gap between the cells and behaviors of complex organisms thereby explaining how the former give rise to the latter.

Until recently there was little hope of formulating testable theories of this sort. Many scientists have tried to identify how the brain creates a working information processing system through its network of neurons, also called the Connectome [2].

© Springer Nature Singapore Pte Ltd. 2019
A. Zeng et al. (Eds.): HBAI 2019, CCIS 1072, pp. 151–169, 2019.
https://doi.org/10.1007/978-981-15-1398-5_11

With new technologies for recording the activity of thousands, even millions of neurons simultaneously, it is now feasible to observe neural activity at a scale and resolution that opens the possibility of inferring such theories directly from data. Chosen the Nature Method of the Year in 2010 [3], the novel field of optogenetics combines genetics and optics to identify the functions in the connectome. Two large scale projects, the NHI Human Connectome Project [4] and the EU co-founded Human Brain Project [5], which are trying to map this interconnected whole, have contributed to a new understanding in scientific research, one which emphasizes the network and the relationships within it rather than the parts.

The Human Connectome Project (HCP), which began in the USA in 2009, aims to map the neural network to elucidate the anatomical and functional interconnectivity of the healthy human brain to create data that would support research into conditions such as dyslexia, autism and Alzheimer's disease. The data obtained from the research carried out through the cooperation of dozens of researchers around the continent are available to the public on an internet based neuroinformatics platform.

Europe's response to the same research goal, but from a more mathematical perspective, the Human Brain Project (HBP) was initiated within the EU in 2013. As one of the largest collective efforts to explain the brain, the HBP tried to understand how information flows through it and whether a supercomputer can be built that can simulate the human brain. The project involved the most sophisticated computers with an eye to building a scientific research platform for scientists all over Europe in fields related to neuroscience, information processing and neuroscience.

The first results of the HBP work were published in 2015 [6], revealing data about the interconnectivity in a 31,000 neuron section of a rat brain. While it turned out that achieving a simulation of the human brain within a decade was unachievable as a goal, the project underlined the premise that Big Data would be a crucial part of discovering how the brain truly works. This showed that further development was necessary in the field of network sciences, mathematics and computerized network sciences.

In a Nobel prize-winning work since 1982, the connectome of the worm "Caenorhabditis Elegans" was mapped [7], finding a network of 383 neurons. In the study on the worm, the scientists incapacitated each neuron in turn, and were able to see the different decisions the worm made and how its life changed. Therefore, how each individual neuron affected this worm's connectome was found. It is this connectome that creates these choices that the worm makes and therefore the life it lives.

By taking the definition of consciousness, a somewhat elusive term, as the ability to make decisions, it might be fair to say that the connectome creates consciousness. Once the connectome is mathematically modeled, that model might also be used as the mathematical model for explaining conscience. The above example of the model with 383 neurons makes it even more compelling to understand a human decision making system. This will only be made possible once the mathematical modelling of such complex structures of interconnectivity is advanced enough. Nevertheless, our deeper current understanding of neurons and the patterns of interconnectivity they work in; i.e., neuronal networks, through studies such as this has fueled advances in artificial intelligence research, and vice versa [8].

2 Human Brain Fundamental Code Unit

Your mobile phone can process around 25 billion instructions per second. This may sound a lot, but best estimates put our own brain processing capacity at around 100 trillion instructions per second, far more powerful. Unlike machines, however, we cannot focus all of our processing power on a single task. We need to keep breathing, stay balanced, keep listening and seeing, and so on, all at the same time. Nevertheless, the fact that we can build devices that implement the same basic operations as those the nervous system uses leads to the inevitable conclusion that we should be able to build entire systems based on the network organizing principles used by the nervous system. The human brain is at least a factor of 1 billion more efficient than our present digital technology, and a factor of 10 million more efficient than the best digital technology that we can imagine [9]. The unavoidable conclusion is that we still have something fundamental to learn from the brain and neurobiology about new ways and much more effective forms of computation representation.

By anatomical and biophysical point of view, estimated adult human brain total neuron number is 86 ± 81 billions and equal numbers of neuronal and nonneuronal cells make the human brain an isometrically scaled-up primate brain [10]. Each of these neurons can have up to 15,000 connections with other neurons via synapses [11]. About 19% of all brain neurons are located in the cerebral cortex (including subcortical white matter) with average cell density (CD) about $10^7/cm^2$ and synapse density (SD) about $10^{11}/cm^2$, while about 80% of all brain neurons are in the cerebellum. The human cerebral cortex is 2 to 4 mm (0.079 to 0.157 in) thick. On the average, adult humans have about 100 trillion (10^{14}) synapses (up to 1,000 trillion, by some estimates). Such an enormous figure gives just one indication of the astonishing flexibility of our brains, as every one of these synapses can be modified in order to let you learn something new.

A systematic account of exploratory neuroscientific research that would allow researchers to form new concepts and formulate general principles of brain connectivity, and to combine connectivity studies with manipulation methods to identify neural entities in the brain can be found in Haueis [12]. The field of connectomics combines such advances with classic methods (e.g., micro-anatomy and electrophysiology) to uncover organizational principles of the human brain. In contrast to hypothesis-driven, task-based research, the discovery science of connectomics often uses data-driven methods and large sample sizes [2, 13].

Human brain is a network of networks [14], but current experimental designs of functional connectivity studies do not provide necessary conditions for identifying large scale networks nor do the different clustering algorithms in such studies equally account for gradually changing connectivity profiles [15]. The validity and integration of system-level results will depend on which organizational units can be experimentally established at the mesoscopic scale. The human brain exhibits several attributes of an efficient network organization, such as a cost-effective small-world modular organization, where there is a strong concentration of connectivity within confined modular subsystems that co-exists with the existence of short global communication routes across the entire brain [16].

There is, however, relatively little knowledge about how microscale molecular processes implement the computations that underlie cognition and ultimately cause observable mesoscale and macroscale behavior. Optogenetic devices may supersede current measurement technologies in a few years with more precise tools for intervention and new options for recording [17], but for now we can still depend on a relatively mature technology accelerated by Moore's law to sustain us for the near future.

One factor that renders the brain difficult to understand is that it consists of ever-changing patterns in the connectome referred to as neuroplasticity [10]. In the case of the brain, the more it is used, the more pronounced a given neural pathway becomes. The pattern at any given moment only exists within that moment; it has never been the same and it never will be. Such constant change and complexity makes it extremely challenging to examine each neuron individually, so scientists simplify them into clusters based on function to examine its fibers as electrochemical rivers. Each fiber is an electrochemical river made up of about 200 to 300 million neurons. This shows the flow of information. Therefore, function also forms anatomy. But a look into the system made up of the neurons would offer a much more detailed image than this. Each fiber here is actually merged functional units.

Most current 2-D microelectrode arrays are on the order 5–10 μm and the latest 3-D optogenetic array from Boyden's lab is on the order of a couple of millimeters with about 150 μm resolution along one of the x or y axis and perhaps a tenth of that along the z axis and the other x or y axis [17]. Current optogenetic data indicate that the neurons within the functional unit receive common inputs, have common outputs, are interconnected, and may well be constituted by fundamental computational sub-units of the cerebral cortex [18]. According to [19], a sub-unit is on the order of 28–40 μm and there are about 2×10^8 sub-units in human brain. Estimates of number of neurons in a sub-unit range from 80–100 neurons in the average and computerized image analysis reveals a fairly consistent range for sub-unit size in humans, between 35 and ∼60 μm, depending on the area examined [19]. In 2000, a study utilizing a novel approach provided a mean value of 80 μm for "inter sub-unit distance" and a 50 μm width for sub-units [20].

Taking into consideration all previous cerebral cortex data, the sub-unit average size is about 6×10^{-12} [m³]. Assuming the sub-unit as networked computational unit (NCU), we can model it as simple harmonic oscillator (SHO) with a resonant frequency of 20 [Hz] and a radius R in Modified Phase Space. In this way, assuming a strength of magnetic field H = ½ picotesla = ½ 10^{-12} T [kg·s^{-2}·A^{-1}] [21], we can estimate the SHO equivalent energy of about 10^{-31} J [J or Kg (m/s)²], corresponding to an associated, hypothetical quantum state. This result effectively indicate that the energy process is at the quantum scale level, and that a small change ΔR in R can give a significant change in the related energy $f(R^2)$.

Understanding the human neural coding remains a major challenge of the 21st century [18] to arrive to the fundamental code unit of the brain (FCU) [22]. In fact, one major goal of computational neuroscience is to produce predictive mesoscale theories of biological computation that bridge the gap between the cells and behaviors of complex organisms thereby explaining how the former give rise to the latter. There is nothing that is done in the nervous system that we cannot emulate with electronics if we understand the principles of neural information processing right [23].

The final goal is to understand how self-awareness emerges when individuals recognize and correct mistakes and investigate the unknown by themselves. What we call "consciousness" may result from specific types of information-processing computations, physically realized by the hardware of the brain. It differs from other theories in being resolutely computational; we surmise that mere information-theoretic quantities [24] do not suffice to define consciousness unless one also considers the nature and depth of the information being processed. Although centuries of philosophical dualism have led us to consider consciousness as unreducible to physical interactions, the empirical evidence is compatible with the possibility that consciousness arises from nothing more than specific computations [23, 25–27]. Once we can spell out in computational terms what the differences may be in humans between conscious and unconsciousness, coding that into computers may not be that hard.

To a certain extent, some types of AI can evaluate their actions and correct them responsively. But do not expect to meet self-aware AI anytime soon. While we are quite close to having machines that can operate autonomously (self-driving cars, robots that can explore an unknown terrain, etc.), we are very far from having conscious machines. The key change performance factors are knowledge and education, solving the major "information double-bind" (IDB) problem in current most advanced research laboratory and instrumentation system, just at the inner core of human knowledge extraction by experimentation in current science [28]. It will be the fundamental dichotomy distinguishing classic, contemporary education from a new one, based on a more reliable control of learning from uncertainty and uncertainty management; discriminating information building on sand (in the past) from information building on rock (in the future).

Therefore, to minimize or overcome major system limitations and to arrive much closer to human-centered symbiotic system (HCSS) [29], we need to extend our traditional system model representation understanding first, taking into consideration even quantum field theory (QFT) main interactions conveniently. We need to integrate our current neural coding reductionist interpretation with new neuroscience insights [30, 31]. We will refer to these new systems generically as neuromorphic anticipatory learning system (ALS) [32]. There is nothing that is done in the nervous system that we cannot emulate with electronics if we understand the principles of neural information processing right.

Taking into consideration recent neurophysiological findings, differently from the past, it is much better to consider ontological uncertainty [1] as an emergent phenomenon out of a complex system, arriving to the basic schema for Ontological Uncertainty Management (OUM) System [1]. Then, our dynamic ontological perspective can be thought as an emergent, natural trans-disciplinary reality level (TRL) [33] out of, at least, a non-dual dichotomy of two fundamental coupled irreducible complementary computational subsystems: (A) reliable predictability subsystem and (B) reliable unpredictability respectively [1].

In fact, although there are many sources of information and uncertainty for human [34], two basic areas of uncertainty that are fundamentally different from each other were recognized as traditional reference knowledge since the beginning of the past century: "natural uncertainty" and "epistemic uncertainty." We already discussed natural uncertainty in previous papers [35, 36]. Here we like to focus epistemic uncertainty in general first. As a matter of fact, all main epistemic uncertainty sources can be referred to three core conceptual areas:

(a) Entropy Generation (Clausius-Boltzmann).
(b) Heisenberg Uncertainty Principle.
(c) Gödel Incompleteness Theorems.

Specifically, we like to deepen the Heisenberg Uncertainty Principle (previous conceptual area b) related to the quantum uncertainty management of single and many-particle systems, with analogies at personal and social level, to get useful suggestion to develop more resilient and antifragile HCSS in the near future.

Therefore, to minimize or overcome major system limitations and to arrive much closer to fourth generation adaptive learning, deep learning (DL), deep thinking (DT) and real machine intelligence systems, we need to extend our traditional system model representation understanding first, taking into consideration quantum field theory (QFT) main interactions conveniently.

3 Heisenberg Uncertainty Principle (HUP)

The original Heisenberg Uncertainty Principle (HUP) states that there is an intrinsic limit to the precision with which we can simultaneously know two complementary variables of a quantum system. For example, the concepts of exact position and exact velocity together have no meaning in nature. The more precisely that you know the position of a particle, the less precisely you can know its momentum, and vice versa. In quantum physics, the space-time distribution of matter and energy has a coarse-grained structure which allows its representation as an ensemble of quanta (particle representation). The local phase invariance is shown to hold if a field exists which is connected to the space-time derivatives of the phase. In the case of a system made up of electrically charged components (nuclei and electrons of atoms), as, for instance, a biological system, this is just the electromagnetic (e.m.) potential A_μ, where μ is the index denoting the usual four space-time coordinates $x_0 = ct$, x_1, x_2, x_3 [37, 38].

Let us, first of all, realize that in quantum physics the existence of gauge fields, such as the e.m. potential, dictated by the physical requirement that the quantum fluctuations of atoms should not be observable directly, prevents the possibility of having isolated bodies. For this reason, the description of a physical system, traditionally, is given in terms of a matter field, which is the space-time distribution of atoms/molecules, coupled to the gauge field with the possible supplement of other fields describing the nonelectromagnetic "granularity" interactions, such as the chemical forces.

When we try to locate an electron we must throw light on it (e.m. radiation), and that disturbs either its position or its momentum. If we use short-wave light to get the position accurately, the large energy of the light disturbs the velocity; if we use long-wave light of low energy we get a less accurate estimate of position. The product of these two inaccuracies or errors is a "unit of uncertainty," and this unit has the same formulation, MV times L, as Planck's quantum of action, where M is mass, V is velocity and L is length. The more precisely the position L of some particle is determined, the less precisely its momentum MV can be known, and vice-versa. This uncertainty, which is the inability of the observer to predict what is going to happen, is the freedom of what is observed to initiate a new action. Thus the uncertainty of the quantum of action is, or if you prefer, allows, "purpose." The original heuristic argument that such a limit should exist was given by German theoretical physicist Werner Karl Heisenberg in 1927, 25 years after the quantum of action was discovered, after whom it is sometimes named, as the "Heisenberg Uncertainty Principle" [39].

The HUP does not just underpin the foundations of quantum mechanics, it also explains phenomena across science such as the stability of stars and the phenomenon of electric currents. We like to show that HUP can originate three different operative interpretations or lines of thought that give rise to three original, consistent physics interpretations, with no contradiction to one another. Even better, they can be thought complementary at arbitrary multiscale and we are free to use them, according to the specific energy and complexity nature of the problem we need to solve.

3.1 First HUP Interpretation

The first HUP interpretation is the classical one for single particle isolated system that is found in every traditional quantum physics book, like previous SHO in Sect. 2. It starts from observing that Planck's quantum of action "h" $= A$, the "unit of uncertainty," is given by MV times L, where M is mass, $V = L/T$ is velocity, L is position and T is time. It considers Position (L) and Momentum (MV) as the fundamental components for physical representation (conjugate variables) and the Planck's quantum of action as the "unit of uncertainty." A related equation looks like the following:

$$\Delta L\, \Delta MV \geq 1/2 \tag{1}$$

One of the more salient and beautiful insights of the HUP is that the relationship between position and momentum is the same as the relationship between sound and frequency. This insight increases our knowledge of how the world works by telling us that deep down, on the smallest levels, everything is made up of waves. If we describe a physical phenomenon in terms of frequency F ("cycles per second"), and we assume that time T is continuous, under the "continuum hypothesis" (CH) assumption, we can calculate the associated general (unstructured) Energy (E) (we know that frequency and energy are related by a simple equation and therefore we can obtain the corresponding energy). Vice-versa, we can start from known general Energy (E) and compute the system Position (L) or its Momentum (MV) "approximately" (by statistical estimation, obtaining an "approximated approximation"). In fact, position and momentum will never be known exactly at the same time. In other words, we can use a continuum representation support system with uncertainty associated to it. From this uncertainty, the well-known "measurement problem" in traditional Science originated.

It is not much of a step to interpret the unit of uncertainty as either "incompleteness" or "opportunity," and thus see entropy and chance as the basic properties of our representation of the cosmos. On that basis scientists have developed a formal understanding based on general rules and statistical algorithms for research inquiry and advancement. Statistical and applied probabilistic theory became the core of classic scientific knowledge and engineering applications at system macroscale level in the past centuries (Science 1.0 approach). It was applied to all branches of human knowledge under the CH assumption, reaching highly sophistication development, and a worldwide audience. Many "Science 1.0" researchers and scientists up to scientific journals assume naively, till nowadays, it is the only ultimate language of Science and it is the traditional instrument of risk-taking at system macroscale level.

Unfortunately, in a continuum-discrete arbitrary multi-scale modeling environment, quite often the "statistical veil" can be quite opaque computationally, and misplaced precision leads to information dissipation and confusion [40].

3.2   Second HUP Interpretation

The second HUP line of thought, related to single particle system interaction, starts from observing that Planck's quantum of action "h," the "unit of uncertainty" or "unit of action" = A, can be given by Kinetic Energy (KE) = $(1/2) M V^2 = (1/2) M (L/T)^2$ times Time (T). Please, note that this time "action" A is Kinetic Energy (KE) times Time (T) and the conjugate variables are time and energy. A related equation looks like the following:

$$\Delta KE \, \Delta T \geq 1/2 \qquad\qquad (2)$$

What does that mean?

It means that action A is a count of so many "cycles per second" (F = frequency) associated with energy (usually, we can forget about the energy because we know that frequency and energy are related by a simple equation and therefore we can calculate the corresponding energy). But this time, we need to be more precise than before. When we say "know the frequency," we always know it as "so many cycles per second," but we do not know, as human beings, fractions of a second phenomenologically in Nature.

Like counting the turns of a corkscrew, we do not know which way the tip of the corkscrew will point. The difference between the count of whole turns and the fraction of a turn left over is the basis of any counting system, like the well known Decimal System. The count in "units" of 10 (or 100 or 1000, etc.) is called "modulo"; what is left is the "residue." Thus the number 73 is modulo 7, residue 3. Thus the residue is the fraction of a whole cycle.

Thus if the time is given as 5:14 p.m., it is 5 h plus 14 min, or 14/60 of an hour. In other words, we must use a discrete representation support system, under the "discreteness hypothesis" (DH) assumption to capture system properties by "exact approximation" [41]. This approach permits us to correlate the quantum of action A to timing, by which is meant a choice of the "exact" time T to hit the ball or pull the trigger. This property is the fundamental tool to deal with system at nanoscale level and beyond.

A tennis player hits the ball in such a way as to direct it where the opponent cannot return it, but he can only control its direction by the time he hits it. Assuming a right-handed player, if he hits it too soon it will go to the left; if he hits it too late it will go to the right. He must hit it at exactly the right time to get it where he wants it to go. Thus the choice of timing is the ultimate dimension of action or "choice of direction." We can conclude that action A is "directed energy" (DE).

Thus, according to present interpretation, the ultimate constituent of the cosmos is not generic, unstructured Energy (E), but "structured energy," Directed Energy (DE). It is not much of a step to translate DE as "purpose," and thus see purpose and syntropy as the basic constituents of our representation of the cosmos this time [42]. Syntropy produces a continuous increase in complexity through the action of attractors that emanate from the future and provides systems with their purpose and design. Rather than generating disorder via increasing differentiation, syntropy draws individuals and systems together by their common characteristics and goals.

The Universe is not a mechanical system of matter only. It operates like a cosmic network that runs on and is connected by information. Information "in-forms" and underlies all of the physical world, including the human body. Syntropy determines our purpose, our identity, our consciousness [43], or Self, which is small and cohesive, whereas entropy is the diverging outside Universe inflating towards infinity. In a way, syntropy can be regarded as the life force that emanates from the unifying action of something which can be called "love" by humans [44].

3.3   Third HUP Interpretation

Intermolecular interactions in living beings take place not as individual and independent events, but as components of a collective net of related events. The issue of these collective dynamics with related bio-communications can be found in the settings of QFT. The interrelation is comprised of a mutual phase agreement between molecules that are tuned with an electromagnetic field of their own production [45]. In fact, according to the principle of complementarity, there is also a third system representation of the HUP for multiple-particle system interactions, where the phase assumes a precise value. This representation which focuses on the wave-like system features cannot be assumed simultaneously with the particle representation. The relation between these two representations is expressed by the uncertainty relation, similar to the HUP relation between Position and Momentum. This time we have:

$$\Delta N\, \Delta \varphi \geq 1/2 \tag{3}$$

connecting the uncertainty of the number of quanta (particle structure of the system) ΔN and the uncertainty of the system phase (which describes the rhythm of fluctuation of the system) $\Delta \varphi$. Consequently, the two representations we have introduced above correspond to the two following extreme cases.

First Asymptotic Case, $\Delta N = 0$

If $\Delta N = 0$, the number of quanta is well defined, so that we obtain an atomistic description of the system, but lose the information on its capability to fluctuate, since $\Delta \varphi$ becomes infinite. This choice corresponds to the usual description of objects in terms of the component atoms/molecules, considered by Classical Physics, where objects interact by exchanging energy. These exchanges are connected with the appearance of forces. Since energy cannot travel faster than light, this interaction obeys the traditional principle of causality.

Second Asymptotic Case, $\Delta\varphi = 0$

If $\Delta\varphi = 0$, the phase is well defined, so that we obtain a description of the movement of the system, but lose the information on its particle-like features which become undefined since ΔN becomes infinite. Such a system having a well-defined phase is termed coherent in the physical jargon. A common phase arises among different objects because of their coupling to the quantum fluctuations and hence to an e.m. potential. In this case there is no propagation of matter and/or energy taking place, and the components of the system "talk" to each other through the modulations of the phase field travelling at the phase velocity, which has no upper limit and can be larger than c, the speed of light.

The process of the emergence of coherent structures out of a crowd of independent component particles has been investigated in the last decades and is presently quite well understood [46, 47]. The presence of this field has received experimental corroboration [48, 49]. Therefore a weak e.m. field is always present in system about equilibrium, where it often merely produces variation around the mean by usual performance measurements.

4 Quantum Waves and Knowledge Representation

The concept of quantum waves stems from a proposal in the early 1920s by a graduate student of physics at Sorbonne University, Prince Louis de Broglie. Reasoning that Einstein's $E = mc^2$ relates mass to energy and that Planck's equation relates energy to the frequency of waves, mass should have a wavelike nature. So, in his doctoral thesis he put forth the notion that a moving electron should have a wave associated with it. His examiners at the Sorbonne found the idea that particles are also waves too fantastic to be taken seriously, though they accepted his thesis defense as a virtuoso performance. But his thesis adviser, Paul Langevin, was not given to passivity; he spoke to Einstein by telephone about the matter and arranged that an extra copy of de Broglie's thesis be sent to him. He did not have to wait very long; Einstein wrote back, "Er hat eine Ecke des grossen Schleiers gelüftet" (German Transl.: "He has lifted a corner of the great veil").

Thus started wave mechanics, a vigorous branch of physics, which within a few years, through Erwin Schrödinger's mathematics, would acquire enormous explanatory and predictive power. Schrödinger's equation describes in probabilistic terms the evolution of the wave, the so-called *"wave function"*, Ψ (pronounced "psi"), which gives all the possible alternatives that are open to a particle system. One of the great achievements of twentieth-century physics, this equation touches nearly all aspects of matter: the structure of the atom and nucleus, the mechanical properties of solids, the conduction of electricity, and the chemical bonds. Today the notion that matter, all fundamental particles of matter, including the quarks, has a wavelike character has firmly taken hold. Much of modern physics is built on it, and on the practical side it yielded the transistor, the superconductor, television, and so on and on.

But why then do we experience matter as something so stiff and sturdy, and not as waves? De Broglie's equation provides a simple answer: the wavelengths are extremely small; they are proportional to Planck's constant, a minuscule number. Matter waves are therefore unnoticeable and unperceivable by our rational mind, at macroscale level, in our day-to-day world. But they do exist, even if they cannot be measured by our current, limited precision instrumentation!

About a century ago, the presence of super weak electromagnetic emission (SWEME) in living organisms was revealed [50, 51]. Unfortunately, even the most sensitive equipment of our time is not yet able to directly detect an objects emission several minutes after its initial excitation. The core problem concerns the precision with which measurement on quantum resonant systems can be used to estimate quantities that appear as classic parameters in the theory at macroscale level, for example time, displacement, rotation, external fields, etc., to overcome the information double-bind (IDB) problem, for reliable and effective quantum knowledge extraction by current scientific experimental set-up [25]. Even our computational information contemporary classic systemic tools (developed under the positivist reductionist paradigm) are totally unable to capture and to tell the difference between an information-rich message (optimally encoded message) and a random jumble of signs that we call "noise" (they are quite fragile). Furthermore, traditional digital computational resources are still unable to capture and to manage not only the full information content of a single Real Number R, but even Rational Number Q is managed by information dissipation (e.g. finite precision machine, truncating, rounding, etc.) In fact, current Number Theory and modern Numeric Analysis use LTR (Left-To-Right) mono-directional interpretation only for numeric group generator and relations, so information entropy generation cannot be avoided in current computational algorithm and application [41]. How does it come we scientists (statisticians) are still in business without having worked out a definitive solution to the problem of the logical relationship between experience and knowledge?

For the moment we wish simply to emphasize the deep tension in our present world between science and experience. In our present world science is so dominant that we give it the authority to explain even when it denies what is most immediate and direct, our everyday, immediate experience. Thus most people would hold as a fundamental truth the scientific account of matter/space as collections of atomic particles, while treating what is given in their immediate experience, with all of its richness, as less profound and true. Yet when we relax into the immediate bodily wellbeing of a sunny day or of the bodily tension of anxiously running to catch a bus, such accounts of space/matter fade into the background as abstract and secondary. When it is cognition or mind that is being examined, the dismissal of experience becomes untenable, even paradoxical. The tension comes to the surface especially in cognitive science because cognitive science stands at the crossroads where the natural sciences and the human sciences meet. It is only by having a sense of common ground between cognitive science and human experience that our understanding of cognition can be more complete and reach a satisfying level [34]. The manifestations of cognitivism are nowhere more visible than in artificial intelligence (AI), which is the literal construal of the cognitivist hypothesis.

Over the years many interesting theoretical advances and technological applications have been made within this orientation, such as expert systems, robotics, and image processing. These results have been widely publicized, and so we need not digress to provide specific examples here. Even though in theory the symbolic level of cognitivism is compatible with many views about the brain, in practice almost all of neurobiology (and its huge body of empirical evidence) has become permeated with the cognitivist, information-processing perspective. More often than not, the origins and assumptions of this perspective are not even questioned. Within our Western tradition, phenomenology was and still is the philosophy of human experience, the only extant edifice of thought that addresses these issues head-on. But above all, it was and still is philosophy as theoretical reflection. In most of the Western tradition since the Greeks, philosophy has been the discipline that seeks to find the truth, including the truth about the mind, purely by means of abstract, theoretical reasoning. Even philosophers who critique or problematize reason do so only by means of arguments, demonstrations, and, especially in our so-called postmodern era, linguistic exhibitions (i.e., by means of abstract thought).

Therefore, to try to be less wrong that in the past, to capture the full information content of any elementary symbolic representation, it is necessary to conceive a "quadratic support space" at least. As an operative example in human knowledge structuring and computer science modeling and simulation, we can start to divide human experience into two, nondual, irreducible, interacting concepts or parts, "Application" and "Domain", in the sense that experience is always gained when an Application is developed to act within a Domain, and a Domain is always investigated by a developed Application. In terms of ultimate truth, a dichotomy of this sort has little meaning but it is quite legitimate when one is operating within the classic mode used to discover or to create a world of "immediate appearance" by narration. In turn, both Domain and Application can be thought of as being either in "simple mode" (SM, linearly structured, technical, unfolded, etc.) or in "complex mode" (CM, non-linearly or quantum structured or unstructured, non-technical, folded, etc.) Representation, as defined in Fiorini [52].

The SM Application or Domain represents the world primarily in terms of "immediate appearance", whereas a CM Application or Domain sees it primarily as "underlying process" in itself. CM is primarily inspirational, imaginative, creative, intuitive; feeling rather than facts predominate initially. "Art", when it is opposed to "Science 1.0" is "feeling transmission" rather than "data transmission." It does not proceed by data, reason or by laws. It proceeds by emotion, feeling, intuition and aesthetic resonance. The SM, by contrast, proceeds by data, reason and by laws, which are themselves underlying forms of rational thought and behavior. Therefore, we can assume, for now, to talk about human experience by referring to SM and CM, Application and Domain, according to the Four-Quadrant Scheme (FQS) of Fig. 1.

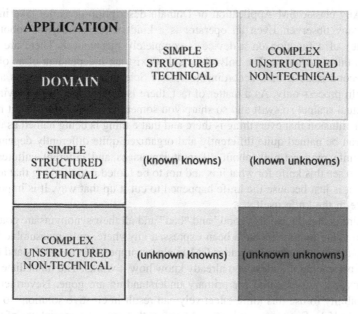

Fig. 1. Four-Quadrant Scheme (FQS) for Application and Domain.

SM is straightforward, unadorned, unemotional, analytic, economical, and carefully proportioned. Its purpose is not to inspire emotionally, but to bring order out of chaos and make the "unknowns known." It is not an aesthetically free and natural style. It is "esthetically restrained." Everything is under control. Its value is measured in terms of the skill with which this control is maintained. From the CM point of view, the SM often appears predictable, dull, awkward, limited and ugly. Everything is in terms of pieces and parts and components and relationships. Nothing is figured out until it is run through the computer a dozen times. Everything has got to be measured and proved. By a SM point of view, however, CM has some appearances of its own; irrational, erratic, unpredictable, untrustworthy, sometime frivolous, etc. By now these battle lines should sound a little familiar. This is the source of current conflict and trouble between the usual two human dominant cultures! Human beings and researchers tend to think and feel exclusively in one mode or the other and in so doing tend to misunderstand and underestimate what the other mode is all about. But no one is willing to give up the truth as he/she sees it, and as far as we know, quite a few individuals now living have been developing any real reconciliation of these truths or modes, which is mandatory to arrive to the new Science 2.0 worldview.

There is no social, formal shared point at which these visions of reality are unified at present. But if you can keep hold of the most obvious observation about SM Application or Domain, some other peculiarities can be observed which are not apparent at first, and which can help to provide and to let us understand a convenient unification point.

The first is that in the traditional Science 1.0 approach, apart from the recent areas of risk analysis within disciplines and computer security, an interacting observer is missing. Any classic SM Application or Domain description does not take into consideration any observer. Even an operator is a kind of personalityless robot whose performance of a function on a device is completely mechanical. There are no real subjects in this description. The only objects that exist are independent of an observer.

The second issue is that, according to classic Science 1.0, dichotomy is a simple cut-and-split process only. As a matter of fact, there is an arbitrary knife moving here: an intellectual scalpel so swift and so sharp you sometimes do not even see it moving. You get the illusion that everything is there and that a thing is being named as it exists. But they can be named quite differently and organized quite differently depending on how the knife moves (think about different languages and different cultures). It is important to see this knife for what it is and not to be fooled into thinking that anything is the way it is just because the knife happened to cut it up that way. It is important to concentrate in the knife itself.

The third is that the words "good" and "bad" and all their synonyms are completely absent. No value judgments have been expressed anywhere, only measurable fact.

The fourth is that anything under CM is almost impossible to understand directly without experiencing it, unless you already know how it works. The immediate surface impressions that are essential for primary understanding are gone. Nevertheless, the masterful ability to use this knife effectively can result in creative solutions to the SM and CM split [53]. For now, you have to be aware that even the special use of the term SM and CM are examples of this knifemanship. Of course, we can apply our dichotomizing process in a recursive way to achieve any precision we like.

5 Discussion

As you saw, we got three consistent physical representation systems. The first one, for single isolated particle, under the "continuum hypothesis" (CH) assumption, considers Position (P) energy conservation as the fundamental components for useful physical representation and the Planck's quantum of action A as the "unit of uncertainty." This worldview is the core of classic scientific knowledge and engineering applications at system macroscale level, inherited from the past century (Science 1.0 approach).

The second one, related to single particle system interaction, under the "discreteness hypothesis" (DH) assumption, assumes Time (T) as the fundamental component for choice of direction and the Planck's quantum of action as DE or "unit of purpose." It allows to build combinatorial pre-spatial arithmetic scheme to overcome and minimize the traditional statistical modeling veil opacity, typical of Science 1.0 approaches. It is the fresh, elementary QFT (quantum field theory) approach offered by Computational Information Conservation Theory (CICT) [36].

The third one, for multiple-particle system interactions, can be treated under CH or DH, according to your system representation and desired results. If the number of particles or quanta is well defined, we obtain an atomistic description of the system, but we lose the information on its capability to fluctuate. If the phase is well-defined, we obtain a description of the movement of the system, but we lose the information on its particle-like features which become undefined since ΔN becomes infinite.

Unfortunately, over the centuries, the above two large scientific research areas (CH based and DH based) have followed separate mathematical development paths with no or quite little, inconsistent synergistic coupling. That is the main reason why QFT is still mostly overlooked by traditional scientific and engineering researchers for arbitrary multi-scale system modeling, from system nano-microscale to macroscale. Unfortunately, the "statistical veil" can be very opaque computationally, in a continuum-discrete arbitrary multi-scale environment, and misplaced precision leads to information dissipation and confusion.

The CICT framework can help us to develop strategies to gather much more reliable experimental information from single experiment and to conserve overall system information. In this way, coherent representation precision leads to information conservation and clarity. The latest CICT claim has been that the "external" world real system physical manifestation properties and related human perception are HG (hyperbolic geometry) scale related representation based, while Euclidean approximated locally.

Science wants to know the origin of the universe, which it currently assumes, according to Science 1.0 interpretation, was the Big Bang. It seeks for fundamental particles, looks for invariants or for pulsars billions of light years away, and tries to fill the vacuum left by philosophy and religion, much as the wren, a small bird, fills the birdhouse made for large birds with space-filling straw.

Today, to solve complex, arbitrary multiscale system problems, we need a unified, integrated mathematical language that can offer an effective and convenient universal framework, by considering information not only on the statistical manifold of model states, but also on the combinatorical manifold of low-level discrete, directed energy generators and empirical measures of noise sources, related to experimental high-level overall perturbation. As a matter of fact, to grasp a more reliable representation of reality, researchers and scientists need two intelligently articulated hands; both statistic and combinatorical approach, synergistically articulated by natural coupling; let's say we need a fresh "Science 2.0" approach. That is the basic proposal of CICT for Human-Centered Symbiotic System Science (HCSSS) [29]. The interested reader eager to dig deeper into Symbiotic Autonomous System (SAS), Symbiotic System Science (SSS), HCSSS and HCSS is referred to [29, 54–56].

6 Conclusion

According to CICT, the fundamental play of human information observation interaction with an external world representation is related by the different manifestation and representation properties of a unique fundamental computational information structuring principle: the Kelvin Transform (KT) [57]. KT is key to efficient scale related information representation, structuring "external space" information to an "internal representation" and vice-versa by projective-inversive geometry [25].

The final goal of HCSSS is to formulate theoretical and practical knowledge required to maximize security, human welfare and individual wellbeing of all humanity in a manner consistent with universal human rights, cultural diversity and civilizational values and what it will mean to live in harmony with Nature. Economic security ensures minimum material needs. Human welfare encompasses a wider range of material and social needs related to safety, health, education, social security and cybersecurity. Individual wellbeing encompasses higher level social, cultural, psychological and spiritual aspirations for freedom of choice, respect, free association, enjoyment, creative self-expression, individual development and self-realization. Sustainability means achieving this in ways that restore the natural systems on which we depend. The objective of economics is not production for its own sake or economic growth for growth's sake. The goal is not to discover immutable, universal, natural laws based on any existing precedent, model or theory, but to identify the laws and first principles of social system suitable for promoting global human welfare and wellbeing.

Values express purpose, intention and commitment, but they are not merely utopian ideals or ethical principles. They represent the highest abstract mental formulations of life principles with immense power for practical accomplishment. They represent the quintessence of humanity's acquired wisdom regarding the necessary foundations for human survival, growth, development and evolution.

Therefore, in order to achieve an antifragile behavior [58, 59], next generation human-made system must have a new fundamental component, able to address and to face effectively the problem of multiscale ontological uncertainty management, in an instinctively sustainable way: active wisdom by design!

Acknowledgements. Author acknowledges the continuous support from the *CICT CORE* Group of Politecnico di Milano University, Milano, Italy, for extensive computational modelling, simulation resources and enlightening talks. Furthermore, the author is grateful to anonymous reviewers for their perceptive and helpful comments, which helped the author substantially improve previous versions of the manuscript.

References

1. Fiorini, R.A.: More effective biomedical experimentation data by CICT advanced ontological uncertainty management techniques. Int. J. Biol. Biomed. Eng. **9**, 29–41 (2015)
2. Sporns, O., Tononi, G., Kötter, R.: The human connectome: a structural description of the human brain. PLoS Comput. Biol. **1**, 245–251 (2005). https://doi.org/10.1371/journal.pcbi. 0010042
3. Deisseroth, K.: Optogenetics. Nat. Methods Comment. (2010). https://doi.org/10.1038/ NMETH.F.324, https://web.stanford.edu/group/dlab/media/papers/deisserothnature2010.pdf
4. Human Connectome Project. http://www.humanconnectomeproject.org/
5. Human Brain Project. https://www.humanbrainproject.eu/en/
6. Markram, H., Muller, E., Ramaswamy, S., Hill, S.L., Segev, I., Schürmann, F., et al.: Reconstruction and simulation of neocortical microcircuitry. Cell **163**(2), 456–492 (2015)
7. Horvitz, H.R.: Worms, life, and death (Nobel lecture). ChemBioChem **4**, 697–711 (2003)
8. Shapshak, P.: Artificial intelligence and brain. Bioinformation **14**(1), 38–41 (2018)
9. Resconi, G.: Geometry of Knowledge for Intelligent Systems. Studies on Computational Intelligence, vol. 407. Springer, Berlin (2013). https://doi.org/10.1007/978-3-642-27972-0
10. Azevedo, F.A.C., et al.: Equal numbers of neuronal and nonneuronal cells make the human brain an isometrically scaled-up primate brain. J. Comp. Neurol. **513**(5), 532–541 (2009)

11. Brotherson, S.: Understanding brain development in young children, FS-609. n.d. NDSU Extension Service, April 2009. http://www.ag.ndsu.edu/pubs/yf/famsci/fs609w.htm
12. Haueis, P.: Meeting the brain on its own terms. Front. Hum. Neurosci. (2014). http://journal.frontiersin.org/article/10.3389/fnhum.2014.00815/full
13. Biswal, B.B., Mennes, M., Zuo, X.-N., Gohel, S., Kelly, C., Smith, S.M.: Toward discovery science of human brain function. Proc. Natl. Acad. Sci. U.S.A. **107**, 4734–4739 (2010). https://doi.org/10.1073/pnas.0911855107
14. Sporns, O.: Networks of the Brain. MIT Press, Cambridge (2011)
15. Sporns, O.: Contributions and challenges for network models in cognitive neuroscience. Nat. Neurosci. **17**, 652–660 (2014). https://doi.org/10.1038/nn.3690
16. Hagmann, P., et al.: Mapping the structural core of human cerebral cortex. PLoS Biol. **6**(7), e159, 1479–1493 (2008)
17. Zorzos, A.N., Scholvin, J., Boyden, E.S., Fonstad, C.G.: Three-dimensional multiwaveguide probe array for light delivery to distributed brain circuits. Opt. Lett. **37**(23), 4841–4843 (2012)
18. Cruz, L., et al.: A statistically based density map method for identification and quantification of regional differences in microcolumnarity in the monkey brain. J. Neurosci. Methods **141**(2), 321–332 (2005)
19. Buxhoeveden, D.P., Casanova, M.F.: The minicolumn hypothesis in neuroscience. Brain **125**(5), 935–951 (2002)
20. Buldirev, S.V., Cruz, L., Gomez-Isla, T., Gomez-Tortosa, E., Havlin, S., Le, R.: Descrimination of microcolumnar ensembles in association cortex and their disruption in Alzheimer and Lewy body dementias. Proc. Natl. Acad. Sci. U.S.A. **97**, 5039–5043 (2000)
21. Blagoev, K.B., et al.: Modelling the magnetic signature of neuronal tissue. Neuroimage **37**, 137–148 (2007)
22. Howard, N., Hussain, A.: The fundamental code unit of the brain: towards a new model for cognitive geometry. Cogn. Comput. **10**(3), 426–436 (2018)
23. Fiorini, R.A.: From computing with numbers to computing with words. In: Howard, N., Wang, Y., Hussain, A., Hamdy, F., Widrow, B., Zadeh, L.A. (eds.) Proceedings of the IEEE 16th International Conference on Cognitive Informatics and Cognitive Computing, pp. 84–91. IEEE Press, New York (2017)
24. Tononi, G., Boly, M., Massimini, M., Koch, C.: Integrated information theory: from consciousness to its physical substrate. Nat. Rev. Neurosci. **17**(7), 450–461 (2016)
25. Fiorini, R.A.: How random is your tomographic noise? A number theoretic transform (NTT) approach. Fundam. Infomaticae **135**(1–2), 135–170 (2014)
26. Wang, Y., et al.: Cognitive intelligence: deep learning, thinking, and reasoning by brain-inspired systems. Int. J. Cogn. Inform. Nat. Intell. **10**(4), 1–21 (2016)
27. Fiorini, R.A.: Brain-inspired systems and predicative competence. In: Howard, N., Wang, Y., Hussain, A., Hamdy, F., Widrow, B., Zadeh, L.A. (eds.) Proceedings of the IEEE 16th International Conference on Cognitive Informatics and Cognitive Computing, pp. 268–275. IEEE Press, New York (2017)
28. Fiorini, R.A.: A cybernetics update for competitive deep learning system. In: Proceedings of the 2nd International Electronic Conference on Entropy and Its Applications. MDPI, 15–30 November 2015. http://sciforum.net/conference/ecea-2/paper/3277
29. Fiorini, R.A.: Human-centered symbiotic system science. In: Soda, P., et al. (eds.) Proceedings of the IEEE ICCI*CC 2019, 18th International Conference on Cognitive Informatics and Cognitive Computing, pp. 286–292. IEEE Press, New York (2019)
30. LeDoux, J.: The Emotional Brain: The Mysterious Underpinnings of Emotional Life. Weidenfeld & Nicolson, Great Britain (1998)

31. LeDoux, J.: Synaptic Self: How Our Brains Become Who We Are. Viking Penguin, New York (2002)
32. Fiorini, R.A., Santacroce, G.F.: Economic competitivity in healthcare safety management by biomedical cybernetics ALS. In: 2013 Proceedings International Symposium, The Economic Crisis: Time for a Paradigm Shift - Towards a Systems Approach, pp. 24–25. Universitat de València, Valencia (2013)
33. Nicolescu, B.: Levels of complexity and levels of reality. In: Pullman, B. (ed.) Proceedings of the Plenary Session of the Pontifical Academy of Sciences on the Emergence of Complexity in Mathematics, Physics, Chemistry, and Biology. Casina Pio IV, Vatican, Pontifical Academy of Sciences, Vatican City, 27–31 October 1992. Princeton University Press, Princeton (1992)
34. Fiorini, R.A.: Evolutive information in the anthropocene era. In: Dodig-Crnkovic, G., Burgin, M. (eds.) Philosophy and Methodology of Information, Part 2. Methodology of Information, pp. 201–261. World Scientific, Singapore (2019)
35. Fiorini, R.A.: From epistemic uncertainty quantification to ontological uncertainty management for system safety and security. In: Proceedings of the IEEE 1st International Forum on Research and Technologies for Society and Industry: Leveraging a Better Tomorrow, Torino, Italy, 16–18 September 2015, pp. 312–319. IEEE Press, Torino (2015)
36. Fiorini, R.A.: Embracing the unknown in intelligent systems. In: Proceedings of the 18th International Conference on Mathematical Methods, Computational Techniques and Intelligent Systems, MAMETICS 2016, Venice, Italy, 29–31 January 2016. WSEAS Press, Venice (2016)
37. Einstein, A.: Über die elektromagnetischen Grundgleichungen für bewegte Körper. Ann. der Phys. **331**, 532–540 (1908)
38. Hestenes, D.: Space-Time Algebra. Gordon and Breach, New York (1966)
39. Cassidy, D.C.: Uncertainty: The Life and Science of Werner Heisenberg. W.H. Freeman and Company, New York (1992)
40. Fiorini, R.A.: Computerized tomography noise reduction by CICT optimized exponential cyclic sequences (OECS) co-domain. Fundam. Inform. **141**, 115–134 (2015)
41. Fiorini, R.A., Laguteta, G.: Discrete tomography data footprint reduction by information conservation. Fundam. Inform. **125**(3–4), 261–272 (2013)
42. Laszlo, E.: Science and the Akashic Field: An Integral Theory of Everything. Amazon Media EU S.à r.l. (2010)
43. Laszlo, E., Tobias, M.: The Tuscany Dialogues: The Earth, Our Future, and the Scope of Human Consciousness. SelectBooks, Incorporated, New York (2018)
44. Di Corpo, U., Vannini, A.: Syntropy: The Spirit of Love. ICRL Press, Princeton (2015)
45. Bono, I., Del Giudice, E., Gamberale, L., Henry, M.: Emergence of the coherent structure of liquid water. Water **4**(3), 510–532 (2012). https://doi.org/10.3390/w4030510
46. Preparata, G.: QED Coherence in Matter. World Scientific, Singapore (1995)
47. Del Giudice, E., Vitiello, G.: Role of the electromagnetic field in the formation of domains in the process of symmetry breaking phase transitions. Phys. Rev. A **74**(2), 1–9 (2006). Article ID 022105
48. Lamb, W.E., Retherford, R.C.: Fine structure of the hydrogen atom by a microwave method. Phys. Rev. **72**(3), 241–243 (1947)
49. Casimir, H.B.G.: On the attraction between two perfectly conducting plates. Proc. K. Ned. Akademie VanWetenschappen B **51**, 793–796 (1948)
50. Gurwitsch, A.A.: A historical review of the problem of mitogenetic radiation. Experientia **44**, 545–550 (1988)
51. Beloussov, L.V., Opitz, J.M., Gilbert, S.F.: Life of Alexander G. Gurwitsch and his relevant contribution to the theory of morphogenetic fields. Int. J. Dev. Biol. **41**, 771–779 (1997)

52. Fiorini, R.A.: Strumentazione Biomedica: Sistemi di Supporto Attivo. CUSL, Collana Scientifica, Milano (1994)
53. De Giacomo, P., Fiorini, R.A.: Creativity mind. Amazon (2019)
54. Fiorini, R.A.: From autonomous systems to symbiotic system science. In: Soda, P., et al. (eds.) Proceedings of the IEEE ICCI*CC 2019, 18th International Conference on Cognitive Informatics and Cognitive Computing, pp. 254–260. IEEE Press, New York (2019)
55. Fiorini, R.A.: Arbitrary multiscale explainable decision-making for symbiotic autonomous systems. Keynote speech. In: IEEE ICCI*CC 2019, 18th International Conference on Cognitive Informatics and Cognitive Computing. Politecnico di Milano, Milano, Italy, 23–25 July 2019, p. 6. IEEE Press, New York (2019)
56. Wang, Y., et al.: On autonomous systems: from reflexive, imperative and adaptive intelligence to autonomous and cognitive intelligence. In: Soda, P., et al. (eds.) Proceedings of the IEEE ICCI*CC 2019, 18th International Conference on Cognitive Informatics and Cognitive Computing, pp. 7–12. IEEE Press, New York (2019)
57. Lützen, J.: Joseph Liouville 1809–1882 – Master of Pure and Applied Mathematics. Springer, Heidelberg (1990). https://doi.org/10.1007/978-1-4612-0989-8
58. Taleb, N.N., Goldstein, D.G.: The problem is beyond psychology: the real world is more random than regression analyses. Int. J. Forecast. 28(3), 715–716 (2012)
59. Taleb, N.N.: Silent Risk: Lectures on Probability, vol. 1, January 2015. https://drive.google.com/file/d/0B8nhAlfIk3QIR1o1dnk5ZmRaaGs/view?pli=1

Implicit Cognition and Understanding Unobserved Human Mind States by Machines

Amy Wenxuan Ding[1,2]($\boxtimes$) (iD)

[1] EMLYON Business School, 23 avenue Guy de Collongue,
69134 Ecully Cedex, France
ding@em-lyon.com
[2] Asia Europe Business School, East China Normal University, Shanghai,
People's Republic of China

Abstract. Humans can unconsciously develop abstract and complex knowledge from the encountered environment stimuli through implicit cognition and learning. In this paper, we examine whether a machine can recognize and establish such an unobserved capability. Using a mobile app for weight loss management to treat obesity as the context, we show that the machine can detect the occurrence of human implicit cognition and identify the dynamics of individual users' unobserved mind states over time. Our empirical testing demonstrates that not all app users engage in implicit cognition and learning. A strong need for weight loss helps develop implicit cognition and learning. The occurrence of implicit learning promotes an activated mind state, and users in the activated state significantly increase their daily steps taken by 57.82% compared to those in the inactivated state when following the health suggestions in the app. Further, a simple home-screen reminder of checking the health suggestions in the app targeting inactivated state users will stimulate implicit learning, and increase their probabilities and time duration in the activated state by 29% and 38.9%, respectively. As a result, generating user mind state-based optimal healthcare interventions in the mobile app is shown to be quite effective.

Keywords: Implicit cognition · Mind · Computational intelligence · Machine awareness

1 Introduction

Implicit cognition and learning plays a significant role in the acquisition of complex knowledge in human brains [6]. It refers to human unconsciously developing abstract, representative knowledge of a complex stimulus environment [8]. Such an acquisition procedure exhibits two key characteristics: (1) it is an unconscious process such that it is unobserved to outside observers; and (2) it produces abstract knowledge from the encountered environment. To understand such an unobserved acquisition process of implicit cognition and learning, researchers often conduct controlled lab experiments. A typical experiment usually consists of an acquisition phase and a test phase. In the acquisition phase, human subjects observe the occurrence of a sequence of rapidly presented events. These event sequences may include a variety of stochastic structures

© Springer Nature Singapore Pte Ltd. 2019
A. Zeng et al. (Eds.): HBAI 2019, CCIS 1072, pp. 170–180, 2019.
https://doi.org/10.1007/978-981-15-1398-5_12

or language grammar structures, which could not be directly observed and is not part of or even remotely similar to the epistemic contents of the typical subject's long-term memory. Subjects are not told when the sequence starts, and they make no prediction responses. In the test phase, some event signals are displayed and the subjects make prediction responses. Researchers examine whether knowledge is acquired through implicit cognition and learning when the subjects are confronted with a stimulus environment in the acquisition phase so that they make a correct or effective response using the acquired knowledge in the test phase. Usually researchers do not know and cannot observe if subjects generate implicit cognition and learning. Therefore, they check the subjects' prediction response rates in the test phase.

In this paper, we replace human researchers with a machine and examine whether a machine – a non-living entity – can discover whether implicit cognition and learning occur in humans, and whether the machine itself generates such an implicit cognition ability. Specifically, we consider a real world situation where humans encounter an environment, and a cognitive machine serves as an observer to watch people's reactions. Humans may (or may not) engage in implicit cognition and learning which are not observed by the cognitive machine. We investigate (1) whether the machine can detect if humans engage in implicit learning; (2) if implicit learning occurs, can the machine identify what implicit knowledge that the human may generate from the stimuli in the environment, and (3) whether the machine itself develops implicit knowledge about unobserved human minds when observing humans' behavior in the environment. Currently, artificial intelligence (AI) and machine learning (ML) often focus on learning from existing observed data (e.g., supervised, unsupervised, deep and reinforcement learning) and ignore unknown unknowns such as the unobserved mechanism that generates these data. For example, given human behavior data, current ML methods *only* focus on finding potential patterns in the data, and do not consider how and why unobserved human minds generate the behavioral data [1, 3]. In fact, behavior data only represents phenomenon rather than essentials, while human minds determine the behaviors.

As AI offers a promising means to increase human and societal well-being, it is critical for a machine to understand human minds in human-machine interactions. Thus, investigating machines' implicit cognition and learning can provide insights on how rich and complex knowledge (i.e., unknown unknowns) is obtained independently of overt, conscious strategies from existing and observed data. This process is ubiquitous in human experiences, but largely ignored in the ML research. We investigate the aforementioned questions in the context of individuals using a mobile app for weight loss management to treat obesity.

This paper is organized as follows. We first describe the characteristics of the application context and related concept definitions. We then present the proposed model on how a machine captures the occurrence of users' unobserved implicit cognition, and how the machine generates an implicit cognition when observing users' behavior. Next, we report empirical test and results, followed by conclusions.

2 Application Context and Important Definitions

Obesity is a major contributor to many chronic diseases including type 2 diabetes, cardiovascular disease, many cancers, and numerous other diseases and conditions. The World Health Organization reports that 1.4 billion adults globally exceed healthy body weight [14]. This rate increases every year, and by 2030 nearly half of the world's adult population will be overweight or obese. In U.S., the projected cost of treating preventable obesity related diseases is expected to increase by $48–66 billion per year [12]. Given the scope of the obesity epidemic, the chronic nature of this condition, and the cost of care, it is urgent and critical to develop effective, efficient, and minimally intrusive treatment approaches [4]. The rapid development of artificial intelligence technologies and mobile applications (apps) provide inexpensive healthcare tools to interact directly with users (or patients), enhance user self-monitoring, motivate users to adhere to treatment protocols, and thereby improve health outcomes while reducing the cost.

Using a mobile app to provide users health intervention for weight loss actually consists of an intertwined cycle of users' offline-online-offline behaviors, reflecting the social cognitive construct of reciprocal causality. Consider a hypothetical case in which a user goes for a one-hour jog one afternoon. After exercising, the user feels increased energy and confidence about doing more to manage weight. The user might then open the mobile app to check sensor-recorded jogging activities (e.g., in terms of calorie or fat reduction, or steps) and then click on and search for more exercise and dietary information. In doing so, the user may be cued, and then subsequently perform other healthy diet and/or physical activities. In this example, the user first performs offline behaviors (i.e., jogging) which are tracked and recorded in the app. This information, displayed in the app, becomes online stimuli that prompt the user to click or browse additional exercise and diet information (i.e., online behavior). Following cumulative exposures to such offline activities and online stimuli, the user is then primed to engage in the suggested diet or physical activity (i.e., offline behavior). This offline-online-offline cycle continues constantly.

Thus far, the AI community in this area focuses on how machine learning can be used to offer personalized health recommendations based on recorded data [2, 7]. Combined with users' preferences and the recorded physical activities in terms of calorie consumption, the app provides *mass* customization and suggests wellness information that the app believes is good to each individual user by implicitly assuming that users' preferences do not change over time. This line of research tends to regard apps as only providing *online* recommendations that prompt offline behaviors, and does not consider whether and how the offline behaviors also prompt subsequent online click or browsing behaviors that, in turn, may elicit further stimuli online.

Obviously, when users access the app, a stimulus environment is structured. Users learn to exploit that structure and their minds may develop an abstract, implicit knowledge from the online information. There is a purported and dynamically evolving unobserved mind state of self-efficacy/motivation for the user's weight loss management due to implicit learning [10, 11]. We label this mind state involving implicit cognition and learning as *activated weight loss engagement*. In reality, after seeing the app information, some users may engage in implicit cognition and learning, and their states of the mind become an activated state concerning weight loss engagement. As a result, they actively respond to health intervention suggestions. However, others may be in an inactivated state where no implicit cognition occurs. Therefore, they are not motivated to follow the suggestions closely.

Furthermore, a user could change from the inactivated state to activated sate from time to time or vice versa, meaning that the occurrence of implicit cognition and learning dynamically changes over time in response to stimuli and information in the app. In any circumstance, if a user stays in an inactivated state and does not respond to health suggestions that the app displays by adjusting her *offline* physical or dietary activities, the effectiveness of health intervention using the app will be low, and a desired weight loss goal may not be achieved [13]. However, this dynamic property of mind states is often ignored by conventional ML methods used in mobile health tools [5, 9]. We propose an innovative model for the machine that observes individual user's *online* browsing behavior in the app and identifies whether implicit learning occurs such that it influences the user's mind state for weight loss engagement. The model then recognizes this unobserved real-time mind state at time t and immediately designs an optimal mind-state based suggestion displayed at time t + 1 to encourage the user to perform the desired weight loss activities *offline* at time t + 1. Our modeling efforts thus offer new knowledge on how AI supported individual-level mind state-based healthcare can be achieved without using other users' information. We show that promoting the occurrence of implicit cognition and learning and remaining in an activated mind state for weight loss engagement can maintain a positive offline-online-offline cycle. Thus, it will increase the effectiveness of the healthcare interventions.

3   The Model

When a user accesses the app, information displayed on the app serves as environmental stimuli S which may influence a person's internal cognitive mind state O. If implicit learning occurs in state O, it may yield abstract knowledge from the induction of the stimuli S in the environment. This implied knowledge then affects her behaviors of offline physical or dietary activities R. If we assume our model resides in the app as a cognitive agent for weight loss management, what the agent can observe is users' physical and dietary activities or weight measures (R) and information displayed in the app (S). Individual user's mind states (O) are not observed. Our goal is to investigate if the agent can detect whether implicit learning occurs, and identify the user's real-time unobserved states of mind (O) when observing S and physical and dietary activities or weight measures R at time t.

Figure 1 displays the logic flow of our agent model, where the solid arrows with numbers (1, .., 5) refer to the sequence of working processes. The cognitive agent consists of three working processes: (a) observation, (b) identification, and (c) mind-state based targeting. An observation process (arrow 1) watches and captures what a user actually does and is exposed to on the app at the page view level. Specifically, this process handles both environmental stimuli information S and the user's observed behaviors R (i.e., the recorded physical and dietary activities or weight measures).

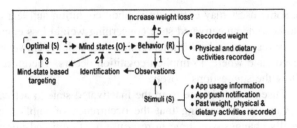

Fig. 1. Model system working processes

Then an identification process (arrow 2) detects whether an implicit cognition and learning occurs by inferring the user's unobserved mind states O at time t. The identification process also performs a simultaneous analysis to identify effects of various observed stimuli S displayed on the app (up to time t) to determine what implied knowledge can be generated to influence individual user's mind states (arrows 3 and 4), which in turn increases the user's offline activities for weight loss (arrow 5). The unobserved implicit cognition under mind state O indicates the user's mental state of activated engagement in weight loss that moderates the impact of stimuli information S on the user's actual behavior R.

Once realizing the user's state of mind, the cognitive agent can generate a mind-state based optimal healthcare intervention at time t + 1 to encourage the user to take a desired offline physical or dietary activity for weight loss. Below is the mathematical treatment of the agent model.

3.1   Mathematical Description

The app's information constitutes a stimulus environment, which conveys meaning to users from which a felt value (i.e., an abstract knowledge) may be developed in the user mind state O. This felt value generated, due to implicit cognition and learning, in user mind state O at time t is unobserved. If we assume that user i unconsciously develops a felt value $U_{io(t+1)}^{j}$ in mind state o at time t + 1 when encountering stimuli information on the app at time t regarding the jth type of physical activity (e.g., a physical/dietary activity), then we have

$$U_{io(t+1)}^{j} = \varphi_{io}U_{iot}^{j} + C_{io}X_{it}^{j} + \varepsilon_{i(t+1)o}^{j}, \varepsilon_{ito}^{j} \sim N[0,\ \sigma^2 I],$$

where subscript o denotes the user's unobserved mind state ($o = 1, \ldots, O$) for user i when accessing the app at page view t. We assume that the mind state o is governed by a first-order hidden Markov process since it is unobserved. X_{it}^{j} corresponds to the perceived stimuli information at page view t from the app. Different users may develop different felt values if implicit learning occurs, when facing the same stimuli on the app at time t. Thus, C_{io} refers to user-and-state specific parameters to capture this user difference. φ_{io} denotes the parameter to capture the effect of individual user's felt value

$\left(U_{iot}^{j}\right)$ at time t. The error terms ε_{ito} are assumed to be distributed as $N[0, \sigma^2 I]$, where I is the identity matrix.

When the unobserved felt value $U_{io(t+1)}^{j}$ is greater than some threshold value (without loss of generality, it is normalized to be zero), we say the user's mind state becomes an activated state which promotes user i to take an offline action $R_{ij(t+1)}$ at time t + 1 such that

$$R_{ij(t+1)} = \begin{cases} 1 & \text{if } U_{io(t+1)}^{j} > 0, \\ 0 & \text{otherwise.} \end{cases} \text{ for } j = 1, \ldots, J.$$

where J refers to the number of different types of individual physical/dietary actions such as walking, eating a low calorie meal, jogging, etc.

As the user's unobserved mind state may change over time, we propose that such a mind state can be captured by a first-order, continuous-time, discrete-state hidden Markov model. We let waiting time represent how long a user will stay in a particular mind state before jumping into another state. The waiting time between transitions (w_{ijt}) from one mind state to another in our continuous-time domain is assumed to follow an exponential function and its probability can be calculated as follows:

$$\Pr\left[w_{ijt}|\gamma_{ijt}\right] = \gamma_{ijto} \exp\left(-w_{ijt} \times \gamma_{ijto}\right)$$

where γ_{ijto} is an intensity parameter for mind state o, and the expected waiting time (until the transition out of the current intent state) is the inverse of this parameter $\left(1/\gamma_{ijto}\right)$.

If a user's mind state changes from one to another, the transition matrix (P_{ijt}) that defines the first-order Markov process is:

$$P_{ijt} = \begin{bmatrix} 0 & P_{ijt12} & \cdots & P_{ijt1O} \\ P_{ijt21} & 0 & \cdots & P_{ijt2O} \\ \vdots & \vdots & \ddots & \vdots \\ P_{ijtO1} & P_{ijtO2} & \cdots & 0 \end{bmatrix}$$

where P_{ijtso} denotes the conditional probability of user i switching to mind state o at time t, given that the previous mind state was s; the rows sum to 1. The diagonal elements equal 0 because the same state transitions (from state o to state o, that is, remaining in state o) can be captured by the waiting time. The transition matrix and the waiting time process will govern the mind state changes. The model is implemented as a hierarchical Bayes model combined with Monte Carlo Markov Chain (MCMC) algorithms.

4 Empirical Testing and Results

Our empirical testing is to verify whether the cognitive agent can detect and infer the occurrence of human unobserved implicit cognition and learning, and whether the cognitive agent itself develops implicit cognition and generates abstract knowledge about human mind states when observing human behavior in the encountered environment. Before reporting the results, we first describe the data set, and then present the model's performance.

4.1 Data Description

The data set consists of 250 overweight users who use a mobile health app to manage their weight loss for a 3-month period. We focus on their daily steps taken. The app displays the user's total and average steps up to pervious day, the steps taken on the current day, and the recommended health intervention (e.g., 20% increase in the average daily steps by far). Thus, the observation information that the agent receives is the stimuli displayed in the app including individual users' past steps, demographics, their clicking behaviors on the app, health interventions received, whether the user follows the intervention, pages viewed in the app, and if the app visit is on a weekend.

On the user demographics, 39.47% and 60.53% of the users are females and males, respectively. The average age is 35.77 with a minimum of 13 and maximum of 60. Out of 250 users, 110 are college employees, 46 are company employees, and 39 are college students. The remaining users' professions include bank staff, government employees, doctors, lawyers, members of non-profit organizations, retirees, etc.

4.2 Results

The results show that implicit learning may not always occur among the app users. When implicit learning occurs, the user's mind state exhibits activated weight loss engagement; otherwise, the user is in the inactivated mind state. On average users have a higher probability (67%) of being in the inactivated state than in the activated state (33%). However, they stay longer in the latter state (4 days) than in the former (2.7 days). After identifying users' states of mind, a simple home-screen reminder message targeting inactivated-state users is quite effective, drastically increasing the user's probability of being in the activated state from 33% to 62% with a significant 29% increase. Also, on average generating a mind-state based intervention to promote implicit cognition reduces the user's stay in the inactivated state from 2.70 days to 1.75 days while increasing her time in the activated state from 4 days to 5.56 days (a 38.9% increase). We find that male users, government employees or retirees, or users aged 50 or above are more likely to be in the activated state than other users, showing that a strong need of weight loss helps develop user implicit cognition and learning.

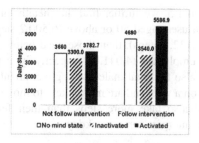

Fig. 2. Impacts of users' mind states

Interestingly, we find that users' mind states with implicit learning significantly moderate the impact of healthcare intervention messages on the daily steps taken. As shown in Fig. 2, when not accounting for user mind states, a user takes 3,660 and 4,680 steps daily when not following and following the health interventions, respectively. However, when user mind states are considered by stimulating the occurrence of implicit learning, activated-state users take dramatically more steps (3,782.7 and 5,586.9 steps in the two above cases) than those in the inactivated state (3,300.0 and 3,540.0 steps). The most noticeable difference between these two groups exists in the case of user following the intervention suggestion (3,540.0 vs. 5,586.9 steps with a 57.8% difference).

As shown in Fig. 3, we also find that the health interventions work differently for female vs. male users in different mind states. Specifically, the results show that, when there is no health intervention, male users tend to take slightly more steps per day than their female counterparts do. Further, users in the activated state take more steps compared to those in the inactivated state regardless of gender. More interestingly, in the presence of the health intervention, male users in the activated state take significantly more steps (6,885.8 steps) than the male users in the inactivated state (3,904.4 steps), with a big increase of 76.4%. This suggests that implicit cognition and learning stimulates users' needs and motive them to take the desired physical activities. Although female users in the activated state also take more steps (4,287.9 steps) than the female users in the inactivated state (3,175.6 steps). Its percentage increase (35.0%) is much lower than that of male users (76.4%). This indicates that health interventions work better for male users, especially when they are in the activated state.

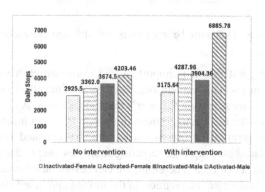

Fig. 3. Difference between female and male users

As shown in Figs. 4 and 5, we further find that health interventions have a significantly larger impact on users aged 50 or above (6,500.2 steps), and users who are government employees (7,132.7 steps), than those aged below 50 (4,673.6 steps) and who are non-government employees (4,041.0), respectively, especially when they are in the activated state. We also find that male users, government employees or retirees, or users aged 50 or above on a weekend are more likely to move from the inactivated to activated mind state, and also take more steps than their female, non-government employees, or younger counterparts on a weekday.

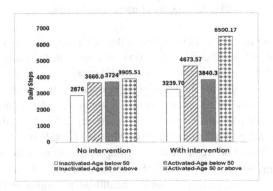

Fig. 4. Difference between age groups

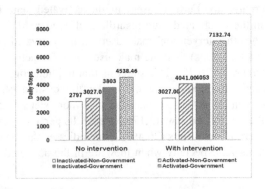

Fig. 5. Difference between users with different profession

These results suggest that it is important to incorporate each user's unobserved mind states of weight loss engagement because they significantly moderate the impact of health intervention messages on the user's daily steps taken. A simple home-screen reminder of checking the health suggestions in the app targeting inactivated-state users is quite effective to prompt the user to move into the activated state. We find that overall the mind-state based optimal targeting increases users' daily steps taken by 19.38% compared to actual data. Therefore, we can design an optimal user mind state-based personalized healthcare intervention in the mobile app based on the dynamics of user mind states in real time, which is proven to be an effective strategy to improve user weight loss management.

In summary, the aforementioned three research questions are all addressed. Specifically, we find that, by checking the dynamic changes of the user's states of mind, the cognitive agent can detect whether a user engages in implicit cognition and learning. Moreover, such unobserved mind states can be inferred by the cognitive agent using limited observations at the individual user level. Thus, in human-machine interactions, a machine can develop an abstract cognition about human unobserved mind states through observing users' behaviors.

4.3   Model Performance Checks

To check the model performance, we considered several benchmark models and conducted a series of model comparison as shown in Table 1. Specifically, the first benchmark model is a simplified and nested model of the proposed model such that individual user heterogeneity and mind states are ignored (labeled as "Agg. model without mind states" in Table 1). The second benchmark model adds individual user heterogeneity only to the first model (labeled as "One-state" model in the table). Next, we allow multiple latent mind states (two-, three-, or four-state models in the table) captured by the hidden Markov process based on the second model. Finally, we use two criterions – the log marginal density (a measure of the model fit to the data, the higher the better) and mean absolute error (a measure of prediction error on the user's daily steps taken, the lower the better), to evaluate the performance of the models. As shown in Table 1, clearly the proposed model with two latent mind states (termed as activated and inactivated engagement states) has the best performance with the highest log marginal density and the lowest mean absolute error. This indicates the importance of accounting for individual user heterogeneity and the existence of the user's multiple unobserved mind states.

Table 1. Model performance

Model	Log marginal density	Mean absolute error
Agg. model without mind states	−2461.52	97.15 (8.03)
One-state	−2375.55	48.92 (4.06)
Two-state	**−2374.47**	**38.97 (3.07)**
Three-state	−2397.82	58.62 (5.09)
Four-state	−2399.85	68.35 (6.01)

5   Conclusions

Humans can unconsciously develop implicit and complex knowledge from the encountered environment through implicit cognition and learning. In this paper, using a mobile app for weight loss engagement as the application context, we show that a machine can also establish such an important capability. Specifically, we present a novel cognitive model that can detect and capture the dynamics of individual users' unobserved mind states over time. Such modeling efforts offer a new method for the machine to establish knowledge about an unknown world such as unobserved real-time human minds, which in turn could enhance individual and social well-being.

References

1. Bacigalupo, R., Cudd, P., Littlewood, C.: Interventions employing mobile technology for overweight and obesity: an early systematic review of randomized controlled trials. Obes. Rev. **14**(4), 279–291 (2013)
2. Boateng, G., Batsis, J.A., Halter, R., Kotz, D.: ActivityAware: an app for real-time daily activity level monitoring on the amulet wrist-worn device. In Proceeding of International Conference on Pervasive Computing and Communication Workshops (2017)
3. Free, C., Phillips, G.: The effectiveness of mobile-health technologies to improve health care service delivery processes: a systematic review and meta-analysis. PLoS Med. **10**(1), e1001363 (2013)
4. Jakicic, J.M., Tate, D.F., Lang, W., Davis, K.K., et al.: Effect of a stepped-care intervention approach on weight loss in adults: a randomized clinical trial. J. Am. Med. Assoc. **307**(24), 2617–2626 (2012)
5. Kumar, S., et al.: Mobile health technology evaluation. Am. J. Prev. Med. **45**(20), 228–236 (2013)
6. Lewicki, P., Czyzewska, M., Hoffman, H.: Unconscious acquisition of complex procedural knowledge. J. Exp. Psychol. Learn. Mem. Cogn. **13**, 523–530 (1987)
7. Manzoni, G.M., Pagnini, F., Corti, S.: Internet-based behavioral interventions for obesity: An updated systematic erview. Clin. Pract. Epidemiol. Ment. Health **7**, 19–28 (2011)
8. Reber, A.S., Lewis, S.: Toward a theory of implicit learning: the analysis of the form and structure of a body of tacit knowledge. Cognition **5**, 333–361 (1977)
9. Riley, W.T.: Health behavior models in the age of mobile interventions: are our theories up to the task? TBM **1**, 53–71 (2011)
10. Spring, B.: Integrating technology into standard weight loss treatment: A randomized controlled trial. JAMA Int. Med. **173**(2), 105–111 (2013)
11. Steinberg, D.M., et al.: The efficacy of a daily self-weighing weight loss intervention using smart scales and e-mail. Obesity (Silver Spring) **21**(9), 1789–1797 (2013)
12. Wang, Y.C., McPherson, K., Marsh, T.: Health and economic burden of the projected obesity trends in the USA and the UK. Lancet **378**(9793), 815–825 (2011)
13. Williams, S.L., French, D.P.: What are the most effective intervention techniques for changing physical activity self-efficacy and physical activity behavior—and are they the same? Health Educ. Res. **26**(2), 308–322 (2011)
14. World Health Organization: Obesity and overweight fact sheet (2013). http://www.who.int/mediacentre/factsheets/fs311/en/

Learning Preferences in a Cognitive Decision Model

Taher Rahgooy[1(✉)] and K. Brent Venable[1,2]

[1] Department of Computer Science, Tulane University, New Orleans, LA, USA
{trahgooy,kvenabl}@tulane.edu
[2] IHMC, Pensacola, FL, USA

Abstract. Understanding human decision processes has been a topic of intense study in different disciplines including psychology, economics, and artificial intelligence. Indeed, modeling human decision making plays a fundamental role in the design of intelligent systems capable of rich interactions. Decision Field Theory (DFT) [3] provides a cognitive model of the deliberation process that precedes the selection of an option. DFT is grounded in psychological principles and has been shown to be effective in modeling several behavioral effects involving uncertainty and interactions among alternatives. In this paper, we address the problem of learning the internal DFT model of a decision maker by observing only his final choices. In our setting choices are among several options which are evaluated according to different attributes. Our approach, based on Recurrent Neural Networks, extracts underlying preferences compatible with the observed choice behavior and, thus, provides a method for learning a rich preference model of an individual which encompasses psychological aspects and which can be used as more realistic predictor of future behavior.

1 Introduction

Preferences play a fundamental role in the understanding of human behavior and in the design of intelligent systems. On the one side, they lie at the core of decision making, a task which is central in describing how humans function in everyday life. On the other hand, qualitative and quantitative measures of satisfaction or utility, are at the basis of optimization in complex problems, a challenge which artificial agents have been successful in tackling.

In this paper we address the challenge of automatically extracting information about an individual's preferences by observing his choice behavior. Preference learning [6,11,15,18] has been a topic of intense investigation by the AI community. This body of work has been crucial in enabling the use of preference models developed in the context of artificial agents as their direct definition is often impractical [6,17]. However, these approaches are less suitable to model human behavior when it comes to decision making. Several properties which are necessary for optimization, such as, transitivity for example, infringe their ability to accommodate behavioral violations of rational principles.

© Springer Nature Singapore Pte Ltd. 2019
A. Zeng et al. (Eds.): HBAI 2019, CCIS 1072, pp. 181–194, 2019.
https://doi.org/10.1007/978-981-15-1398-5_13

On the other hand, in the area of psychology, cognitive computational models have been designed for the purpose of faithfully capturing human behavior in decision making. In these models, the parameters are often defined by hand in order to accurately replicate average behavior of individuals and, to the best of our knowledge, no method capable of automatically inferring them has been proposed.

In this paper we focus on Multialternative Decision Field Theory (MDFT) a dynamic-cognitive approach to decision making based on the idea that the process of deliberation consists of a sequential sampling and accumulation of information over time. MDFT formally generalizes other models of decision making such as the classical multi-attribute decision model [9] and preferential choice model [5,20]. MDFT is able to replicate fundamental aspects of human decision making such as, for example, violation to transitivity, preference reversal under time pressure and the well known effects of similarity, attraction and compromise [3].

In this paper we present a method based on machine learning and, in particular Recurrent Neural Networks, capable of inferring an underlying MDFT model compatible with the observed choice behavior on an individual. A key aspect of our method is that it learns in the presence of uncertainty and partial information. In fact, the training data contains only examples of choices and deliberation times and does not include how attention was allocated to the attributes during the deliberation process. In our experimental results we compare the original and learned models in terms of similarity of both the produced choice distributions and the initial evaluations for the options. As shown in Sect. 7, our learning approach is able to recover a model which is extremely close to the original one in terms of both measures.

Our work is novel as it tackles the problem of learning automatically a cognitive architecture of human decision making. From the preference learning perspective, it provides a way to extract multi-attribute preferences in the context of a complex systems involving stochasticity and bounded rationality. From a cognitive standpoint, our method allows to use these architectures at the level of the individual. Learned MDFT models can be used as behaviorally more accurate predictors of future choices in the context of recommender systems. Our work is also useful in settings where sets of options are presented simultaneously to a user (e.g., option slates). In fact, since the learned model inherits the characteristics of MDFT it is able to predict how choices change if different options are presented as competitors. Moreover, our results are relevant in the context of artificial personal assistants which often need to recover a model of the supported individuals by observing their behavior. The capability of automatically inferring an MDFT model of the user can allow the agent to have more realistic representation of his decision making behavior.

The paper is organized as follows. The first two sections provide background on MDFT and Recurrent Neural Networks. In Sect. 4 we discuss related work. In Sect. 5 we formally define the learning problem which we tackle in Sect. 6. In Sect. 7 we describe the results of our experimental study and we then conclude, in the last section, with future work directions.

2   Multialternative Decision Field Theory

Decision field theory (DFT) is a dynamic-cognitive approach that models human decision making based on psychological principles [3]. DFT models the preferential choice as an accumulative process in which the decision maker attends to a specific attribute at each time to derive comparisons among options and update his preferences accordingly. Ultimately the accumulation of those preferences forms the decision maker's choice. DFT has been extended by [16] to multialternative preferential choice (denoted MDFT, for Multialternative DFT), where an agent is confronted with multiple options and equipped with an initial personal evaluation for them according to different criteria called attributes. For example, a student who needs to chose a main course among those offered by the cafeteria will have in mind an initial evaluation of the options in terms of how tasty and healthy they look. More formally, MDFT, in its basic formulation [16], is composed of:

Personal Evaluation: We assume a set of options $\{o_1, \ldots, o_n\}$ and a set of attributes $\{A_1, \ldots, A_J\}$. The subjective value of option o_i on attribute A_j is denoted by m_{ij} and stored in matrix $\mathbf{M}$ for all options and attributes. In our example, let us assume that the cafeteria options for main course are *Salad (S)*, *Burrito (B)* and *Vegetable pasta (V)* and that the attributes considered are *Taste* and *Health*. Matrix $\mathbf{M}$ containing the student's initial preferences for the three options according to the two attributes could be defined as follows:

$$\mathbf{M} = \begin{bmatrix} 1 & 5 \\ 5 & 1 \\ 2 & 3 \end{bmatrix}$$

In this matrix the rows correspond to the options in order (S, B, V) and the columns to the attributes *Taste* and *Health*. For example, we can see that *Burrito* has a high preference in terms of taste but low in terms of nutritional value.

Attention Weights: Attention weights are used to express how much attention is allocated to each attribute at each particular time t during the deliberation process. We denote them by a one-hot column vector $\mathbf{W}(t)$ where $W_j(t)$ is a value denoting the attention to attribute j at time t. We adopt the common simplifying assumption that, at each point partial, the decision maker attends to only one attribute. Thus, $W_j(t) \in \{0, 1\}, \forall t, j$. In our example, where we have two attributes, at any point in time t, we will have $\mathbf{W}(t) = [1, 0]$, or $\mathbf{W}(t) = [1, 0]$, representing that the student is attending to, respectively, *Taste* or *Health*. In general, the attention weights change across time according to a stationary stochastic process with probability distribution $\mathbf{w}$, where w_j is the probability of attending to attribute A_j. In our example, defining $w_1 = 0.55$ and $w_2 = 0.45$ would mean that at each point in time, the student will be attending *Taste* with probability 0.55 and *Health* with probability 0.45. In other words, *Taste* matters slightly more to this particular student than *Health*.

Contrast Matrix: Contrast matrix $\mathbf{C}$ is used to compute the advantage (or disadvantage) of an option with respect to the other options. For example, $\mathbf{C}$ can be defined by contrasting the initial evaluation of one alternative against the average of the evaluations of the others. In this case, for three options, we have:

$$\mathbf{C} = \begin{bmatrix} 1 & -1/2 & -1/2 \\ -1/2 & 1 & -1/2 \\ -1/2 & -1/2 & 1 \end{bmatrix}$$

At any moment in time, each alternative in the choice set is associated with a **valence** value. The valence for option o_i at time t, denoted $v_i(t)$, represents its momentary advantage (or disadvantage) when compared with other options on some attribute under consideration. The valence vector for n options $o_1, \ldots, o_n$ at time t, denoted by column vector $\mathbf{V}(t) = [v_1(t), \ldots, v_n(t)]^T$, is formed by:

$$\mathbf{V}(t) = \mathbf{C} \times \mathbf{M} \times \mathbf{W}(t) \tag{1}$$

In our example, the valence vector at any time point in which $\mathbf{W}(t) = [1, 0]$, is $\mathbf{V}(t) = [1 - 7/2, 5 - 3/2, 2 - 6/2]^T$.

In MDFT preferences for each option are accumulated across the iterations of the deliberation process until a decision is made. This is done by using the **Feedback matrix**, which defines how the accumulated preferences affect the preferences computed at the next iteration. This interaction depends on how similar the options are in terms of their initial evaluation contained in matrix $\mathbf{M}$. Intuitively, the new preference of an option is affected positively and strongly by the preference it had accumulated so far, it is strongly inhibited by the preference of other options which are similar and this lateral inhibition decreases as the dissimilarity between options increases.

Clearly, the concept of similarity plays a crucial role. A common way to define it is to project the initial evaluations contained in $\mathbf{M}$ on the directions of indifference and dominance respectively [8]. Formally, this is done by defining distance matrix $\mathbf{D} = [D_{ij}]$ where $D_{ij} = (\mathbf{M}_i - \mathbf{M}_j) \times \mathbf{H}_b \times (\mathbf{M}_i - \mathbf{M}_j)^T$ and $\mathbf{H}_b$ is defined as

$$\mathbf{H}_b = \frac{1}{2} \times \begin{bmatrix} b+1 & b-1 \\ b-1 & b+1 \end{bmatrix} \tag{2}$$

where constant b determines the ratio of emphasis on the dominance direction with respect to the indifference direction.

Intuitively, the difference between competitive options will have a larger component along the line of indifference while the difference between two options where one is dominating will have a stronger component along the line of dominance. In order to simulate the common human behavior where dominated options are rapidly discarded during a decision process, more emphasis should be given to differences in the dominance direction than in the indifference direction. This is achieved whenever $b > 1$. At this point matrix $\mathbf{S}$ can be defined by mapping the distance via Gaussian function:

$$\mathbf{S} = \delta - \phi_2 \times \exp\left(-\phi_1 \times \mathbf{D}^2\right) \tag{3}$$

where δ, ϕ_1, ϕ_2 are the identity matrix, the decay parameter, and the sensitivity parameter respectively. The identity matrix δ is used to model positive self feedback. We can also see that when $i \neq j$, and, thus, $\delta_{ij} = 0$, we have a lateral inhibition $-\phi_2 \times \exp\left(-\phi_1 \times \mathbf{D}^2\right)$ which depends on the distance $\mathbf{D}$ between options. In our example, if we set $b = 10$, $\phi_1 = 0.01$ and $\phi_2 = 0.1$ we get the following $\mathbf{S}$ matrix:

$$\mathbf{S} = \begin{bmatrix} +0.9000 & -0.0000 & -0.0405 \\ -0.0000 & +0.9000 & -0.0047 \\ -0.0405 & -0.0047 & +0.9000 \end{bmatrix}$$

At any moment in time, the preference of each alternative is calculated by

$$\mathbf{P}(t+1) = \mathbf{S} \times \mathbf{P}(t) + \mathbf{V}(t+1) \tag{4}$$

where $\mathbf{S} \times \mathbf{P}(t)$ is the contribution of the past preferences and $\mathbf{V}(t+1)$ it the valence computed at that iteration. Usually the initial state $\mathbf{P}(0)$ is defined as $\mathbf{0}$, unless defined otherwise due, for example, to prior knowledge on past experiences.

As, feedback matrix $\mathbf{S}$ is a function of personal evaluations $\mathbf{M}$ and parameters $\theta = \langle \phi_1, \phi_2, b \rangle$ and for us $\mathbf{C}$ is always defined as described above, we will refer to an MDFT model by $\langle \mathbf{M}, \theta, \mathbf{w} \rangle$. Given an MDFT model one can simulate the process of deliberating among the options by accumulating the preferences for a number of iterations. The process can be stopped either by setting a threshold on the preference value and selecting whichever option reaches it first or, by fixing the number of iterations and then selecting the option with highest preference at that point. In general, different runs of the same MDFT model may return different choices because of the uncertainty on the attention weights distribution. This allows MDFT to effectively replicate behaviors observed in humans [4].

3   Recurrent Neural Networks

Artificial neural networks [19] are one of the most powerful and expressive learning models that are successfully used in many real world problems. However, conventional neural networks are not suitable for sequential problems with variable length where the current prediction depends on the previous predictions. Recurrent neural networks (RNNs) [19] are an extension of conventional neural networks designed to deal with such problems. In their simplest form, at any given point in time t, RNNs maintain a state variable h_t as a function of current input x_t and the value of the previous state h_{t-1}, that is, $h_t = f_\eta(x_t, h_{t-1})$ where

η is the set of parameters to be learned. In addition, a loss function $L(y_t, h_t)$, where y_t is the observed target value at time t, is appropriately defined to quantify the error of prediction at each time. The learning objective is to minimize an aggregate function of losses (e.g. the average, the sum or, simply, the last loss value) subject to parameters η. This objective is achieved by iteratively running back-propagation algorithm [19], or one of its improved versions [1], on the training data.

4   Related Work

Preference learning [6] is about inducing predictive preference models from empirical data. Although learning preferences can be reduced to conventional machine learning approaches in some cases, in general, it is a more challenging task because of the complexity of the output (which usually takes the form of rankings or partial orders) and the incompleteness of the input (such as indirect feedback or implicit preference information) [6]. Most preference learning tasks are defined by an option input space and a label output space. The output space is used to define the orderings. For example in *label ranking* the goal is to learn a ranking function mapping the input space into permutations of the labels. The training data for these tasks is usually a set of pairwise comparisons. Our setting is significantly different from those considered in these tasks. First of all our training data is made of choices, and not pairwise comparison. Furthermore, these choices are only the final outcome of a dynamic process, which we aim at replicating as a whole.

In another related research, [2] presents a model which combines utility-based models of preference in economics with Bayesian inference to learn complex structured preferences. Their model predicts the user's choice based on previous choices and also on the relationships between new and old options. Our work is different in that we focus on cognitive models of preferences, rather than economic models, and, while they assume prior knowledge about relations between options, we do not rely on any local information on options' preferences.

5   Problem Formulation

In this section we formalize the problem of learning initial evaluations compatible with a decision maker's observed choice behavior assuming an underlying MDFT model.

Problem Formulation. We consider a setting in which a user is confronted with choosing among a set of options $\{o_1, \ldots, o_n\}$ taking into account a set of attributes $\{A_1, \ldots, A_J\}$. Given a dataset of observed choices $\mathcal{D} = \{\langle c_1, T_1 \rangle, \ldots, \langle c_k, T_k \rangle\}$, where T_i is the deliberation time (i.e., number of iterations) for choice c_i, we want to find a $\hat{\mathbf{M}}$ in such a way that the MDFT $\hat{\mathcal{M}} = \langle \hat{\mathbf{M}}, \theta, \mathbf{w} \rangle$ generates a similar choice distribution as the one observed in $\mathcal{D}$.

Evaluation. One option to compare two choice probability distributions is the Kullback-Leibler (KL) divergence [12]. It is a measure that quantifies in bits how far a probability distribution $p = \{p_i\}$ is from another distribution $q = \{q_i\}$, formally $D_{kl}(p||q) = \sum_i p_i \log(\frac{p_i}{q_i})$.

However, a problem with using KL-Divergence as a distance measure is that it is not symmetric. We, thus, use the Jensen-Shannon Divergence [13] which is an extension of KL-Divergence that overcomes this problem:

$$D_{js}(p||q) = \frac{D_{KL}(p||\frac{p+q}{2}) + D_{KL}(q||\frac{p+q}{2})}{2} \tag{5}$$

Let, $h_\mathcal{D}, h_{\hat{\mathcal{M}}}$ denote the histogram of choices in $\mathcal{D}$ and generated by $\hat{\mathcal{M}}$, respectively. In the next sections we will describe a learning approach and show how it minimizes $D_{js}(h_\mathcal{D}||h_{\hat{\mathcal{M}}})$.

6   Learning Preference in a MDFT Model

We recall that each time a MDFT model is run on the set of options $\{o_1, \ldots, o_n\}$, an option is selected after a sequence of deliberation steps, where, at each step, attention to attributes is allocated according to a specific attention vector (see Sect. 2). We can thus associate the deliberation sequence with a sequence of attention vectors: $\langle \mathbf{W}(1), \ldots, \mathbf{W}(T) \rangle$, which we will call attention sequence for short. In our running example, if the student first considered health, then taste and then health again, the attention sequence would be $\langle [1,0], [0,1], [1,0] \rangle$. It is easy to see, that if, in addition to dataset $\mathcal{D}$ we also had the associated attention sequences, then we could easily map the problem of learning an MDFT model of the user's behavior into a multi-class classification problem. Options $1, \ldots n$ would correspond to n classes, each sequence of attention vectors $\langle \mathbf{W}(1), \ldots, \mathbf{W}(T) \rangle$ would be an input, and the selected option would be the output. In what follows we propose a learning approach based on this intuition which designed to bypass the absence of information on the attention sequences.

6.1   Learning Architecture

As a first step we show how we can map an MDFT model into a recurrent neural network architecture as the one depicted in Fig. 1. A pass over the network, from input to output, at time t corresponds to one iteration of the MDFT model. The network is structured into two sub-networks, respectively at the top and bottom of Fig. 1. The top sub-network is responsible for computing the valences (as defined in Eq. 1), while the bottom one corresponds to the preference update (as defined in Eq. 4). As it can be seen, there is a one-to-one correspondence between networks' weights and the parameters of the MDFT. More in detail, starting from the top sub-network, the first layer of nodes, denoted with $\{1, \ldots, J\}$, corresponds to the attributes and the weights of their inputs, $\{w_1^t, \ldots w_J^t\}$ are the elements of the attention weight vector (at time t). The weights of the connections between this first layer of nodes and the second one correspond to the initial evaluations contained in matrix $\mathbf{M}$ and the weights between the second and third layer correspond to the values of contrast matrix $\mathbf{C}$. Notice that the third layer of nodes corresponds to the valence values, $v_1^t, v_2^t, \ldots, v_n^t$, one for each option. The inputs of the bottom sub-network are the preferences from the previous iteration $p_1^{t-1}, p_2^{t-1}, \ldots, p_n^{t-1}$, and the weights between the two layers are the values of the $\mathbf{S}$ matrix. The output of the two sub-networks are combined to synthesize the new preferences at time t, $P_1^t, P_2^t, \ldots, P_n^t$.

One deliberation process of length T is simulated by cycling over the network for T times and obtaining final preferences $\{P_1^T, P_2^T, \ldots, P_n^T\}$. We treat the final preferences as scores of a multi-class classifier and use hinge loss to optimize the parameters:

$$\text{loss}(\mathbf{P}, c) = \frac{\sum_{i \neq c}^{|\mathbf{P}|} \max(0, \mathrm{m} - P_c + P_i))}{|\mathbf{P}| - 1} \tag{6}$$

where $\mathbf{P}$ is the predicted preference vector, c is the ground-truth choice with predicted preference P_c, and m is the margin parameter of hinge loss. During training the $\mathbf{C}$ parameters are fixed as defined in the description of the contrast matrix $\mathbf{C}$ in Sect. 2. $\mathbf{M}$ parameters are updated by error propagation and $\mathbf{S}$ parameters are recomputed given the new $\mathbf{M}$ parameters and also ϕ_1 and ϕ_2 (see Eq. 3) which are maintained fixed during learning.

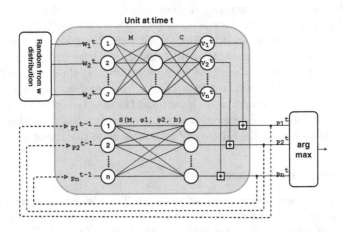

Fig. 1. Recurrent neural network representing an MDFT model.

6.2   Training

It is easy to see that it is not possible to train the RNN described above using choice dataset $\mathcal{D}$ because we don't have any information about the attention sequences that generated the choices. However, attention sequences are the only way in which uncertainty is manifested in the MDFT model, that is, it is a difference in attention sequences which makes it possible to obtain different choices from the same set of initial evaluations. Given this, we conjecture that sequences that generate the same options will have a common trend in terms of overall attention allocated to each attribute during deliberation. We corroborate our hypothesis with an extensive experimental study. In Fig. 2 we show results for 4 samples, generated from a single MDFT model with three options and two attributes, and consisting each of 100 deliberation simulations involving 100 iterations each. The plots show, for each option and for each iteration, the percentage of previous iterations at which attention was allocated to the first attribute (i.e., when the attention vector was W_2, as defined in Sect. 2). The different colors correspond to different choices (o_1, o_2 and o_3, respectively) and the legends in each of the 4 sub-figures show the number of times that a particular option was returned over the 100 trials. From the figure we can see that each option has an attention allocation trend that, on average, is completely different from the other options. We can also see that different samples generate very similar trends for the same options, confirming our hypothesis.

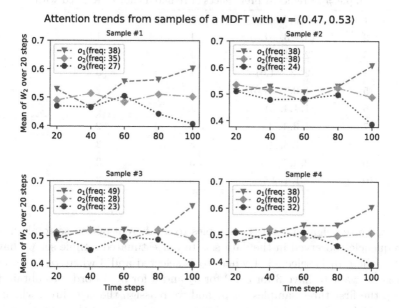

Fig. 2. Average percentage of iterations at which attribute A_1 is attended for a given number of deliberation steps. Each sub-figure is the average over 100 samples. All samples are generated by the same MDFT. (Color figure online)

In conclusion we see that the final choice will be the same for all attention sequences that follow a particular option trend. Therefore, we can use any subset of those sequences interchangeably for training our model as long as the average trend approximately remains the same. Based on this, we design an algorithm that adjusts the output of the RNN so that it aligns with the frequencies of returned options in the dataset.

We explain this algorithm with a simplified example. Consider an MDFT with three options $\{o_1, o_2, o_3\}$ and two attributes A_1 and A_2, similar to the one described in Sect. 2. Let us assume that we run this model for 10 times and that three options are returned with frequencies $\langle 3, 2, 5 \rangle$. In other words, o_1 was selected 3 times out of 10, o_2 2 times and o_3 the remaining 5. Now let us assume that we run the estimated model represented by RNN 10 times and that the three options are returned with the following frequencies: $\langle 6, 1, 3 \rangle$. In Table 1 (first three columns) we show an example of returned sample set with final preferences and choices. In the first phase of the algorithm, we sort the samples generated for each option by the RNN in decreasing order of the preference they assign to the selected option (as shown in Table 1). The intuition is that samples with higher preference are better representatives for the selected option.

Table 1. Samples generated from the learned model. * indicates re-assigned choice.

Sample #	Predicted preferences	Predicted choice	Aligned with
1	$\langle 5, 3, 1.5 \rangle$	1	1
2	$\langle 5, -3, -1.5 \rangle$	1	1
3	$\langle 2.5, 1, 1.5 \rangle$	1	1
4	$\langle 2, .3, -1.5 \rangle$	1	3^*
5	$\langle 1, 0.3, -1.5 \rangle$	1	2^*
6	$\langle 1, 1.4, .5 \rangle$	1	3^*
7	$\langle 1, 3, 1.5 \rangle$	2	2
8	$\langle -1, 3, 10 \rangle$	3	3
9	$\langle 2, 4, 7 \rangle$	3	3
10	$\langle -1, 1, 2.5 \rangle$	3	3

Next, we reassign some of the samples to a different option so to align with the frequencies observed in the data set. In our estimated sample set we have 6 samples where o_1 is selected, 1 where o_2 is selected and 3 where o_3 is selected, whereas we want to have 3 for o_1, 2 for o_2 and 5 for o_3. In order to obtain this we keep the first three samples for o_1 and we reassign the last three, which are in excess and weaker representatives for o_1, assigning one of them to o_2 and the other two to o_3. Reassignments can be done randomly (as in our implementation), or based on the preference assigned by the sample to the choice they have been reassigned to. The result of the reassignment is shown in the last column of Table 1.

At this point the hinge loss error defined in Eq. 6 can be computed and propagated (e.g., for sample 4 of Table 1 we have $P_c = -1.5$ and $P_1 = 1$). In this way, the training procedure penalizes the miss-aligned samples and the error propagation causes the personal evaluation of more frequent options to shift towards most frequent attention sequences and vice-versa. The training algorithm, thus, iteratively improves the alignments and finds the appropriate attention sequence for each option.

Summarizing, given data set $\mathcal{D} = \{\langle c_1, T_1 \rangle, \ldots, \langle c_k, T_k \rangle\}$ of size k, training proceeds as follows:

1. **Initialization:** All parameters of the RNN network are initialized randomly, except for the contrast parameters $\mathbf{C}$ and ϕ_1 and ϕ_2 which are fixed as previously described.
2. **Sample generation and preference prediction:** The RNN is used to generated k new samples. Each sample is generated by cycling through the network a number of times equal to the number of deliberation iterations of the corresponding sample in the data set. For example, the first sample is generated with T_1 iterations over the network. For each sample, the selected choice is computed by applying **argmax** to the final preferences.
3. **Alignment:** An alignment between each sample in the data set and one in the new sample set is obtained as described above.
4. **Parameter update:** Hinge error for all samples is computed using Eq. 6 and finally personal evaluation values $\mathbf{M}$ are updated accordingly using back-propagation algorithm. Once the $\mathbf{M}$ are computed, the $\mathbf{S}$ values are updated accordingly.

7 Experimental Results

In this section we report experimental results obtained from synthetic datasets generated from MDFT models. For each dataset, we generate 100 different MDFT models randomly according to uniform distributions in $[0.002, -0.05]$, $[1, 20]$, $[0.3, 0.7]$ and $[1, 5]$ for ϕ_1, ϕ_2, b, w, and $\mathbf{M}$, respectively. Given an MDFT model, we use it to produce sample sets of different sizes, consisting of (choice, deliberation-time) pairs as defined in Sect. 5. In our experiments we fix the deliberation time at $T = 100$.

We use *Pytorch* library [14] to implement the Recurrent Neural Network described in Sect. 6. We use *RMSprop* optimizer [7] with learning rate 0.005, hinge loss(*MultiMarginLoss*) with margin 0.01. We train each model for 1000 iterations. We also stop training early whenever loss error drops under 10^{-5}.

After training is completed, the learned models are used to produce choice distributions over the options (denoted with $h_{\hat{\mathcal{M}}}$ in Sect. 5).

In Fig. 3 we show results comparing the choice distributions of the learned models with the ones produced by the original MDFTs with the Jensen-Shannon distance D_{js} (defined in Sect. 5). We consider problems with 5 to 9 options and training sample sets ranging from 20 to 150. For each combination, after training, we first generate 10000 samples from the ground-truth and the learned model to obtain their histograms, then we calculate Jensen-Shannon distance. We repeat this process for 100 sample sets in each dataset and report the average distances.

As it can be seen the two distributions are already very close with smaller training sample sizes (e.g., 30) and the divergence of the two distributions decreases significantly as the sample size increases. The number of options also has a mild impact on the similarity between the distributions. The number of options has a more significant impact on the training times, as shown in Fig. 4. In fact, each iteration considers all the pairs in the sample set and involves all the steps summarized at the end of Sect. 6. Moreover, the size of the output produced by the RNN (before **argmax** is applied) also corresponds to the sample size. Nevertheless, by looking at the results in Figs. 3 and 4 we can see that very good performance can be reached with a sample set of size 30 and a training time of less than 300 s.

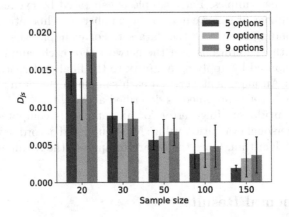

Fig. 3. Average D_{js} with their 95% confidence interval.

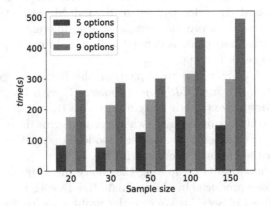

Fig. 4. Average training time.

We recall that our primary goal is to learn an MDFT model capable of generating a decision making behavior similar to the one observed. However, since our data is generated starting from MDFTs, we also check the similarity of the orderings of the options, with respect to each attribute, between the ground truth $\mathbf{M}$ matrix and in the learned matrix $\mathbf{M}'$. To do this we consider Kendall's τ ranking correlation coefficient [10]. This measure quantifies the distance between two rankings as the ratio of the number of pairwise miss-orderings to the number of all possible pairs. Figure 5 shows the results for sample size 150 and when the orderings do not include relations among never chosen options. As it can be seen, our learning method comes very close to recovering the initial rankings for options that are not systematically discarded.

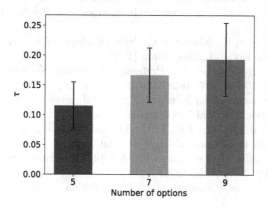

Fig. 5. Average Kendall's τ with their 95% confidence interval.

8   Conclusion and Future Work

Current preference learning approaches build on assumptions that are sometimes in contrast with cognitive models of decision making. In this paper we present a method that combines a cognitive model of choice with recurrent neural networks to learn the decision maker's preferences from his final choices. Experimental results show that the proposed method is effectively learning preferences compatible with ground-truth behavior.

In the future, we plan to expand this model to simultaneously learn other parameters of the architecture, such as, the decision maker's attention distribution over attributes, $\mathbf{w}$, and the parameter controlling how an individual evaluates the interaction among different options, (b). While we have focused on the basic version of MDFT, additional parameters can be added to model more sophisticated behaviors and can be subject to learning. We also plan to consider datasets involving choices from different sets of options as well as scenarios where multiple interdependent decisions are made via MDFT.

References

1. Bengio, Y., Boulanger-Lewandowski, N., Pascanu, R.: Advances in optimizing recurrent networks. In: 2013 IEEE International Conference on Acoustics, Speech and Signal Processing, pp. 8624–8628. IEEE (2013)
2. Bergen, L., Evans, O., Tenenbaum, J.: Learning structured preferences. In: Proceedings of the Annual Meeting of the Cognitive Science Society, vol. 32 (2010)
3. Busemeyer, J.R., Diederich, A.: Survey of decision field theory. Math. Soc. Sci. **43**(3), 345–370 (2002)
4. Busemeyer, J.R., Townsend, J.T.: Decision field theory: a dynamic-cognitive approach to decision making in an uncertain environment. Psychol. Rev. **100**(3), 432 (1993)
5. De Soete, G., Feger, H., Klauer, K.C.: New Developments in Probabilistic Choice Modeling. North-Holland, Amsterdam (1989)
6. Fürnkranz, J., Hüllermeier, E.: Preference Learning. Springer, Boston (2010). https://doi.org/10.1007/978-0-387-30164-8
7. Hinton, G., Srivastava, N., Swersky, K.: Neural networks for machine learning lecture 6A overview of mini-batch gradient descent
8. Hotaling, J.M., Busemeyer, J.R., Li, J.: Theoretical developments in decision field theory: comment on Tsetsos, Usher, and Chater (2010)
9. Keeney, R.L., Raiffa, H.: Decisions with Multiple Objectives: Preference and Value Tradeoffs. Wiley, New York (1976)
10. Kendall, M.G.: A new measure of rank correlation. Biometrika **30**(1/2), 81–93 (1938)
11. Koriche, F., Zanuttini, B.: Learning conditional preference networks. Artif. Intell. **174**(11), 685–703 (2010)
12. Kullback, S.: Information Theory and Statistics. Courier Corporation, North Chelmsford (1997)
13. Lin, J.: Divergence measures based on the Shannon entropy. IEEE Trans. Inf. Theory **37**(1), 145–151 (1991)
14. Paszke, A., et al.: Automatic differentiation in PyTorch. In: NIPS-W (2017)
15. Raedt, L.D., Passerini, A., Teso, S.: Learning constraints from examples. In: Proceedings of the Thirty-Second AAAI Conference on Artificial Intelligence, (AAAI 2018), pp. 7965–7970. AAAI (2018)
16. Roe, R.M., Busemeyer, J.R., Townsend, J.T.: Multialternative decision field theory: a dynamic connectionst model of decision making. Psychol. Rev. **108**(2), 370 (2001)
17. Rossi, F., Venable, K., Walsh, T.: A Short Introduction to Preferences: Between Artificial Intelligence and Social Choice. Morgan and Claypool, San Rafael (2011)
18. Rossi, F., Sperduti, A.: Learning solution preferences in constraint problems. J. Exp. Theor. Artif. Intell. **10**(1), 103–116 (1998)
19. Rumelhart, D.E., Hinton, G.E., Williams, R.J.: Learning representations by back-propagating errors. Nature **323**(6088), 533 (1986)
20. Thurstone, L.L.: The Measurement of Values. University of Chicago Press, Chicago (1959)

Neural Networks as Model Selection with Incremental MDL Normalization

Baihan Lin[1,2,3](✉)

[1] Center for Theoretical Neuroscience, Columbia University,
New York, USA
Baihan.Lin@Columbia.edu
[2] Zuckerman Mind Brain Behavior Institute, Columbia University,
New York, USA
[3] Department of Applied Mathematics, University of Washington, Seattle, USA

Abstract. If we consider the neural network optimization process as a model selection problem, the implicit space can be constrained by the normalizing factor, the minimum description length of the optimal universal code. Inspired by the adaptation phenomenon of biological neuronal firing, we propose a class of reparameterization of the activation in the neural network that take into account the statistical regularity in the implicit space under the Minimum Description Length (MDL) principle. We introduce an incremental version of computing this universal code as normalized maximum likelihood and demonstrated its flexibility to include data prior such as top-down attention and other oracle information and its compatibility to be incorporated into batch normalization and layer normalization. The empirical results showed that the proposed method outperforms existing normalization methods in tackling the limited and imbalanced data from a non-stationary distribution benchmarked on computer vision and reinforcement learning tasks. As an unsupervised attention mechanism given input data, this biologically plausible normalization has the potential to deal with other complicated real-world scenarios as well as reinforcement learning setting where the rewards are sparse and non-uniform. Further research is proposed to discover these scenarios and explore the behaviors among different variants.

Keywords: Neuronal adaption · Minimum description length · Model selection · Universal code · Normalization method in neural networks

1 Introduction

The Minimum Description Length (MDL) principle asserts that the best model given some data is the one that minimizing the combined cost of describing the model and describing the misfit between the model and data [16] with a goal to maximize regularity extraction for optimal data compression, prediction and communication [6]. Most unsupervised learning algorithms can be understood using the MDL principle [17], treating the neural network as a system communicating the input to a receiver.

© Springer Nature Singapore Pte Ltd. 2019
A. Zeng et al. (Eds.): HBAI 2019, CCIS 1072, pp. 195–208, 2019.
https://doi.org/10.1007/978-981-15-1398-5_14

If we consider the neural network training as the optimization process of a communication system, each input at each layers of the system can be described as a point in a low-dimensional continuous constraint space [20]. If we consider the neural networks as population codes, the constraint space can be subdivided into the input-vector space, the hidden-vector space, and the *implicit space*, which represents the underlying dimensions of variability in the other two spaces, i.e., a reduced representation of the constraint space. For instance, if we are given a image of an object, the rotated or scaled version of the same image still refers to the same objects, then each image instance of the same object can be represented by a code assigned position on a 2D implicit space with one dimension as orientation and the other as size of the shape [20]. The relevant information about the implicit space can be constrained to ensure a minimized description length of the neural networks.

This type of constraint can also be found in biological systems. In biological brains of primates, high-level brain areas are known to send top-down feedback connections to lower-level areas to encourage the selection of the most relevant information in the current input given the current task [4], a process similar to the communication system above. This type of modulation is performed by collecting statistical regularity in a hierarchical encoding process between these brain areas. One feature of the neural coding during the hierarchical processing is the adaptation: in vision neuroscience, vertical orientation reduce their firing rates to that orientaiton after the adaptation [2], while the cell responses to other orientations may increase [5]. These behaviors contradict to the Bayesian assumption that the more probable the input, the larger firing rate should be, but instead, well match the information theoretical point-of-view that the most relevant information (saliency), which depends on the statistical regularity, have higher "information", just as the firing of the neurons. As [15] hypothesized that the firing rate represent the code length instead of the probability, similarly, the more regular the input features are, the lower it should yield the activation. We introduce the minimum description length (MDL), such that the activation of neurons can be analogous to the code length of the model (a specific neuron or neuronal population) - a shorter code length would be assigned to a more regular input (such as after adaptation), and a longer code length to a more rare input or event.

In this paper, we adopt the similar definition of implicit space as in [20], but extend it beyond unsupervised learning, into a generical neural network optimization problem in both supervised and unsupervised setting. In addition, we consider the formulation and computation of description length differently, given the neuroscience inspiration described above. Instead of considering neural networks as population codes, we formulate each layer of neural networks during training a state of module selection. In our setup, the description length is computed not in the scale of the entire neural networks, but by the unit of each layer of the network. In addition, the optimization objective is not to minimize the description length, but instead, to take into account the minimum description length as part of the normalization procedure to reparameterize the activation of each neurons in each layer. The computation of the description length (or model cost as in [20]) aims to minimize it, while we directly compute the minimum description length in each layer not to minimize anything, but to reassign the weights based on statistical regularities. Finally, we compute the description length by an optimal universal code obtained by the batch input distribution in an online incremental fashion.

We begin our presentation in Sect. 2, with a short overview of related works in normalization methods and MDL in neural networks. Section 3 formulated the problem setting in neural networks where we consider the training as a layer-specific model selection process under MDL principle. We then introduce the proposed class of incremental MDL normalization method, its standard formulation (regularity normalization), its implementation, and the online incremental tricks for batch computation. We also present several variants of the regularity normalization (RN) by incorporating batch and layer normalizations, termed regularity batch normalization (RBN) and regularity layer normalization (RLN), as well as including the data prior as a top-down attention mechanism during the training process, termed saliency normalization (SN). In Sect. 5, we present the empirical results on the imbalanced MNIST dataset and a reinforcement learning problem to demonstrate that our approach is advantageous over existing normalization methods in different imbalanced scenarios. In the last section, we conclude our methods and point out several future work directions as the next step of this research.

2 Related Work

2.1 Normalization in Neural Networks

Batch normalization (BN) performs global normalization along the batch dimension such that for each neuron in a layer, the activation over all the mini-batch training cases follows standard normal distribution, reducing the internal covariate shift [8]. Similarly, layer normalization (LN) performs global normalization over all the neurons in a layer, and have shown effective stabilizing effect in the hidden state dynamics in recurrent networks [1]. Weight normalization (WN) applied normalization over the incoming weights, offering computational advantages for reinforcement learning and generative modeling [19]. Like BN and LN, we apply the normalization on the activation of the neurons, but as an element-wise reparameterization (over both the layer and batch dimension). In Sect. 4.2, we also proposed the variant methods based on our approach with batch-wise and layer-wise reparameterization, the regularity batch normalization (RBN) and regularity layer normalization (RLN).

2.2 Description Length in Neural Networks

[7] first introduced the description length to quantify neural network simplicity and develop an optimization method to minimize the amount of information required to communicate the weights of the neural network. [20] considered the

neural networks as population codes and used MDL to develop highly redundant population code. They showed that by assuming the hidden units reside in low-dimensional implicit spaces, optimization process can be applied to minimize the model cost under MDL principle. Our proposed method adopt a similar definition of implicit space, but consider the implicit space as data-dependent encoding statistical regularities. Unlike [20] and [7], we consider the description length as a indicator of the data input and assume that the implicit space is constrained when we normalize the activation of each neurons given its statistical regularity. Unlike the implicit approach to compute model cost, we directly compute the minimum description length with optimal universal code obtained in an incremental style.

3   Problem Setting

3.1   Minimum Description Length

Given a model class Θ consisting of a finite number of models parameterized by the parameter set θ. Given a data sample x, each model in the model class describes a probability $P(x|\theta)$ with the code length computed as $-\log P(x|\theta)$. The minimum code length given any arbitrary θ would be given by $L(x|\hat{\theta}(x)) = -\log P(x|\hat{\theta}(x))$ with model $\hat{\theta}(x)$ which compresses data sample x most efficiently and offers the maximum likelihood $P(x|\theta(\hat{x}))$ [6].

However, the compressibility of the model, computed as the minimum code length, can be unattainable for multiple non-i.i.d. data samples as individual inputs, as the probability distributions of most efficiently representing a certain data sample x given a certain model class can vary from sample to sample. The solution relies on the existence of a universal code, $\bar{P}(x)$ defined for a model class Θ, such that for any data sample x, the shortest code for x is always $L(x|\hat{\theta}(x))$, as proposed and proven in [18].

3.2   Normalized Maximum Likelihood

To select for a proper optimal universal code, a cautious approach would be to assume a worst-case scenario in order to make "safe" inferences about the unknown world. Formally, the worst-case expected regret is given by $R(p\|\Theta) = \max_q E_q[\ln \frac{f(x|\hat{\theta}_x)}{p(x)}]$, where the "worst" distribution $q(\cdot)$ is allowed to be any probability distribution. Without referencing the unknown truth, [18] formulated finding the optimal universal distribution as a mini-max problem of computing $p* = \arg_p \min_p \max_q E_q[\ln \frac{f(x|\hat{\theta}_x)}{p(x)}]$, the coding scheme that minimizes the worst-case expected regret. Among the optimal universal code, the normalized maximum likelihood (NML) probability minimizes the worst-case regret and avoids assigning an arbitrary distribution to Θ. The minimax optimal solution is given by [14]:

$$P_{NML}(x) = \frac{P(x|\hat{\theta}(x))}{\sum_{x'} P(x'|\hat{\theta}(x'))} \tag{1}$$

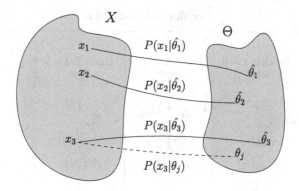

Fig. 1. Normalized maximal likelihood. Shown here in the schematic illustration, data sample x_i are drawn from the entire data distribution X and model $\hat{\theta}_i$ is the optimal model that describes data x_i with the shortest code length. θ_j is an arbitrary model that is not $\hat{\theta}_3$, so $P(x_3|\theta_j)$ is not considered when computing optimal universal code according to NML formulation.

where the summation is over the entire data sample space. Figure 1 describes the optimization problem of finding optimal model $P(x_i|\hat{\theta}_i)$ given data sample x_i among model class Θ. The models in the class, $P(x|\theta)$, are parameterized by the parameter set θ. x_i are data sample from data X. With this distribution, the regret is the same for all data sample x given by [6]:

$$
\begin{aligned}
COMP(\Theta) &\equiv regret_{NML} \\
&\equiv -\log P_{NML}(x) + \log P(x|\hat{\theta}(x)) \\
&= \log \sum_{x'} P(x'|\hat{\theta}(x'))
\end{aligned}
\tag{2}
$$

which defines the model class complexity as it indicates how many different data samples can be well explained by the model class Θ.

3.3   Neural Networks as Model Selection

In the neural network setting where optimization process are performed in batches (as incremental data sample x_j with j denoting the batch j), the model selection process is formulated as a partially observable problem (as in Fig. 2). Herein to illustrate our approach, we consider a feedforward neural network as an example, without loss of generalizability to other architecture (such as convolutional layers or recurrent modules). x_j^i refers to the activation at layer i at time point j (batch j). θ_j^i is the parameters that describes x_j^i (i.e. weights for layer $i-1$) optimized after $j-1$ steps (seen batch 0 through $j-1$). Because one cannot exhaust the search among all possible θ, we assume that the optimized parameter $\hat{\theta}_j^i$ at time step j (seen batch 0 through $j-1$) is the optimal model

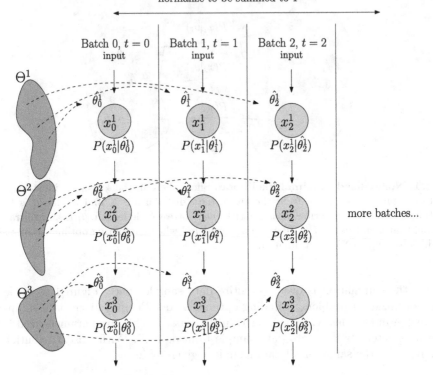

Fig. 2. Model selection in neural network. If we consider each time step of the optimization (drawn here to be batch-dependent) as the process of choose the optimal model from model class Θ^i for ith layer of the neural networks, the optimized parameter $\hat{\theta}^i_j$ with subscript j as time step $t = j$ and superscript i as layer i can be assumed to be the optimal model among all models in the model class Θ^i. The normalized maximum likelihood can be computed by choosing $P(x^i_j|\hat{\theta}^i_j)$, the "optimal" model with shortest code length given data x^i_j, as the summing component in the normalization.

$P(x^i_j|\hat{\theta}^i_j)$ for data sample x^i_j. Therefore, we generalize the optimal universal code with NML formulation as:

$$P_{NML}(x_i) = \frac{P(x_i|\hat{\theta}_i(x_i))}{\sum_{j=0}^i P(x_j|\hat{\theta}_j(x_j))} \tag{3}$$

where $\hat{\theta}_i(x_i)$ refers to the model parameter already optimized for $i-1$ steps and have seen sequential data sample x_0 through x_{i-1}. This distribution is updated every time a new data sample is given, and can therefore be computed incrementally, as in batch-based training.

4   Incremental MDL Normalization

4.1   Standard Formulation

We first introduce the standard formulation of the class of incremental MDL normalization: the regularity normalization (RN). Regularity normalization is outlined in Algorithm 1, where the input would be the activation of each neurons in certain layer and batch. Parameters $COMP$ and θ are updated after each batch, through the incrementation in the normalization and optimization in the training respectively. As the numerator of P_{NML} at this step of normalization, the term $P(x_i|\hat{\theta}_t(x_i))$ is computed to be stored as a log probability of observing sample x_i in $N(\mu_{i-1}, \sigma_{i-1})$, the normal distribution with the mean and standard deviation of all past data sample history $(x_0, x_1, \cdots, x_{i-1})$, with a Gaussian prior for $P(x|\hat{\theta}(x))$. The selection for the Gaussian prior is based on the assumption that each x is randomly sampled from a Gaussian distribution, and the parameter sets from model class Θ are Gaussian, while further research can explore other possible priors and inference methods for arbitrary priors.

As defined in Eq. 2, $COMP$ is the denominator of the P_{NML} taken log, so the "increment" function takes in the $COMP_t$ storing $\sum_{i=0}^{t-1} P(x_i|\hat{\theta}_i(x_i))$ and the latest batch of $P(x_i|\hat{\theta}_t(x_i))$ to be added in the denominator, stored as $COMP_{t+1}$. The incrementation step involves computing the log sum of two values, which can be easily numerically stabilized with the log-sum-exp trick[1]. The normalization factor is then computed as the shortest code length L given the NML distribution, the universal code distribution in Eq. 1.

4.2   Variant: Saliency Normalization

NML distribution can be modified to also include a data prior function, $s(x)$, given by [21]:

$$P_{NML}(x) = \frac{s(x)P(x|\hat{\theta}(x))}{\sum_{x'} s(x')P(x'|\hat{\theta}(x'))} \qquad (4)$$

Algorithm 1. Regularity Normalization (RN)

Input: Values of x over a mini-batch: $\mathcal{B} = \{x_{1,\cdots,m}\}$;
Parameter: $COMP_t$, $\hat{\theta}_t$
Output: $y_i = RN(x_i)$

$COMP_{t+1} = \text{increment}(COMP_t, P(x_i|\hat{\theta}_t(x_i)))$
$L_{x_i} = COMP_{t+1} - \log P(x_i|\hat{\theta}_t(x_i))$
$y_i = L_{x_i} * x_i$

---

[1] In continuous data streams or time series analysis, the incrementation step can be replaced by integrating over the seen territory of the probability distribution X of the data.

Table 1. Heavy-Tailed Scenario 1: Under-represented Minorities Test errors of the imbalanced permutation-invariant MNIST 784-1000-1000-10 task

	"Balanced"	"Rare minority"		
	$n = 0$	$n = 1$	$n = 2$	$n = 3$
Baseline	4.80 ± 0.15	14.48 ± 0.28	23.74 ± 0.28	32.80 ± 0.22
BN	$\mathbf{2.77 \pm 0.05}$	12.54 ± 0.30	21.77 ± 0.25	30.75 ± 0.30
LN	3.09 ± 0.11	8.78 ± 0.84	14.22 ± 0.65	20.62 ± 1.46
WN	4.96 ± 0.11	14.51 ± 0.44	23.72 ± 0.39	32.99 ± 0.28
RN	4.91 ± 0.39	8.61 ± 0.86	14.61 ± 0.58	19.49 ± 0.45
RLN	5.01 ± 0.29	9.47 ± 1.21	$\mathbf{12.32 \pm 0.56}$	22.17 ± 0.94
LN+RN	4.59 ± 0.29	$\mathbf{8.41 \pm 1.16}$	12.46 ± 0.87	$\mathbf{17.25 \pm 1.47}$
SN	7.00 ± 0.18	12.27 ± 1.30	16.12 ± 1.39	24.91 ± 1.61

where the data prior function $s(x)$ can be anything, ranging from the emphasis of certain inputs, to the cost of certain data, or even top-down attention. For instance, we can introduce the prior knowledge of the fraction of labels (say, in an imbalanced data problem where the oracle informs the model of the distribution of each label in the training phase); or in a scenario where we wish the model to focus specifically on certain feature of the input, say certain texture or color (just like a convolution filter); or in the case where the definition of the regularity drifts (such as the user preferences over years): in all these possible applications, the normalization procedure can be more strategic given these additional information. Therefore, we formulate this additional functionality into our regularity normalization, to be saliency normalization (SN), where the P_{NML} is computed with the addition of a pre-specified data prior function $s(x)$.

4.3   Variant: Beyond Elementwise Normalization

In our current setup, the normalization is computed elementwise, considering the implicit space of the model parameters to be one-dimensional (i.e. all activations across the batch and layer are considered to be represented by the same implicit space). Instead, the definition of the implicit can be more than one-dimensional to increase the expressibility of the method, and can also be user-defined. For instance, we can also perform the normalization over the dimension of the batch, such that each neuron in the layer should have an implicit space to compute the universal code. We term this variant regularity batch normalization (RBN). Similarly, we can perform regularity normalization over the layer dimension, as the regularity layer normalization (RLN). These two variants have the potential to inherit the innate advantages of batch normalization and layer normalization.

5   Empirical Evaluations

5.1   Imbalanced MNIST Problem with Feedforward Neural Network

As a proof of concept, we evaluated our approach on MNIST dataset [10] and computed the total number of classification errors as a performance metric. As

Table 2. Heavy-Tailed Scenario 2: Over-represented Minorities Test errors of the imbalanced permutation-invariant MNIST 784-1000-1000-10 task

	"Highly imbalanced"				"Dominant oligarchy"	
	$n = 4$	$n = 5$	$n = 6$	$n = 7$	$n = 8$	$n = 9$
Baseline	42.01 ± 0.45	51.99 ± 0.32	60.86 ± 0.19	70.81 ± 0.40	80.67 ± 0.36	90.12 ± 0.25
BN	40.67 ± 0.45	49.96 ± 0.46	59.08 ± 0.70	67.25 ± 0.54	76.55 ± 1.41	80.54 ± 2.38
LN	26.87 ± 0.97	34.23 ± 2.08	36.87 ± 0.64	41.73 ± 2.74	$\mathbf{41.20 \pm 1.13}$	$\mathbf{41.26 \pm 1.30}$
WN	41.95 ± 0.46	52.10 ± 0.30	60.97 ± 0.18	70.87 ± 0.39	80.76 ± 0.36	90.12 ± 0.25
RN	$\mathbf{23.35 \pm 1.22}$	33.84 ± 1.69	41.47 ± 1.91	60.46 ± 2.88	81.96 ± 0.59	90.11 ± 0.24
RLN	23.76 ± 1.56	32.23 ± 1.66	43.06 ± 3.56	57.30 ± 6.33	88.36 ± 1.77	89.55 ± 0.32
LN+RN	25.65 ± 1.91	$\mathbf{28.71 \pm 1.97}$	$\mathbf{33.14 \pm 2.49}$	$\mathbf{36.08 \pm 2.09}$	44.54 ± 1.74	82.29 ± 4.44
SN	31.07 ± 1.41	41.87 ± 1.78	52.88 ± 2.09	68.44 ± 1.42	83.34 ± 1.85	82.41 ± 2.30

we specifically wish to understand the behavior where the data inputs are non-stationary and highly imbalanced, we created an imbalanced MNIST benchmark to test seven methods: batch normalization (*BN*), layer normalization (*LN*), weight normalization (*WN*), and regularity normalization (*RN*), as well as three variants: saliency normalization (*SN*) with data prior as class distribution, regularity layer normalization (*RLN*) where the implicit space is defined to be layer-specific, and a combined approach where RN is applied after LN (*LN+RN*).

Given the nature of regularity normalization, it should better adapt to the regularity of the data distribution than other methods, tackling the imbalanced data issue by up-weighting the activation of the rare sample features and down-weighting those of the dominant sample features.

To simulate changes in the context (input) distribution, in each epoch we randomly choose n classes out of the ten, and set their sampling probability to be 0.01 (only 1% of those n classes are used in the training). In this way, the training data may trick the models into preferring to classifying into the dominant classes. For simplicity, we consider the classical 784-1000-1000-10 feedforward neural network with ReLU activation functions for all six normalization methods, as well as the baseline neural network without normalization. As we are looking into the short-term sensitivity of the normalization method on the neural network training, one epoch of trainings are being recorded (all model face the same randomized imbalanced distribution). Training, validation and testing sets are shuffled into 55000, 5000, and 10000 cases. In the testing phase, the data distribution is restored to be balanced, and no models have access to the other testing cases or the data distribution. Stochastic gradient decent is used with learning rate 0.01 and momentum set to be 0.9.

The imbalanced degree n is defined as following: when $n = 0$, it means that no classes are downweighted, so we termed it the *"fully balanced"* scenario; when $n = 1$ to 3, it means that a few cases are extremely rare, so we termed it the *"rare minority"* scenario. When $n = 4$ to 8, it means that the multi-class distribution are very different, so we termed it the *"highly imbalanced"* scenario;

when $n = 9$, it means that there is one or two dominant classes that is 100 times more prevalent than the other classes, so we termed it the *"dominant oligarchy"* scenario. In real life, *rare minority* and *highly imbalanced* scenarios are very common, such as predicting the clinical outcomes of a patient when the therapeutic prognosis data are mostly tested on one gender versus the others, or in reinforcement learning setting where certain or most types of rewards are very sparse.

Tables 1 and 2 report the test errors (in %) with their standard errors of eight methods in 10 training conditions over two heavy-tailed scenarios: labels with under-represented and over-represented minorities. In the balanced scenario, the proposed regularity-based method doesn't show clear advantages over existing methods, but still managed to perform the classification tasks without major deficits. In both the "rare minority" and "highly imbalanced" scenarios, regularity-based methods performs the best in all groups, suggesting that the proposed method successfully constrained the model to allocate learning resources to the "special cases" which are rare and out of normal range, while BN and WN failed to learn it completely (as in the confusion matrices not shown here). In the "dominant oligarchy" scenario, LN performs the best, dwarfing all other normalization methods. However, as in the case of $n = 8$, LN+RN performs considerably well, with performance within error bounds to that of LN, beating other normalization methods by over 30%. It is noted that LN also managed to capture the features of the rare classes reasonably well in other imbalanced scenarios, comparing to BN, WN and baseline. The hybrid methods RLN and LN+RN both displays excellent performance in the imbalanced scenarios, suggesting that combining regularity-based normalization with other methods is advantageous.

These results are mainly in the short term domain as a proof of concept. Further analysis need to be included to fully understand these behaviors in the long term (the converging performance over 100 epochs). However, the major test accuracy differences in the highly imbalanced scenario (RN over BN/WN/baseline for around 20%) in the short term provides promises in its ability to learn from the extreme regularities.

5.2 Reinforcement Learning Problem with Deep Q Network

We further evaluated the benefit of the proposed approach in the game setting of the reinforcement learning problem, where the rewards can be sparse. For simplicity, we consider the classical deep Q network [13] and tested it in OpenAI Gym's LunarLander-v2 environment [3]. In this game, the agent learns to land on the exact coordinates of the landing pad (0,0) during a free fall motion starting from zero speed to the land with around 100 to 140 actions, with rewards fully dependent on the location of the lander (as the state vector) on the screen in a non-stationary fashion: moving away from landing pad loses reward; crashes yields -100; resting on the ground yields $+100$; each leg ground contact yields $+10$; firing main engine costs -0.3 points each frame; fuel is infinite. Four discrete actions are available: do nothing, fire left orientation engine, fire main engine, fire

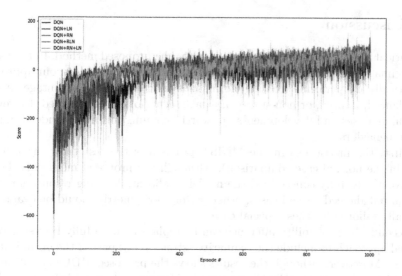

Fig. 3. The learning curves of five agents in LunarLander-V2 environment.

right orientation engine. Five agents (DQN, DQN+LN, DQN+RN, DQN+RLN, DQN+RN+LN) are being considered and evaluated in the speed to master the game, computed as the final scores over 1000 episodes of training.

The Q networks consist of with two hidden layers of 64 neurons. With experience replay [12], the learning of the DQN agents was implemented with the discount factor $\gamma = 0.99$, the soft update rate $\tau = 0.001$, the learning rate $lr = 0.001$, epsilon greedy exploration from 1.0 to 0.01 with decay rate of 0.95, the buffer size 10,000, the batch size 50 and optimization algorithm Adam [9]. To adopt the proposed incremental MDL normalization method, we installed the normalization to both the local and target Q networks.

Figure 3 demonstrated the learning curves of the five competing agents over 1000 episodes of learning with their standard errors. Evaluating by the averaged final scores over 1000 episodes, DQN+RN (76.95 ± 4.44) performs the best among all five agents, followed by DQN+RN+LN (65.82 ± 10.91) and DQN+RLN (49.27 ± 40.35). All three proposed agents beat DQN (37.17 ± 8.82) and DQN-LN (-1.54 ± 39.14) by a large marginal. These numerical results suggested the proposed method has the potential to benefit the neural network training in reinforcement learning setting. On the other hand, certain aspects of these behaviors are worth further exploring. For example, the proposed methods with highest final scores do not converge as fast as DQN+LN, suggesting that regularity normalization resembles some type of adaptive learning rate which gradually tune down the learning as scenario converges to stationarity.[2]

---

[2] The raw data and code to reproduce the results can be downloaded at https://app.box.com/s/ruycgz8p7rh30taj38d8dkc0h1ptltg1.

6 Discussion

Empirical results offered a proof of concept to the proposed method. In the tasks of the image classification and the reinforcement learning problem, our approach empirically outperforms existing normalization methods its advantage in the imbalanced, limited, or non-stationary data scenario as hypothesized. However, several analyses and developments are worth pursuing to further understanding of the behaviors.

First, the metric use in the MNIST problem is the test error (as usually used in the normal case comparison). Although the proposed method is shown to have successfully constrained the model to allocate learning resources to the several imbalanced special cases, other performance metric should be evaluated specially tailored for these special cases.

Second, the probability inference can be replaced with a fully Bayesian variational approach to include the regularity estimation as part of the optimization process. Moreover, although the results shows the proposed MDL normalization has an improvement on MNIST, it would be interesting to record the overall loss or probability as the computation of NML makes selection on the model, as a partially observable routing process of representation selection [11].

Last but not least, in traditional model selection problems, MDL can be regarded as ensemble modeling process and usually involves multiple models. However, in our neural network problem, we assume that the only model trained at each step is the local "best" model learned so far, but local maximal likelihood may not be a global best approach for model combinations. In another word, the generation of optimized parameter set for a specific layer currently adopts greedy approach, such that the model selection could be optimized for each step, but we haven't theoretically demonstrated that it is the best global selection.

7 Conclusion and Future Work

Inspired by the neural code adaptation of biological brains, we propose a biologically plausible normalization method taking into account the regularity (or saliency) of the activation distribution in the implicit space, and normalize it to upweight activation for rarely seen scenario and downweight activation for commonly seen ones. We introduce the concept from MDL principle and proposed to consider neural network training process as a model selection problem.

We compute the optimal universal code length by normalized maximum likelihood in an incremental fashion, and showed this implementation can be easily incorporated with established methods like batch normalization and layer normalization. In addition, we proposed saliency normalization, which can introduce top-down attention and data prior to facilitate representation learning. Fundamentally, we implemented with an incremental update of normalized maximum likelihood, constraining the implicit space to have a low model complexity and short universal code length.

One main next direction of this research include the inclusion of top-down attention given by data prior (such as feature extracted from signal processing, or task-dependent information). For instance, the application of top-down attention $s(x)$ to modulate the normalization process can vary in different scenarios. Further investigation of how different functions of $s(x)$ behave in different task settings may complete the story of having this method as a top-down meta learning algorithm potentially advantageous for continual multitask learning.

In concept, the regularity-based normalization can also be considered as an unsupervised attention mechanism imposed on the input data, with the flexibility to directly install top-down attention from either oracle supervision or other meta information. As the next stage, we are currently exploring this method to convolutional and recurrent neural networks, and applying to popular state-of-the-art neural network architectures in multiple modalities of datasets, as well as more complicated reinforcement learning setting where the rewards can be very sparse and non-uniform.

References

1. Ba, J.L., Kiros, J.R., Hinton, G.E.: Layer normalization. arXiv preprint arXiv:1607.06450 (2016)
2. Blakemore, C., Campbell, F.W.: Adaptation to spatial stimuli. J. physiol. **200**(1), 11P–13P (1969)
3. Brockman, G., et al.: Openai gym. arXiv preprint arXiv:1606.01540 (2016)
4. Ding, S., Cueva, C.J., Tsodyks, M., Qian, N.: Visual perception as retrospective Bayesian decoding from high-to low-level features. Proc. Nat. Acad. Sci. **114**(43), E9115–E9124 (2017)
5. Dragoi, V., Sharma, J., Sur, M.: Adaptation-induced plasticity of orientation tuning in adult visual cortex. Neuron **28**(1), 287–298 (2000)
6. Grünwald, P.D.: The Minimum Description Length Principle. MIT press, Cambridge (2007)
7. Hinton, G., Van Camp, D.: Keeping neural networks simple by minimizing the description length of the weights. In: In Proceedings of the 6th Annual ACM Conference on Computational Learning Theory. Citeseer (1993)
8. Ioffe, S., Szegedy, C.: Batch normalization: Accelerating deep network training by reducing internal covariate shift. arXiv preprint arXiv:1502.03167 (2015)
9. Kingma, D.P., Ba, J.: Adam: A method for stochastic optimization. arXiv preprint arXiv:1412.6980 (2014)
10. LeCun, Y.: The MNIST database of handwritten digits. http://yann.lecun.com/exdb/mnist/ (1998)
11. Lin, B., Bouneffouf, D., Cecchi, G.A., Rish, I.: Contextual bandit with adaptive feature extraction. In: 2018 IEEE International Conference on Data Mining Workshops (ICDMW), pp. 937–944. IEEE (2018)
12. Lin, L.J.: Self-improving reactive agents based on reinforcement learning, planning and teaching. Mach. Learn. **8**(3–4), 293–321 (1992)
13. Mnih, V., et al.: Playing atari with deep reinforcement learning. arXiv preprint arXiv:1312.5602 (2013)
14. Myung, J.I., Navarro, D.J., Pitt, M.A.: Model selection by normalized maximum likelihood. J. Math. Psychol. **50**(2), 167–179 (2006)

15. Qian, N., Zhang, J.: Neuronal firing rate as code length: a hypothesis. Comput. Behav. pp. 1–20 (2019)
16. Rissanen, J.: Modeling by shortest data description. Automatica **14**(5), 465–471 (1978)
17. Rissanen, J.: Stochastic Complexity in Statistical Inquiry. World Scientific, Singapore (1989)
18. Rissanen, J.: Strong optimality of the normalized ML models as universal codes and information in data. IEEE Trans. Inf. Theory **47**(5), 1712–1717 (2001)
19. Salimans, T., Kingma, D.P.: Weight normalization: A simple reparameterization to accelerate training of deep neural networks. In: Advances in Neural Information Processing Systems, pp. 901–909 (2016)
20. Zemel, R.S., Hinton, G.E.: Learning population coes by minimizing description length. In: Unsupervised Learning, pp. 261–276. Bradford Company (1999)
21. Zhang, J.: Model selection with informative normalized maximum likelihood: Data prior and model prior. In: Descriptive and Normative Approaches To Human Behavior, pp. 303–319. World Scientific (2012)

Tensor Super-Resolution with Generative Adversarial Nets: A Large Image Generation Approach

Zihan Ding[1]($\boxtimes$), Xiao-Yang Liu[2], Miao Yin[3], and Linghe Kong[4]

[1] Imperial College London, London, UK
zd2418@ic.ac.uk
[2] Columbia University, New York, USA
xl2427@columbia.edu
[3] University of Electronic Science and Technology of China, Chengdu, China
yinmiaothink@gmail.com
[4] Shanghai Jiao Tong University, Shanghai, China
linghe.kong@sjtu.edu.cn

Abstract. Deep generative models have been successfully applied to many applications. However, existing methods experience limitations when generating large images (the literature usually generates small images, e.g., 32×32 or 128×128). In this paper, we propose a novel scheme using tensor super-resolution with adversarial generative nets (TSRGAN), to generate large high-quality images by exploring tensor structures. Essentially, the super resolution process of TSRGAN is based on tensor representation. First, we impose tensor structures for concise image representation, which is superior in capturing the pixel proximity information and the spatial patterns of elementary objects in images, over the vectorization preprocess in existing works. Secondly, we propose TSRGAN that integrates deep convolutional generative adversarial networks and tensor super-resolution in a cascading manner, to generate high-quality images from random distributions. More specifically, we design a tensor super-resolution process that consists of tensor dictionary learning and tensor coefficients learning. Finally, on three datasets, the proposed TSRGAN generates images with more realistic textures, compared with state-of-the-art adversarial autoencoders and super-resolution methods. The size of the generated images is increased by over 8.5 times, namely 374×374 in PASCAL2.

Keywords: GAN · Generative model · Super-resolution · Tensor sparse coding · Tensor representation

1 Introduction

With the great successes of deep learning, deep generative models have been investigated widely. However, existing generative adversarial nets (GAN) experience limitations when generating large images. With the growing scale of images,

© Springer Nature Singapore Pte Ltd. 2019
A. Zeng et al. (Eds.): HBAI 2019, CCIS 1072, pp. 209–223, 2019.
https://doi.org/10.1007/978-981-15-1398-5_15

conventional GAN is hard to produce high-quality natural images because it is difficult for the generator and the discriminator to achieve the optimality simultaneously. When processing high-dimensional images, the computational complexity and the training time increase significantly. The challenge is that the image has too many pixels and it is hard for a single generator G to learn the empirical distribution. Therefore, the traditional GAN [7] does not scale well for the generation of large images.

The variations of GAN such as deep convolutional GAN (DCGAN) [23], super-resolution GAN (SRGAN) [16], Laplacian Pyramid GAN (LAPGAN) [2] and StackGAN [30] are promising candidates for generative models in unsupervised learning. Moreover, other types of generative models include adversarial autoencoders (AAE) [20], combining the GANs and variational autoencoders (VAE) [12], etc. [8]. However, even with DCGAN, the bottleneck of GAN exposes easily for large images, since increasing the complexity of the generator does not necessarily improve the image quality. Moreover, StackGAN [30] uses a two-stage GAN to generate images of size 256×256, which are relatively large images for state-of-the-art generative models. Another work is progressive growing of GANs [11], which applies an approach of growing network size for both the generator and the discriminator to generate high-resolution images. However, this method requires large amounts of computation during the progressively increasing of network size. Our proposed method only needs much less computation resources to obtain high-resolution images of large size.

For image super-resolution, approaches including deep neural networks [3,4,26], sparsity-based [29], local regression [9] are proposed in recent years. The super-resolution via sparse representation (ScSR) [29] applies the sparse representation with an over-complete dictionary in super-resolution. The enforced similarity of sparse representations between the low-resolution and high-resolution images makes it possible to achieve super-resolution. Instead of applying popular deep neural networks for super-resolution, our work is based on sparse representation, and changes the representation space from pixel space to tensor space, to exploit the benefits of tensor representation for large images generation.

To solve the challenge of efficient large image generation, we apply a new perspective to change the representation space through combining the GAN and tensor super-resolution process. Traditional GAN-based methods operates in pixel space to generate images while tensor-based methods work in tensor space. Tensor representation [13] and its derivative methods such as tensor sparse coding [6] and tensor super-resolution have a better representation of images, especially for large images. Multi-dimensional tensor sparse coding uses t-linear combination to obtain a more concise and smaller dictionary for representing the images, and the corresponding coefficients have richer physical explanations than the traditional methods.

In this paper, we present a novel generative model called TSRGAN as shown in Fig. 1, cascading a DCGAN and tensor-based super-resolution to generate large high-quality images (e.g. 374×374). The contribution of the proposed

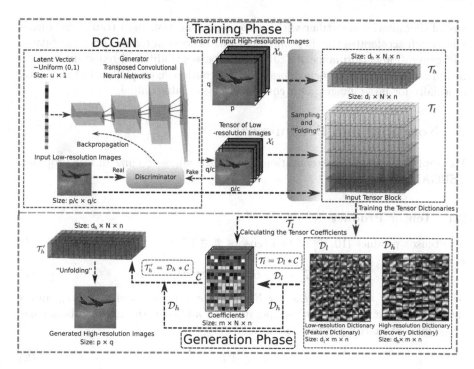

Fig. 1. The architecture of TSRGAN. The latent vectors are sampled from random distributions. During the training phase, the DCGAN are trained with the input low-resolution images, to generate low-resolution image tensors from latent vectors. Through a sampling and "folding" process, the high-resolution and low-resolution image tensors are transformed into tensor blocks, $\mathcal{T}_h$ and $\mathcal{T}_l$, respectively. The feature dictionary (low-resolution) $\mathcal{D}_l$ and recovery dictionary (high-resolution) $\mathcal{D}_h$ are trained with these input tensor blocks. In the generation phase, low-resolution tensor images are generated with DCGAN from the latent vectors. The tensor coefficients $\mathcal{C}$ are obtained using $\mathcal{T}_l = \mathcal{D}_l * \mathcal{C}$, where $\mathcal{D}_l$ is the low-resolution tensor feature dictionary derived from the training phase. High-resolution tensor images can be obtained via $\mathcal{T}_h' = \mathcal{D}_h * \mathcal{C}$, where $\mathcal{D}_h$ is the trained high-resolution tensor recovery dictionary. The final 2D images X' are transformed from the high-resolution tensor images $\mathcal{T}_h'$. (Note that during the training phase $\mathcal{T}_l$ is derived from input low-resolution images while for the generation phase it is from images generated with DCGAN.)

TSRGAN has threefold: (i) We apply tensor representation and tensor sparse coding for images representation in generative models. This is testified to have advantages of more concise and efficient representation of images with less loss on spatial patterns. (ii) We incorporate the tensor representation into the super-resolution process, which is called tensor super-resolution. The tensor super-resolution is cascaded after a DCGAN with transposed convolutional layers, which generates low-resolution images directly from random distributions. (iii) The DCGAN and tensor dictionaries in tensor super-resolution are both pre-trained with a large number of high-resolution and low-resolution images. The size of dictionaries is smaller with tensor representation than traditional methods, which accelerates the dictionary learning process in tensor super-resolution. The generation performance of TSRGAN surpasses traditional generative models including adversarial autoencoders [20] in inception score [24] on test datasets, especially for large images. Our codes will be available online.

2   Notations and Preliminaries

We apply the tensor representation and tensor sparse coding in our proposed TSRGAN scheme.

2.1   Tensor Product

The tensor product [10,19] of two tensors $\mathcal{A} \in \mathbb{R}^{n_1 \times n_2 \times n_3}$ and $\mathcal{B} \in \mathbb{R}^{n_2 \times n_4 \times n_3}$ is defined as

$$\mathcal{T} = \mathcal{A} * \mathcal{B} \in \mathbb{R}^{n_1 \times n_4 \times n_3}, \tag{1}$$

where $\mathcal{T}(i,j,:) = \sum_{s=1}^{n_2} \mathcal{A}(i,s,:) \bullet \mathcal{B}(s,j,:)$ for $i \in [n_1]$ and $j \in [n_4]$, and $\bullet$ denotes the circular convolution operation. In addition, the tensor product has an equivalent matrix-product form:

$$\underline{\mathcal{T}} = \underline{\mathcal{A}}^c \underline{\mathcal{B}}. \tag{2}$$

2.2   Tensor Sparse Coding for Images

Considering r input images X of size $p \times q$, we first sample the image tensor $\mathcal{X} \in \mathbb{R}^{p \times q \times r}$ using tensor cubes and reshape it to be the input tensor block $\mathcal{T} \in \mathbb{R}^{d \times N \times n}$ (detailed relationships of d, N, n with p, q, r and the tensor cubes are shown in Sect. 4). $\mathcal{T}$ can be approximated with an overcomplete tensor dictionary $\mathcal{D} \in \mathbb{R}^{d \times m \times n}$, $m > d$ as follows [6]:

$$\mathcal{T} = \mathcal{D} * \mathcal{C} = \mathcal{D}_1 * \mathcal{C}_1 + ... + \mathcal{D}_m * \mathcal{C}_m, \tag{3}$$

where $\mathcal{C} \in \mathbb{R}^{m \times N \times n}$ is the tensor coefficient with slice $\mathcal{C}_j = \mathcal{C}(j,:,:)$.

One of the proposed schemes for tensor sparse coding is based on the ℓ_1-norm of the coefficient. The sparse coding problem in tensor representation is as follows:

$$\min_{\mathcal{D}, \mathcal{C}} \quad \frac{1}{2} \|\mathcal{T} - \mathcal{D} * \mathcal{C}\|_F^2 + \lambda \|\mathcal{C}\|_1$$

$$\text{s.t.} \quad \|\mathcal{D}(:,j,:)\|_F^2 \leqslant 1, j \in [m], \tag{4}$$

where the size of the dictionary $\mathcal{D}$ is $d \times m \times n$, $m > d$. However, traditional sparse coding requires the size of the dictionary to be $(d \times n) \times m, m > d \times n$, which significantly increases with the increase in dimensionality, as shown in [6]. A smaller dictionary is easier to learn in tensor sparse coding, which is a more efficient way to encode images compared with traditional sparse coding methods.

Our proposed TSRGAN scheme are based on tensor representation, to reduce the dictionary size and improve the dictionary learning efficiency, which is the key advantage of the proposed method over other more advanced approaches like BigGANs [1], Progressive GAN [11], SNGAN [21], etc. Moreover, our proposed framework of cascading tensor super-resolution with DCGAN is actually orthogonal to those advanced GAN methods, which means the DCGAN can actually be replaced by more advanced GANs to leverage the advantages of tensor sparse coding as well.

3   TSRGAN Scheme

As a generative model with tensor super-resolution, the TSRGAN scheme could be divided into two phases: the training phase and the generation phase. First of all, two-dimensional (2D) images are transformed into the tensor space as a preprocess. In the generation phase: using pretrained DCGAN to generate low-resolution image tensors from random distributions, we apply tensor super-resolution for transforming low-resolution image tensors to high-resolution image tensors. High-resolution 2D images can be derived from the obtained high-resolution image tensors. The tensor dictionaries we used in the tensor super-resolution process and the DCGAN are both pretrained with large numbers of high-resolution and low-resolution image tensors in the training phase. The training phase is ahead of the generation phase in implementations. Our proposed approach combines DCGAN with tensor-based super-resolution, to directly generate high-resolution images.

3.1   Tensor Representation in TSRGAN

An important motivation of applying the tensor representation for large-image generation is the advantage of smaller size of both the dictionary and the sparse coefficients, as shown in Sect. 2.2. For instance, a tensor of size $T \in \mathbb{R}^{d \times N \times n}$ with tensor sparse coding has both the dictionary size and size of sparse coefficients at least n times smaller than the traditional sparse coding methods. Moreover, there are other advantages including the invariance of shifting [6,18] and more concise representation of images, which make the proposed TSRGAN scheme to have larger potential to be effective in practice. We make the assumption [25] that the inner patterns of images can be at least approximately sparsely represented with a learned dictionary. For tensor dictionary representation, $T = \mathcal{D} * \mathcal{C}$, where $T \in \mathbb{R}^{d \times N \times n}, \mathcal{D} \in \mathbb{R}^{d \times m \times n}, \mathcal{C} \in \mathbb{R}^{m \times N \times n}$. Therefore, tensor representation of images is necessary, which acts as the main representation of images in our workflows.

3.2   Data Preprocess: "Folding" and "Unfolding"

We obtain the tensor input block $\mathcal{T}$ with original images $X \in \mathbb{R}^{p \times q}$ with the "folding" process as follows. We first concatenate r images shifted from the same original image $X \in \mathbb{R}^{p \times q}$ for high-resolution or $X \in \mathbb{R}^{\frac{p}{c} \times \frac{q}{c}}$ for low-resolution (first upsampling it to be $X \in \mathbb{R}^{p \times q}$ in the generation phase) with different pixels to obtain the image representation tensor $\mathcal{X} \in \mathbb{R}^{p \times q \times r}$, as shown in Fig. 2. Then we sample N_0 image tensors $\mathcal{T}$ in all dimensions with the tensor block of size $a \times a \times a$ to obtain N sample blocks, where $N = N_0 \times (p - a + 1) \times (q - a + 1) \times (r - a + 1)$. Therefore, the size of image representation tensor is $(a \times a \times a) \times (p - a + 1) \times (q - a + 1) \times (r - a + 1)$. The tensor is reshaped to be input tensor blocks $\mathcal{T} \in \mathbb{R}^{d \times N \times n}$, where $d = a \times a, n = a$. For training phase, X are 2D images from the training set; and for generation phase, X are generated with DCGAN from random distributions. Note that the tensor dictionary $\mathcal{D} \in \mathbb{R}^{d \times m \times n}$ is independent of the number of samples N.

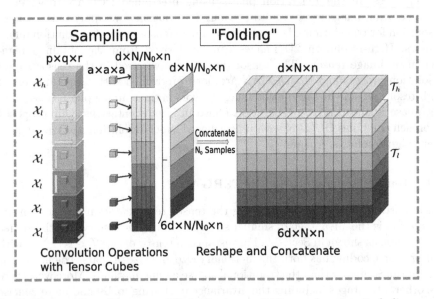

Fig. 2. Preparation of the tensor blocks for tensor dictionary learning, including sampling and "folding". With the concatenated high-resolution image tensors $\mathcal{X}_h$ and low-resolution image tensors $\mathcal{X}_l$ (upsampled to have same size with $\mathcal{X}_h$) from the same original image, we sample (through a convolution operation) $\mathcal{X}_l$ in all dimensions and $\mathcal{X}_h$ in one dimension with the tensor cubes of size $a \times a \times a$, to obtain N sample blocks and reshape them. With a batch of original images, we could obtain the tensor blocks $\mathcal{T}_l \in \mathbb{R}^{d_l \times N \times n}$ and $\mathcal{T}_h \in \mathbb{R}^{d_h \times N \times n}$, where $d_l = 6 \times d, d_h = d$.

The inverse process of the above "folding" process is called the "unfolding" process, which is used for recovering the high-resolution 2D images from the obtained high-resolution tensor output blocks. The "unfolding" is just a trivial combination of inversing each step in "folding".

3.3 The Training Phase: DCGAN Training and Tensor Dictionary Learning

In our model, we first downsample the original images $X \in \mathbb{R}^{p \times q}$ in the training set to high-resolution images $\boldsymbol{X}_h \in \mathbb{R}^{p \times q}$ and low-resolution images $\boldsymbol{X}_l \in \mathbb{R}^{\frac{p}{c} \times \frac{q}{c}}$ at the downsampling rate c, and we further transform them into tensor representation $\mathcal{X}_l, \mathcal{X}_h$. Then we train DCGAN with X_l to generate low-resolution tensor images $\mathcal{T}_G \in \mathbb{R}^{\frac{p}{c} \times \frac{q}{c} \times r}$ from random distributions $\mathbf{r} \sim \text{Uniform}(0, 1)$. The reconstruction loss and adversarial loss are formulated as a minimax game:

$$\min_{G} \max_{D} L(G, D) = \mathbb{E}_{\mathbf{r} \sim U} \left[\log(1 - D(G(\mathbf{r}))) \right]$$
$$+ \mathbb{E} \left[\log D(X_l) \right], \tag{5}$$

where G, D denote generator and discriminator of DCGAN, and $\mathbf{r}, U$ denote the latent vector and uniform distributions. The images in tensor representation $\mathcal{X}_l$ and $\mathcal{X}_h$ are further transformed to be input tensor blocks $\mathcal{T}_l$ and $\mathcal{T}_h$ (as shown in the data preprocess of Sect. 3.2) for training the dictionaries $\mathcal{D}_l$ and $\mathcal{D}_h$ in tensor super-resolution. We have tensor product relationships in tensor sparse coding: $\mathcal{T}_h = \mathcal{D}_h * \mathcal{C}_h$ and $\mathcal{T}_l = \mathcal{D}_l * \mathcal{C}_l$, where $\mathcal{C}_h, \mathcal{C}_l$ denotes tensor sparse coefficients for high-resolution images and low-resolution images respectively. Note that, in tensor super-resolution, it is reasonable to set $\mathcal{C}_h = \mathcal{C}_l$ and denote it with $\mathcal{C}$ [29]. This treatment for the coefficients in super-resolution is derived from the intuition that images can be represented well with sparse codes and appropriate over-complete dictionaries, for both low- and high-resolution images.

3.4 Details About Tensor Super-Resolution

The goal for tensor super-resolution is to transform low-resolution images X_l into high-resolution images X_h through the tensor spares coding approach. For an input tensor $\mathcal{T} \in \mathbb{R}^{d \times N \times n}$, tensor dictionary learning is similar to (the only difference is the dimensions) the tensor sparse coding in Sect. 3.2, where $\mathcal{D} \in \mathbb{R}^{d \times m \times n}$ is the tensor dictionary, and its slice $\mathcal{D}(:, j, :)$ is a basis, $\mathcal{C} \in \mathbb{R}^{m \times N \times n}$ is the tensor sparse coefficient. The first and second term uses the Frobenius norm and ℓ_1-norm in Eq. (6), respectively.

If taking the sparse coding process of different resolution images as similar patterns with respect to different bases, we could consider that high-resolution and low-resolution tensor images from the same origins have sparse and approximate tensor coefficients $\mathcal{C}$. Therefore the constraints of two dictionaries could be combined as follows (neglect the normalization constraints here):

$$\mathcal{D} = \arg \min_{\mathcal{D}, \mathcal{C}} ||\mathcal{T} - \mathcal{D} * \mathcal{C}||_F^2 + \lambda ||\mathcal{C}||_1, \tag{6}$$

where

$$\mathcal{T} = \begin{bmatrix} \frac{1}{\sqrt{N_h}} \mathcal{T}_h \\ \frac{1}{\sqrt{N_l}} \mathcal{T}_l \end{bmatrix}, \mathcal{D} = \begin{bmatrix} \frac{1}{\sqrt{N_h}} \mathcal{D}_h \\ \frac{1}{\sqrt{N_l}} \mathcal{D}_l \end{bmatrix}, \lambda = \frac{\lambda_h}{N_h} + \frac{\lambda_l}{N_l}, \tag{7}$$

where $\mathcal{T}_h, \mathcal{T}_l$ represent input tensor blocks of high-resolution and low-resolution images and N_h, N_l denote the first dimensional size of $\mathcal{T}_h, \mathcal{T}_l$ respectively. We then apply the Lagrange dual method and the iterative shrinkage threshold algorithm based on tensor-product to solve the tensor dictionaries and tensor sparse coefficients, using an alternative minimization approach [17]. The minimization problem can be rewritten as:

$$\min_{\mathcal{C}} f(\mathcal{C}) + \lambda g(\mathcal{C}) \tag{8}$$

where $f(\mathcal{C})$ stands for $\frac{1}{2}||\mathcal{T} - \mathcal{D} * \mathcal{C}||_F^2$ and $g(\mathcal{C})$ stands for $||\mathcal{C}||_1$ (coefficient $\frac{1}{2}$ can be absorbed in λ). At the $(s+1)$-th iteration,

$$\mathcal{C}_{s+1} = \arg\min_{\mathcal{C}} f(\mathcal{C}_s) + \langle \nabla f(\mathcal{C}_s), \mathcal{C} - \mathcal{C}_s \rangle$$
$$+ \frac{L_{s+1}}{2} ||\mathcal{C} - \mathcal{C}_s||_F^2 + \lambda g(\mathcal{C}), \tag{9}$$

where L_{s+1} is a Lipschitz constant. Therefore,

$$\mathcal{C}_{s+1} = \arg\min_{\mathcal{C}} \frac{1}{2} ||\mathcal{C} - (\mathcal{C}_s - \frac{1}{L_{s+1}} \nabla f(\mathcal{C}_s))||_F^2$$
$$+ \frac{\lambda}{L_{s+1}} ||\mathcal{C}||_1, \tag{10}$$

We can obtain the Lipschitz constant that $L = \sum_{b=1}^{n} ||\tilde{\mathcal{D}}^{(b)H} \tilde{\mathcal{D}}^{(b)}||_F^2$, $\tilde{\mathcal{D}}^{(b)}$ is the discrete fourier transformation (DFT) of the third-dimension slice $\mathcal{D}^{(b)}(:, j), b \in [n]$, and subscript H implies that it is a conjugate transpose. In the implemented algorithm for the training process of $\mathcal{C}$, we use $\mathbf{Prox}_{\beta/L}$ to solve the above equations, which is the proximal operator [22]. We therefore obtain the tensor sparse coding coefficients $\mathcal{C}$ through iteratively solving Eq. (10).

For learning the dictionary $\mathcal{D}$ with fixed $\mathcal{C}$, the optimization problem can be decoupled for each of the n slices of $\mathcal{D}$ according to the frequency domain:

$$\min_{\mathcal{D}^{(b)} \in \mathbb{R}^{d \times m}, b \in [n]} ||\tilde{\mathcal{T}}^{(b)} - \tilde{\mathcal{D}}^{(b)} \cdot \tilde{\mathcal{C}}^{(b)}||_F^2$$
$$\text{s.t. } ||\tilde{\mathcal{D}}^{(b)}(:, j)||_F^2 \leqslant 1, j \in [m], b \in [n]. \tag{11}$$

Therefore, with the Langrange dual, we obtain

$$\mathcal{L}(\tilde{\mathcal{D}}, \Omega) = \sum_{b=1}^{n} ||\tilde{\mathcal{T}}^{(b)} - \tilde{\mathcal{D}}^{(b)} \cdot \tilde{\mathcal{C}}^{(b)}||_F^2$$
$$+ \sum_{j=1}^{m} \omega_j (\sum_{b=1}^{n} ||\tilde{\mathcal{D}}^{(b)}(:, j)||_F^2 - n). \tag{12}$$

Thus, the optimal formulation of $\widehat{\mathcal{D}}^{(b)}$ satisfies:

$$\tilde{\mathcal{D}}^{(b)} = (\tilde{\mathcal{T}}^{(b)} \tilde{\mathcal{C}}^{(b)H})(\tilde{\mathcal{C}}^{(b)} \tilde{\mathcal{C}}^{(b)H} + \Omega)^{-1}. \tag{13}$$

Algorithm 1. TSRGAN - Training Phase

1: **Input:** original images $X \in \mathbb{R}^{p \times q}$, training iteration T, S, sparsity parameter λ;
2: Initialize the parameters, transform the data into tensor representation space and train the DCGAN.
3: **for** $k = 1$ to T **do**
4:    *# Solve tensor coefficient $\mathcal{C}$.*
5:    **for** $s = 1$ to S **do**
6:       Set $L_s = \eta_s(\sum_{b=1}^{n} \|\widehat{\mathcal{D}}^{(b)^H} \widehat{\mathcal{D}}^{(b)}\|_F)$;
7:       Compute $\nabla f(\mathcal{C}_s)$;
8:       Compute $\mathcal{C}_s$ via $\mathbf{Prox}_{\beta / L_s}(\mathcal{C}_s - \frac{1}{L_s}\nabla f(\mathcal{C}_s))$;
9:       $t_{s+1} = \frac{1+\sqrt{1+4t_s^2}}{2}$;
10:      $\mathcal{C}_{s+1} = \mathcal{C}_s + \frac{t_s - 1}{t_{s+1}}(\mathcal{C}_s - \mathcal{C}_{s-1})$;
11:   **end for**
12:   *# Solve tensor dictionaries $\mathcal{D}_h, \mathcal{D}_l$.*
13:   Take Fourier transformation for $\mathcal{T} = [1/\sqrt{N_h}\mathcal{T}_h, 1/\sqrt{N_l}\mathcal{T}_l]^T$ to obtain $\tilde{\mathcal{T}}$ and $\tilde{\mathcal{C}}$;
14:   Solve Equ. (14) for ω via Newton's method;
15:   Derive $\tilde{\mathcal{D}}^{(b)}$ from Equ. (13), $l \in [n]$;
16:   Take inverse Fourier transformation of $\tilde{\mathcal{D}}$ to derive $\mathcal{D}$. $\mathcal{D}$ includes feature dictionary $\mathcal{D}_l$ and recovery dictionary $\mathcal{D}_h$.
17: **end for**
18: **Output:** feature and recovery dictionaries: $\mathcal{D}_l$ and $\mathcal{D}_h$.

Therefore,

$$\mathcal{L}(\Omega) = -\sum_{b=1}^{n} \mathbf{Tr}(\tilde{\mathcal{C}}^{(b)^H} \tilde{\mathcal{T}}^{(b)} \tilde{\mathcal{D}}^{(b)^H}) - n \sum_{j=1}^{m} \omega_j. \tag{14}$$

Equation (14) can be solved with Newton's method. Substitute the derived Lagrange multiplier $\Omega = \{\omega_j\}, j \in [m]$ in Eq. (13). Thus, we can derive the dictionary $\mathcal{D}$ through inverse fourier transformation of $\tilde{\mathcal{D}}^{(b)}$.

3.5 The Generation Phase

In the generation phase, we first generate low-resolution images $\mathcal{T}_G \in \mathbb{R}^{p \times q}$ with the trained DCGAN model directly from latent vectors $\mathbf{r}$ in random distribution, and concatenate them to make image tensors $\mathcal{T}_G \in \mathbb{R}^{p \times q \times r}$. Then, we set $\mathcal{T}_l = \mathcal{T}_G$ to derive the tensor sparse coefficients $\mathcal{C}$ with the relationship $\mathcal{T}_l = \mathcal{D}_l * \mathcal{C}$ and trained dictionary $\mathcal{D}_l$ with $\mathcal{C}$. Finally we use $\mathcal{T}_h' = \mathcal{D}_h * \mathcal{C}$ to generate high-resolution output tensor block $\mathcal{T}_h'$ with derived dictionary $\mathcal{D}_h$. The output high-resolution 2D images $X' \in \mathbb{R}^{p \times q}$ are obtained through "unfolding" the generated high-resolution tensor block $\mathcal{T}_h'$.

Algorithm 2. TSRGAN - Generation Phase

1: **Input:** $\mathcal{D}_h \in \mathbb{R}^{d_h \times m \times n}, \mathcal{D}_l \in \mathbb{R}^{d_l \times m \times n}$;
2: Use the trained DCGAN to generate low-resolution images $T_G \in \mathbb{R}^{\frac{p}{c} \times \frac{q}{c}}$ from the latent vector $\mathbf{r} \in \mathbb{R}^{u \times 1}$ in random distributions, and further concatenate r images T_G to image tensors $\mathcal{T}_G \in \mathbb{R}^{\frac{p}{c} \times \frac{q}{c} \times r}$;
3: Reshape $\mathcal{T}_G$ to be $\mathcal{T}_l' \in \mathbb{R}^{d_l \times N' \times n}$ through sampling and "folding", and use $\mathcal{T}_l' = \mathcal{D}_l * \mathcal{C}$ to obtain tensor sparse coding coefficients $\mathcal{C}$ with feature dictionary $\mathcal{D}_l$ derived above;
4: Derive $\mathcal{T}_h' = \mathcal{D}_h * \mathcal{C}$;
5: Transform $\mathcal{T}_h'$ into 2D images $X' \in \mathbb{R}^{p \times q}$ through the "unfolding" process;
6: **Output:** Generated high-resolution 2D images X'.

---

4   Performance Evaluation

In this section, we present the results of proposed TSRGAN scheme on three datasets: MNIST [15], CIFAR10 [14], PASCAL2 VOC [5]. The image size of these three datasets applied in our model is $28 \times 28, 32 \times 32, 374 \times 374$ (downscaled from original 375×500 pixels), repectively.

4.1   Experiments Setting

DCGAN neural network parameters: the generator network has one fully connected layer and three transposed convolutional layers, with a decreasing number of 5×5 filter kernels, decreasing by a factor of 2 from 4×64 to 64 kernels and finally one channel of output images. The discriminator has three convolutional layers, with an increasing number of 5×5 filter kernels consistent with the generator. We use LeakyReLu [28] with parameter $\alpha = 0.2$ to avoid max-pooling. Strided convolutions of size $[1, 2, 2, 1]$ are used in each convolutional layer and tranposed convolutional layer. The learning rate is set to 1×10^{-4} and stochastic gradient descent is applied with a mini-batch size of 32.

By default, $u = 128, d_h = 16, d_l = 96, m = 128, n = 4, N = 10000, N' = 2500$. The number of directions for pixel-shifting is $r = 7$. The number of iterations $T = 10, S = 50$. The sparsity parameter $\lambda = 0.05$. β in **Prox** method is 0.05. For MNIST data, original images of size $p \times q, p = 28, q = 28$ (size values are set accordingly for other two datasets), downsampling rate $c = 2$.

4.2   Inception Score of Generation Results

We adopt the inception score (IS) metric [24, 27] to compare performance of different schemes. The metric compares three kinds of samples, including our generated images, other generated images from similar generative methods and the real images. The inception score metric is $\exp [\mathbb{E}_{\mathbf{x} \sim X'} \mathbb{KL}(p(y|\mathbf{x}) \| p(y))]$. The comparison results of the AAE and our TSRGAN model are shown in Table 1. The proposed TSRGAN achieves better results in all three datasets, especially for larges-sized PASCAL2 images (e.g. 374×374). Its inception score of 4.02 for PASCAL2 images significantly outperforms AAE of 3.81.

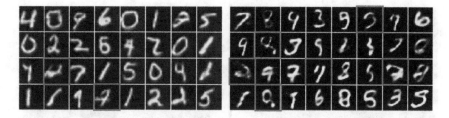

Fig. 3. MNIST samples of 28 × 28 pixels: for TSRGAN and AAE model, we pick the generated digital number images which are hard to recognize (in red borders). The number of the obscure images of TSRGAN (left) and AAE (right) is 2 and 6, respectively. (Color figure online)

Table 1. The inception score estimates metric are measured for AAE and proposed TSRGAN on CIFAR10 and Pascal2 VOC datasets.

Dataset	CIFAR 10	Pascal2 VOC
AAE [20]	3.98	3.81
TSRGAN	**4.05**	**4.02**

4.3 Generated Images of TSRGAN

Some of the testing results on benchmark datasets are shown in the end of the paper. Figure 3 shows the comparison of MNIST images generation with TSRGAN and AAE. The TSRGAN model provides images with more precise features of digital numbers, which benefits from its concise and efficient representation in tensor space. The effects of tensor super-resolution are shown in Fig. 4 for MNIST images with ablation studies. The images generated with general DCGAN have much coarser features without the tensor-based super-resolution process, which testifies that tensor super-resolution can significantly increase the

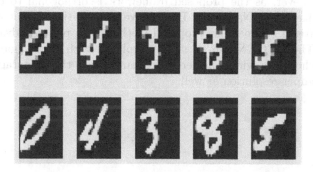

Fig. 4. Ablation studies: MNIST samples using TSRGAN with (below) or without (above) tensor super-resolution. This testifies the significant effects of tensor-based super-resolution process.

Fig. 5. PASCAL2 samples of 374 × 374 pixels: we show the large size airplane samples generated by TSRGAN, compared with the same-sized samples generated by AAE for airplane images in PASCAL2.

image quality with more convincing details. Figures 5 and 6 shows the generation results on PASCAL2 and CIFAR10 datasets, both testify the capability of TSR-GAN in generating images with better quality, especially for large images (e.g. 374 × 374) in PASCAL2. Images generated with TSRGAN have more precise features and convincing details than images generated by AAE. This testifies that TSRGAN preserves spatial structures and local proximal information in a better way than traditional methods. Generally, the DCGAN generates basic shapes, structures, and colors of images, while the cascading tensor super-resolution process improves the images with more details.

It is worth noticing that the DCGAN applied in our proposed framework is a simple and straightforward method for illustrating our original ideas of combining tensor super-resolution. And experiments show the advantages of cascading tensor super-resolution with GAN methods for large image generation in a tensor space. However, as the proposed framework is orthogonal to other GAN approaches, like BigGANs [1] and Progressive GAN [11], it is not a necessary or fair comparison between our proposed method with present advanced GAN approaches. The DCGAN can be simply replaced with those more advanced GAN approaches to provide a better performance, with the advantages of leveraging tensor super-resolution as well.

Fig. 6. CIFAR10 samples of 128 × 128 pixels (4 × 4 image matrix of 32 × 32 pixels images): TSRGAN and AAE model. We show three kinds of samples: airplane, bird, and car. Above are generated by TSRGAN, and below are AAE.

5   Conclusion

In this paper, we proposed a TSRGAN scheme that integrates DCGAN model and tensor super-resolution, which is able to generate large-sized high-quality images. The proposed scheme applies tensor representation space as main operation space for image generation, which shows better results than traditional generative models working in image pixel space. Essentially, the adversarial process of TSRGAN takes place in a tensor space. Note that in the tensor super-resolution process, tensor sparse coding brings several advantages: (i) the size of dictionary, which accelerates the training process for deriving the representation dictionary; (ii) more concise and efficient representation for images, which is verified in the generated images in our experiments. TSRGAN is superior in preserving spatial structures and local proximity information in images. Accordingly, the tensor super-resolution benefits from tensor representation to generate higher-quality images, especially for large images. Our proposed cascading TSR-

GAN scheme surpasses the generative model AAE on three datasets (MNIST, CIFAR10, and PASCAL2).

References

1. Brock, A., Donahue, J., Simonyan, K.: Large scale GAN training for high fidelity natural image synthesis. arXiv preprint arXiv:1809.11096 (2018)
2. Denton, E.L., Chintala, S., Fergus, R., et al.: Deep generative image models using a laplacian pyramid of adversarial networks. In: Advances in Neural Information Processing Systems, pp. 1486–1494 (2015)
3. Dong, C., Loy, C.C., He, K., Tang, X.: Learning a deep convolutional network for image super-resolution. In: Fleet, D., Pajdla, T., Schiele, B., Tuytelaars, T. (eds.) ECCV 2014. LNCS, vol. 8692, pp. 184–199. Springer, Cham (2014). https://doi.org/10.1007/978-3-319-10593-2_13
4. Dong, C., Loy, C.C., He, K., Tang, X.: Image super-resolution using deep convolutional networks. IEEE Trans. Pattern Anal. Mach. Intell. 38(2), 295–307 (2016)
5. Everingham, M., Gool, L., Williams, C.K., Winn, J., Zisserman, A.: The pascal visual object classes (VOC) challenge. Int. J. Comput. Vis. 88(2), 303–338 (2010)
6. Fei, J., Liu, X.-Y., Lu, H., Shen, R.: Efficient multi-dimensional tensor sparse coding using t-linear combinations. In: Association for the Advancement of Artificial Intelligence (2018)
7. Goodfellow, I., et al.: Generative adversarial nets. In: Advances in Neural Information Processing Systems, pp. 2672–2680 (2014)
8. Gregor, K., Danihelka, I., Graves, A., Rezende, D.J., Wierstra, D.: Draw: a recurrent neural network for image generation. arXiv preprint arXiv:1502.04623 (2015)
9. Gu, S., Sang, N., Ma, F.: Fast image super resolution via local regression. In: Proceedings of the 21st International Conference on Pattern Recognition (ICPR 2012), pp. 3128–3131. IEEE (2012)
10. Hao, N., Kilmer, M.E., Braman, K., Hoover, R.C.: Facial recognition using tensor-tensor decompositions. SIAM J. Imaging Sci. 6(1), 437–463 (2013)
11. Karras, T., Aila, T., Laine, S., Lehtinen, J.: Progressive growing of GANs for improved quality, stability, and variation. arXiv preprint arXiv:1710.10196 (2017)
12. Kingma, D.P., Welling, M.: Auto-encoding variational bayes. In: International Conference on Learning Representations (2014)
13. Kolda, T.G., Bader, B.W.: Tensor decompositions and applications. SIAM Rev. 51(3), 455–500 (2009)
14. Krizhevsky, A., Hinton, G.: Learning multiple layers of features from tiny images. Technical report. Citeseer (2009)
15. LeCun, Y., Bottou, L., Bengio, Y., Haffner, P.: Gradient-based learning applied to document recognition. Proc. IEEE 86(11), 2278–2324 (1998)
16. Ledig, C., et al.: Photo-realistic single image super-resolution using a generative adversarial network. In: CVPR, vol. 2, p. 4 (2017)
17. Liu, X.-Y., Aeron, S., Aggarwal, V., Wang, X.: Low-tubal-rank tensor completion using alternating minimization. arXiv preprint arXiv:1610.01690 (2017)
18. Liu, X.-Y., Aeron, S., Aggarwal, V., Wang, X., Wu, M.-Y.: Adaptive sampling of RF fingerprints for fine-grained indoor localization. IEEE Trans. Mob. Comput. 15(10), 2411–2423 (2015)
19. Liu, X.-Y., Wang, X.: Fourth-order tensors with multidimensional discrete transforms. arXiv preprint arXiv:1705.01576 (2017)

20. Makhzani, A., Shlens, J., Jaitly, N., Goodfellow, I., Frey, B.: Adversarial autoencoders. In: International Conference on Learning Representations (2016)
21. Miyato, T., Kataoka, T., Koyama, M., Yoshida, Y.: Spectral normalization for generative adversarial networks. arXiv preprint arXiv:1802.05957 (2018)
22. Parikh, N., Boyd, S., et al.: Proximal algorithms. Found. Trends® Optim. **1**(3), 127–239 (2014)
23. Radford, A., Metz, L., Chintala, S.: Unsupervised representation learning with deep convolutional generative adversarial networks. arXiv preprint arXiv:1511.06434 (2015)
24. Salimans, T., Goodfellow, I., Zaremba, W., Cheung, V., Radford, A., Chen, X.: Improved techniques for training GANs. In: Advances in Neural Information Processing Systems, pp. 2234–2242 (2016)
25. She, B., Wang, Y., Liang, J., Liu, Z., Song, C., Hu, G.: A data-driven avo inversion method via learned dictionaries and sparse representation. Geophysics **83**(6), 1–91 (2018)
26. Shi, W., et al.: Real-time single image and video super-resolution using an efficient sub-pixel convolutional neural network. In: Proceedings of the IEEE Conference on Computer Vision and Pattern Recognition, pp. 1874–1883 (2016)
27. Szegedy, C., Vanhoucke, V., Ioffe, S., Shlens, J., Wojna, Z.: Rethinking the inception architecture for computer vision. In: Proceedings of the IEEE Conference on Computer Vision and Pattern Recognition, pp. 2818–2826 (2016)
28. Xu, B., Wang, N., Chen, T., Li, M.: Empirical evaluation of rectified activations in convolutional network. arXiv preprint arXiv:1505.00853 (2015)
29. Yang, J., Wright, J., Huang, T.S., Ma, Y.: Image super-resolution via sparse representation. IEEE Trans. Image Process. **19**(11), 2861–2873 (2010)
30. Zhang, H., et al.: StackGAN: text to photo-realistic image synthesis with stacked generative adversarial networks. In: IEEE International Conference on Computer Vision, pp. 5907–5915 (2017)

Avoiding Implementation Pitfalls of "Matrix Capsules with EM Routing" by Hinton *et al.*

Ashley Daniel Gritzman(✉) ⓘ

IBM Research, Johannesburg, South Africa
`ashley.gritzman@za.ibm.com`

Abstract. The recent progress on capsule networks by Hinton *et al.* has generated considerable excitement in the machine learning community. The idea behind a capsule is inspired by a cortical minicolumn in the brain, whereby a vertically organised group of around 100 neurons receive common inputs, have common outputs, are interconnected, and may well constitute a fundamental computation unit of the cerebral cortex. However, Hinton's paper on "Matrix Capsule with EM Routing" was unfortunately not accompanied by a release of source code, which left interested researchers attempting to implement the architecture and reproduce the benchmarks on their own. This has certainly slowed the progress of research building on this work. While writing our own implementation, we noticed several common mistakes in other open source implementations that we came across. In this paper we share some of these learnings, specifically focusing on three implementation pitfalls and how to avoid them: (1) parent capsules with only one child; (2) normalising the amount of data assigned to parent capsules; (3) parent capsules at different positions compete for child capsules. While our implementation is a considerable improvement over currently available implementations, it still falls slightly short of the performance reported by Hinton *et al.* (2018). The source code for this implementation is available on GitHub at the following URL: https://github.com/IBM/matrix-capsules-with-em-routing.

Keywords: Capsules · EM routing · Hinton · CNN

1 Introduction

Geoffrey Hinton has been talking about "capsule networks" for a long time, so when his team published their recent progress on this topic, it naturally created quite a stir in the machine learning community. The idea behind a capsule is inspired by a cortical minicolumn in the brain, whereby a vertically organised group of around 100 neurons receive common inputs, have common outputs, are interconnected, and may well constitute a fundamental computation unit of the cerebral cortex [2]. In the context of machine learning, a capsule is a group of

© Springer Nature Singapore Pte Ltd. 2019
A. Zeng et al. (Eds.): HBAI 2019, CCIS 1072, pp. 224–234, 2019.
https://doi.org/10.1007/978-981-15-1398-5_16

neurons whose outputs represents not only the probability that an entity exists, but also different properties of the same entity. Capsules may encode information such as orientation, scale, velocity, and colour. Layers in a capsule network learn to assemble these entities to form parts of a larger whole.

In computer graphics, a scene is represented in abstract form comprising objects and their corresponding instantiation parameters (e.g. x, y location, and angle). A rendering function then converts this abstract representation into an image. Hinton argues that the brain does 'inverse graphics' [3], which essentially means deconstructing visual information received by the eyes into a hierarchical representation of the world, and then trying to match it with already learned patterns and relationships stored by the brain. A capsule network is basically a neural network that tries to perform inverse graphics.

Hinton *et al.* [4] first introduced the concept of capsule networks in 2011 when they used a transformation matrix in a "transforming auto-encoder" that learned to transform a stereo pair of images into a stereo pair from a slightly different viewpoint. But it was only towards the end of 2017 that Sabour *et al.* [13] published a capsule network architecture featuring dynamic routing-by-agreement that managed to reach state-of-the-art performance on MNIST [9], and considerably better results than CNNs on MultiMNIST [13] (a variant with overlapping pairs of different digits). Then in 2018, Hinton *et al.* [6] published "Matrix Capsules with EM Routing" to address some of the deficiencies of Sabour *et al.* [13], and reported a reduction in the test error on smallNORB [10] of 45% compared to state-of-the-art.

The matrix capsule version of a capsule network is described as follows [6]: "each capsule has a logistic unit to represent the presence of an entity and a 4×4 matrix which could learn to represent the relationship between that entity and the viewer (the pose). A capsule in one layer votes for the pose matrix of many different capsules in the layer above by multiplying its own pose matrix by trainable viewpoint-invariant transformation matrices that could learn to represent part-whole relationships. Each of these votes is weighted by an assignment coefficient. These coefficients are iteratively updated for each image using the Expectation-Maximization algorithm such that the output of each capsule is routed to a capsule in the layer above that receives a cluster of similar votes."

Sabour *et al.* [13] made their code for "Dynamic Routing between Capsules" available on GitHub [12], but unfortunately Hinton *et al.* [6] did not do the same for "Matrix Capsules with EM Routing", which may somewhat explain the slower progress in research building on this work. While implementing this work ourselves, we noticed several common mistakes in other implementations that we came across, and also discovered a couple of pitfalls which may prevent the network from operating as intended.

In this paper we share some of these learnings, specifically focusing on three implementation pitfalls and how to avoid them: (1) parent capsules with only one child; (2) normalising the amount of data assigned to parent capsules; (3) parent capsules at different positions compete for child capsules.

To make this paper slightly easier to consume for readers not entirely familiar the work, we try to simplify the terminology where possible, for example we use the terms "child capsules" to represent capsules in lower layer L, and "parent capsules" to represent capsules in higher layer $L + 1$. However, we do assume that the reader is already familiar with Hinton's paper [6], which is necessary in order to understand the discussion on the pitfalls that follows below.

2 Understanding and Avoiding Pitfalls

2.1 Parent Capsules with only One Child

The EM routing algorithm is a form of cluster finding which iteratively adjusts the assignment probabilities between child capsules and parent capsules. Figure 1 illustrates this process: at the start of EM routing, the output of each child capsule is evenly distributed to all of the parent capsules. As the EM algorithm proceeds, the affinity of parent capsules for particular child capsules increases, and eventually each child capsule may contribute to only one parent capsule. This phenomenon does not cause a problem if each parent capsule comprises multiple child capsules, however the situation may arise whereby a parent capsule comprises only one child capsule. This situation is similar to a clustering scenario whereby a cluster has only one data point. Since the EM routing algorithm fits a Gaussian distribution to each of the parent capsules, it is necessary to calculate the mean μ_j^h and variance $(\sigma_j^h)^2$ of each parent capsule. If the parent capsule comprises only one child capsule, then the variance of the parent capsule is 0. This causes numerical instability when calculating the activation cost in Eq. (1), as $log(\sigma_j^h)$ is undefined at $\sigma_j^h = 0$. Furthermore, a Gaussian distribution with a variance of 0 is the unit impulse centered at the mean μ_j^h, so $p_j(\mu_j^h) = \infty$ which causes numerical overflow.

$$cost^h \leftarrow \left(\beta_u + log(\sigma_j^h)\right) \sum_i R_{ij} \tag{1}$$

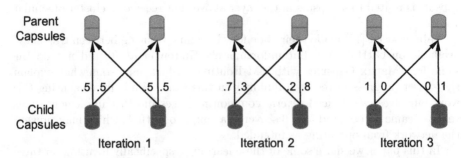

Fig. 1. Illustration of assignment probabilities between two capsule layers over three iterations of EM routing. At iteration 3 each parent capsule receives input from only one child capsule.

This problem of parent capsules having only one child capsule occurs more frequently as the number of routing iterations increases, whereby the assignment probabilities tend to either 0 or 1. In our experiments with the *smaller* capsule network configuration of $A = 64$, $B = 8$, $C = D = 16$, the problem did not occur during training with one or two iterations, but occurred consistently for *iterations* $\geqslant 3$.

Furthermore, the occurrence of this problem also depends on the ratio of child capsules to parent capsules. If the ratio is high, meaning many child capsules feeding fewer parent capsules, then the problem only occurs at higher routing iterations. Whereas, if the ratio is low and approaches 1:1, or even lower (i.e. more parent capsules than child capsules), then the problem starts occurring at a lower number of routing iterations.

To address this problem in our implementation, we impose a lower bound on the variance $(\sigma_j^h)^2$ by adding $\epsilon = 10^{-4}$.

2.2 Normalising the Amount of Data Assigned to Parent Capsules

In Eq. (1) computing the activation cost, $\sum_i R_{ij}$ is the amount of data assigned to parent capsule j from all child capsules.

For the convolutional capsule layers, each child capsule within the kernel feeds to one spatial location in the parent layer containing O types of capsules. If all child capsules within a convolutional kernel assign their data to only one parent capsule type, then the maximum data that a parent capsule can receive is give by:

$$max\_data = K \times K \times I \tag{2}$$

where K is the kernel size, and I is the number of input capsule types.

The mean data received by parent capsules (assuming that all child capsules are active) is the total number of child capsules divided by the total number of parent capsules:

$$mean\_data = \frac{child\_W \times child\_H \times I}{parent\_W \times parent\_H \times O} \tag{3}$$

where W and H denote the spatial width and height of the tensors containing the capsules, and O is the number of output capsule types.

For the final output layer denoted *class_caps*, the spatial dimensions of the child tensor is flattened such that the child capsules are fully connected to the *class* capsules.

Table 1 shows a summary of the layers in the *smaller* capsule network configuration. For capsule layers connected with EM routing, the maximum and mean assignment data is calculated with Eqs. (2) and (3). The mean assignment data is similar for both the *conv_caps1* and *conv_caps2* layers at 2.61 and 1.96 respectively, however notice that the mean data of the *class_caps* layer is ≈30× larger at 80.0. The larger assignment data for the *class_caps* layer occurs since each parent capsule in this layer is fully connected to all child capsules in *conv_caps2* layer. Therefore, the $5 \times 5 \times 16 = 400$ capsules in the *conv_caps2* layer feed to just 5 capsules in the *class_caps* layer.

Table 1. Summary of layers in the *smaller* capsule network configuration ($A = 64$, $B = 8$, $C = D = 16$) showing the maximum and mean assignment data between layers with EM routing. K is the kernel size, S is the stride, Ch is the number of channels in a regular convolution, I is the number of input capsule types, O is the number of output capsule types, W and H are the spatial width and height. The *Output shape* shows the dimensions of the tensor containing the *activations (batch size, W, H, Ch or O)*; the tensor containing the *poses* would have additional dimensions 4×4 for the *pose* matrix.

Layer	Details	Output shape	EM Rt. Data	
			Max	Mean
input		(?, 32, 32, 1)		
↪relu_conv1	K = 5, S = 2, Ch = 64	(?, 16, 16, 64)		
↪primary_caps	K = 1, S = 1, Ch = 8	(?, 16, 16, 8)		
↪conv_caps1	K = 3, S = 2, O = 16	(?, 7, 7, 16)	72	2.61
↪conv_caps2	K = 3, S = 1, O = 16	(?, 5, 5, 16)	144	1.96
↪class_caps	flatten, O = 5	(?, 1, 1, 5)	400	80.0

We now consider the effects of the large discrepancy in assignment data between the *class_caps* layer and the other layers. While the mean data was calculated under the assumption that all child capsules are active (which is unlikely), nevertheless the actual data assigned to a parent capsule $\sum_i R_{ij}$ will be proportional to the mean value of the layer.

Consider the computation of the parent activations from the M-step of Procedure 1 in [6]:

$$a_j \leftarrow logistic\left(\lambda\left(\beta_a - \sum_h \left(\beta_u + log(\sigma_j^h)\right) \sum_i R_{ij}\right)\right)$$

Since β_u is per capsule type and does not depend on h:

$$a_j \leftarrow logistic\left(\lambda\left(\beta_a - \sum_i R_{ij}\left(H\beta_u + \sum_h log(\sigma_j^h)\right)\right)\right) \qquad (4)$$

Finally:

$$a_j \leftarrow logistic\left(\lambda\beta_a - \lambda\sum_i R_{ij}\left(H\beta_u + \sum_h log(\sigma_j^h)\right)\right) \qquad (5)$$

Consider the second term in Eq. 4, notice that the cost of activating a parent capsule is scaled by the total amount of data received by that capsule $\sum_i R_{ij}$. In Eq. (5) the first term $\lambda\beta_a$ sets the operating point on the logistic curve, and the second term determines the perturbations about this point. If the $\sum_i R_{ij}$ scaling is too small, then all the output activations will not deviate from the operating point. But if the $\sum_i R_{ij}$ scaling is too large, then all the parent capsules will either be fully active or inactive. The most desirable situation occurs when the input to the logistic function is nicely distributed over a useful range (e.g. $[-5,5]$), so the output of the logistic function is nicely distributed over the range $[0,1]$.

The impact of the $\approx 30\times$ difference in assignment data is that the range of the input to the logistic function will not be distributed over a useful range for all capsule layers. The values β_a and β_v are learned discriminatively for each layer, and can to some extent compensate for this effect. However, since β_a and β_v are initialised randomly, the problem will be more pronounced at the start of training and may prevent the network from learning.

This problem can be addressed to an extent by carefully initialising β_a and β_v, which will need to be different for the *class_caps* layer and the preceding *conv_caps1* and *conv_caps2* layers. It will also be necessary to ensure that the λ scaling value ensures a useful range for the input to the logistic function at every layer. In our implementation we adopt a different approach, and instead scale the amount of data assigned to a parent capsule ($\sum_i R_{ij}$) relative to the mean data in a particular layer (see Table 1 for scaling values). We find this approach to be more robust to the initial values of β_a and β_v.

2.3   Parent Capsules at Different Positions Compete for Child Capsules

Consider the case of a 1D convolutional capsule layer, with a kernel size of 3 and a stride of 1, and where both child and parent layers contain only 1 capsule type. In the M-step shown in Fig. 2, the kernel slides over the child capsules resulting in each parent receiving votes from 3 child capsules. In the E-step, child capsules towards the edges receive feedback from fewer parent capsules, while capsules towards the center receive feedback from up to K parent capsules. In the example of Fig. 2, $\{C_1, C_5\}$ receive feedback from one parent capsule each, $\{C_2, C_4\}$ each receive feedback from two parent capsules, and $\{C_3\}$ receives feedback from three parent capsules.

It is clear from Fig. 2 that child capsules receive feedback from parent capsules at different spatial positions, and therefore these parent capsules must compete for the vote of the child capsule. The competition happens in the update of the assignment probabilities in the E-step, where we normalise across all parent capsules competing for a particular child capsule. This point was further clarified by the paper authors in response to a question on OpenReview.net [1].

We reviewed several open source implementations on GitHub, and found that incorrect normalisation in the E-step is a common mistake. In particular, the implementations normalise only across parent capsule types, and not across parent capsule positions. This has the unintended effect of preventing parent capsules at different positions from competing for child capsules. The correct method is to normalise across all parent capsules that receive input from a particular child capsule, which will include normalising across parent capsule types and parent capsule positions.

We found this important detail somewhat tricky to implement, so we describe our implementation below.

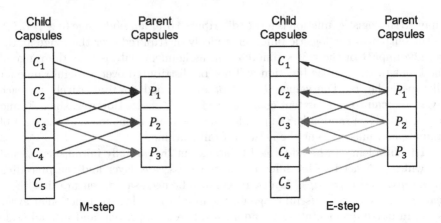

Fig. 2. Connectivity between parent capsules and child capsules resulting from 1D convolution with a kernel size of 3 and a stride of 1. In the **M-step**, all parent capsules receive input from 3 child capsules; in **E-step**, child capsules towards the edges receive feedback from fewer parent capsules, while capsules at towards the center receive feedback from up to 3 parent capsules.

With reference to Fig. 3, the first step in computing the votes is tiling the child capsules according to the convolution kernel. The subsequent mapping between child capsules and parent capsules is stored a 2D binary matrix called the *spatial routing map*. The tiled representation is then multiplied by a tensor containing K transformation matrices (3 in our example), which are learned discriminatively with backpropagation during training. The tiled child capsules at each spatial location are multiplied by the same transformation matrices. The votes are then scaled by the corresponding assignment probabilities R_{ij} and used in the M-step to compute the mean μ_j, standard deviation σ_j, and activation a_j of each parent capsule.

Our implementation of the E-step is shown in Fig. 4. The probability density p_{ij} of vote V_{ij} is computed from the Gaussian distribution of parent capsule P_j. The probability densities are then converted to sparse representation using the *spatial routing map* that was stored during the convolution operation. In the sparse representation the probability densities of each child capsule are aligned in one column, thereby enabling us to normalise over all parent capsules competing for a child capsule C_i.

Extending from 1D to 2D Convolution. The above description of our implementation refers to the case of 1D capsule convolution, with a stride of 1. In order to extend to 2D convolution, we unroll the spatial dimension of the child capsules and parent capsules. Figure 5 shows an example of the *spatial routing map* produced from 2D capsule convolution with a 3×3 kernel and of stride 2. The rows of the *spatial routing map* correspond to parent capsules, and the columns correspond to child capsules.

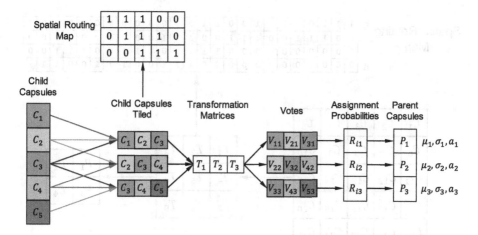

Fig. 3. Votes are computed by tiling the child capsules feeding to each parent capsule, and multiplying by the transformation matrix. The *spatial routing map* is a binary matrix which stores the spatial connectivity between child capsules and parent capsules resulting from the convolution operation. V_{ij} denotes the vote from child capsule i to parent capsule j. The votes are scaled by the corresponding assignment probabilities R_{ij} and used in the M-step to calculate the mean μ_j, standard deviation σ_j, and activation a_j of each parent capsule.

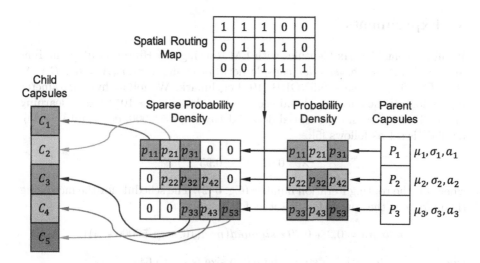

Fig. 4. Feedback of parent capsules to child capsules in the E-step of EM routing (follow diagram from right to left). p_{ij} denotes the probability density of vote V_{ij} under the Gaussian distribution of the parent capsule j. The *spatial routing map*, which stores the spatial connectivity between child capsules and parent capsules, is used to convert the probability densities to sparse representation thereby aligning by child capsule. Finally, the probability densities are used to update the routing assignments R_{ij} by normalising over columns of the sparse representation.

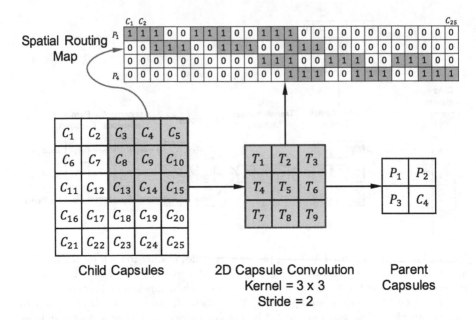

Fig. 5. Example of *spatial routing map* produced by 2D capsule convolution with a 3×3 kernel and stride of 2.

3   Experiments

We implement "Matrix Capsules with EM Routing" by Hinton *et al.* [6] in TensorFlow, and test the *smaller* capsule network configuration ($A = 64$, $B = 8$, $C = D = 16$) on the smallNORB [10] benchmark. We follow hyperparameter suggestions of the authors [7] and use a weight decay of 2×10^{-7}, and a learning rate of 3×10^{-3} with exponential decay: decay steps = 2000, decay rate = 0.96. Lambda is set as follows [5]:

$$\lambda = 0.01 * (1 - 0.95^{i+1})$$

where i is the routing iteration number (e.g. 0–2). The schedule for the increasing the margin in the spread loss is set as follows [5]:

$$margin = 0.2 + 0.79 * sigmoid\big(min(10, step/50000 - 4)\big)$$

where *step* is the training step. The batch size is set to 64.

Figure 6 shows the test accuracy of the matrix capsule model after each training epoch for 1–3 iterations of EM routing. Whereas Hinton *et al.* [6] report the maximum test accuracy at 3 routing iterations, in our implementation the maximum test accuracy of 95.4% occurs with 2 routing iterations, and with 3 iterations we record an accuracy of 93.7%.

In Table 2 we compare our implementation to other open source implementations available on GitHub. The accuracy of our implementation at

95.4% is a 3.8% point improvement on the previous best open source implementation by Zhang (www0wwwjs1) [14] at 91.8%, however it is still below the accuracy reported in Hinton *et al.* [6]. At this time, our implementation is currently the best open source implementation available.

Table 2. Comparison of test accuracy on smallNORB dataset for different implementations of "Matrix Capsules with EM Routing" by Hinton *et al.* [6]. For the open source implementations on GitHub, the test accuracy is reported as at 28/05/2019, and the specific commit is noted in the reference.

Implementation	Framework	Routing iterations	Test accuracy
Hinton [6]	Not available	3	**97.8%**
yl-1993 [11]	PyTorch	1	74.8%
yl-1993 [11]	PyTorch	2	89.5%
yl-1993 [11]	PyTorch	3	82.5%
www0wwwjs1 [14]	Tensorflow	2	91.8%
Officium [8]	PyTorch	3	90.9%
Ours	TensorFlow	1	86.2%
Ours	TensorFlow	2	**95.4%**
Ours	TensorFlow	3	93.7%

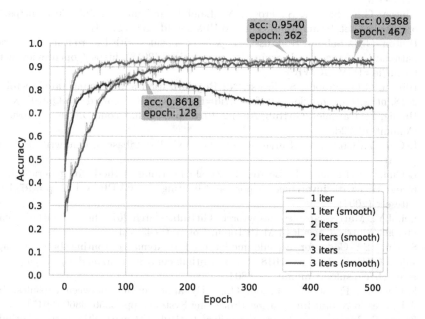

Fig. 6. Test accuracy of our implementation with 1–3 iterations of EM routing after each training epoch. Smoothed with exponentially-weighted moving window $\alpha = 0.25$.

4 Conclusion

In this paper we discuss three common pitfalls when implementing "Matrix Capsules with EM Routing" by Hinton *et al.*, and how to avoid them. While our implementation performs considerably better than other open source implementations, nevertheless it still falls slightly short of the performance reported by Hinton *et al.* (2018). The source code for this implementation is available on GitHub at the following URL: https://github.com/IBM/matrix-capsules-with-em-routing.

References

1. Calvano, G.S.: Some clarification on the convolution topology? July 2018. https:// openreview.net/forum?id=HJWLfGWRb&noteId=BJgX7Iy04m
2. Cruz, L., et al.: A statistically based density map method for identification and quantification of regional differences in microcolumnarity in the monkey brain. J. Neurosci. Methods **141**(2), 321–332 (2005)
3. Hinton, G., Krizhevsky, A., Jaitly, N., Tieleman, T., Tang, Y.: Does the brain do inverse graphics? In: Brain and Cognitive Sciences Fall Colloquium, vol. 2 (2012)
4. Hinton, G.E., Krizhevsky, A., Wang, S.D.: Transforming auto-encoders. In: Honkela, T., Duch, W., Girolami, M., Kaski, S. (eds.) ICANN 2011. LNCS, vol. 6791, pp. 44–51. Springer, Heidelberg (2011). https://doi.org/10.1007/978-3-642-21735-7_6
5. Hinton, G.E., Sabour, S., Frosst, N.: Lambda and margin, July 2018. https:// openreview.net/forum?id=HJWLfGWRb&noteId=BkelcSxC47
6. Hinton, G.E., Sabour, S., Frosst, N.: Matrix capsules with EM routing. In: International Conference on Learning Representations (2018). https://openreview.net/forum?id=HJWLfGWRb
7. Hinton, G.E., Sabour, S., Frosst, N.: Regularization and learning rate? October 2018. https://openreview.net/forum?id=HJWLfGWRb&noteId=rJeQnSsE3X
8. Huang, Y.: Capsules. GitHub, April 2019. https://github.com/Officium/Capsules. Commit: e1f02d3
9. LeCun, Y., Cortes, C., Burges, C.J.: The MNIST database of handwritten digits (1998)
10. LeCun, Y., Huang, F.J., Bottou, L., et al.: Learning methods for generic object recognition with invariance to pose and lighting. In: CVPR, vol. 2, pp. 97–104. Citeseer (2004)
11. Lei, J.Y.: Matrix-capsules-em-pytorch. GitHub, March 2019. https://github.com/yl-1993/Matrix-Capsules-EM-PyTorch. Commit: c4547bf
12. Sabour, S.: Code for capsule model used in dynamic routing between capsules. GitHub, January 2018. https://github.com/Sarasra/models/tree/master/research/capsules. Commit: cac8804
13. Sabour, S., Frosst, N., Hinton, G.E.: Dynamic routing between capsules. In: Advances in Neural Information Processing Systems, pp. 3856–3866 (2017)
14. Zhang, S.: Matrix-capsules-em-tensorflow. GitHub, February 2018. https://github.com/www0wwwjs1/Matrix-Capsules-EM-Tensorow. Commit: 0196ead

Adaptive Joint Attention
with Reinforcement Training
for Convolutional Image Caption

Ruoyu Chen, Zhongnian Li, and Daoqiang Zhang[✉]

College of Computer Science and Technology,
MIIT Key Laboratory of Pattern Analysis and Machine Intelligence,
Nanjing University of Aeronautics and Astronautics, Nanjing, China
{rychen,zhongnianli,dqzhang}@nuaa.edu.cn

Abstract. A convolutional decoder for image caption has proven to be easier to train than the Long Short Term Memory (LSTM) decoder [2]. However, previous convolutional image captioning methods are not good at capture the relationship between generated words, which could lead to failure in predicting visually unrelated words. To address this issue, we propose an Adaptive Joint Attention (AJA) module for the convolutional decoder, by incorporating self-attention to explore the correlation between generated words automatically. Specifically, we develop a word gate with multi-head self-attention to directly capture words' relationship. An adaptive combination strategy is proposed to learn which word is less related to image information. Besides, reinforcement learning is applied for directly optimizing the non-differentiable metrics while avoiding the exposure bias during inference. Extensive evaluations on two public data sets demonstrate that our method outperforms several state-of-the-art approaches in image captioning task.

Keywords: Computer vision · Image caption · Nature language generation

1 Introduction

The Encoder-Decoder framework [22] has been widely used for image captioning task. In this kind of framework, a LSTM is usually adopted as the language generation model. Generally speaking, LSTM takes the previous word embedding of ground-truth as inputs and then outputs a probability distribution over the predefined vocabulary for the next word. With a sequential prediction progress, LSTM is able to generate captions with variable length for input images. Although LSTM works well in image captioning task, it can not explicitly model the hierarchical structure of nature language [19]. Also, in contrast

This research was supported by the National Natural Science Foundation of China (61876082, 61861130366, 61732006, 61473149).

© Springer Nature Singapore Pte Ltd. 2019
A. Zeng et al. (Eds.): HBAI 2019, CCIS 1072, pp. 235–247, 2019.
https://doi.org/10.1007/978-981-15-1398-5_17

to convolutional neural networks (CNNs), that are non-sequential, LSTM often requires more careful engineering, when considering a novel task [2].

Recently, a convolutional sequence to sequence learning method (ConvS2S) [6] has emerged as a new architecture for machine translation. ConvS2S has also been successfully applied to some other challenging tasks like conditional image generation [16] and text summarization [23]. Inspired by these works, a convolutional sequence decoder was proposed to replace the LSTM language model in image captioning task [2].

Most of the previous captioning models based on a convolutional decoder are not good at capture the relationship between generated words, especially the long range ones [20]. What's more, some visually unrelated words like 'of' and 'on' can be reasoned from previous generated ones. The model may make mistakes if it pays more attention to image information when generating these words. As a result, relationship between generated words should be taken into account in a convolutional decoder and an adaptive combination strategy should be built into the model to learn when to put more weights on image information.

Inspired by the recent successes of attention models in machine translation [20], we propose an Adaptive Joint Attention (AJA) module for obtaining a better caption generator. In contrast to the existing convolutional image captioning models, our proposed method can directly model the inner relationship between generated words by a word self-attention block. In particular, we develop an adaptive combination strategy to automatically learn which word is less related to image information. In order to solve the exposure bias [3], we optimize our proposed model by employing reinforcement training [18], which can also directly use the non-differentiable metrics as rewards to guide the training progress. Figure 1(B) gives an example of captions generated by our method. The main contributions of this paper include:

- We propose an Adaptive Joint Attention (AJA) module, which incorporates multi-head self-attention mechanism to capture the inner relationship between generated words automatically. An adaptive combination mechanism for convolutional image captioning model is developed to learn which word is less visually related.
- We employ the reinforcement training technique in ConvS2S to directly optimize the model with respect to the non-differentiable metric CIDER, which also remedies the exposure bias issue.
- Extensive evaluations on two public data sets demonstrate that our model outperforms all previous convolutional image captioning models and gets a competitive result to some state-of-the-art methods.

2   Related Work

Image captioning has been widely investigated. Many approaches have been proposed to address this challenging task. Among all these methods, an encoder-decoder framework takes the main position in recent years [11]. The first encoder-decoder based image captioning model was proposed in [22]. Based on this work,

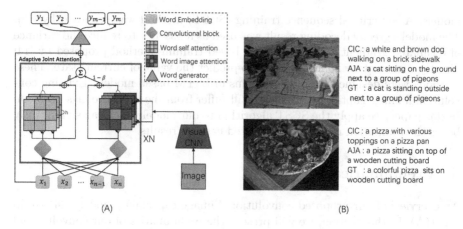

(A)   (B)

Fig. 1. (A) An graphical illustration of our proposed model. n, m means the length of input and output words respectively. h indicates the number of heads, β is the adaptive rate for combining two attention results. We stack N layer to obtain our final language model. (B) Captions generated by our Adaptive Joint Attention (AJA) model are compared to the Convolutional Image Captioning (CIC) model and ground-truth (GT) caption. As shown in the first row, visually unrelated phrases such as 'next to', 'a group of' can be better generated by our proposed method. In the second row, we randomly chose an image together with the generated captions to show that our model gets a closer result to the ground-truth caption.

an attention image captioning model was proposed in [26], which tries to describe the salient contents of an image automatically. Although using an attention mechanism can significantly improve the captioning result, [15] argued that it does not need to attend visual signals when generating some words or phases (e.g., a, of). As a result, LSTM with visual sentinel was proposed to learn when to focus on image regions and when to focus on word features.

Although LSTM is powerful enough to achieve good results on image captioning task, its inherent sequential processing prevents it from training in parallel. Inspired by recent success of convolutional sequence to sequence methods, an image captioning model totally based on convolutional architecture was proposed by [2]. However, the quantity of captions generated by this model is still not good enough. Different from the model proposed by [2,24] developed a hierarchical attention module to connect the visual-CNN with language-CNN. A gated hierarchical attention method which merges low-level concepts into high-level ones was also proposed by [25]. All these convolutional methods can not get competitive results with the state-of-the-art LSTM models and none of them investigates the importance of words' inner relationships for convolutional image captioning. In this paper, our proposed AJA module can jointly model the relationship of both word-image and generated words.

The training process based on a cross entropy loss brings exposure bias and training-inference error to this image captioning task. To solve these issues, reinforcement learning was incorporated to optimize LSTM based captioning models. A self-critical sequence training (SCST) method was proposed by [18]. The model's greedy decoding result was used as a baseline to reduce the variance of estimated gradient. The actor-critic based training method proposed by [14] directly uses another neural network to predict the value of current state. These methods were designed to solve problems in LSTM based models. Existing convolutional image captioning methods still suffer from the exposure bias problem. In this paper, we apply the SCST algorithm to our model which can significantly boost the evaluation metrics of generated caption results.

3 Preliminaries

An overview of our proposed convolutional image captioning model is shown in Fig. 1(A). In this section, we will present the preliminaries of our convolutional captioning model.

3.1 Image Feature Extractor

We use a ResNet-101 [10] which is pre-trained on the ImageNet dataset to obtain the image feature. We apply an adaptive average pooling mechanism on the feature maps from last layer of the last residual block. A bottom-up feature [1] obtained from faster R-CNN can also be used as image features.

3.2 Input Embeddings

Given a ground truth sentence denoted as $\mathbf{x} = (x_1, \cdots, x_n)$, we first embed them into a distribution space $\mathbf{w} = (w_1, \cdots, w_n)$. Here, n is the maximum length of an input sentence, x_i is the one-hot representation of a word and $w_i \in \mathbb{R}^d$ is a column vector in an embedding matrix $D \in \mathbb{R}^{T \times d}$ with T being the size of vocabulary. In order to learn the position information of input words, we use the encoding strategy as described in [20]. We denote the positional encoding of the input sequence as $\mathbf{p} = (p_1, \cdots, p_n)$. Thus, the final embedding for the input words is $\mathbf{e} = (w_1 + p_1, \cdots, w_n + p_n)$.

3.3 Convolutional Block

We adopt the gated linear unit (GLU) [4] as our basic convolutional block. Different from previous ConvS2S methods, we add a word gate $\mathbf{s} \in \mathbb{R}^d$ to inference the inner relationship between input words (Fig. 1). The original gate $\mathbf{c} \in \mathbb{R}^d$ is left to deal with the image features. Suppose we have an input $X \in \mathbb{R}^{k \times d}$ which contacts k input embedding in a dimension d. Take the word gate as an example, the convolution kernel matrix is denoted as $W_s \in \mathbb{R}^{2d \times kd}$, $b_s \in \mathbb{R}^{2d}$. Applying the convolution operation on the input, we will get:

$$Y = W_s * X + b_s \tag{1}$$

where $Y = [A; B] \in \mathbb{R}^{2d}$, $A, B \in \mathbb{R}^d$ is the output intermediate states. Then we apply a non-linearity operation given by [4]:

$$\mathbf{s} = f([A; B]) = A \otimes \sigma(B) \tag{2}$$

$\otimes$ indicates the point-wise multiplication and σ stands for the sigmoid function. Outputs of this gated operation is the half size of Y which results in a dimension of d. The gates $\sigma(B)$ controls how much contents of inputs A will be sent to the next layer. This performs similarly as the input gate of LSTM. We denote the input to l-th convolution block as $\mathbf{h}^l = (h_1^l, \cdots, h_n^l)$, then the final output of the word gate $\mathbf{s}^l = (s_1^l, \cdots, s_n^l)$ can be formulated as:

$$\mathbf{s}_i^l = f(W_s^l[h_{i-k/2}^l, \cdots, h_{i+k/2}^l] + b_s^l) \tag{3}$$

Similarly, we can get the context vector $\mathbf{c}^l = (c_1^l, \cdots, c_n^l)$ from the context gate.

We denote the output of top decoder layer at j-th position as h_j^L and compute the distribution over T possible next target elements y_{j+1} by the following equation:

$$p(y_{j+1}|y_1, ..., y_j, \mathbf{x}) = \text{softmax}(W_p h_j^L + b_p) \tag{4}$$

where W_p and b_p represent the learned parameters of this linear projection layer.

4 The Proposed Method

4.1 Multi-head Word Self-Attention

In order to directly capture the inner relationship between the input words, we adopt the multi-head attention proposed in [20] as our word attention module. The original paper used this method in machine translation task, while in this paper, we just use it as an attention mechanism. Again, word features obtained from a convolution block are denoted as $\mathbf{s} = (s_1, \cdots, s_n)$, we define three linear projection matrix $W_i^q \in \mathbb{R}^{d \times q}, W_i^k \in \mathbb{R}^{d \times k}, W_i^v \in \mathbb{R}^{d \times v}$ to project high dimensional word features into its subspace, here i indicates the order of head and we use h to represent the total number of heads. The input to these three matrices is equal to $\mathbf{s}$. As a result, the subspace dimension of each head can be calculated by $q = k = v = d/h$. After Applying the projection, we can get three feature matrix Q_i, K_i, V_i. For simplicity, we write the dimension of all the three matrix as m, then we compute the scaled dot production attention by:

$$\text{Attention}(Q_i, K_i, V_i) = \text{softmax}(\frac{Q_i K_i^T}{\sqrt{m}})V_i \tag{5}$$

Note that this is similar to the dot-product attention in [6] except for a scaling factor $\frac{1}{\sqrt{m}}$. For a large value of m, the dot products grow large in magnitude which will result in a small score under the softmax function. Thus, this scaling factor is designed to counteract this growing effect and get more 'clear' score maps for the captioning model. Remember that we have h number of heads for this attention module, thus the final output of this layer is calculated by:

$$\text{MultiHead}(\mathbf{s}) = \text{concat}(\text{head}_1, \cdots, \text{head}_h)W_O \tag{6}$$

where $W_O \in \mathbb{R}^{hm \times d}$ and head_i can be calculated by Eq. (5). This multi-head attention allows the model to learn information from different representation subspace. Adding this multi-head word self-attention in captioning model can significantly boost the performance in some evaluation metrics.

4.2 Multi-head Word-Image Attention

Previous convolutional captioning methods [2,25] apply a single head attention between word and image features. However, we empirically find that increasing the number of heads can improve model's ability to generate better caption. As illustrated in the previous section, the convolutional gate $\mathbf{c}$ is designed to deal with the image features. We use feature maps $U \in \mathbb{R}^{d_c \times d_c \times D_c}$ obtained from Resnet-101 as image features, here d_c indicates the height and width of the feature maps and D_c is the channels of convolution kernels (for resnet it is 2048). We resize it as $\mathbf{u} = [u_1, \cdots, u_N]$ where $N = d_c^2$ and $u_i \in \mathbb{R}^{D_c}$ to obtain a vector representation of an input image. Then we apply a linear projection on these vectors to ensure the image features and word features are in the same dimensionality. As a result, the final representation of an input image is defined as $\tilde{\mathbf{u}} = [\tilde{u}_1, \cdots, \tilde{u}_N]$ where $\tilde{u}_i = u_i W_u$ and $W_u \in \mathbb{R}^{D_c \times d}$. In this attention module, we set the Q matrix as projection of $\mathbf{c}$ and K, V matrix as projection of image features $\tilde{\mathbf{u}}$. The other operations stay the same with word self-attention.

4.3 Adaptive Combination Strategy

Inspired by [15], some words such as "the" and "of" may require no visual information while other words like "horse" and "fields" may totally depend on image features. Giving same weight coefficients to both image and word informations may result in a noisy feature for captioning model.

To address this issue, we propose an adaptive combination strategy for our multi-head joint attention. The attention score map of head_i is calculated by:

$$\alpha_i = \frac{1}{\sqrt{m}} Q_i K_i^T \tag{7}$$

for both word and image-word attention. We define $\alpha_u \in \mathbb{R}^{h \times n \times N}$ as image-word attention score maps and $\alpha_w \in \mathbb{R}^{h \times n \times n}$ as word self-attention score maps. We average the last dimension of word self attention score maps which result in $\overline{\alpha}_w \in \mathbb{R}^{h \times n \times 1}$ to obtain an expectation of how much attention does the captioning model pay for word informations. Then we can calculate the weight coefficients by:

$$\hat{\alpha} = \text{mean}(\text{softmax}(\text{concat}(\alpha_u, \overline{\alpha}_w))) \tag{8}$$

where $\hat{\alpha} \in \mathbb{R}^{n \times (N+1)}$. Note that the average is calculated over all heads and we interpret the last column of this score map to be the weight coefficient vector $\beta = \hat{\alpha}[:, N+1]$. Finally, the output of l-th adaptive joint attention (AJA) block is

$$\mathbf{h}^{l+1} = \beta * \mathbf{s}^l + (1 - \beta) * \mathbf{c}^l \tag{9}$$

where $\mathbf{s}^l$ and $\mathbf{c}^l$ are the outputs of word self-attention and image-word attention module in l-th convolutional block respectively.

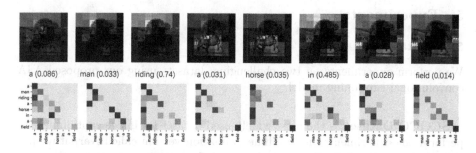

Fig. 2. An example of word-image attention and word self-attention. We average the attention scores over 8 heads in layer 3 for word-image attention which is shown in first row. The model pays less attention on darker regions. Each generated word is followed by an adaptive weight in between parentheses. Higher weight indicates the model pay more attention on word features. Word self-attention are shown in the second row. Darker colour indicates higher attention score. These 8 heads of attention scores from 5th layer of decoder perform different tasks in a low dimension subspace. (Colour figure online)

4.4   Objective and RL Training

Given a target ground truth sentence $y^\star_{1:T}$ with paired image I, we first minimize the following cross entropy loss:

$$L_{XE}(\theta) = -\sum_{t=1}^{T} \log(\pi_\theta(y^\star_t | y^\star_{1:t-1}, I)) \tag{10}$$

where θ denotes model parameters. Note that this is a supervised training process and needs large quantity of image-sentence pairs which is different from reinforcement learning.

This teacher forcing algorithm has two disadvantages called exposure bias and training-inference error. In order to address such issues, we utilize self-critic sequence training (SCST) algorism [18] to optimize CIDER score after few "warm up" epochs under cross entropy loss. We write the reinforcement training loss as:

$$L_{RL}(\theta) = -\mathbb{E}_{y_{1:T} \sim \pi_\theta}[r(y_{1:T})] \tag{11}$$

where r is the CIDER score function. In [18], a greedy decoding result $\hat{y}_{1:T}$ of captioning model is obtained as baseline to reduce the variance of gradient, namely,

$$\nabla_\theta L_{RL}(\theta) \approx -(r(y_{1:T}^s) - r(\hat{y}_{1:T}))\nabla_\theta \log \pi_\theta(y_{1:T}^s) \tag{12}$$

where $y_{1:T}^s$ is obtained from a sampling distribution (e.g., multinomial distribution). Intuitively speaking, SCST algorithm increases the probability of sampled caption y^s which gets a higher CIDER score than greedy decoding caption $\hat{y}$.

5   Experiments

5.1   Datasets

We perform experiments on two challenging datasets using our proposed AJA convolutional captioning model.

MSCOCO Dataset is the most widely used dataset for image captioning. We perform our experiments on an offline evaluation version called Karpathy split [12] which contains 113287 images along with 5 captions for each one. We use a set of 5 K images for validation and report our result on a test set of 5 K images as well. We preprocess the captions by mapping words that occur less than 5 times to a special "UNK" token, and create a vocabulary for all the remaining words which result in a size of 9488.

Flicker30k Dataset contains 31783 images together with 5 captions for each of them. Following [12], we use 1000 images for validation and 1000 images for testing. We do the same preprocessing on this dataset as MSCOCO. The vocabulary size is 7001.

5.2   Implementation Details

We use a pre-trained Resnet-101 [10] as our basic image encoder. All the input images have a size of 256×256 without resize or cropping. We apply an adaptive pooling on the last layer of last block to obtain 7×7 feature maps. Bottom-up features [1] pre-trained on Visual Genome dataset are also used to train our proposed model. The hidden size of both word and image embeddings are set to 512 and the convolution kernel size is set to 3. We stack 6 layers of our adaptive convolutional block and 8 heads for each attention module to obtain our final language model. Dropout (with probability of 0.1) and layer normalization are applied to every layer. The model parameters are initialized by Xivaer method [7]. We use Adam as our optimizer. The learning rate is set to 5e-5 for teacher forcing training and 1e-5 for reinforcement learning. Momentum is 0.9 and 0.999 for both case. Batch size is 16 and 8 for teacher forcing and reinforcement learning respectively. We implement our model based on this repository[1] in pytorch

---

[1] https://github.com/ruotianluo/ImageCaptioning.pytorch.

environment. Training our model with cross entropy loss for 20 epochs takes about 5 h on a single GTX1080Ti. After teacher forcing training, we start a RL training progress and stop it when CIDER score do not increase for 3 epochs.

Table 1. Performance on MSCOCO Karpathy split. We bring these results from their papers. We give detailed descriptions of these models in Sect. 5.3. '-' means unknown metrics. All values are reported as percentage (the raw value of CIDER score could beyond 1). Bold numbers indicate highest values. Among all metrics, higher values indicate better performances. Our model gets best scores over all the convolutional based methods.

Method	BLEU-1	BLEU-2	BLEU-3	BLEU-4	METEOR	ROUGE-L	CIDER
Hard-ATT [26]	71.8	50.4	35.7	25.0	23.04	-	-
Soft-ATT [26]	70.7	49.2	34.4	24.3	23.90	-	-
Ada-ATT [15]	74.2	58.0	43.9	33.2	26.6	-	108.5
Up-Down [1]	**79.8**	-	-	36.3	**27.7**	56.9	120.1
StackCap [8]	78.6	62.5	47.9	36.1	27.4	56.9	120.4
SCST [18]	-	-	-	34.2	26.7	55.7	114.0
ACST [14]	-	-	-	34.4	26.7	55.8	116.2
CIC [2]	72.2	55.3	41.8	31.6	25.0	53.1	95.2
CNN+CNN [24]	68.5	51.1	36.9	26.7	23.4	51.0	84.4
GHA [25]	73.3	56.4	42.6	32.1	25.5	53.8	99.9
CNN+RHN [9]	72.3	55.3	41.3	30.6	25.2	-	98.9
AJA (Resnet, XE)	74.0	57.5	43.7	33.2	26.7	54.7	106.8
AJA (R-CNN, XE)	75.9	59.6	45.9	35.3	27.6	56.3	112.5
AJA (Resnet, RL)	78.0	61.8	47.1	35.4	27.0	56.4	116.7
AJA (R-CNN, RL)	79.3	**63.6**	**48.8**	**36.8**	**27.7**	**57.4**	**121.1**

5.3 Compared Methods

We compare our model with Resnet and bottom-up features under cross entropy loss and RL loss. Four state-of-the-art models based on LSTM: hard-ATT [26] (VGG, XE) and soft-ATT [26] (VGG, XE), Ada-ATT [15] (Resnet, XE), Up-Down [1] (R-CNN, RL), StackCap [8] (Resnet, RL) are included in our comparing list. We also compare with two reinforcement captioning methods: SCST [18] (Resnet, RL) and ACST [14] (Resnet, RL). The newest CNN based captioning methods: CIC [2] (VGG, XE), CNN+CNN [24] (Resnet, XE) and GHA [25] (Resnet, XE) are also compared with our model.

5.4 Evaluation Metrics

We evaluate our model on the following metrics: BLEU-1,2,3,4 [17], METEOR [5], ROUGE-L [13], CIDER [21]. These metrics are computed using MSCOCO caption evaluation tool[2]. For all metrics, higher values indicate better performance.

---
[2] https://github.com/tylin/coco-caption.

6   Results and Analysis

6.1   Results on MSCOCO

Our results on MSCOCO dataset are shown in Table 1. For fair comparison, we report results of both Resnet and bottom-up features. Performances of our models training under cross entropy loss and reinforcement learning loss are also reported in Table 1. Over all the convolutional captioning models, our model gets the best scores of all metrics. The worst result of our model(training under cross entropy with Resnet image features) exceeds the best convolutional method about 6 points on CIDER score. This result is competitive with Ada-ATT [15] which is trained under the same conditions. Bottom-up features can boost our model performance to a new level. Training under reinforcement learning with bottom-up features yields best performance over all metrics except BLUE-1.

Another advantage of our proposed model is that we have faster training and converging time under cross entropy loss. Our model contains 180M parameters and a training time of 0.09 s per batch. All the models trained under cross entropy get their best performance on validation set at about 18 epochs.

Table 2. Performance on Flickr30k dataset. We re-implement the CIC [2] model and perform experiments on this dataset. Other results are borrowed from their original papers. '-' means unknown metrics. All values are reported as percentage (the raw value of CIDER score could beyond 1). Bold numbers indicate highest values. Among all metrics, higher values indicate better performances. Our model gets best scores over all the convolutional based methods.

Method	BLEU-1	BLEU-2	BLEU-3	BLEU-4	METEOR	ROUGE-L	CIDER
Hard-ATT [26]	66.9	43.9	29.6	19.9	18.5	-	-
Soft-ATT [26]	66.7	43.4	28.8	19.1	18.5	-	-
Ada-ATT [15]	67.7	49.4	35.4	25.1	20.4	-	53.1
CIC [2]	63.7	44.4	30.4	20.6	17.8	43.4	38.3
CNN+CNN [24]	60.7	42.5	29.2	19.9	19.1	44.2	39.5
AJA (Resnet, XE)	68.4	50.0	35.8	25.5	20.5	47.2	54.0
AJA (Resnet, RL)	**71.0**	**51.8**	**36.9**	**25.9**	**20.8**	**48.3**	**60.1**

6.2   Results on Flicker30k

Since Flickr30k dataset is not as much used as MSCOCO dataset, we pick out models which have results on this dataset as comparison methods. Because there are no pre-trained bottom-up features for Flickr30k dataset, we only report results of models trained with Resnet-101 features. As shown in Table 2, our model gets the highest scores over all metrics under both supervised and reinforcement training.

6.3   Qualitative Analysis

Figure 1(B) gives a qualitative comparison of captions generated by our model and CIC [2] model. Our results show that captions generated by our method are more close to the ground-truth sentences. Also, some visually unrelated phrases can be better predicted by our method.

We visualize both word-image and word-self attention in Fig. 2. A multi-head mechanism in word-image attention exhibits behaviour that looks like ensemble learning. Interestingly, attentions about objects in the real world are formed in the 3th layer of convolutional decoder. The result shows that our model can learn to focus on salient objects when predicting these words. In case of word self-attention, we directly plot all heads in 5th layer of word attention module. As shown in the last row of Fig. 2, different heads seem to learn different tasks for word prediction.

Table 3. Performance of our model with different attention modules. The "Base" model is one that only has a convolutional decoder and a scaled dot-product attention (attention module between image and words) with a head number of 1. The "Base+Word-Image ATT" model contains a multi-head version of the scaled dot-product attention. The "Base+AJA" is our full model as described in Sect. 4. We report results training on MSCOCO dataset with a Resnet image feature extractor. Bold numbers indicate highest values. Among all metrics, higher values indicate better performance.

Method	B-1	B-2	B-3	B-4	ME	R-L	CD
Base (XE)	73.7	57.4	43.1	32.0	25.3	53.4	100.7
Base+Word-Image ATT (XE)	**74.5**	**58.0**	**43.9**	33.1	26.4	54.6	105.7
Base+AJA (XE)	74.0	57.5	43.7	**33.2**	**26.7**	**54.7**	**106.8**
Base (RL)	76.8	60.6	45.7	34.0	26.3	55.6	112.6
Base+Word-Image ATT (RL)	77.0	60.7	45.9	34.2	26.4	55.8	114.1
Base+AJA (RL)	**78.0**	**61.8**	**47.1**	**35.4**	**27.0**	**56.4**	**116.7**

6.4   Effectiveness of Attention Modules

We perform experiments with different attention modules to verify their effectiveness. As shown in Table 3, a multi-head version of scaled product attention can improve CIDER score of 5 points under teacher forcing training. While adding an adaptive word attention can slightly boost the CIDER score under this training method. Note that some metrics get slightly worse after adding a word attention. We think this may due to the disadvantages of teacher forcing training. Results of reinforcement training method can give us a clear eye of how much effect does these modules have on our basic model. All the metrics increased after applying a multi-head image-word attention. Our proposed adaptive joint attention module can push the evaluation metric to an even higher score.

7   Conclusion and Future Work

In this paper, we propose an adaptive joint attention module for convolutional image captioning. Our multi-head attention and adaptive word self-attention can improve the model performance in two stages. Captioning with our proposed model can get a competitive result with some state-of-the-art LSTM based models. Future works may focus on the efficiency and parallelism on reinforcement training for convolutional architecture. Other useful informations like grammar and image objects' relationship can also be included to our model following the same structure as word self-attention.

References

1. Anderson, P., et al.: Bottom-up and top-down attention for image captioning and visual question answering. In: 2018 IEEE Conference on Computer Vision and Pattern Recognition (CVPR) (2018)
2. Aneja, J., Deshpande, A., Schwing, A.G.: Convolutional image captioning. In: 2018 IEEE Conference on Computer Vision and Pattern Recognition (CVPR) (2018)
3. Bengio, S., Vinyals, O., Jaitly, N., Shazeer, N.: Scheduled sampling for sequence prediction with recurrent neural networks. In: Advances in Neural Information Processing Systems (NeurIPS) (2015)
4. Dauphin, Y., Fan, A., Auli, M., Grangier, D.: Language modeling with gated convolutional networks. In: Proceedings of the International Conference on Machine Learning (ICML) (2017)
5. Denkowski, M.J., Lavie, A.: Meteor universal: language specific translation evaluation for any target language. In: ACL (2014)
6. Gehring, J., Auli, M., Grangier, D., Yarats, D., Dauphin, Y.: Convolutional sequence to sequence learning. In: Proceedings of the International Conference on Machine Learning (ICML) (2017)
7. Glorot, X., Bengio, Y.: Understanding the difficulty of training deep feedforward neural networks. In: AISTATS 2010 (2010)
8. Gu, J., Cai, J., Wang, G., Chen, T.: Stack-captioning: coarse-to-fine learning for image captioning. In: Proceedings of the Conference on Artificial Intelligence (AAAI) (2018)
9. Gu, J., Wang, G., Cai, J., Chen, T.: An empirical study of language CNN for image captioning. In: 2017 IEEE International Conference on Computer Vision (ICCV), pp. 1231–1240 (2017)
10. He, K., Zhang, X., Ren, S., Sun, J.: Deep residual learning for image recognition. In: 2016 IEEE Conference on Computer Vision and Pattern Recognition (CVPR), pp. 770–778 (2016)
11. Hossain, M.Z., Sohel, F.A., Shiratuddin, M.F., Laga, H.: A comprehensive survey of deep learning for image captioning. CoRR abs/1810.04020 (2018)
12. Karpathy, A., Fei-Fei, L.: Deep visual-semantic alignments for generating image descriptions. In: 2015 IEEE Conference on Computer Vision and Pattern Recognition (CVPR), pp. 3128–3137 (2015)
13. Lin, C.Y.: Rouge: a package for automatic evaluation of summaries. In: ACL (2004)
14. Lin, X., et al.: Actor-critic sequence training for image captioning. CoRR abs/1706.09601 (2017)

15. Lu, J., Xiong, C., Parikh, D., Socher, R.: Knowing when to look: adaptive attention via a visual sentinel for image captioning. In: 2017 IEEE Conference on Computer Vision and Pattern Recognition (CVPR), pp. 3242–3250 (2017)
16. van den Oord, A., Kalchbrenner, N., Vinyals, O., Espeholt, L., Graves, A., Kavukcuoglu, K.: Conditional image generation with PixelCNN decoders. In: Advances in Neural Information Processing Systems (NeurIPS) (2016)
17. Papineni, K., Roukos, S., Ward, T., Zhu, W.J.: Bleu: a method for automatic evaluation of machine translation. In: ACL (2002)
18. Rennie, S.J., Marcheret, E., Mroueh, Y., Ross, J., Goel, V.: Self-critical sequence training for image captioning. In: 2017 IEEE Conference on Computer Vision and Pattern Recognition (CVPR), pp. 1179–1195 (2017)
19. Shen, Y., Tan, S., Sordoni, A., Courville, A.: Ordered neurons: integrating tree structures into recurrent neural networks. In: International Conference on Learning Representations (2019). https://openreview.net/forum?id=B1l6qiR5F7
20. Vaswani, A., et al.: Attention is all you need. In: Advances in Neural Information Processing Systems (NeurIPS) (2017)
21. Vedantam, R., Zitnick, C.L., Parikh, D.: Cider: consensus-based image description evaluation. In: 2015 IEEE Conference on Computer Vision and Pattern Recognition (CVPR), pp. 4566–4575 (2015)
22. Vinyals, O., Toshev, A., Bengio, S., Erhan, D.: Show and tell: a neural image caption generator. In: 2015 IEEE Conference on Computer Vision and Pattern Recognition (CVPR), pp. 3156–3164 (2015)
23. Wang, L., Yao, J., Tao, Y., Zhong, L., Liu, W., Du, Q.: A reinforced topic-aware convolutional sequence-to-sequence model for abstractive text summarization. In: Proceedings of the International Joint Conference on Artificial Intelligence (IJCAI) (2018)
24. Wang, Q., Chan, A.B.: CNN+CNN: convolutional decoders for image captioning. CoRR abs/1805.09019 (2018)
25. Wang, Q., Chan, A.B.: Gated hierarchical attention for image captioning. CoRR abs/1810.12535 (2018)
26. Xu, K., et al.: Show, attend and tell: neural image caption generation with visual attention. In: Proceedings of the International Conference on Machine Learning (ICML) (2015)

Visualizing Emotional States: A Method Based on Human Brain Activity

Yanfang Long[1], Wanzeng Kong[1,2(✉)], Xuanyu Jin[1], Jili Shang[1], and Can Yang[3]

[1] Hangzhou Dianzi University, Hangzhou 310018, Zhejiang, China
yanfang_longsun@163.com, kongwanzeng@hdu.edu.cn, JXuanyu599@163.com, jilishang_hdu@163.com
[2] Fujian Key Laboratory of Rehabilitation Technology, Fuzhou 350003, China
[3] Hong Kong University of Science and Technology, Kowloon, Hong Kong, China
macyang@ust.hk

Abstract. Recently, how to infer one's emotional state by nonverbal components has attracted great attention from the scientific community. If we can decode and visualize the emotional states from human brain activity, what an amazing thing that would be? The research in this paper found a way to decode and visualize different emotional states from human brain activity. In our experiments, at first, the power spectral density (PSD) was extracted from EEG signals evoked by visual stimulation of different emotional facial images. PSD can be viewed as a clue containing specific emotional states in human brain. After that, we use the conditional variational auto-encoder (VAE) to decode and visualize the emotional state, which takes the extracted PSD feature as input and generates the corresponding image. Specifically, VAE is a framework consisting of an encoder and a decoder. The former is used to learn low-dimension potential features of specific emotional state from the input PSD, and the later outputs an image containing the corresponding emotional state. Finally, our method was trained and tested on the EEG data from six subjects while they were looking at images from the Chinese Facial Affective Picture System (CFAPS) and obtained some promising results.

Keywords: Human brain activity · Emotional states · PSD · VAE

1 Introduction

For centuries, psychologists and scientists have been trying to read and decode the natural visual and emotional cognitive mechanisms of the human brain. The central question is whether people's thoughts and emotional states can be decoded or translated from brain activity. With the development of brain imaging techniques such as EEG, MRI and fMRI, researchers have made initial results in the study of neural coding and decoding.

© Springer Nature Singapore Pte Ltd. 2019
A. Zeng et al. (Eds.): HBAI 2019, CCIS 1072, pp. 248–258, 2019.
https://doi.org/10.1007/978-981-15-1398-5_18

Several recent studies have explored how to decode visual and linguistic content from the brain activity [8,9,19,22]. They used the EEG or fMRI equipment to record brain activities when people participated in verbal or visual tasks. These efforts have shown some promising results, because they have demonstrated that brain activities contain information about the visual or linguistic object. In other words, it is demonstrated that the EEG or fMRI data contains and reflects the representation of stimulus information in human brain.

Inspired by these works, we hope to go further and study the brain activity of a person with different emotional states. Emotional state is a subjective experience such as anger, happiness, and sadness. This experience is internal, private, and difficult to describe in words. Our goal is to use low-cost EEG devices to find clues from brain activity that encode specific emotional states and ultimately visualize people's emotions. To address those, we proposed a novel method named Brain-Conditioned VAE (BC-VAE) and conducted experiments on the Chinese Facial Affective Picture System (CFAPS) [22]. The main contributions in this paper as follows:

- First, we introduced the problem of explaining and visualizing human emotional states.
- Second, we proposed a novel variational auto-encoder that conditioned by the specific brain activity.
- At last but not least, we demonstrated our method is suitable for the small database, and it can convert the emotion-related EEG signal into specific emotion image.

The structure of this paper is as follows. In Sect. 2, we discuss the related work about using EEG or fMRI data to visualize human minds and identify emotional states. In Sect. 3, we provide detailed information on how to encode emotional cues and generate images. In Sect. 4, we present the experimental results and analyze the performance. Finally, in Sect. 5, we draw some conclusions and possible directions for future work.

2 Related Work

Research in neuroscience and neuroimaging [7,15] have shown that non-invasive imaging techniques (such as fMRI, EEG and MEG) can be used to analyze the states of human visual and emotional perception. In particular, these studies provided the evidence that the possibility of decoding human visual content and emotional experience from brain activity. Nevertheless, these methods are primarily designed to identify pattern differences in brain activity between cognitive states. Our work is different because it can not only do this, but it also attempts to visualize cognitive state from specific brain activities. In [22], the author proposed a dynamic natural visual nerve encoding-decoding method based on the fMRI data. In terms of the objectives, their work is closely related to ours. In addition, some researchers used the fMRI data from early visual areas to reconstruct simple geometric patterns [14]. While fMRI data has shown great potential in process of generating mind, the cost of it is also expensive and that is the main limitation. However, this disadvantage can be overcome by low-cost techniques such as electroencephalography (EEG). EEG signals provide higher temporal resolution compared with fMRI, but it is influenced by lower spatial resolution and noise data. Therefore, it is difficult to analyze the recognition states. It is worth mentioning that the author [10,20] proposed using EEG signals to extract features of visual stimuli in brain activity. And they generated corresponding object stimulation successfully through the VAE [11] and GAN [5]. The difference between above work and ours: (a) The evoking stimulation of EEG signals, ie whether there is emotional difference in visual content; (b) The feature extraction method from the original EEG signal; (c) The generating model architecture on the experimental data set.

3   Method

This paper attempts to 'translate' the emotion-related EEG signals into expression images. In order to prevent overfitting and unstable training on the acquired data set, we chose VAE instead of GAN eventually. In addition, the VAE has been widely applied in unsupervised learning and several fields such as the generation of text, text-image, and synthetic music [4,6,18,24]. Especially, the VAE model based on the encoder-decoder framework is more suitable for modeling neural encoding-decoding problems. As shown in Fig. 1, our brain-conditioned VAE mainly consists of four parts: (1) EEG signal acquisition. EEG data is collected by visual stimuli of different emotional facial images. (2) Extracting the features of the raw EEG signal. The power spectral density (PSD) is extracted from EEG data, which can be regarded as cues encoded specific emotional states in human brain. (3) Learning the potential features of specific emotional states from the input PSD via the encoder. (4) Generating an image containing a emotional state from the potential features by the decoder.

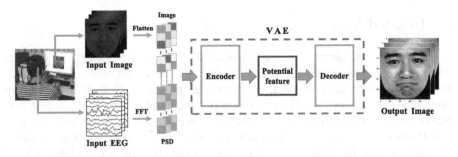

Fig. 1. The framework of visualization method of emotional states based on human brain activity.

3.1   EEG Signal Acquisition

In this paper, we recorded EEG signals from six subjects. They are 23–25 years old (1:1 for male and female) and have similar educational backgrounds. Each of them sat comfortably on the front of the computer screen. The images in our experiments are from the CFAPS, which collects 870 emotional faces, including 74 anger, 47 disgust, 64 fear, 95 sadness, 150 surprise, 222 neutrality, 248 happiness. Each image is presented in category order for 0.5 s, and then there is a black image of 10 s between different emotions. The experimental paradigm parameters are shown in Table 1. The design of the experimental paradigm is based on the related work [3]. Finally, we obtained 870-segment 62-channel EEG signals, and the data was filtered at 1–75 Hz.

Table 1. Experimental paradigm parameter.

Number of classes	7
Total number of images	870
Time for each image	0.5 s
Pause between classes	10 s
Sampling rate	1000 Hz
Number of channels	62
Filtered frequency	1–75 Hz

3.2   Power Spectral Density Feature Extraction

Since the signal-to-noise ratio of EEG signals is usually low, it is necessary to extract features from the original signals before analyzing the cognitive state. Related studies have shown that spectral power changes in EEG signals are highly correlated with emotional neural representation [12,17,23]. Thus, we used the Fast Fourier Transform (FFT) to extract Power Spectral Density (PSD) in five different sub-bands (delta (1–4 Hz), theta (4–8 Hz), alpha (8–13 Hz), beta (13–30 Hz), gamma (30–40 Hz)). Additionally, the Pyeeg [2] and MATLAB tools are used to plot the brain topography with un-normalized PSD in the gamma band, as shown in Fig. 2. Although there are significant differences in PSD features between different emotion states, there are also common phenomena. That is to say, high energy is mainly concentrated in the occipital region and the prefrontal region. This is most likely because the occipital region function is associated with visual stimuli and the forehead region is associated with emotional cognition of the brain. These two points about the occipital lobe and the forehead area involve some other literature [3,13].

3.3   Learning Potential Features (Encoder)

In the previous section, we extracted the PSD features to represent the emotional state. If we want to visualize these states, we need to use features further to

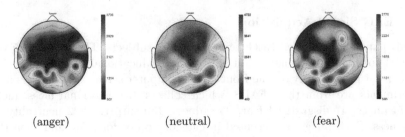

(anger)   (neutral)   (fear)

Fig. 2. The brain topographic map of different emotional states based on PSD and gamma band.

generate emotion-related images. Therefore, we proposed a brain-conditioned VAE model. Compared with the basic VAE, the latent variable z learns potential features from images and PSDs rather than learning directly from images, which is remarked as $E(z|I, c)$. I indicates that the $i-$th image with 100×100 size, and will be flattened as 10000-dimension vector. c represents the corresponding PSD condition of the corresponding EEG signal evoked by the I stimulation, and the dimension is $310 = 62 \times 5$. z(2-dimension) represents the potential features learned from the encoder. We collected EEG signals from six students on the whole, but the c we choose is the best result of the seven emotional classification problem. As shown in Fig. 3, the structure of the encoder consists of five fully connected layers. The first four layers are designed with Relu activation, except that the last one is linear.

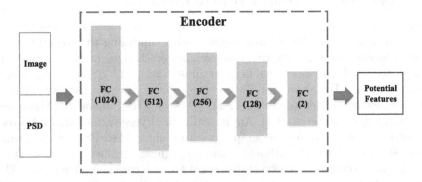

Fig. 3. The structure of an encoder for the brain-conditioned VAE.

3.4   Convering Potential Features into Images (Decoder)

Again, in the decoder part of the basic VAE, it only models I directly based on the latent variable z. Therefore, we will model I from the hidden variable z with c conditional distribution so that the emotional cues of EEG signals can be visualized as corresponding facial expressions, which remarked as $D(\widehat{I}|z, c)$.

Since the decoder performs an inverse operation with the encoder, it should have a similar structure to the encoder. As shown in Fig. 4, all of the first four layers are activated using Relu, except for the last layer with sigmoid.

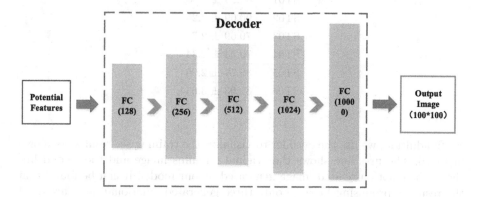

Fig. 4. The structure of a decoder for the brain-conditioned VAE.

The loss function of the brain-conditioned VAE is formulated as follows:

$$\mathcal{L}_{VAE} = KL[D(\widehat{I}|z,c)||E(z|I,c)] + MSE(\widehat{I}, I) \tag{1}$$

The purpose of the training is to minimize two things. On the one hand, it is the reconstruction error of the picture, which we can measure by the mean squared error. On the other hand, we can use KL divergence to measure the distribution difference of our potential features and the Gaussian distribution.

4   Results and Performance Analysis

The data in our experiment was randomly divided into training set, validation set and test set according to 60%:20%:20%. The KNN classifier was used for the seven classification problem based on each subject, and the average results of 5-fold cross-validation are shown in Table 2.

As can be seen from Table 2, the emotion recognition based on PSD features is different between subjects, which is most likely due to the data collection environment and the difference in emotional response. In this paper, considering the encoder to learn effective potential features, the most discriminating PSD is selected from the subjects. The implementation of the brain-conditioned VAE model is based on the open source framework keras [1]. And the hyperparameters batch size is 29, optimizer is Adam, learning rate is 0.001, and a total number of iterations is 400. The model converges quickly with one 1080Ti GPU environment and the time is around about 5 min. The KL-loss and reconstruction loss of our method on training and validating data sets are shown in Fig. 5.

Table 2. The results of seven classification problem for each subject using normalized PSD features and KNN classifier.

Subject	Accuracy(%)
ST01	85.29 ± 2.08
ST02	90.69 ± 2.25
ST03	70.69 ± 2.73
ST04	79.54 ± 2.34
ST05	89.71 ± 2.06
ST06	82.93 ± 3.05

In addition, we use the decoder to visualize the training set results, as shown in Fig. 6. The first line shows the original stimulus image and the second line shows the emotion-related image generated by our model. It can be found that the result is promising because only three generated emotional faces are a bit fuzzy and not compatible with the real images.

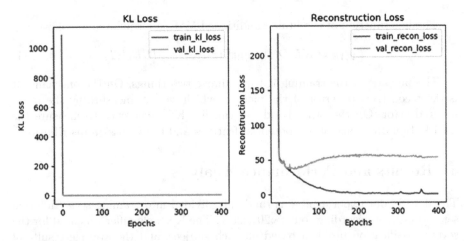

Fig. 5. The KL-loss and reconstruction loss of our method on training and validating sets.

Similarly, Figs. 7, 8, 9, 10, 11, 12 and 13 shows the result of the decoder generating different emotional states using the potential features of the test set. The visual performance here has some minor drawbacks. We can notice that the results can be explained because each face in the test set is different from the training set and the validation set. Therefore, we can only visualize the underlying features of each real image into a picture containing similar facial expressions.

Fig. 6. The true and generated results of different emotions on the training set.

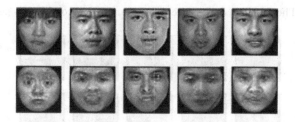

Fig. 7. The first line is the true anger and the second line is generated.

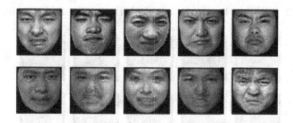

Fig. 8. The first line is the true disgust and the second line is generated.

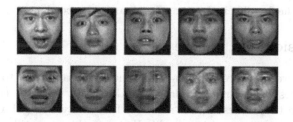

Fig. 9. The first line is the true fear and the second line is generated.

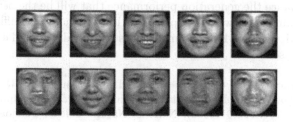

Fig. 10. The first line is the true happy and the second line is generated.

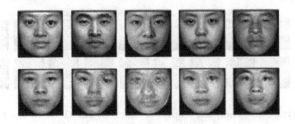

Fig. 11. The first line is the true neutral and the second line is generated.

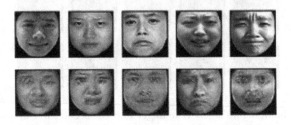

Fig. 12. The first line is the true sad, the second line is generated.

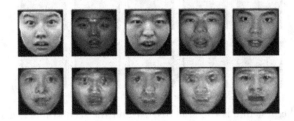

Fig. 13. The first line is the true surprise and the second line is generated.

5   Conclusion and Future Work

In this paper, we proposed a brain-conditioned VAE approach to visualize the emotional states from emotion-related EEG signals. And we conducted the experiments on the Chinese Facial Affective Picture System (CFAPS). Eventually, we obtained some promising results. However, there are still many improvements in this work, such as using VQ-VAE [16, 21] to express discrete potential features to enhance the generation performance that will be the next part of our work. At the same time, we will explore this idea further on a sufficient number of subjects and visualize human emotional states in different data sets, which makes more sense.

Acknowledgement. This work was supported by National Key R&D Program of China for Intergovernmental International Science and Technology Innovation Cooperation Project (2017YFE0116800), National Natural Science Foundation of China (61671193), Key Science and Technology Program of Zhejiang Province (2018C04012), Science and technology platform construction project of Fujian science and Technology Department (2015Y2001).

References

1. (2013). https://github.com/keras-team/keras
2. Bao, F.S., Liu, X., Zhang, C.: PyEEG: an open source python module for EEG/MEG feature extraction. Comput. Intell. Neurosci. (2011)
3. DeYoe, E.A., et al.: Mapping striate and extrastriate visual areas in human cerebral cortex. Proc. Natl. Acad. Sci. **93**(6), 2382–2386 (1996)
4. Dieleman, S., van den Oord, A., Simonyan, K.: The challenge of realistic music generation: modelling raw audio at scale. In: Advances in Neural Information Processing Systems, pp. 7989–7999 (2018)
5. Goodfellow, I., et al.: Generative adversarial nets. In: Advances in Neural Information Processing Systems, pp. 2672–2680 (2014)
6. Gupta, A., Agarwal, A., Singh, P., Rai, P.: A deep generative framework for paraphrase generation. In: Thirty-Second AAAI Conference on Artificial Intelligence (2018)
7. Haynes, J.D., Rees, G.: Neuroimaging: decoding mental states from brain activity in humans. Nat. Rev. Neurosci. **7**(7), 523 (2006)
8. Huth, A.G., de Heer, W.A., Griffiths, T.L., Theunissen, F.E., Gallant, J.L.: Natural speech reveals the semantic maps that tile human cerebral cortex. Nature **532**(7600), 453 (2016)
9. Huth, A.G., Lee, T., Nishimoto, S., Bilenko, N.Y., Vu, A.T., Gallant, J.L.: Decoding the semantic content of natural movies from human brain activity. Front. Syst. Neurosci. **10**, 81 (2016)
10. Kavasidis, I., Palazzo, S., Spampinato, C., Giordano, D., Shah, M.: Brain2image: converting brain signals into images. In: Proceedings of the 25th ACM International Conference on Multimedia, pp. 1809–1817. ACM (2017)
11. Kingma, D.P., Welling, M.: Auto-encoding variational bayes. arXiv preprint arXiv:1312.6114 (2013)
12. Lin, Y.P., et al.: EEG-based emotion recognition in music listening. IEEE Trans. Biomed. Eng. **57**(7), 1798–1806 (2010)
13. Miller, E.K., Cohen, J.D.: An integrative theory of prefrontal cortex function. Annu. Rev. Neurosci. **24**(1), 167–202 (2001)
14. Naselaris, T., Prenger, R.J., Kay, K.N., Oliver, M., Gallant, J.L.: Bayesian reconstruction of natural images from human brain activity. Neuron **63**(6), 902–915 (2009)
15. Ray, W.J., Cole, H.W.: EEG alpha activity reflects attentional demands, and beta activity reflects emotional and cognitive processes. Science **228**(4700), 750–752 (1985)
16. Razavi, A., van den Oord, A., Vinyals, O.: Generating diverse high-resolution images with VQ-VAE (2019)
17. Rozgić, V., Vitaladevuni, S.N., Prasad, R.: Robust EEG emotion classification using segment level decision fusion. In: 2013 IEEE International Conference on Acoustics, Speech and Signal Processing, pp. 1286–1290. IEEE (2013)
18. Serban, I.V., et al.: A hierarchical latent variable encoder-decoder model for generating dialogues. In: Thirty-First AAAI Conference on Artificial Intelligence (2017)
19. Spampinato, C., Palazzo, S., Kavasidis, I., Giordano, D., Souly, N., Shah, M.: Deep learning human mind for automated visual classification. In: Proceedings of the IEEE Conference on Computer Vision and Pattern Recognition, pp. 6809–6817 (2017)

20. Tirupattur, P., Rawat, Y.S., Spampinato, C., Shah, M.: Thoughtviz: visualizing human thoughts using generative adversarial network. In: 2018 ACM Multimedia Conference on Multimedia Conference, pp. 950–958. ACM (2018)

21. Vandenhende, S., De Brabandere, B., Neven, D., Van Gool, L.: A three-player GAN: generating hard samples to improve classification networks. arXiv preprint arXiv:1903.03496 (2019)

22. Wen, H., Shi, J., Zhang, Y., Lu, K.H., Cao, J., Liu, Z.: Neural encoding and decoding with deep learning for dynamic natural vision. Cereb. Cortex **28**(12), 4136–4160 (2017)

23. Xu, H., Plataniotis, K.N.: Affective states classification using EEG and semi-supervised deep learning approaches. In: 2016 IEEE 18th International Workshop on Multimedia Signal Processing (MMSP), pp. 1–6. IEEE (2016)

24. Yan, X., Yang, J., Sohn, K., Lee, H.: Attribute2Image: conditional image generation from visual attributes. In: Leibe, B., Matas, J., Sebe, N., Welling, M. (eds.) ECCV 2016. LNCS, vol. 9908, pp. 776–791. Springer, Cham (2016). https://doi.org/10.1007/978-3-319-46493-0_47

Unified Image Aesthetic Prediction via Scanpath-Guided Feature Aggregation Network

Xiaodan Zhang$^{(\boxtimes)}$, Xinbo Gao, Wen Lu, Ying Yu, and Lihuo He

State Key Laboratory of Integrated Services Networks,
School of Electronic Engineering, Xidian University, Xi'an 710071, China
xdanzhang@stu.xidian.edu.cn

Abstract. The performance of automatic aesthetic prediction has achieved significant improvement by utilizing deep convolutional neural networks (CNNs). However, existing CNN methods can only achieve limited success because (1) most of the methods take one fixed-size patch as the training example, which loses the fine-grained details and the holistic layout information, and (2) most of the methods ignore the biologically cues such as the gaze shifting sequence in image aesthetic assessment. To address these challenges, we propose a scanpath-guided feature aggregation model for aesthetic prediction. In our model, human fixation map and the view scanpath are predicted by a multi-scale network. Then a sequence of regions are adaptively selected according to the scanpath. These attended regions are then progressively fed into the CNN and LSTM network to accumulate the information, yielding a compact image level representation. Extensive experiments on the large scale aesthetics assessment benchmark AVA and Photo.net data set thoroughly demonstrate the efficacy of our approach for unified aesthetic prediction tasks: (i) aesthetic quality classification; (ii) aesthetic score regression; and (iii) aesthetic score distribution prediction.

Keywords: Image quality assessment · Image aesthetic prediction · Long short-term memory network

With the popularization of digital cameras, images have been experiencing an unprecedented growth. Thus, automatic image aesthetic prediction is receiving increasing attention. And it also plays an important role in many applications such as image recommendation system, content management and image enhancement [1,19,27].

Early attempts [2,3,22] in this area mainly adopt hand-craft features which are designed based on the photographic rules. But most photographic rules are too abstract to be modeled mathematically. Recently, deep convolutional networks have been used to extract effective aesthetics features [6,23,25]. However, the performance is frustrated by the fixed input size restriction. The input images need to be pre-processed via cropping, scaling, or padding. These additional operations alter the global composition and reduce the image resolution which are

© Springer Nature Singapore Pte Ltd. 2019
A. Zeng et al. (Eds.): HBAI 2019, CCIS 1072, pp. 259–271, 2019.
https://doi.org/10.1007/978-981-15-1398-5_19

quite important in aesthetic assessment. In order to alleviate this restriction, [14] mimics the variable input sizes by using multiple fixed-size inputs which are scaled from the original images. It is apparently still far from arbitrary size input. Other methods [10,11] address this restriction by designing multiple column neural networks to simultaneously take random cropping patches as input. However, the random cropping strategy undermines the integrity of semantic information (Fig. 1).

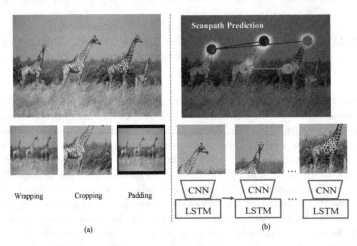

Fig. 1. (a) Conventional CNN methods transform images via cropping, warping and padding. (b) The proposed scanpath-guided feature aggregation networks take multiple glimpse and aggregate the fine grained details into a compact image level features via LSTM network.

In human perception process, one does not process the whole scene in its entirety at once. Instead humans sequentially allocate the attention on the parts of the visual space and integrate the information from different fixations over time [16]. The sequence of eye fixations is called a scanpath. A scanpath provides a graphic record of how information from an image is selected and processed. Existing researches [9,28] have demonstrated that the scanpath has close relationship with image aesthetic prediction.

In this work, we mimic human attention system and propose a scanpath-guided feature aggregation model for unified aesthetic prediction tasks. This model sequentially attends to different locations according to the predicted scanpath, and aggregates the information via LSTM network to build up a compact image-level representation. The main contributions of our method are summarized as follows.

- We are the first to incorporate the scanpaths into deep networks for image aesthetic prediction. With the guidance of scanpaths, the network can sequentially focus on the key areas to extract vision features just as HVS do.
- We design a novel network architecture that can deal with arbitrary size images and process them at their original aspect ratio without any

transformations. This is quite important in image aesthetic prediction since most of the existing deep networks are compromised by the fixed-sized constraint.

– We conduct comprehensive experiments for unified aesthetic prediction tasks: aesthetic classification, aesthetic regression and aesthetic label distribution. For all these tasks, the proposed model achieves superior performance over the state-of-the-art approaches on public datasets.

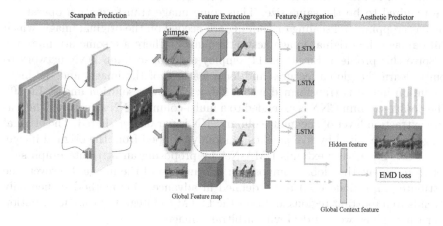

Fig. 2. The overall architecture of our scanpath-guided feature aggregation model.

1 Related Work

Image aesthetic prediction can be roughly divided into: personalized image aesthetics prediction [18,24] and public image aesthetic prediction. This paper focuses on the public aesthetic prediction. In the past decades, many attempts have been made in the direction of public aesthetic assessment. These attempts can be divided into two categories: extraction of more advanced features and utilization of more sophisticated learning algorithms. Thus we review the related work from these two aspects: the visual representations and learning algorithms.

1.1 Visual Representations

Traditional methods manually design features by explicitly modeling existing photography rules and psychological rules, such as rule of thirds, color balance and rule of simplicity [2,12,22]. Research [2,22] shows that both global features and local features of the image are important for the aesthetic quality evaluation of the image. For example, the composition of the image is a global feature, and the sharpness or noise of the image belongs to the local feature. However, these methods require strong expert knowledge and engineering skills, and these rules are descriptive so they are difficult to model accurately. Some methods [15] directly use generic image features to predict the aesthetic quality of the image.

SIFT, Bag-of-Visual-Words (BOV) and Fisher Vector (FV) are most commonly used descriptors. These methods are not optimal because they are not specifically designed for aesthetic quality assessment task.

Recently, deep learning method is applied to image aesthetic quality assessment and the performance is greatly improved compared to the previous non-deep method. One problem needs to be solved when applying deep neural networks to image aesthetic quality evaluation is the fixed-size constraint. Because the number of fully connected neurons in the network is fixed, the input images are required to be the same size. Thus some image transformation operations such as cropping and scaling or padding are needed on the original image, which will damage the original image aesthetic quality. There are some attempts try to solve this problem. Lu et al. [11] employ a double-column DNN network to jointly learn the global features and local features of the image, and the high-resolution image is transformed into a 256×256 low-resolution image. In [10], The double-column CNN is extended to a multi-column CNN structure. The feature extraction layer of the multi-column CNN is parameter-shared. The original image is represented by five patches randomly cropped from the original image. Ma et al. [13] further extends DMA-Net by proposing an attribute graph subnet to represent the global composition information of the image. However, the attribute graph node need to be defined in advance. Our method sequentially attends to important regions and uses the LSTM to integrate visual information over time. Thus, we can deal with arbitrary images.

1.2   Learning Algorithms

Most of the previous methods cast image aesthetic quality assessment as a binary classification problem [6,10,13,15], distinguishing images into high quality and low quality, or as a regression problem [7], giving a score to the image. However, the evaluation of image aesthetic quality is very subjective. Different people's evaluation of the same image are not exactly the same. Classification or regression does not reflect the subjectivity of an image. Some methods use label distribution to solve this problem. In [5], a new CJS loss was proposed to predict the aesthetic label distribution instead of a single scalar value. Other method [21] treated the scores as ordered classes and used squared EMD loss to predict the score distributions. However, this mechanism seriously degrades the performance when the ground-truth score distribution contains zeros. In this paper, we adopt the label smoothing mechanism to regularize the aesthetic prediction layer. Experimental results demonstrate that it can boost the performance.

2   Proposed Models and Algorithms

The overall framework is illustrated in Fig. 2. The proposed architecture consists of four major components: a fixation map and scanpath predictor, an image feature extractor, a LSTM network for feature aggregation and a unified image aesthetic predictor. Given an image, we first use the fixation map and scanpath predictor to predict the human view path and generate the multi-scaled glimpse images. We further extract CNN features of these attended regions and propose an active fusion model to aggregate them into an image level representation. Finally, the global context features and the output of LSTM block is concatenated and passed onto the unified image aesthetic predictor. In the following, we describe each of the aforementioned parts in detail.

2.1 Eye Fixation Map and Scanpath Prediction

Previous works have shown that the fixation map is best predicted when features are considered from multiple scales. Thus we adopt the DVA model [26] to predict the eye fixation map in this paper. DVA model is based on a skip-layer network with an encoder-decoder architecture. The encoder network is topologically identical to the five convolutional blocks in the VGG16 network. In order to preserve more spatial information of the feature map, the final pooling layer (pool5) is omitted. The decoder network aims to upsample feature maps and construct an output that maintains the original resolution. It consists of multiple deconvolution layers connected to *conv3-3*, *conv4-3* and *conv5-3* layers. Finally, these multi-level output layers are merged together by a 1×1 convolution layer.

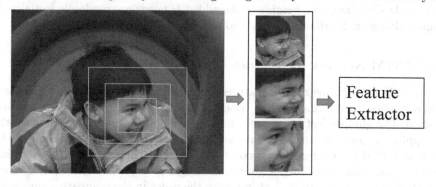

Fig. 3. Each glimpse is a multi-resolution image.

After getting the fixation map, the scanpath can be obtained via Winner-Take-All (WTA) and Inhibition Of Return (IOR) mechanism [4]. The WTA network naturally converges towards the most salient locations, and the IOR allows the model to rapidly shift the attention to new locations instead of being bound to the maximal saliency location. Figure 4 shows the predicted fixation maps and the scanpath of some example images.

The structure of the glimpse images is shown in Fig. 3. Each glimpse is a multi-scaled attended regions, which have a high-resolution around the fixation point l but a progressively lower resolution further from l. The goal is to emulate a "foveal" structure with the higher visual acuity in the center and lower resolution toward the periphery.

2.2 Visual Feature Extraction

In our model, We initially used a truncated version of $VGG16$ [8] to perform the task of automatic feature learning. The standard VGG16 consists of five

Fig. 4. Visualizations of the predicted fixation map and scanpath. The first column: original images. Second column: predicted fixation map and scanpath.

convolutional blocks and three fully connected layers. Considering the number of parameter, we replace the last two fully connected (*fc*) layers with one FC-1024 layer. The features are normalized before sending into the LSTM network. The weights of the filters in the five convolution blocks and the first fc layers are initialized from the VGG16 [8], which is trained on ImageNet database for the task of classification. The weights of the added *fc* layers are randomly initialized from a Gaussian distribution with zero mean and standard deviation of 0.01.

2.3   LSTM Network for Feature Aggregation

The LSTM network aggregates features extracted from the individual glimpses and combines the information in a coherent manner that preserves spatial information. The glimpse feature vector g from the visual feature extraction network is supplied as input to the LSTM network at each time step. In particular, each node in LSTM network is composed of a memory cell state c_t and three gates, i.e. the input gate i, the output gate o, the forget gate f. Give the input x_t and the previous hidden state h_{t-1} (t indicates the order in the scanpath sequence), LSTM network updates as follows:

$$i_t = \sigma(W_{xi}x_t + W_{ci}c_{t-1} + W_{hi}h_{t-1} + b_i) \tag{1}$$
$$f_t = \sigma(W_{xf}x_t + W_{cf}c_{t-1} + W_{hf}h_{t-1} + b_f) \tag{2}$$
$$g_t = \tanh(W_{xc}x_t + W_{hc}h_{t-1} + b_c) \tag{3}$$
$$o_t = \sigma(W_{xo}x_t + W_{co}c_{t-1} + W_{ho}h_{t-1} + b_o) \tag{4}$$
$$c_t = f_t c_{t-1} + i_t g_t \tag{5}$$
$$h_t = o_t \tanh(c_t) \tag{6}$$

where σ is the logistic sigmoid function, W_* is the weight matrices and b_* is the bias vectors. The (temporally) last output of the LSTM network then serves as the aggregated feature vector. Thus, the LSTM network can learn to aggregate the features to the deeper nodes and selectively forget noisy ones in the meantime.

2.4   Unified Image Aesthetic Prediction

The traditional methods often formulate the aesthetic assessment as binary classification, i.e. to predict whether a given image is of "high" or "low" quality from an aesthetic perspective. The binary labels are typically derived from a distribution of scores. However, the single binary label removes the useful information to investigate the consensus and diversity of opinions among annotators. In this paper, we aim to predict the unified aesthetic assessment tasks: aesthetic classification, aesthetic regression, and aesthetic label distribution.

Each image in the dataset consists of its ground truth ratings q. Let $q = [q_{s_1}, q_{s_2}, q_{s_N}]$ denote the score distributions of the images. $s = \{s_1, s_2, \ldots s_N\}$ represents the ordered score. N is the total number of score buckets. q_{s_i} denotes the number of voters that give a discrete score of s_i to the image. The score distributions are l_1-normalized as a preprocessing step. Thus $\sum_{i=1}^{N} q_{s_i} = 1$. For each training example x, label distribution models aim to learn a mapping $x \rightarrow q$. The loss function [21] used in our paper is defined as follows:

$$EMD(q, \hat{q}) = (\frac{1}{N} \sum_{k=1}^{N} |CDF_q(k) - CDF_{\hat{q}}(k)|^r)^{\frac{1}{r}}, \tag{7}$$

where $CDF_q(k)$ is the cumulative distribution function, r is set as 2 to penalize the Euclidean distance between the CDFs.

Label Smoothing Module. In the network, in order to guarantee that the final cumulative distribution function equals to 1, the predicted quality probabilities are fed to a soft-max function before output. This mechanism seriously limits the performance when the groundtruth score distribution contains zeros (Mathematically, the predicted outputs of softmax should never be zero). Inspired by [20], we smooth the ground-truth score distribution as follows:

$$q_s = (1 - \epsilon)q + \epsilon/N, \tag{8}$$

where N is the total number of score buckets, q is the ground-truth score distribution.

3   Experimental Results and Discussion

3.1   Dataset

AVA Dataset: The AVA aesthetic dataset [17] is considered as the largest public available dataset for image aesthetic assessment, which contains $250,000$ images. The images are collected from www.dpchallenge.com. Each image has about 200 aesthetic ratings ranging from one to ten. We follow the standard train/test split as the previous work [10,13,14], i.e. $230,000$ images for training and validation, the rest $19,000$ images for testing.

Table 1. Evaluation Criteria corresponded to three tasks.

Tasks	Method
Image aesthetic score regression	SRCC
	PLCC
	MAE
	RMSE
Image aesthetic classification	Overall accuracy
Image aesthetic label distribution	EMD

Photo.net Dataset: The Photo.net dataset [2] is collected from www.photo. net. It contains of $20,278$ images but only $17,200$ images have aesthetic label distribution. Distribution (counts) of aesthetics ratings are in 1–7 scale. $15,000$ images are used to train, 1000 images are used for validation and the rest 1200 images are used for test.

3.2   Experimental Settings

In the proposed framework, we directly use open source model [26] to predict the fixation map. We extract 10 glimpse in each image. The glimpse images consist of three-resolution. The high-resolution patch is extracted from square 112×112. The medium-resolution patch is from a square that is twice the side length of the high-resolution patch, i.e. 224×224. The low resolution patch is also twice the side length of the medium-resolution patch, i.e. 448×448. Finally, all the multi-scaled glimpse images are resized to 224×224 and sent to feature extractor for further processing. Each input image is normalized through mean RGB-channel subtraction. The feature extractor module is based on VGG-16 [8], which is pre-trained on AVA dataset and is freezed while training the LSTM networks. For the LSTM module, the number of hidden units is 512, and the lengths of LSTM networks are fixed to 10. The ϵ in the label smoothing module is 0.01. Each mini-batch consists of 32 images. We use Adam optimization method with initial learning rate 0.001 and reduced by a factor of 10 every 10 epochs. The weight decay is 1×10^{-8}. The training continues until the validation loss reaches a plateau for 5 epochs. We implement our model by the open-source library PyTorch.

Table 2. Ablation study.

Network architecture	Accuracy (%) ↑	SRCC (mean) ↑	LCC (mean) ↑	MAE↓	RMSE↓	EMD↓
Random cropping	76.06	0.5753	0.5831	0.4753	0.6054	0.05031
max pooling	75.38	0.5420	0.5532	0.4825	0.6157	0.0533
mean pooling	75.16	0.5375	0.5449	0.4861	0.6194	0.0536
Our model+EMD	80.74	0.6113	0.6209	0.4688	0.6024	0.05
Our model (label smoothing)	81.56	0.6452	0.6537	0.4242	0.5211	0.046

3.3 Evaluation Metrics

Unlike most traditional methods that are designed to perform the binary classification, we evaluate our proposed method with respect to three aesthetic quality tasks: (i) aesthetic score regression, (ii) aesthetic quality classification, and (iii) aesthetic score distribution prediction. For the aesthetic score regression task, we compute the mean score of the label distribution via $\mu = \sum_{i=1}^{N} s_i \times q_{s_i}$. For the aesthetic quality classification, images with predicted scores above 5 are categorized as high quality and vice versa. The evaluation metrics corresponding to three tasks are summarized in Table 1. For image aesthetic score regression task, we use the most significant metrics for testing the performance of an IQA method, i.e. the Spearman rank-order correlation coefficient (SRCC), Pearson linear correlation coefficient (LCC), root mean square error (RMSE) and mean absolute error (MAE). Of these criteria, SRCC measures the prediction monotonicity, and the LCC provides an evaluation of prediction accuracy. Both SRCC and LCC range from 0 to 1, and larger value indicates better result. While for MAE and RMSE, the smaller value indicates the better results. For image aesthetic quality classification task, we report the overall accuracy, defined as $Accuracy = \frac{TP+TN}{P+N}$. And for image aesthetic score distribution task, we report the EMD values. The EMD measures the closeness of the predicted and ground truth rating distribution with $r = 1$ in Eq. 8.

3.4 Ablation Study

Effect of the Scanpath. In order to verify the effect of the scanpath prediction module in our proposed framework, we compare with a baseline which uses random cropping strategies to get the glimpse images. The baseline network is optimized based on the EMD loss. The comparison results are shown in Table 2. Our proposed scanpath guided feature aggregation framework achieves remarkable improvement to the baseline (from 76.06% to 80.74% in overall accuracy, from 0.5753 to 0.6113 in SRCC), which demonstrates the effectiveness of the scanpath prediction module.

Effect of LSTM-Based Feature Aggregation. To evaluate the effectiveness of the LSTM feature aggregation module, we compare with two baselines, i.e., mean pooling and max pooling. In the two baseline networks, the features of glimpse images are aggregated via max pooling or mean pooling before sending into the aesthetic predictor. EMD loss is used to optimize the networks. The comparison results are shown in Table 2. The proposed LSTM fusion method brings more than 5% classification improvement to the mean pooling and max pooling scheme, indicating that LSTM feature aggregation network is more effective.

Effect of Label Smoothing. When the groundtruth score distribution contains zeros, it is difficult for EMD loss to optimize. In this paper, we add the label smoothing module to the ground truth score distribution. The comparison results are shown in Table 2. As can be seen, the classification results has been improved about 0.82% (from 80.74% to 81.56%), and the SRCC has been improved about 3.39% (from 0.6113 to 0.6452).

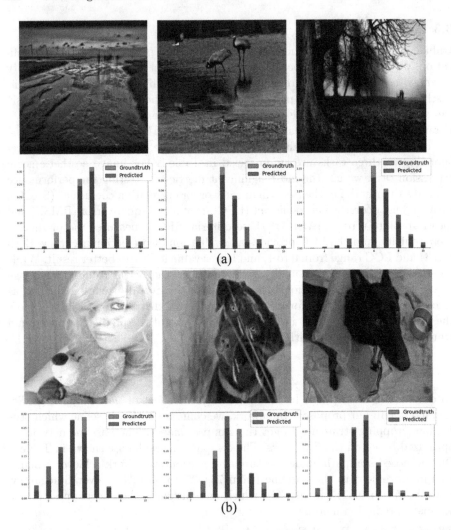

Fig. 5. Test images that are considered of high quality and low quality by our method. Predicted score distribution and ground-truth distribution has been showed. (a) High quality images. (b) Low quality images.

3.5 Comparison on AVA Dataset

We quantitatively compare our method with several state-of-the-art methods: *i.e. NIMA* [21], *MTRLCNN* [6], *A-Lamp* [13], *MNA-CNN* [14], *RAPID* [11], *DMA-Net* [10] on AVA dataset. Table 3 shows the comparison results. Note that methods of [6, 10, 11, 13, 14] are designed to perform binary classification on the aesthetic scores. Only aesthetic quality classification results are reported. The results of these methods are obtained from their papers. As can be seen, our method achieves the best performance across the board. *NIMA* [21] also utilizes the EMD loss to optimize their network, but our method outperforms it by a large margin (0.592 vs. 0.6452 in SRCC). *RAPID* [11], *DMA-Net* [10] and *A-Lamp* [13] are all take the global and local information into consideration, but they ignore the scanpath information. Our method, on the other hand, incorporates the scanpath information in aesthetic prediction framework, and uses the *LSTM* network to aggregate information, enabling better performance. Figure 5 shows some examples of the test images that are considered of high quality and low quality by our method. Plots of the ground-truth and predicted distributions are also shown. As can be seen, distribution of the ground truth scores is closely predicted by the proposed model.

Table 3. Comparison with state-of-the-art methods on AVA dataset.

Network architecture	Accuracy (%)↑	SRCC (mean)↑	LCC (mean)↑	MAE↓	RMSE↓	EMD↓
RAPID [11]	74.2	–	–	–	–	–
DMA-Net [10]	75.42	–	–	–	–	–
MNA-CNN [14]	76.1	–	–	–	–	–
A-Lamp [13]	82.5	–	–	–	–	–
MTRLCNN [6]	78.46	–	–	–	–	–
NIMA [21]	80.6	0.592	0.610	–	–	0.052
Our mothod	**81.56**	**0.6452**	**0.6537**	**0.4242**	**0.5211**	**0.046**

Table 4. Comparison with state-of-the-art methods on Photo.net dataset.

Network architecture	Accuracy (%)↑	SRCC (mean)↑	LCC (mean)↑	MAE↓	RMSE↓	EMD↓
GIST_SVM	59.90	–	–	–	–	–
FV_SIFT_SVM	60.8	–	–	–	–	–
MTCNN(VGG16)	65.2	–	–	–	–	–
VGG16	70.69	0.4097	0.4214	0.4621	0.5623	0.0761
Our method	**75.32**	**0.5247**	**0.5324**	**0.4322**	**0.5311**	**0.075**

3.6   Comparison on Photo.net Dataset

In order to demonstrate the robustness of proposed method, we compare the proposed model with state-of-the-art methods. Table 4 illustrates the comparison results. The comparison methods includes the deep learning models proposed in [6], VGG16 and the traditional feature extraction models [15]. For VGG16, the last layer was replaced with a fully connected layer which has 7 neurons followed by *softmax* activations (the scale of the Photo.net dataset is 1–7). The parameters in VGG16 are initialized with models trained on ImageNet. We can find that the proposed method outperforms the baselines by a large margin, achieving 75.32% accuracy rate. This is around 10.12% better than MTCNN, and 14.52% better than traditional handcraft methods.

4   Conclusion

In this paper, we present a novel scanpath guided feature aggregation model for photo aesthetic assessment. Humans sequentially allocate the attention on the parts of the visual space and integrate the information from different fixations. We are inspired by this attention mechanism and propose to use the scanpath to guide the fine details feature extraction. These fine-details features are aggregated via LSTM network. The proposed method not only can handle images with arbitrary size, but also can incorporate the gaze shifting sequence into the aesthetic framework. The experimental results on the large-scale AVA and Photo.net datasets show that our method is significantly superior to state-of-the-art methods on three tasks: aesthetic quality classification, aesthetic score regression and aesthetic score distribution prediction.

References

1. Bhattacharya, S., Sukthankar, R., Shah, M.: A framework for photo-quality assessment and enhancement based on visual aesthetics. In: Proceedings of the 18th ACM International Conference on Multimedia, pp. 271–280 (2010)
2. Datta, R., Joshi, D., Li, J., Wang, J.Z.: Studying aesthetics in photographic images using a computational approach. In: Leonardis, A., Bischof, H., Pinz, A. (eds.) ECCV 2006. LNCS, vol. 3953, pp. 288–301. Springer, Heidelberg (2006). https://doi.org/10.1007/11744078_23
3. Guo, L., Xiong, Y., Huang, Q., Li, X.: Image esthetic assessment using both hand-crafting and semantic features. Neurocomputing **143**, 14–26 (2014)
4. Itti, L., Koch, C.: Computational modelling of visual attention. Nat. Rev. Neurosci. **2**(3), 194 (2001)
5. Jin, X., et al.: Predicting aesthetic score distribution through cumulative Jensen-Shannon divergence. In: Proceedings of the AAAI Conference on Artificial Intelligence, pp. 77–84 (2018)
6. Kao, Y., He, R., Huang, K.: Deep aesthetic quality assessment with semantic information. IEEE Trans. Image Process. **26**(3), 1482–1495 (2017)
7. Kong, S., Shen, X., Lin, Z., Mech, R., Fowlkes, C.: Photo aesthetics ranking network with attributes and content adaptation. In: Leibe, B., Matas, J., Sebe, N., Welling, M. (eds.) ECCV 2016. LNCS, vol. 9905, pp. 662–679. Springer, Cham (2016). https://doi.org/10.1007/978-3-319-46448-0_40
8. Krizhevsky, A., Sutskever, I., Hinton, G.E.: ImageNet classification with deep convolutional neural networks. In: NIPS, pp. 1097–1105 (2012)
9. Locher, P.: The usefulness of eye movement recordings to subject an aesthetic episode with visual art to empirical scrutiny. Psychol. Sci. **48**(2), 106 (2006)
10. Lu, X., Lin, Z., Shen, X., Mech, R., Wang, J.Z.: Deep multi-patch aggregation network for image style, aesthetics, and quality estimation. In: ICCV, pp. 990–998 (2015)
11. Lu, X., Lin, Z., Jin, H., Yang, J., Wang, J.Z.: Rating image aesthetics using deep learning. IEEE Trans. Multimed. **17**(11), 2021–2034 (2015)
12. Luo, Y., Tang, X.: Photo and video quality evaluation: focusing on the subject. In: Forsyth, D., Torr, P., Zisserman, A. (eds.) ECCV 2008. LNCS, vol. 5304, pp. 386–399. Springer, Heidelberg (2008). https://doi.org/10.1007/978-3-540-88690-7_29

13. Ma, S., Liu, J., Chen, C.W.: A-lamp: adaptive layout-aware multi-patch deep convolutional neural network for photo aesthetic assessment. In: CVPR, pp. 722–731 (2017)

14. Mai, L., Jin, H., Liu, F.: Composition-preserving deep photo aesthetics assessment. In: CVPR, pp. 497–506 (2016)

15. Marchesotti, L., Perronnin, F., Larlus, D., Csurka, G.: Assessing the aesthetic quality of photographs using generic image descriptors. In: ICCV, pp. 1784–1791 (2011)

16. Mnih, V., Heess, N., Graves, A., Kavukcuoglu, K.: Recurrent models of visual attention. In: NIPS, pp. 2204–2212 (2014)

17. Murray, N., Marchesotti, L., Perronnin, F.: AVA: a large-scale database for aesthetic visual analysis. In: CVPR, pp. 2408–2415 (2012)

18. Ren, J., Shen, X., Lin, Z.L., Mech, R., Foran, D.J.: Personalized image aesthetics. In: ICCV, pp. 638–647 (2017)

19. Samii, A., Měch, R., Lin, Z.: Data-driven automatic cropping using semantic composition search. Comput. Graph. Forum **34**(1), 141–151 (2015)

20. Szegedy, C., Vanhoucke, V., Ioffe, S., Shlens, J., Wojna, Z.: Rethinking the inception architecture for computer vision. In: CVPR, pp. 2818–2826 (2016)

21. Talebi, H., Milanfar, P.: NIMA: neural image assessment. IEEE Trans. Image Process. **27**(8), 3998–4011 (2018)

22. Tang, X., Luo, W., Wang, X.: Content-based photo quality assessment. IEEE Trans. Multimed. **15**(8), 1930–1943 (2013)

23. Tian, X., Dong, Z., Yang, K., Mei, T.: Query-dependent aesthetic model with deep learning for photo quality assessment. IEEE Trans. Multimed. **17**(11), 2035–2048 (2015)

24. Wang, G., Yan, J., Qin, Z.: Collaborative and attentive learning for personalized image aesthetic assessment. In: IJCAI, pp. 957–963 (2018)

25. Wang, W., Zhao, M., Wang, L., Huang, J., Cai, C., Xu, X.: A multi-scene deep learning model for image aesthetic evaluation. Sig. Process. Image Comm. **47**, 511–518 (2016)

26. Wang, W., Shen, J.: Deep visual attention prediction. IEEE Trans. Image Process. **27**(5), 2368–2378 (2018)

27. Zhang, F.L., Wang, M., Hu, S.M.: Aesthetic image enhancement by dependence-aware object recomposition. IEEE Trans. Multimed. **15**(7), 1480–1490 (2013)

28. Zics, B.: Eye gaze as a vehicle for aesthetic interaction: affective visualisation for immersive user experience. In: Proceedings of the 17th International Symposium on Electronic Arts, Istanbul, Turkey, pp. 2204–2212, September 2014

Consistent and Specific Multi-view Relative-Transform Classification

Siyuan Ping, Long Zhang, Xing Wang, and Guoxian Yu[(✉)] [ID]

College of Computer and Information Sciences, Southwest University,
Chongqing 400715, China
gxyu@swu.edu.cn

Abstract. In many practical problems, the same objects can be described in many different ways or from different angles. These multiple descriptions constitute multiple views of objects. Multi-view classification methods try to exploit information from all views to improve the classification performance and reduce the effect of noises. However, how to efficiently exploit the consistency and specificity in multiple views remains a challenge. In addition, it is also worth to explore the processing results of multi-view data more inline with human cognition. For this reason, we propose a new multi-view classification algorithm, Consistent and Specific Multi-View Relative-transform Classification (CSMRtC). CSMRtC firstly explores the underlying subspace structure of different views exhaustively, to evacuate consistency and specificity of multi-view data. Next, these data matrices are processed using the relative transform technique. As for the consistency and specificity, consistent matrix stores the shared information of multiple data matrices, specificity captures the characteristic of each view. Then, we use the relative transformations to transform data from raw space to relative spaces, to achieve the purpose of suppress noise in the data and improve the distinction between the data. Comprehensive evaluations with several state-of-the-art competitors demonstrate the efficiency and the superiority of the proposed method.

Keywords: Multi-view learning · Classification · Relative transformation

1 Introduction

With the development of information technology, multi-view data have met a widespread increase over the last few decades. In many real-world applications, the data sets are naturally comprised of multiple views [10,12,17,32,37]. For example, web pages can be described based on either the page content (text) or hyperlink information [4,12], social networks based on user profile or the

Supported by NSFC (61872300 and 61873214), Fundamental Research Funds for the Central Universities (XDJK2019B024), NSF of CQ CSTC (cstc2018jcyjAX0228).

friend links [33], images based on the pixel arrays or the captions associated with them [13]. Each individual view can only partially express the data. To address this problem, multi-view learning [11,23,30] has emerged with the goal of jointly learning features from multi-view data, which can provide diverse and complementary information to each other effectively [28,36].

Many multi-view learning algorithms have been proposed, according to the fusion strategy of view information, they can be simply divided into three categories (early, intermediate and late). For the early fusion techniques, the information is combined before any training process is performed. For example, Zilca *et al.* [25] achieved the fusion by means of a simple concatenation of the data from all views. Here, one has the freedom to model the views differently, which is a strong advantage when the data is inherently different over the views (e.g. in the case of text data and pixel arrays). However, with the continuous development of multi-view classification methods, late fusion has become a more common processing strategy. For example, Bekker *et al.* [3] used a stochastic combination of two classifiers to determine whether a breast micro calcification is benign or malignant. Mayo and Frank [20] performed multi-view multi-instance learning by a weighted combination of separate classifiers on each view and used it to do image classification. Wozniak and Jackowski [29] gave a comparative overview of methods and performed classification based on a weighted voting of the results of separate classifiers on the views individually. A third option is to combine the benefits of both fusion types, it firstly combines the information from different views before training, and at the end of the training phase a weighted combination of the classifiers is taken as the final classifier. Minh *et al.* [2] use this technique to develop a multi-view semi-supervised classification model based on Support Vector Machines (SVM) with within-view as well as between-view regularization.

However most existing multi-view methods only consider the consistency of multi-view data [14,15,35], or only explore the specific of different subspace representations [5]. Although we can simply concatenate all the features, this strategy ignores the correlation among views and may lead to a severe curse of dimensionality. In addition, the real world is by nature and merely considering consistency or diversity is not adequate. Thus, these methods do not explore the underlying data distribution among different views comprehensively. How to efficiently exploit the consistency and specificity in multiple views remains a challenge.

To multi-view data, excepting the reasonable use of the consistency and specific between views, how to effectively remove the noise in the data is also a challenge. Some studies have tried to remove the noise [6], but in many cases this is not appropriate. Firstly, the noise is difficult to accurately identify. Secondly, some noise-like data is essential for analysis. Finally, many of the noise is not isolated, but rather pollution of normal data points. It is therefore appropriate to remove the effect of noise on the normal point rather than eliminating the noise itself.

Two manifold machine learning methods published in "Science": local linear embedding algorithm and isometric embedded learning algorithm can be considered as cognitive-based methods [24,27]. The manifold concept is the core of the manifold machine learning method. It is for this reason that these two methods have original innovation, which has led to extensive research. Experience has shown that human perception is relative, for example, when observing the two circles X and Y in Fig. 1, X is often considered to be larger than Y, but in fact the two circles are the same size.

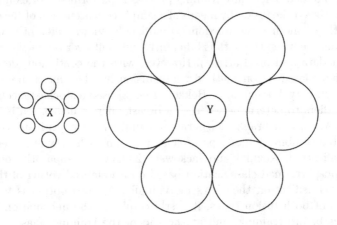

Fig. 1. Human perception on image is relative

Inspired by the cognitive relativity, Wen *et al.* [1] presented a relative transformation for machine learning to build the relative space from the original space of data. By comparing experiments of the SVM and R-SVM in processing of noise data, it is proved that the relative transformation can effectively suppress noise.

Wen *et al.* added a figure in their paper [1] to explain the role of relative transformation more intuitively. As shown in Fig. 2, X_4 may be noise data, but $d(X_3, X_1) = d(X_3, X_4)$ in the original space, which makes X_1 and X_4 have the same chance to become the neighbors of X_3, which is inconsistent with our intuition. In relative space, $d(X_3, X_1) < d(X_3, X_4)$, which means that the noise point data is farther away from the normal data points.

Looking at the multi-view classification method, some only consider the consistency between views, some only consider the specificity between views [5]. All of them lack effective solutions to combine the two. At the same time, multi-view data still has the problem of data noise. In order to solve the above two problems, we have proposed a consistent and specific multi-view relative-transform classification (CSMRtC). CSMRtC can explore the structure between views, taking into account the commonalities and differences between views. In addition, CSMRtC also uses relative transformation techniques to suppress noise in the data and make the data more indexable, which is more in line with people's cognitive rules. Experimental results on five multi-view datasets show that

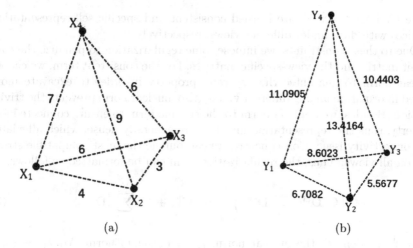

(a)   (b)

Fig. 2. Relative transformation can weaken the influence of noise. (a) The original space and (b) The constructed relative space.

the proposed CSMRtC achieves superior performance against state-of-the-art approaches across various evaluation criteria.

2   Method

In order to use the consistency and specificity information between views, and make the data distribution more in line with people's cognitive concepts, the overall algorithm is divided into two steps, one is using the consistency and specificity of multi-view data for matrix representation learning, the second is constructing a new data space using a relative transformation method.

2.1   Formulation

Let $\mathbf{X}^{(v)} \in \mathbb{R}^{d_v \times N}$ denote the feature matrix corresponding to the v-th view, d_v indicate the dimensionality of the data in the v-th ($v \in \{1, 2, \cdots, V\}$) view. Define $\mathbf{Z}^{(v)} \in \mathbb{R}^{N \times N}$ the learned subspace representation in each view. If we just consider the consistency term of all views, the multi-view self-representation formula can be written as

$$\mathbf{X}^{(V)} = \mathbf{X}^{(V)}\mathbf{Z} \tag{1}$$

Furthermore, though the common representation which remains unchanged among all views is considered in above equation, the unique part in each view is not considered, and it is obviously not enough or accurate to merely leverage this small part for data modeling. We consider

$$\mathbf{X}^{(v)} = \mathbf{X}^{(v)}\left(\mathbf{C} + \mathbf{D}^{(v)}\right), v \in V \tag{2}$$

where $\mathbf{C}$, $\mathbf{D}^{(v)} \in \mathbb{R}^{N \times N}$ are learned consistent and specific self-representation matrices with data under different views, respectively.

Due to these constraints, we impose some regularization to penalize the consistent matrix and the view-specific matrices. For the consistent term, we choose nuclear norm to guarantee the low rank property in order to excavate more shared information among different views. Also, nuclear norm prevents the trivial solution. Besides, we apply l_2 norm to the specific term to ensure connectedness property, thus the representation matrices are generally dense, which alleviates the connectivity issue. Consequently, we can pursue the most compatible structure on all views. Thus, the regularization term can be formatted as follows:

$$\Omega\left(\mathbf{C}, \mathbf{D}^{(1)}, \ldots, \mathbf{D}^{(V)}\right) = \lambda_C \|\mathbf{C}\|_* + \lambda_D \sum_{v=1}^{V} \left\|\mathbf{D}^{(v)}\right\|_2^2 \tag{3}$$

where $\| \cdot \|_*$ denotes the nuclear norm, $\| \cdot \|_2$ is the l_2 norm, $\lambda_D, \lambda_C \in (0, 1]$ are trade-off parameters. Consequently, combining all the conditions discussed above together leads to the objective function of the proposed method:

$$\min_{\mathbf{C}, \mathbf{D}^{(v)}} \lambda_C \|\mathbf{C}\|_* + \lambda_D \sum_{v=1}^{V} \left\|\mathbf{D}^{(v)}\right\|_2^2 \tag{4}$$

$$s.t. \quad \mathbf{X}^{(v)} = \mathbf{X}^{(v)}\left(\mathbf{C} + \mathbf{D}^{(v)}\right) \tag{5}$$

By solving above equation with multi-view features, a consistent and a series of specific representations can be extracted and the data is represented more naturally. With the learned representations, we construct the affinity matrix with respect to the consistency and the specificities

$$\mathbf{S} = \frac{|\mathbf{C}| + |\mathbf{C}|^T}{2} + \frac{1}{V} \sum_{v=1}^{V} \frac{\left|\mathbf{D}^{(v)}\right| + \left|\mathbf{D}^{(v)}\right|^T}{2} \tag{6}$$

Now we use the relative transformation method to project the data into the new space. For any point, its distance from all other points in the original space constitutes its coordinates in the new space S^Γ.

$$s_i^r = \left(d\left(s_i, s_1\right), d\left(s_i, s_2\right) \ldots, d\left(s_i, s_{|x|}\right)\right) \tag{7}$$

where $S = \{s_1, s_2, \ldots, s_{|S|}\}$, $|S|$ is the number of elements of the set S. The space constructed by relative transformation is called relative space S^r. Then we apply the k-NN to the data in relative space to get the final classification result.

2.2 Optimization

Our objective function simultaneously learns the consistent and specific representations from multiple views. However, directly finding the optimal solution of the problem is extremely difficult. Thus, we leverage a convex relaxation and develop an alternating optimization algorithm to jointly recover the corresponding data representations. Firstly, we introduce variables $\mathbf{K}$, $(\mathbf{W})^{(v)} \in \mathbb{R}^{N \times N}$ as surrogates of $\mathbf{C}$ in nuclear norm, where $\langle \cdot, \cdot \rangle$ is the standard Euclidean inner product of two matrices, $\| \cdot \|_F$ denotes Frobenius norm,

$$\min_{\mathbf{C}, \mathbf{D}^{(v)}, \mathbf{W}^{(v)}, \mathbf{K}} \lambda_C \|\mathbf{K}\|_* + \lambda_D \sum_{v=1}^{V} \left\| \mathbf{D}^{(v)} \right\|_2^2 + \sum_{v=1}^{V} \left\| \mathbf{W}^{(v)} \right\| \tag{8}$$

This problem can be solved by the Augmented Lagrange Multiplier (ALM) method [18], which minimizes the augmented Lagrange function of the form. $\left\{ \mathbf{Y}_1^{(v)}, \mathbf{Y}_2^{(v)}, \mathbf{Y}_3^{(v)} \right\}_{v \in V}$, $\mathbf{Y}_2$ are Lagrange multipliers and $\mu > 0$ is a penalty parameter.

$$\lambda_C \|\mathbf{K}\|_* + \lambda_D \sum_{v=1}^{V} \left\| \mathbf{D}^{(v)} \right\|_2^2 + \sum_{v=1}^{V} \left\| \mathbf{W}^{(v)} \right\|_{2,1} + \sum_{v=1}^{V} \left\langle \mathbf{Y}_1^{(v)}, \mathbf{X}^{(V)} - \mathbf{X}^{(V)}(\mathbf{C} + \mathbf{D}) \right\rangle$$

$$+ \frac{\mu}{2} \sum_{v=1}^{V} \left\| \mathbf{X}^{(V)} - \mathbf{X}^{(V)}(\mathbf{C} + \mathbf{D}) \right\| + \langle \mathbf{Y}_2, \mathbf{C} - \mathbf{K} \rangle + \frac{\mu}{2} \|\mathbf{C} - \mathbf{K}\|_F^2$$

$$+ \sum_{v=1}^{V} \left\langle \mathbf{Y}_3^{(v)}, -\mathbf{W}^{(V)} \right\rangle + \frac{\mu}{2} \sum_{v=1}^{V} \left\| -\mathbf{W}^{(v)} \right\|_F^2 \tag{9}$$

To tackle this issue, we divide the above unconstrained problem into six sub-problems and alternatively optimize them by fixing the other variables. The Algorithm 1 is depicted below.

2.3 Complexity Analysis

Assume that the number of views is V. CSMRtC consists of $3V + 3$ sub-problems and the complexities of the subproblems are analyzed as follows. The complexity of updating $\mathbf{C}, \mathbf{D}^{(v)}$ and $\mathbf{K}$ derived from matrix inversion and nuclear norm are $O(N^3)$, where N is the number of data samples. The complexity of updating $\mathbf{W}^{(V)}$ is $O(dN)$, where d is the maximal dimensionality of data towards all views. The relative transformation complexity is $O(N^2)$. Overall, the complexity is $O((V + 2)N^3 + 2VdN)$ for each iteration, where V is the number of views. Considering the number of iterations, the complexity of Algorithm 1 is $O(MVN(N^2 + d) + N^2)$, where M is the number of iterations.

3 Experimental Results

3.1 Data Set

we compare our method, CSMRtC, to the state-of-the-art methods on multi-view face classification datasets. Five benchmark datasets are adopted in our evaluation.

Algorithm 1. Consistent and Specific Multi-View Relative-transform Classification (CSMRtC)

Input:

The data set $\mathbf{X}$ with multiple types of feature $\left\{\mathbf{X}^{(v)}\right\}_{v\in[V]}$, the parameters λ_C and λ_D.

1: Initialize coefficient matrices $\mathbf{C} = \mathbf{K} = \mathbf{Y}_1^{(v)} = \mathbf{Y}_2 = \mathbf{Y}_3^{(v)} = 0$, generate $\left\{\mathbf{D}^{(v)}\right\}_{v\in[V]}$ by the method proposed by Cao *et al.* [5], set parameters $\mu = 10^{-6}, \mu_{\max} = 10^6, \rho = 1.1$, maximum iterations $\mathbf{M} = 60$ and stopping threshold $\varepsilon = 10^{-6}$.

2: **For** $t < M$

3:    Fix the others and update $\mathbf{C}$ using
$$\mathbf{C} = \left(\sum_{v=1}^V \left(\mathbf{X}^{(v)}\right)^T \mathbf{X}^{(v)} + \mathbf{I}\right)^{-1} \times$$
$$\left(\sum_{v=1}^V \left(\mathbf{X}^{(v)}\right)^T \left(\mathbf{X}^{(v)} - \mathbf{X}^{(v)}\mathbf{D}^{(v)} + \frac{\mathbf{Y}_1^{(v)}}{\mu}\right) + \mathbf{K} - \frac{\mathbf{Y}_2}{\mu}\right)$$

4:    Fix the others and update $\mathbf{K}$ using
$$\mathbf{K} = \arg\min \frac{\lambda_C}{\mu}\|\mathbf{K}\|_* + \frac{1}{2}\left\|\mathbf{K} - \left(\mathbf{C} + \frac{\mathbf{Y}_2}{\mu}\right)\right\|_F^2$$

5:    **For** $v \in [V]$

6:       Fix the others and update $D^{(v)}$ using
$$\mathbf{D}^{(v)} = \left(\mu\left(\mathbf{X}^{(v)}\right)^T \mathbf{X}^{(v)} + 2\lambda_D\mathbf{I}\right)^{-1} \times \mu\left(\mathbf{X}^{(v)}\right)^T \left(\mathbf{X}^{(v)} - \mathbf{X}^{(v)}\mathbf{C} + \frac{\mathbf{Y}_1}{\mu}\right)$$

7:       Fix the others and update $\mathbf{W}^{(v)}$ using
$$\mathbf{W}^{(v)} = \arg\min \frac{1}{\mu}\left\|\mathbf{W}^{(v)}\right\|_{2,1} + \frac{1}{2}\left\|\mathbf{W}^{(v)} - \frac{\mathbf{Y}_3^{(v)}}{\mu}\right\|_F^2$$

8:       Update the multipliers
$$\mathbf{Y}_{1(t+1)}^{(v)} = \mathbf{Y}_{1(t)}^{(v)} + \mu\left(\mathbf{X}^{(v)} - \mathbf{X}^{(v)}\left(\mathbf{C} + \mathbf{D}^{(v)}\right)\right)$$
$$\mathbf{Y}_{3(t+1)}^{(v)} = \mathbf{Y}_{3(t)}^{(v)} - \mu\mathbf{W}^{(v)}$$

9:    **End For**

10:   Update the multipliers
$$\mathbf{Y}_{2(t+1)}^{(v)} = \mathbf{Y}_{2(t)} + \mu(\mathbf{C} - \mathbf{K})$$

11:   Construct the affinity matrix S using Eq.(6)

12:   **For** $s \in [S]$ $S_i^\tau = \left(d\left(s_i, s_1\right), d\left(s_i, s_2\right)\ldots, d\left(s_i, s_{|x|}\right)\right)$

13:   **End For**

14:   Apply the k-NN algorithm on S

15: **End For**

Output:

The predicted label of S.

- **ORL** face dataset contains 400 images of 40 distinct subjects. For each category, images were taken at different times, lights, facial expressions (open/closed eyes, smiling or not) and facial details (with glasses/without glasses).
- **Yale** is a widely used face dataset which contains 165 grayscale images, 15 individuals with 11 images of each category. Variations of the data include

center light, with glasses, happy, left light, without glasses, normal, right light, sad, sleepy, surprised and wink.

- **Notting-Hill Video Face** is derived from the movie Notting-Hill. The faces of five main casts are collected, including 4,660 faces in 76 tracks. We randomly sample 110 images of each cast.
- **BBCsport** Contains 544 documents from the BBC Sport website of sports news articles in five topical areas in 2004–2005.
- **Caltech 101-7** consists of 101 classes of images for objective recognition. Due to the unbalance of the data quantity in each class of Caltech101, we select the commonly-used 7 categories for the subsequent evaluations, including Face, Motorbikes, Dolla-Bill, Garfield, Snoopy, Stop-Sign, and Windsor-Chair with 1474 images in total, referred to as Caltech101-7.

For face datasets, we resize the images to 48×48 and extract three types of features: View1 intensity (4096 dimensions), View2 LBP [21] (3304 dimensions) and View3 Gabor [16] (6750 dimensions). The standard LBP feature is extracted from 72×80 loosely cropped images with a histogram size of 59 over 9×10 pixel patches. The Gabor feature is extracted with one scale $\lambda = 4$ at four orientations $\theta = \{0°, 45°, 90°, 135°\}$ with a loose face crop at the resolution of 25×30 pixels. BBCSport dataset only has two views, View1: 3183 dimensions and View2: 3203 dimensions, respectively. All descriptors except the intensity are scaled to have unit norm. As for Caltech 101-7 dataset, five public features are adopted for the experiments, including Gabor [16], Wavelet Moments (WM), CENTRIST [31], HOG [7], GIST [22], and LBP [21].

3.2 Experimental Setup

We compare our proposed method with six state-of-the-art methods, including k-NN classification algorithm, a conventional single-view classification method, i.e., SVM [9], supervised dimension reduction method, i.e., LDA [8], supervised multi-view learning method SimpleMKL [19], multiple kernels prediction algorithm for protein function prediction ProMK [34] and Matrix Completion for multi-view Weak label Learning McWL [26].

We also compare with three baseline algorithm. One of them is CSMC which is removed the part of the relative transformation in CSMRtC. The other two methods are variants of CSMRtC. CMRtC represents consistent multi-view relative-transform classification, which uses the consistent part as self-representation matrix $\mathbf{Z}$. SMRtC stands for specific multi-view relative-transform classification, which uses the specific part as the self-representation matrix $\mathbf{Z}$.

In our experiments, we tune the parameter λ_C and λ_D in the range of $(0, 1]$ and report the best results. We run each experiment 30 times and report the average score and standard deviation. For all the compared methods, we have tuned the parameters to the best.

3.3   Performance Evaluation

Three widely used multi-view evaluation metrics are adopted for performance comparisons, i.e., Accuracy (ACC), Average Precision (AP) and Average Recall (AR). Accuracy (ACC) reflects the ability of the classifier to determine the entire sample. Average Precision (AP) reflects the proportion of true positive samples in the positive case determined by the classifier. Average Recall (AR) reflects the proportion of positive cases that are correctly judged to all positive cases. Their metrics are defined as follows:

$$ACC = \frac{TP + TN}{TP + TN + FP + FN} \tag{10}$$

$$PE = \frac{TP}{TP + FP}, AP = \frac{1}{Q}\sum_{q=1}^{Q} PE(q) \tag{11}$$

$$RE = \frac{TP}{TP + FN}, AR = \frac{1}{Q}\sum_{q=1}^{Q} RE(q) \tag{12}$$

where TP (true positive) is the number that are correctly predicted, TN (true negative) is the number of true non-interacting pairs that are correctly predicted, FP (false positive) is the number of the wrongly predicted interacting pairs, and FN (false negative) is the number of the true interacting pairs that are failed to be predicted, q is one specific query image, n is the number of the query images.

Table 1. Accuracy (ACC) compare results (mean ± standard deviation)

Method	ORL	Yale	Notting-Hill	BBCsport	Caltech 101-7
CSMRtC	**0.9982 ± 0.0347**	**0.9784 ± 0.0113**	**0.9953 ± 0.0052**	**0.9697 ± 0.0259**	**0.9475 ± 0.0148**
CSMC	0.9753 ± 0.0165	0.9155 ± 0.0485	0.9951 ± 0.0059	0.9311 ± 0.0137	0.9279 ± 0.0215
CMRtC	0.8342 ± 0.0125	0.6284 ± 0.0234	0.2094 ± 0.0068	0.3796 ± 0.0478	0.4756 ± 0.0321
SMRtC	0.8654 ± 0.0354	0.6774 ± 0.0245	0.7764 ± 0.0241	0.7654 ± 0.0134	0.6324 ± 0.0231
ProMK	0.9725 ± 0.0235	0.9145 ± 0.0652	0.9345 ± 0.0235	0.9345 ± 0.0235	0.9201 ± 0.2164
McWL	0.9789 ± 0.0154	0.9316 ± 0.0454	0.9924 ± 0.0164	0.9401 ± 0.0165	0.9214 ± 0.2264
simpleMKL	0.9786 ± 0.0116	0.9042 ± 0.0124	0.9946 ± 0.0204	0.9265 ± 0.0317	0.9176 ± 0.0069
SVM	0.9732 ± 0.0158	0.8732 ± 0.0158	0.9934 ± 0.0214	0.8991 ± 0.0223	0.8879 ± 0.0155
LDA	0.9635 ± 0.0218	0.9142 ± 0.0403	0.9951 ± 0.0245	0.9157 ± 0.0114	0.9201 ± 0.0082
k-NN	0.7985 ± 0.0419	0.7200 ± 0.0676	0.9951 ± 0.0590	0.9043 ± 0.0224	0.8709 ± 0.0082

From Table 1, we can see that the overall accuracy of CSMRtC is ranging from 94.75% to 99.53%. In order to comprehensively evaluate the performance of CSMRtC, the results with respect to other two evaluation metrics (including AP, AR) are also included. CSMRtC achieves competent prediction performance with an, average precision of 97.78%, average precision of 97.84%. As shown, multi-view methods mostly outperform single view methods, which demonstrates the necessity of extracting multiple view information for classification. Our proposed method significantly outperforms other methods on BBCsport, ORL and Catech 101-7 datasets, and shows very competitive performance on Yale dataset. In the three aspects of ACC, AP, AR, respectively, higher than the second best method by 6.98%, 5.78%, 6.79%, respectively. **Boldface** data in each rows is the significantly best (or comparable best) results among these comparing methods (Tables 2 and 3).

Table 2. Average Precision (AP) compare results (mean ± standard deviation)

Method	ORL	Yale	Notting-Hill	BBCsport	Caltech 101-7
CSMRtC	**0.9945 ± 0.0205**	**0.9736 ± 0.0121**	0.9947 ± 0.0015	**0.9698 ± 0.0124**	**0.9565 ± 0.0201**
CSMC	0.9735 ± 0.0134	0.9204 ± 0.0435	0.9916 ± 0.0035	0.9334 ± 0.0154	0.9243 ± 0.0235
CMRtC	0.8573 ± 0.0176	0.6734 ± 0.0245	0.2034 ± 0.0024	0.3281 ± 0.0442	0.4724 ± 0.0375
SMRtC	0.8345 ± 0.0335	0.6354 ± 0.0235	0.7476 ± 0.0234	0.7453 ± 0.0123	0.6846 ± 0.0235
ProMK	0.9724 ± 0.0227	0.9164 ± 0.0675	0.9324 ± 0.0276	0.9364 ± 0.0227	0.9234 ± 0.2146
McWL	0.9721 ± 0.0146	0.9321 ± 0.0465	**0.9948 ± 0.0157**	0.9502 ± 0.0126	0.9243 ± 0.2243
simpleMKL	0.9745 ± 0.0175	0.9015 ± 0.0145	0.9946 ± 0.0246	0.9234 ± 0.0325	0.9115 ± 0.0076
SVM	0.9764 ± 0.0124	0.8775 ± 0.0165	0.9924 ± 0.0224	0.8834 ± 0.0224	0.8842 ± 0.0115
LDA	0.9624 ± 0.0224	0.9147 ± 0.0465	0.9918 ± 0.0218	0.9135 ± 0.0143	0.9235 ± 0.0084
k-NN	0.7831 ± 0.0427	0.7534 ± 0.0645	0.9934 ± 0.0576	0.9043 ± 0.0215	0.8747 ± 0.0076

Table 3. Average Recall (AR) compare results (mean ± standard deviation)

Method	ORL	Yale	Notting-Hill	BBCsport	Caltech 101-7
CSMRtC	**0.9956 ± 0.0217**	**0.9787 ± 0.0189**	**0.9986 ± 0.0034**	**0.9708 ± 0.0145**	**0.9485 ± 0.0121**
CSMC	0.9734 ± 0.0135	0.9164 ± 0.0235	0.9924 ± 0.0059	0.9243 ± 0.0134	0.9349 ± 0.0204
CMRtC	0.8456 ± 0.0204	0.6567 ± 0.0234	0.2094 ± 0.0068	0.4453 ± 0.0089	0.5038 ± 0.0247
SMRtC	0.8675 ± 0.0256	0.6254 ± 0.0248	0.7764 ± 0.0241	0.7358 ± 0.0112	0.6725 ± 0.0247
ProMK	0.9743 ± 0.0224	0.9258 ± 0.0354	0.9345 ± 0.0235	0.9354 ± 0.0105	0.9201 ± 0.0154
McWL	0.9724 ± 0.0207	0.9403 ± 0.0278	0.9924 ± 0.0164	0.9354 ± 0.0258	0.9304 ± 0.0264
simpleMKL	0.9735 ± 0.0134	0.9157 ± 0.0104	0.9946 ± 0.0204	0.9445 ± 0.0276	0.9527 ± 0.0255
SVM	0.9765 ± 0.0124	0.8835 ± 0.0168	0.9934 ± 0.0214	0.8766 ± 0.0358	0.8976 ± 0.0286
LDA	0.9596 ± 0.0208	0.9124 ± 0.0348	0.9951 ± 0.0245	0.9134 ± 0.0175	0.9316 ± 0.0107
k-NN	0.8031 ± 0.0201	0.7586 ± 0.0341	0.9951 ± 0.0590	0.9204 ± 0.0135	0.8856 ± 0.0154

3.4   Ablation Study

We analyze the improvement of the proposed CSMRtC by comparing to CSMC which is removed the part of the relative transformation. It is observed in Fig. 3 that our CSMRtC substantially outperforms CSMC on five datasets. This is because CSMC does not use relative changes to denoise, resulting in poor classification results.

We further analyse the improvement of the proposed CSMRtC by comparing to CMRtC which merely considers consistency, and SMRtC which does not consider the consistent part. It is observed that our CSMRtC substantially outperforms CMRtC on five datasets and thus numerically indicates that considering the view-specific terms of each view has merits. Besides, our proposed method performs better than SMRtC, consequently declares that isolating the consistent representation from representations of all views can enhance performance. The two baselines do not discover the underlying subspace structure of different views exhaustively and usually incur inferior classification performance. In conclusion, the proposed method efficiently combines consistency and specificity associated with multi-view data and thus outperforms baselines which only consider either term.

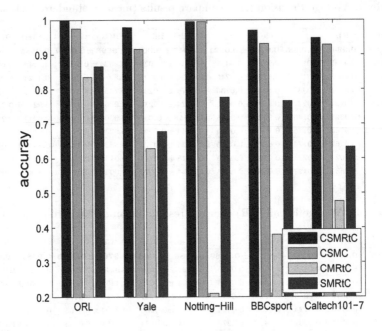

Fig. 3. Performance comparison between CSMRtC, CSMC, CMRtC, SMRtC.

3.5   Parameter Sensitivity

In this section, we conduct a sensitivity test for the parameter λ_C and λ_D by varying them from 0.001 to 1. Figure 4 shows the influence of different parameter values with respect to accuracy on ORL and Notting-Hill datasets. It can be observed that, when λ_C or λ_D approaches to zero, the performance drops sharply, which is consistent with our Ablation study. This is because in the process of the consistency and specificity of multi-view data for matrix representation learning, too small λ_C or λ_D will cause the loss of consistency and specificity information. Moreover, our method performs much stable when λ_C and λ_D becomes larger. This result confirms that joint study of the consistency and specificity make a big contribution in improving the performance of multi-view classification.

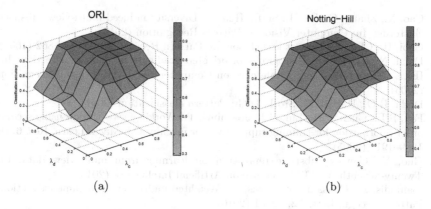

Fig. 4. Sensitivity test on (a) ORL and (b) Notting-Hill

4   Conclusion

In this paper, we proposed a new multi-view classification algorithm called Consistent and Specific Multi-View Relative-transform Classification (CSMVRtC). CSMRtC firstly explores the underlying subspace structure of different views exhaustively, which uses the consistency and specificity of data for representation learning, and then these data matrices are processed using the relative transform technique to reduce the impact of noise. Specifically, consistency models the common properties among all views, while specificity captures the inherent difference in each view. We then use relative transformations to transform data from raw space to relative spaces, to achieve the purpose of suppress noise in the data and improve the distinction between the data. Experimental comparison with competitive methods on five broadly-used benchmark datasets demonstrate the superiority of CSMVRtC in multi-view classification. The main restriction of the proposed method is the relatively long training time. As future work, we intend to speedup our algorithm with efforts into different initialization and optimization techniques.

References

1. Wen, G.: Relative transformation-based neighborhood optimization for isometric embedding **72**(4–6), 1205–1213 (2009)
2. Bazzani, L., Murino, V.: A unifying framework in vector-valued reproducing kernel Hilbert spaces for manifold regularization and co-regularized multi-view learning (2014)
3. Bekker, A., Shalhon, M., Greenspan, H., Goldberger, J.: Multi-view probabilistic classification of breast microcalcifications. IEEE Trans. Med. Imaging **35**(2), 645 (2016)
4. Blum, A., Mitchell, T.: Combining labeled and unlabeled data with co-training. In: Conference on Computational Learning Theory (1998)

5. Cao, X., Zhang, C., Fu, H., Si, L., Hua, Z.: Diversity-induced multi-view subspace clustering. In: Computer Vision & Pattern Recognition (2015)
6. Choi, H., Choi, S.: Robust kernel isomap. Pattern Recogn. **40**(3), 853–862 (2007)
7. Dalal, N., Triggs, B.: Histograms of oriented gradients for human detection. In: IEEE Computer Society Conference on Computer Vision & Pattern Recognition (2005)
8. Duda, R.O., Hart, P.E., Stork, D.G.: Pattern classification (2001)
9. Fan, R.E., Chen, P.H., Lin, C.J., Joachims, T.: Working set selection using second order information for training support vector machines. J. Mach. Learn. Res. **6**(4), 1889–1918 (2005)
10. Guo, Y.: Convex subspace representation learning from multi-view data. In: Twenty-Seventh AAAI Conference on Artificial Intelligence (2013)
11. Ioannidis, A., Chasanis, V., Likas, A.: Weighted multi-view key-frame extraction. Pattern Recogn. Lett. **72**, 52–61 (2016)
12. Jing, X.Y., Qian, L., Fei, W., Xu, B., Zhu, Y., Chen, S.: Web page classification based on uncorrelated semi-supervised intra-view and inter-view manifold discriminant feature extraction. In: International Conference on Artificial Intelligence (2015)
13. Kolenda, T., Hansen, L.K., Larsen, J., Winther, O.: Independent component analysis for understanding multimedia content. In: IEEE Workshop on Neural Networks for Signal Processing (2002)
14. Kumar, A., Iii, H.D.: A co-training approach for multi-view spectral clustering. In: International Conference on Machine Learning (2011)
15. Kumar, A., Rai, P., Daum, H.: Co-regularized multi-view spectral clustering. In: International Conference on Neural Information Processing Systems (2011)
16. Lades, M., et al.: Distortion invariant object recognition in the dynamic link architecture. IEEE Trans. Comput. **42**(3), 300–311 (1993)
17. Li, G., Chang, K., Hoi, S.C.H.: Multiview semi-supervised learning with consensus. IEEE Trans. Knowl. Data Eng. **24**(11), 2040–2051 (2012)
18. Lin, Z., Chen, M., Yi, M.: The augmented lagrange multiplier method for exactrecovery of corrupted low-rank matrices. Eprint Arxiv **9** (2010)
19. Luss, R., D'Aspremont, A.: Support vector machine classification with indefinite kernels. Math. Program. Comput. **1**(2–3), 97–118 (2008)
20. Mayo, M., Frank, E.: Experiments with multi-view multi-instance learning for supervised image classification. In: Image and Vision Computing New Zealand (2011)
21. Ojala, T., Pietikäinen, M., Mäenpää, T.: Multiresolution gray-scale and rotation invariant texture classification with local binary patterns. IEEE Trans. Pattern Anal. Mach. Intell. **24**(7), 971–987 (2002)
22. Oliva, A., Torralba, A.: Modeling the shape of the scene: a holistic representation of the spatial envelope. Int. J. Comput. Vis. **42**(3), 145–175 (2001)
23. Rongali, S., Chandar, A.P.S., Ravindran, B.: From multiple views to single view: a neural network approach (2015)
24. Roweis, S.T., Saul, L.K.: Nonlinear dimensionality reduction by locally linear embedding. Science **290**(5500), 2323–2326 (2000)
25. Zilca, R.D., Bistritz, Y.: Feature concatenation for speaker identification. In: European Signal Processing Conference (2010)
26. Tan, Q., Yu, G., Wang, J., Carlotta, D.: Multi-view weak-label learning based on matrix completion. In: Data Mining, pp. 450–458 (2018)
27. Tenenbaum, J.B., De Silva, V., Langford, J.C.: A global geometric framework for nonlinear dimensionality reduction. Science **290**(5500), 2319–2323 (2000)

28. Wang, Q., Lv, H., Yue, J., Mitchell, E.: Supervised multiview learning based on simultaneous learning of multiview intact and single view classifier. Neural Comput. Appl. **28**(8), 2293–2301 (2017)

29. Wozniak, M., Jackowski, K.: Some remarks on chosen methods of classifier fusion based on weighted voting. In: Corchado, E., Wu, X., Oja, E., Herrero, Á., Baruque, B. (eds.) HAIS 2009. LNCS (LNAI), vol. 5572, pp. 541–548. Springer, Heidelberg (2009). https://doi.org/10.1007/978-3-642-02319-4_65

30. Wu, F., Jing, X.Y., You, X., Yue, D., Hu, R., Yang, J.Y.: Multi-view low-rank dictionary learning for image classification. Pattern Recogn. **50**(C), 143–154 (2016)

31. Wu, J., Rehg, J.M.: CENTRIST: a visual descriptor for scene categorization. IEEE Trans. Pattern Anal. Mach. Intell. **33**(8), 1489–1501 (2010)

32. Xu, C., Tao, D., Xu, C.: Multi-view learning with incomplete views. IEEE Trans. Image Process. **24**(12), 5812–5825 (2015)

33. Yang, Y., Chao, L., Li, X., Bo, L., Huan, J.: Automatic social circle detection using multi-view clustering. In: ACM International Conference on Information & Knowledge Management (2014)

34. Yu, G., Zhu, H., Domeniconi, C.: Predicting protein functions using incomplete hierarchical labels. BMC Bioinform. **16**(1), 1 (2015)

35. Zhang, C., Fu, H., Si, L., Liu, G., Cao, X.: Low-rank tensor constrained multiview subspace clustering. In: IEEE International Conference on Computer Vision (2015)

36. Zhu, Y., Jing, X., Wang, Q., Wu, F., Feng, H., Wu, S.: Multi-view sparse embedding analysis based image feature extraction and classification. In: Zha, H., Chen, X., Wang, L., Miao, Q. (eds.) CCCV 2015. CCIS, vol. 547, pp. 51–60. Springer, Heidelberg (2015). https://doi.org/10.1007/978-3-662-48570-5_6

37. Zhuangabc, F., Heaa, Q.: Multi-view learning via probabilistic latent semantic analysis. Inf. Sci. **199**(15), 20–30 (2012)

Affinity Propagation Clustering Using Centroid-Deviation-Distance Based Similarity

Yifan Xie, Xing Wang, Long Zhang, and Guoxian Yu$^{(\boxtimes)}$ ⓘ

College of Computer and Information Sciences, Southwest University,
Chongqing 400715, China
gxyu@swu.edu.cn

Abstract. Clustering is a fundamental and important task in data mining. Affinity propagation clustering (APC) has demonstrated its advantages and effectiveness in various domains. APC iteratively propagates information between affinity samples, updates the responsibility matrix and availability matrix, and employs these matrices to choose cluster centroid (or exemplar) of the respective clusters. However, since it chooses the sample points as the exemplars, these exemplars may not be the realistic centroids of the clusters they belong to. There may be some deviation between exemplars and the realistic cluster centroids. As a result, samples near the decision boundary may have a relatively large similarity with other exemplar they don't belong to, and they are easy to be clustered incorrectly. To mitigate this problem, we propose an improved APC based on centroid-deviation-distance similarity (APC-CDD). APC-CDD firstly takes advantages of k-means on the whole samples to explore the more realistic centroid of the cluster, and then calculates the approximate centroid deviation distance of each cluster. After that, it adjusts the similarity between pairwise samples by subtracting the centroid deviation distance of the clusters they belong to. Next, it utilizes APC based on centroid-deviation-distance similarity to group samples. Our empirical study on synthetic and UCI datasets shows that the proposed APC-CDD has better performance than original APC and other related approaches.

Keywords: Clustering · Affinity propagation · Decision boundary · Centroid-Deviation-Distance based similarity

1 Introduction

With the rapid development of information technology, a large influx of data has emerged. Making full use of these data can have a greater guiding role in people's work and life. So there have been a series of methods for data processing such as clustering. Clustering is one of the most important research topics in machine

Supported by NSFC (61872300 and 61873214), Fundamental Research Funds for the Central Universities (XDJK2019B024), NSF of CQ CSTC (cstc2018jcyjAX0228).

learning and data mining communities. It aims at grouping samples into several clusters, samples in the same cluster are similar and samples in different clusters are dissimilar as much as possible. In real life, clustering has been applied in many areas, such as genomic data analysis [16], image segmentation [24], social network [13], anomaly detection [17] and so on.

MacQueen et al. [14] proposed a classic clustering algorithm called k-means, which aims to minimize within-cluster sum-of-squares criterion to get the suitable clusters. In order to solve the local minimum problem caused by selecting some bad initial points, Arthur and Vassilvitskii [1] proposed an improved method named k-means++ to initialize the centroids be generally distance from each other, and produced provably better results than random initialization. Sculley et al. [18] proposed Mini Batch k-means algorithm to deal with the problem of very large datasets. In the first step, it randomly selects b samples to form a mini-batch, which are then assigned to the nearest centroid. In the second step, the centroids are updated. Compared to k-means, this algorithm converges faster.

To combat with challenge that the amount of samples increases sharply, Frey et al. [8] proposed a clustering technique called affinity propagation clustering (APC), which propagates affinity message between samples to search a high-quality set of clusters [4]. APC has been shown its usefulness in image segmentation [7,26], gene expressions [15] and text summarization [28]. Wang et al. [22] proposed a semi-supervised APC to utilize pairwise constraints (must-link constraint that two samples are known in the same cluster, and cannot-link that two samples belong to different clusters [20]) to adjust the similarity between samples. It is a hard task for APC to choose a suitable p (predefined preference of choosing a sample as the cluster center). To mitigate this issue, Wang et al. [23] suggested to adaptively scan preference values in the search space and seek the optimal clustering results. Recently, Serdah et al. [19] proposed another efficient algorithm to accelerate the speed of APC on large-scale datasets and ensure the accuracy. This algorithm uses random fragmentation or k-means to divide the samples into several subsets. Then, it uses k-affinity propagation (KAP) [27] to group each subset into k clusters and gets local cluster exemplars (representative point of a cluster) in each subset. Next, inverse weighted clustering algorithm [2] is utilized on all local cluster exemplars to select well-suited global exemplars of all the samples. Finally, non-exemplars are assigned to the respective cluster based on their similarity with respect to global exemplars.

For better handing the datasets with relatively complex structure. Walter [21] suggested a path-based similarity for APC (pAPC) to explore the complex structure of samples. Particularly, for pairwise samples, pAPC finds out the longest segment for each path directly and indirectly connecting these two samples. Then it chooses the shortest segment from all the found segments and takes the length of that segment as the path-based similarity between the pairwise samples. Next, pAPC inputs this similarity into APC to cluster samples. Zhang et al. [25] proposed APC based on geodesic distances (APCGD). APCGD uses the negative geodesic distance between samples as the similarity between samples, instead of the negative Euclidean distance. These approaches improve the performance of APC on datasets with complex structures. However, their performance is found to be unstable, APCGD involves tuning more than two scale parameters, and both of them are very time consuming. Guo *et al.* [10] applied k-path edge centrality [5] on social networks to efficiently compute the similarity between network nodes and then employed APC based on that similarity to discovery communities.

All these optimization methods show improved performance of APC. However, these algorithms do not take into account that points near the decision boundary are easily clustered by errors (see Fig. 1 for example). APC selects a sample point as the exemplar. Unavoidably, this exemplar may not be the realistic centroid of the cluster it belongs to. There may be some deviation between exemplar and the realistic cluster centroid instead. Therefore, samples near the decision boundary may have a relatively large similarity with other exemplar they don't belong to. In other words, the similarity between non-exemplar points and other exemplars may be high. This circumstance will lead to the incorrect clustering.

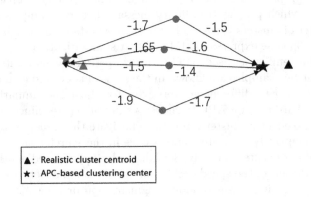

Fig. 1. Four samples are incorrectly grouped due to the bad exemplars.

In this paper, to reduce the deviation distance of exemplar to the realistic cluster centroid, and reduce the similarity between non-exemplar points near the decision boundary and exemplars they don't belong to, we propose a method called Affinity Propagation Clustering using Centroid-Deviation-Distance based similarity (APC-CDD). APC-CDD applies k-means clustering on the whole samples to explore the more realistic cluster centroid of each cluster. Then it calculates the distance from the sample points to their centroids, selecting the shortest distance as the deviation distance of the cluster. APC-CDD adjusts the similarity between pairwise samples based on this deviation distance. If pairwise samples belong to different cluster based on k-means, the similarity between them will be reduced on the basis of the original, otherwise the similarity is unchanged. In this way, the information of realistic centroid of each cluster and deviation distance revealed by k-means is embedded into the adjusted similarity matrix.

Next, APC-CDD applies affinity propagation based on the adjusted similarity to group samples. Our experimental results on both synthetic and UCI datasets shows that APC-CDD achieves better results than original APC, APCGD and other representative clustering algorithms.

2   Method

Suppose $\mathbf{X} = [\mathbf{x}_1; \mathbf{x}_2; \dots; \mathbf{x}_n] \in \mathbb{R}^{n \times d}$ be a data matrix of n samples, and each vector $\mathbf{x}_i$ correspond to a d-dimensional sample. APC-CDD is composed with three steps: executing k-means on the whole samples to get a more realistic cluster centroid and deviation distance; adjusting the similarity between pairwise samples based on their cluster's deviation distance; then applying affinity propagation on the whole samples using adjusted similarity. The following subsections introduce these three steps in details.

2.1   Centroid Deviation Distance

To explore a more realistic cluster centroid, we first perform k-means [14] on the whole samples. In order to improve the stability of the k-means algorithm and avoid falling into local optimum, we use k-means++ [1] to initialize the centroids. Suppose the final clustering results are $\mathcal{C} = \{\mathcal{C}_1, \mathcal{C}_2, \dots, \mathcal{C}_m\}$. m is the number of clusters and $\mathcal{C}_{m_1}$ represents the m_1-th cluster. $\mathcal{C}_{m_1} \cap \mathcal{C}_{m_2} = \emptyset \ (\forall m_1 \neq m_2, m_1, m_2 = 1, 2, \dots, m)$ and $E_{m_1=1}^m \mathcal{C}_{m_1} = \mathbf{X}$. The cluster centroid of the i-th cluster is:

$$E_{m_1} = \frac{\sum_{\mathbf{x}_i \in \mathcal{C}_{m_1}} \mathbf{x}_i}{|\mathcal{C}_{m_1}|} \tag{1}$$

$|\mathcal{C}_{m_1}|$ is the number of samples in the m_1-th cluster. $E_{m_1} \in \mathbb{R}^d$ is the m_1-th cluster centroid. Next, we calculate the nearest distance from the cluster centroid to all its sample points as the cluster's centroid deviation distance. The formula is defined as below:

$$D_{m_1} = \min_{\mathbf{x}_i \in \mathcal{C}_{m_1}} \|\mathbf{x}_i - E_{m_1}\|^2 \tag{2}$$

D_{m_1} is the cluster's centroid deviation distance. Clearly, when there is a sample closer to the realistic cluster center, the deviation distance is smaller.

2.2   Adjusting Similarity Between Samples by Centroid Deviation Distance

We define the original 'similarity' (APC can absorb a negative similarity value) between samples by calculating the Euclidean distance between pairwise samples as follow:

$$\mathbf{S}_{ij} = -\|\mathbf{x}_i - \mathbf{x}_j\|^2 \tag{3}$$

where $\|\mathbf{x}_i - \mathbf{x}_j\|^2$ is the Euclidean distance between $\mathbf{x}_i$ and $\mathbf{x}_j$. When $i = j = k$, all samples are initially viewed as the potential exemplar, each diagonal of $\mathbf{S}$ is set as p, which reflects the preference of choosing a sample as the exemplar. p can be adjusted to get an appropriate number of exemplars. In most cases, p is set as the median of $\mathbf{S}$. Frey *et al.* [8] suggested that p can be adjusted to produce an expected (or user-specified) number of clusters. The smaller the value of p, the fewer the clusters are.

A large number of previous studies have proved that constructing a similarity matrix by Euclidean distance is simple and effective. But there is still a problem: APC algorithm selects the sample points as the exemplars. Unavoidably, there may be some deviation between the exemplars and the realistic cluster centroids. Hence, samples near the decision boundary may have a relatively large similarity with other exemplar they don't belong to. In other words, the similarity between non-exemplar points and other exemplars may be high. For this reason, they are easy to be clustered by errors. To mitigate this problem, we would like to reduce the deviation distance of exemplars to the realistic cluster centroids, reduce the similarity between the non-exemplar points and other exemplars that they don't belong to. At the same time, we keep the similarity between the non-exemplar points and their own exemplars. In order to achieve this goal, we use the predefined centroid deviation distance to adjust the similarity between pairwise samples.

To facilitate the adjustment, we define an indicative vector I:

$$I_i = m_1, \text{ if } \mathbf{x}_i \in \mathcal{C}_{m_1}; i = 1, 2, 3, \dots, n \tag{4}$$

Next, we adjust the original similarity matrix S as follow:

$$\hat{\mathbf{S}}_{ij} = \mathbf{S}_{ij} - w \left(D_{I_i} + D_{I_j} \right) \tag{5}$$

w is a positive deviation coefficient. D_{I_i} and D_{I_j} represent the centroid deviation distance of different clusters. Apparently, $\hat{\mathbf{S}}_{ij} < \mathbf{S}_{ij}$, if $\mathbf{x}_j$ and $\mathbf{x}_j$ belong to different clusters based on k-means, and $\hat{\mathbf{S}}_{ij} = \mathbf{S}_{ij}$ otherwise. In other words, if two samples belong to different clusters, the similarity between them will be reduced on the basis of the original, otherwise unchanged. From this perspective, the similarity between non-exemplar points and other exemplars can be reduced. We apply APC using the adjusted similarity.

2.3   Applying Affinity Propagation Based on the Adjusted Similarity

APC iterates with two matrices: the responsibility matrix ($\mathbf{R} \in \mathbb{R}^{n \times n}$) and availability matrix ($\mathbf{A} \in \mathbb{R}^{n \times n}$). $\mathbf{R}(i, j)$ measures the accumulated evidence of how well-suited sample $\mathbf{x}_j$ serves as the exemplar for sample $\mathbf{x}_i$. $\mathbf{A}(i, j)$ measures the accumulated evidence of how appropriate $\mathbf{x}_i$ chooses $\mathbf{x}_j$ as its exemplar. At the beginning, the responsibility and availability matrices are initialized to zero. Then, the responsibilities are computed using the follow formula:

$$\mathbf{R}^{(t)}(i, j) = \hat{\mathbf{S}}_{ij} - \max_{h \neq j} \left\{ \mathbf{A}^{(t-1)}(i, h) + \hat{\mathbf{S}}(i, h) \right\} \tag{6}$$

where $\mathbf{R}^{(t)}(i,j)$ is the updated $\mathbf{R}(i,j)$ in the t-th iteration, and $\mathbf{A}^{(t-1)}(i,h)$ is the updated $\mathbf{A}(i,h)$ in the $(t-1)$-th iteration. $\mathbf{A}^{(t-1)}(i,h) + \hat{\mathbf{S}}(i,h)$ measures the potentiality of taking $\mathbf{x}_h$ as the exemplar of $\mathbf{x}_i$. $\mathbf{R}^{(t)}(i,j)$ reflects the ability of $\mathbf{x}_j$ to compete for ownership of $\mathbf{x}_i$ with the most potential exemplar $\mathbf{x}_h$. If $\mathbf{R}^{(t)}(i,j)$ is larger than zero, $\mathbf{x}_j$ is more powerful as an exemplar of $\mathbf{x}_i$ than $\mathbf{x}_h$. The larger the value of $\mathbf{R}^{(t)}(i,j)$, the larger the likelihood $\mathbf{x}_j$ as an exemplar of $\mathbf{x}_i$ is. For special case, $i = j$, $\mathbf{R}^{(t)}(i,j)$ reflects accumulated evidence that $\mathbf{x}_j$ is an exemplar based on the initial preference value p.

The available matrix $\mathbf{A}$ is iteratively updated as:

$$\mathbf{A}^{(t)}(i,j) = \min\left\{0, \mathbf{R}^{(t)}(i,j) + \sum_{h \neq i, h \neq j} \max\left\{0, \mathbf{R}^{(t)}(h,j)\right\}\right\} \quad (7)$$

where $\max\left\{0, \mathbf{R}^{(t)}(h,j)\right\}$ means only the positive portions of incoming $\mathbf{R}^{(t)}(h,j)$ are added, since it is only necessary for a good exemplar to explain some samples well (positive responsibility). To limit the influence of strong incoming positive responsibilities, the total sum is thresholded so that it cannot go above zero. The diagonal entry of $\mathbf{A}^{(t)}(i,i)$ is calculated as:

$$\mathbf{A}^{(t)}(i,i) = \sum_{h \neq i} \max\left\{0, \mathbf{R}^{(t)}(h,j)\right\} \quad (8)$$

$\mathbf{A}^{(t)}(i,i)$ reflects the possibility of $\mathbf{x}_j$ as an exemplar based on its all positive responsibilities.

In order to avoid numerical oscillations that arise in some circumstances, APC introduces a damping factor $\lambda \in [0,1)$ and updates responsibility matrix and availability matrix as follow:

$$\mathbf{R}^{(t)}(i,j) = (1-\lambda)\left(\hat{\mathbf{S}}(i,j) - \max_{h \neq j}\left\{\mathbf{A}^{(t-1)}(i,h) + \hat{\mathbf{S}}(i,h)\right\}\right) + \lambda\mathbf{R}^{(t-1)}(i,j) \quad (9)$$

$$\mathbf{A}^{(t)}(i,j) = (1-\lambda)\min\left\{0, \mathbf{R}^{(t)}(i,j) + \sum_{h \neq i, h \neq j}\max\left\{0, \mathbf{R}^{(t)}(h,j)\right\}\right\} + \lambda\mathbf{A}^{(t-1)}(i,j) \quad (10)$$

$$\mathbf{A}^{(t)}(i,i) = (1-\lambda)\sum_{h \neq i}\max\left\{0, \mathbf{R}^{(t)}(h,j)\right\} + \lambda\mathbf{A}^{(t-1)}(i,i) \quad (11)$$

Responsibility matrix and availability matrix are updated iteratively using Formula (9)–(11). For each $\mathbf{x}_i$, the value of j that maximizes $\mathbf{A}(i,j) + \mathbf{R}(i,j)$ either identifies $\mathbf{x}_i$ as an exemplar if $j = i$, or identifies $\mathbf{x}_j$. Formula (9)–(11) describe the basic procedure of APC. After finding out exemplars, non-exemplar samples are assigned to the most suitable cluster.

3 Experimental Results and Analysis

3.1 Experimental Setup

We construct a toy dataset to illustrate APC-CDD algorithm intuitively, and compare our proposed method with four clustering algorithms on four UCI datasets. These comparison algorithms include original APC [8], APCGD [25], pAPC [21], expectation maximization (EM) [3,6]. In the following experiments, λ for APC, APCGD, pAPC and APC-CDD is set as 0.5, k for APC, APCGD, EM and APC-CDD is fixed as the number of ground truth labels. For APCGD, we set the nearest neighbors and ε as 5 on the whole datasets. Detail information of these UCI datasets is listed in Table 1. To avoid randomness, we repeat each algorithm on each dataset 15 times and report the average and standard deviation.

Table 1. Data-sets used in the experiment.

Data-set	#Samples	#Dimensions	#Classes
Glass	214	9	6
Synthetic	600	60	6
Breast	277	9	2
Seeds	210	7	3

Two evaluation matrices are adopted to evaluate the quality of clustering, adjusted rand index (ARI) [9] and Fowlkes-Mallows Index (FMI) [11]. ARI measures the similarity of the two assignments. Suppose $\mathcal{C}$ is a ground truth class assignment and $\mathcal{K}$ is the computed cluster assignment, a is the number of pairs of elements that are in the same set in $\mathcal{C}$ and in the same set in $\mathcal{K}$, b is the number of pairs of elements that are in different sets in $\mathcal{C}$ and in different sets in $\mathcal{K}$. The unadjusted Rand index [12] is given by:

$$\text{RI} = \frac{a+b}{C_n^2} \tag{12}$$

where C_n^2 is the total number of possible pairs in the dataset (without ordering).

However, the RI score does not guarantee that random label assignments will get a value close to zero. To mitigate this effect, ARI is defined as follows:

$$\text{ARI} = \frac{RI - E(RI)}{\max(RI) - E|RI|} \tag{13}$$

where $E|RI|$ is the expected of $|RI|$.

FMI is another commonly-applied metric for clustering and defined as:

$$\text{FMI} = \sqrt{\frac{m}{m+t} \times \frac{m}{m+q}} \tag{14}$$

where m is the number of samples of the same label and grouped into the same cluster, t is the number of samples of the same label but grouped into different clusters, and q is the number of samples of different labels but grouped in the same cluster.

3.2   Results on the Toy Dataset

In this paper, we would like to reduce the deviation distance of exemplars to the realistic cluster centroids, and reduce the similarity between the non-exemplar points near the decision boundary and other exemplars that they don't belong to, and thus to boost the performance of APC. For this purpose, we generate a toy dataset (Fig. 2(a)) composed with 200 samples of two clusters, each cluster has 100 samples. For comparison and illustration, We labeled the realistic centroid and the centroid based on the APC algorithm, respectively. In addition, we draw four pairs of lines. Each pair of lines represents the negative Euclidean distance (similarity) from the non-exemplar point near the decision boundary to APC algorithm's exemplars (see Fig. 2(a)). Figure 2(c) shows the adjusted similarity between the non-exemplar points and exemplars. Figure 2(b) and (d) reveal the clustering of APC and APC-CDD, respectively.

From Fig. 2(a), we can observe that the deviation distance of exemplar to the realistic cluster centroid is large. Hence, the similarity between non-exemplar points near the decision boundary and other exemplars they don't belong to is large, and even larger than that with their own exemplars. Given that, they would be clustered incorrectly. After k-means clustering, the centroid deviation distance of cluster1 is 0.0022, the centroid deviation distance of cluster2 is 0.0019. Based on these deviation distances, we adjusted the similarity. And the exemplars move back to the realistic cluster centroids, the deviation distance is reduced, and the adjusted similarity between the non-exemplar points near the decision boundary and other exemplars that they don't belong to is turned down (see Fig. 2(c)). Therefore, non-exemplar points near the decision boundary are less likely to be assigned to the wrong exemplars. This observation corroborates the advantages of adjusted similarity based on centroid deviation distance. Particularly, we can see four non-exemplar points, whose original similarity to cluster2's exemplar are -0.650, -0.353, -0.297, -0.331, are incorrectly clustered by APC in Fig. 2(b), whereas they are correctly clustered by APC-CDD in Fig. 2(d). The improvement of clustering is mainly because APC-CDD utilizes adjusted similarity based on centroid deviation distance, whereas APC uses the original similarity between pairwise samples.

Overall, this toy dataset demonstrates that, adjusting similarity between samples by centroid deviation distance can reduce the deviation distance of exemplar to the realistic cluster centroid, reduce the similarity between the non-exemplar points near the decision boundary and other exemplars that they don't belong to, and alleviate the issues of error clustering non-exemplar points that near the decision boundary. Thus, the adjusted similarity based on centroid deviation distance can improve the performance of APC.

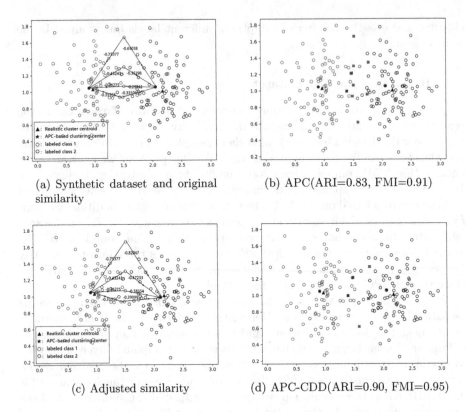

(a) Synthetic dataset and original similarity

(b) APC(ARI=0.83, FMI=0.91)

(c) Adjusted similarity

(d) APC-CDD(ARI=0.90, FMI=0.95)

Fig. 2. The toy dataset and the original similarity, clustering by APC, adjusted similarity, clustering by APC-CDD. Samples incorrectly grouped by APC and APC-CDD are highlighted by ×.

3.3 Clustering Results on UCI Datasets

The average results and standard deviation of these algorithms are listed in Tables 2 and 3. In the tables, **boldface** data in each row is the significantly best (or comparable best) results among these comparing methods. The significance is assessed at 95% confidence level.

Table 2. Experimental results (average standard deviation) on UCI datasets under evaluation metric Fowlkes-Mallows Index (FMI). The numbers in boldface denote the best performance

Method	Synthetic control	Breast	Glass identification	Seeds
EM	0.5934 ± 0.0545	0.6573 ± 0.0130	0.4768 ± 0.0397	0.7663 ± 0.0528
APCGD	0.4752 ± 0.0000	$\mathbf{0.7077 \pm 0.0372}$	0.4798 ± 0.0239	0.7583 ± 0.0472
APC	0.6373 ± 0.0000	0.5491 ± 0.0263	0.4943 ± 0.0000	0.7999 ± 0.0232
pAPC	0.6127 ± 0.0000	0.5526 ± 0.0231	0.4608 ± 0.0000	0.5239 ± 0.0066
APC-CDD	$\mathbf{0.6439 \pm 0.0000}$	$\mathbf{0.6830 \pm 0.0181}$	$\mathbf{0.5047 \pm 0.0000}$	$\mathbf{0.8005 \pm 0.0279}$

Table 3. Experimental results (average standard deviation) on four datasets under evaluation metric Adjusted Rand index (ARI). The numbers in boldface denote the best performance

Method	Synthetic control	Breast	Glass identification	Seeds
EM	0.4810 ± 0.0431	0.1413 ± 0.0239	0.2079 ± 0.0175	0.6490 ± 0.0425
APCGD	0.3964 ± 0.0000	$\mathbf{0.2254 \pm 0.0255}$	0.2101 ± 0.0217	0.6248 ± 0.0388
APC	0.5429 ± 0.0000	0.1000 ± 0.0186	0.2478 ± 0.0000	0.6998 ± 0.0114
pAPC	0.5182 ± 0.0000	0.0185 ± 0.0021	0.1593 ± 0.0000	0.6815 ± 0.0395
APC-CDD	$\mathbf{0.5632 \pm 0.0000}$	0.2124 ± 0.0177	$\mathbf{0.2664 \pm 0.0000}$	$\mathbf{0.7016 \pm 0.0285}$

From these two tables, we have clear observation that none of these comparing methods are always performing better than others. The reason is that different algorithms have some preferences for different datasets and these four UCI data-sets are also distributed with different structures.

The performance of EM is worse than APC and APC-CDD in most cases. The most likely reason is that EM algorithm is based on the assumption that samples are normally distributed. However, the assumption in these four data sets is not suitable. Hence, it leads to a bad result.

APC-CDD has a very stable performance although it utilizes k-means algorithm firstly. The reason is that we use k-means++ to select the initial centroids, increasing the stability of k-means. In addition, APC have completely different clustering processes from k-means, hence a suitable deviation coefficient of APC-CDD can avoid the effects of instability of k-means. Through analysis and experimentation, we set the coefficient between 1.55 and 1.65, which overcomes the instability of k-means.

APC-CDD also significantly performs better than APC in most cases under different evaluation matrices and it often performs as well as the best of the other four methods in terms of ARI and FMI. APC only uses the original Euclidean distance between pairwise samples, APC-CDD exploits adjusted similarity instead. The adjusted similarity contains the information about the realistic cluster centroid and centroid deviation. Therefore, APC-CDD produces better results than APC, and the FMI and ARI are improved by an average of 3.6% and 3.8%, respectively. Based on these results, we can draw a conclusion that APC-CDD can distinguish the samples near the decision boundary better and thus to improve the accuracy of APC.

APCGD and pAPC also utilizes different techniques to measure the similarity between samples rather than the original negative Euclidean distance. But they still lose to APC-CDD in most cases. APCGD defines a neighborhood graph at first, then it takes the shortest path between pairwise samples in the graph as the geodesic distance between them. Next, APCGD takes the negative geodesic distance as the similarity between them and performs APC based on this similarity. However, it is rather difficult to construct a suitable neighborhood graph for APCGD, and an inappropriate neighborhood graph can bring direct connection between two samples, which belong to two different clusters. For this reason, the performance of APCGD often loses to APC-CDD, the FMI and ARI are lose by an average of 7.9% and 10%, respectively. We note that APCGD performs better than APC on Breast dataset, the reason is that we construct a suitable neighborhood graph for APCGD. pAPC finds out the longest segment for each path directly and indirectly connecting these two samples. Then it chooses the shortest segment from all the found segments and takes the length of that segment as the path-based similarity between the pairwise samples. Next, it performs APC based on this similarity. However, the shortest segments from all the found segments may be much similar to the direct distance between pairwise samples on the four datasets. Given that, the performance of pAPC often loses to APC-CDD, and the FMI and ARI values are lower by an average of 12.1% and 6.7%, respectively.

3.4 Sensitivity of the Deviation Coefficient (w) on APC-CDD

APC-CDD uses adjusted similarity based on centroid deviation distance. From Formula (5), we can see that the deviation coefficient is important for adjusting the similarity. In order to get a more suitable adjusted similarity matrix. We analyzed the impact of deviation coefficient's changes on the final clustering results. w should not be too small or too large. If w is too small, the centroid deviation distance is not compensated, and the deviation exemplars will not move back to the realistic centroid. In addition, the clustering result will be affected by the k-means more. Therefore, the clustering results will not change significantly compared to APC algorithm. If w is too big, the similarity changes sharply. This will lead to drastic changes of exemplars. In our previous experiments, we set w between 1.55 and 1.65. To investigate the sensitivity of w on APC-CDD, we conduct experiments to investigate the influence of w. In the following experiments, we increase w from 1.0 to 1.7 for APC-CDD and report the average FMI and ARI under each w in Figs. 3 and 4.

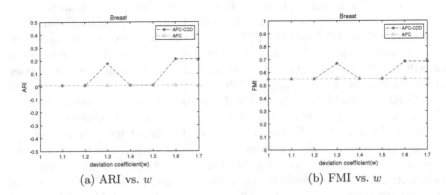

(a) ARI vs. w (b) FMI vs. w

Fig. 3. Results of APC and APC-CDD on the Breast dataset with different input values of deviation coefficient w.

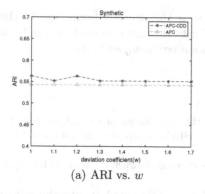 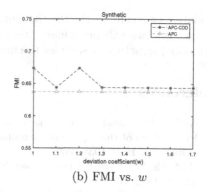

(a) ARI vs. w (b) FMI vs. w

Fig. 4. Results of APC and APC-CDD on the Synthetic control chart dataset with different input values of deviation coefficient w

As to Fig. 3, we can see that when w is small, the results of APC and APC-CDD are similar. However, as w increases, APC-CDD begins to outperform APC. The cause of this change is that w is too small at the start, hence the second term in Formula (5) is too small to remedy the deviation distance, and exemplars doesn't move back to the realistic centroid, but when w reaches the threshold, the deviation distance is reduced and exemplars move back to the realistic centroid. On the other hand, we can easy see that when w reaches the threshold, APC-CDD is always significantly better than APC, irrespective of ARI or FMI. The reason is that APC-CDD employs the centroid-deviation-distance based similarity to assign a non-exemplar sample to cluster. In contrast, APC takes the negative Euclidean distance between two samples as the similarity between them and it assigns a non-exemplar sample to its most similar exemplar based on this similarity. This observation justifies our motivation to incorporate the centroid-deviation-distance similarity to improve the performance of APC.

As to Fig. 4, APC-CDD also produces higher results than APC on the Synthetic control chart time series data-set. Different from Fig. 3, FMI and ARI of APC-CDD is larger than APC at the beginning and always stable. The reason is that the deviation distance in synthetic control chart time series dataset is shorter than that in breast dataset. Hence, a relatively small deviation coefficient can compensate for the centroid deviation. From the above results, we can find that selecting the number between 1.55 and 1.65 as the deviation coefficient can steadily improve clustering for most situations.

4 Conclusions and Future Work

In this paper, to improve the performance of APC on samples near the decision boundary, we introduce an algorithm called Affinity Propagation Clustering using Centroid-Deviation-Distance based similarity (APC-CDD). The experimental results on toy dataset and UCI datasets show APC-CDD outperforms other related algorithms. Our study shows the centroid-deviation-distance based similarity can help to cluster the samples near the decision boundary. In the future work, we will investigate other similarity measures to capture the local and global structure of samples to cluster boundary samples better.

References

1. Arthur, D., Vassilvitskii, S.: k-means++: the advantages of careful seeding. In: Proceedings of the Eighteenth Annual ACM-SIAM Symposium on Discrete Algorithms, pp. 1027–1035 (2007)
2. Barbakh, W., Fyfe, C.: Inverse weighted clustering algorithm. Comput. Inf. Syst. **11**, 10–18 (2007)
3. Bradley, P.S., Fayyad, U., Reina, C., et al.: Scaling EM (expectation-maximization) clustering to large databases. Technical report (1998)
4. Brusco, M.J., Hans-Friedrich, K.: Comment on "clustering by passing messages between data points". Science **319**(5864), 726 (2008)
5. De Meo, P., Ferrara, E., Fiumara, G., Ricciardello, A.: A novel measure of edge centrality in social networks. Knowl.-Based Syst. **30**, 136–150 (2012)
6. Dempster, A.P., Laird, N.M., Rubin, D.B.: Maximum likelihood from incomplete data via the EM algorithm. J. Roy. Stat. Soc. **39**(1), 1–38 (1977)
7. Du, H., Wang, Y., Duan, L.: A new method for grayscale image segmentation based on affinity propagation clustering algorithm. In: 2013 Ninth International Conference on Computational Intelligence and Security, pp. 170–173. IEEE (2013)
8. Frey, B.J., Delbert, D.: Clustering by passing messages between data points. Science **315**(5814), 972–976 (2007)
9. Gates, A.J., Ahn, Y.Y.: The impact of random models on clustering similarity. J. Mach. Learn. Res. **18**(1), 3049–3076 (2017)
10. Guo, K., Guo, W., Chen, Y., Qiu, Q., Zhang, Q.: Community discovery by propagating local and global information based on the MapReduce model. Inf. Sci. **323**, 73–93 (2015)
11. Halkidi, M., Batistakis, Y., Vazirgiannis, M.: On clustering validation techniques. J. Intell. Inf. Syst. **17**(2–3), 107–145 (2001)
12. Hubert, L., Arabie, P.: Comparing partitions. J. Classif. **2**(1), 193–218 (1985)
13. Kang, J.H., Lerman, K., Plangprasopchok, A.: Analyzing microblogs with affinity propagation. In: Proceedings of the First Workshop on Social Media Analytics, pp. 67–70. ACM (2010)
14. MacQueen, J., et al.: Some methods for classification and analysis of multivariate observations. In: Proceedings of the Fifth Berkeley Symposium on Mathematical Statistics and Probability, Oakland, CA, USA, vol. 1, pp. 281–297 (1967)
15. Michele, L., Martin, W.: Clustering by soft-constraint affinity propagation: applications to gene-expression data. Bioinformatics **23**(20), 2708–2715 (2007)
16. Napolitano, F., Raiconi, G., Tagliaferri, R., Ciaramella, A., Staiano, A., Miele, G.: Clustering and visualization approaches for human cell cycle gene expression data analysis. Int. J. Approximate Reasoning **47**(1), 70–84 (2008)
17. Papalexakis, E.E., Beutel, A., Steenkiste, P.: Network anomaly detection using co-clustering. In: Alhajj, R., Rokne, J. (eds.) Encyclopedia of Social Network Analysis and Mining, pp. 1054–1068. Springer, New York (2014). https://doi.org/10.1007/978-1-4614-6170-8
18. Sculley, D.: Web-scale k-means clustering. In: Proceedings of the 19th International Conference on World Wide Web, pp. 1177–1178. ACM (2010)

19. Serdah, A.M., Ashour, W.M.: Clustering large-scale data based on modified affinity propagation algorithm. J. Artif. Intell. Soft Comput. Res. **6**(1), 23–33 (2016)
20. Wagstaff, K., Cardie, C., Rogers, S., Schrödl, S., et al.: Constrained k-means clustering with background knowledge. In: ICML, vol. 1, pp. 577–584 (2001)
21. Walter, S.: Clustering by affinity propagation. Ph.D. thesis (2007)
22. Wang, K.J., Jian, L.I., Zhang, J.Y., Chong-Yang, T.U.: Semi-supervised affinity propagation clustering. Comput. Eng. **33**(23), 197–198 (2007)
23. Wang, K., Zhang, J., Li, D., Zhang, X., Guo, T.: Adaptive affinity propagation clustering. ArXiv Preprint ArXiv:0805.1096 (2008)
24. Wei, F.P., Shu, D., Fu, X.L.: Unsupervised image segmentation via affinity propagation. Appl. Mech. Mater. **610**, 464–470 (2014)
25. Zhang, L., Du, Z.: Affinity propagation clustering with geodesic distances. J. Comput. Inf. Syst. **6**(1), 47–53 (2010)
26. Zhang, R.: Two similarity measure methods based on human vision properties for image segmentation based on affinity propagation clustering. In: 2010 International Conference on Measuring Technology and Mechatronics Automation, vol. 3, pp. 1054–1058. IEEE (2010)
27. Zhang, X., Wang, W., Norvag, K., Sebag, M.: K-AP: generating specified K clusters by efficient affinity propagation. In: 2010 IEEE International Conference on Data Mining, pp. 1187–1192. IEEE (2010)
28. Zhao, C., Peng, Q., Sun, S.: Chinese text automatic summarization based on affinity propagation cluster. In: 2009 Sixth International Conference on Fuzzy Systems and Knowledge Discovery, vol. 1, pp. 425–429. IEEE (2009)

Model and Simulation of Microwave Ablation with Single Antennas on Irregular Hepatic Cancerous Tissue

Yonghua Lao[1], Tianqi Zhang[2], Jinhua Huang[2], and R. Yang[1,3(⊠)]

[1] Department of Biomedical Engineering, South China University of Technology,
Guangzhou 510006, China
bmeyrq@gmail.com
[2] Department of Minimally Invasive Interventional Radiology,
Sun Yat-sen University Cancer Center, State Key Laboratory of Oncology
in South China, and Collaborative Innovation Center for Cancer Medicine,
Sun Yat-sen University, Guangzhou, China
[3] Department of Therapeutic Radiology, School of Medicine, Yale University,
333 Cedar Street, New Haven, CT 06520, USA

Abstract. There is a lot of numerical simulation on microwave ablation which studied the models of the microwave antennas (MA) design and thermal-dielectric properties of tissues. However, few studies focused on the efficient and accurate treatment planning to configure MA in various kinds of irregular tumor, especially irregular hepatic cancerous tissue (IHCT). This work proposed a modelling approach to analyzing the heating performance and thermal lesion of microwave ablation model with different MA inserting directions, inserting depth rates and powers. The specific absorption rate and thermal lesion results showed that the long axis of irregular tissue could be the better MA inserting direction, along which microwave power could be sent to ablate more IHCT. The MA inserting depth rate influenced the power absorption rate and axial thermal lesion of the MA axis under different powers. The temperature field of 60 °C expanded when power gave rise on, which were proposed to predict the thermal lesion zone of IHCT. The results simulated microwave ablation with single MA on IHCT, and thus, the method could also be applied to treatment situations where multiple MAs or more complicated operation are required under image-guided surgical navigation.

Keywords: Irregular hepatic cancerous tissue · Microwave ablation ·
Model and simulation · Treatment planning

This research was funded by the National Natural Scientific Foundation of China under Grant No. 81671788, Guangdong Provincial Science and Technology Program under Grant Nos. 2016A020220006, 2017B020210008, and 2017B010110015, Fundamental Research Funds for Central Universities under Grant No. 2017ZD082, and Guangzhou Science and Technology Program under Grant No. 201704020228, the Chinese Scholarship Fund under Grant No. 201806155010.

A. Zeng et al. (Eds.): HBAI 2019, CCIS 1072, pp. 300–309, 2019.
https://doi.org/10.1007/978-981-15-1398-5_22

1 Introduction

Microwave ablation therapy is fast becoming a key treatment in unresectable large hepatocellular carcinoma [1,2]. As a minimally invasive technique, microwave ablation navigated by clinical image can inactivate cancerous cells and reserve normal cells as much as possible. However, many hepatocellular carcinomas own irregular shape so that it cannot be destroyed completely within the ellipsoid zone of ablation treatment [3]. The residual cancerous cells after ablation surgery will propagate faster to damage patient health and make the treatment failure. Therefore, treatment planning for an ablation zone that is sufficiently wide to cover all the cancerous tissue is one of the leading causes of success in microwave hepatic ablation.

In surgical ablation procedures, the aim of treatment planning is to properly insert the microwave antennas (MA) into the targeted tumor and place the antennas at reasonable positions for the best ablation effect. Microwave ablation procedure relies on the generation of high temperatures (55–60 °C) in the surgical target zones near MA which send electromagnetic energy at microwave frequencies (typically 915 MHz or 2.45 GHz) [4]. It is commonly found that MA can radiate to achieve a thermal lesion that owns some given ablated zone corresponding to microwave power. The shape of the ablated zone near the MA is like an ellipsoid [4–8]. The size of ellipsoid zone is obviously decided by microwave power [5], but the position of ellipsoid zone need adjustment through MAs inserting direction and depth in order to cover the irregular hepatic cancerous tissue (IHCT). It means that the matching of MA ellipsoid zone and IHCT is the key point of treatment planning of microwave ablation.

With the assistance of a computer model, treatment planning can be more reasonably set by the surgeon. Numerical simulation has been used extensively in the studies of microwave ablation as it offers an efficient and accurate way to analyze the curative effect of treatment planning. There were several model studies on the curative effect of microwave ablation reported. Labonte et al. used finite-element analysis to compare and found that the antennas of metal-tip monopole provided the smoothest temperature distribution in the surrounding tissue than other two antennas of open-tip and dielectric-tip monopole [9]. Keangin et al. reported that maximum specific absorption rate (SAR) and temperature appears in the liver tissue in case of single slot antenna which is higher than those of double slot antenna [7], but Karampatzakis et al. predicted that double-slot antennas with slot-to-tip and slot-to-slot distances close to 10 mm make a good design choice for its relatively large, uniform, and localized near their tip SAR field [6]. In addition, Karampatzakis et al. found that triangular and square antenna arrays can create respectively spherical and flatter ablation zones [10]. From the above numerical experimental results, it can be found that MA design and configuration take effect in microwave ablation, but the ellipsoid zone dimensions of MA ablation had not described estimating the thermal lesion of the simplest structure MA with one slot.

To simulate the real clinical situation, it is of interest to investigate the influence of treatment planning in the way MA is inserted and positioned in IHCT for the best curative effect. In this paper, a dynamical treatment simulation model was considered, looking at the effects of MAs inserting direction, depth, and power, for the prediction of the temperature distribution and SAR in the zone of ablation. MAs design was chosen as the common single-slot type and the electro-thermal properties of tissue were obtained from the reported literature. Such an investigation is carried out in this study, in order to provide some insight that is necessary in case-specific clinical scenarios.

2   Method

The microwave simulation model was established by the finite element method (FEM) with the radio-frequency module and heat transfer module. The temperature distribution in the tissue can be computed using the bio-heat equation.

2.1   Modelling

Tissue. As a sample model of irregular tissue, a $72 \times 115 \times 90$ mm geometrical model of a hepatic tumor was taken into account from computed tomography (CT) scan (see Fig. 1a). In most of studies, tissue has typically modeled as a homogenous block, ignoring the irregular shape. However, all cancerous cells in this irregular target region should be killed in order to achieve the success of microwave ablation and avoid the reproduction of cancerous cells. Sphere and ellipsoid models of tumor have often proposed in clinical treatment planning, so our IHCT model is treated as a ellipsoid similar to the thermal lesion zone of MA. After the contour extraction, filtering and smoothing of image processing, our tumor model was built to own long diameter Dtl of 136 mm and short diameter Dts of 63 mm, and the middle axis of the shadow middle CT transverse plane with length $Dma = 92$ mm (see Fig. 1b). The initial temperature was set to that of blood (37 °C) and the hepatic characteristics of density, relative permittivity, electric conductivity, and thermal conductivity were 1078.75 kg/m3, 43.03, 1.69 S/m and 0.56 W/(m*K), respectively.

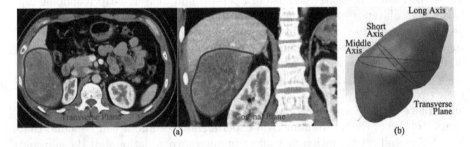

(a)   (b)

Fig. 1. Model of irregular hepatic cancerous tissue (IHCT). (a) Segmented result from the computed tomography (CT) image; (b) Model construction after image processing.

Microwave Antenna. The MA used in the model was semirigid coaxial catheter made of polytetrafluoroethylene (PTFE) and having a diameter Da of 1.79 mm (see Fig. 2a). A 1 mm (Ls) ring-shaped slot was cut on the outer conductor 5 mm (Lst) from the terminal end of the antenna to transfer microwave power at 2.45 GHz frequency of the dielectric into cancerous tissue. The inner and outer diameter, Ddi and Ddo, of the dielectric were set to 0.29 mm and 0.94 mm. And diameter Dco of the outer conductor was 1.19 mm. In addition, the relative permittivity of dielectric and catheter were 20.3 and 20.6, respectively. These geometrical dimensions and material properties of the MA model were incorporated in all FE models in this study.

Model Simulating Treatment Planning. In clinical applications, the MA should be usually manual inserted into the target cancerous region from the intercostal space (see Fig. 2b), avoiding large blood vessels, gallbladder and other tissues. However besides the direction along the middle axis of the shadow middle CT transverse plane, other two MA directions which could be operated in the future surgical robot were designed as the direction along the long axis and short axis of the ellipsoid IHCT model. In term of estimating the heating performance of microwave ablation and analyzing thermal lesion of IHCT, five different powers (30 W, 90 W, 180 W, 450 W, and 900 W) and five insertion depth rates (80%, 85%, 90%, 95% and 100% of tumor length along the MA inserting direction) of MA are modeled. The range of five powers and MA inserting depth rates is chosen assumable according to the scope of clinical use and the actual ablation energy demand of tumor size. The simulated time was supposed as 10 min just like a common clinical operation.

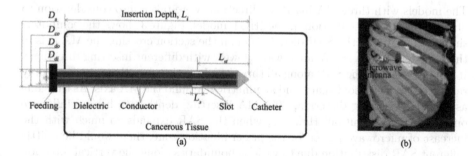

Fig. 2. Model of Microwave antenna (MA). (a) MA structure; (b) Inserting method in the clinical treatment.

2.2   Numerical Methods

Electromagnetic Field Computing. Microwave energy is propagating through the MA and emitted into the cancerous tissue from the MA slot. The electromagnetic field in the simulation was excited by a voltage applied between the inner and outer conductors of the sufficiently long coaxial MA at 2450 MHz before the wave entered the cancerous tissue model. The electric and magnetic field intensity of the MA can be calculated by Keangin et al.'s method [7]. For a discrete finite region, the geometry of the MA was truncated some distance using a similar absorbing boundary condition without excitation. The microwave power was loaded on the truncated surface of the MA.

Bioheat Transfer Analysis. The heat is transferred in biological tissues via blood flow. So the analysis of heat transfer in IHCT is assumed to use frequently Pennes bioheat equation (PBE) introduced by Pennes [11]. The equation includes a special term that describes the heat exchange between hepatic arterial blood flow and IHCT. To evaluate the heating performance of microwave ablation, the specific absorption rate (SAR) distribution is widely used [7,8]. SAR quantifies the electromagnetic power deposited per unit mass in IHCT (W/kg).

Thermal Lesion Estimation. Many studies reported that thermal lesion of tissue formed where the temperature rose to some specific value such as 50 °C [8,10,12] and 60 °C [13,14]. Temperature field can be calculated through FEM or measured by temperature sensors in the ex vivo experiment. In our numerical model, higher temperature 60 °C (T60) was chosen as the critical value of tissue thermal lesion.

3   Results

3.1   Specific Absorption Rate Distribution on Heating Performance

The models with three MA inserting directions were taken into consideration to observe the SAR distribution in the IHCT model. Figure 3 shows the computer-simulated results of the SAR distribution on the section crossing the MA axis in three models, under 180 W microwave power, with different inserting directions. It can be seen that the SAR along all three MA inserting directions are commonly referred to as a ellipsoid shape and symmetrical around the MA axis. As the same as the MA inserting direction, 80% MA inserting depth rate has no influence on the SAR distribution. However, when the SAR expands so much with the increase of microwave power for the larger ablation zone, there would be a little different SAR distribution due to various boundaries along the vertical direction of the MA axis of three models, especially the model with the MA inserting direction along the long axis of the IHCT. A parametric analysis was carried out in order to investigate the effects of the microwave power on the SAR. In the case of the model simulated by inserting MA at 80% depth rate along the long axis of the ellipsoid tissue, 30 W, 90 W, 180 W, 450 W, and 900 W microwave power were loaded. Figure 4 shows the normalized SAR distribution parallel to the MA axis at a distance of 0.9 mm away from the MA and into the tissue. For the model with three MA inserting directions, the MA inserting depth influences on the power absorption rate of total power dissipation at input power. As shown

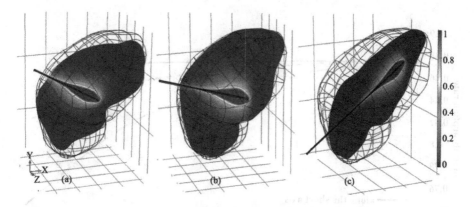

Fig. 3. The specific absorption rate (SAR) of hepatic cancerous tissue near the MA in three models, which are at 80% depth rate of different inserting directions along: (a) the short axis, (b) the middle axis of middle CT transverse plane, and (c) the long axis of the ellipsoid tissue, under the power 180 W.

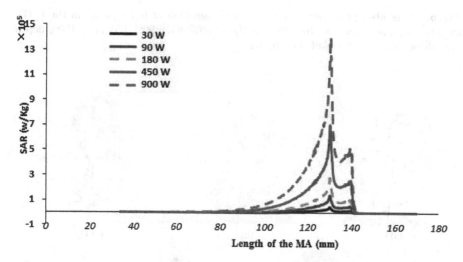

Fig. 4. The SAR along a line parallel to the MA and at a distance 0.9 mm from the MA axis in the IHCT models, which are simulated by inserting MA at 80% depth rate along the long axis of the ellipsoid tissue, under five different powers 30 W, 90 W, 180 W, 450 W, and 900 W.

in Fig. 5, the deeper the MA was inserted, the lower the power absorption rate turn. In addition, the curve of the model with the inserting direction along the long axis of the ellipsoid tissue declined fast from 0.8741 to 0.7427, while the curve of the model with inserting direction along the short axis of the ellipsoid tissue had gentle trend from 0.8732 to 0.8482.

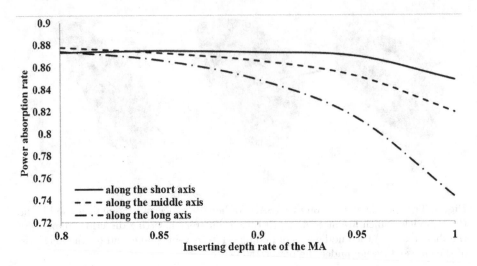

Fig. 5. Power absorption rate of total power dissipation at input power in the IHCT models, which are simulated by inserting MA at 80%, 85%, 90%, 95%, and 100% depth rate along three directions of the tumour.

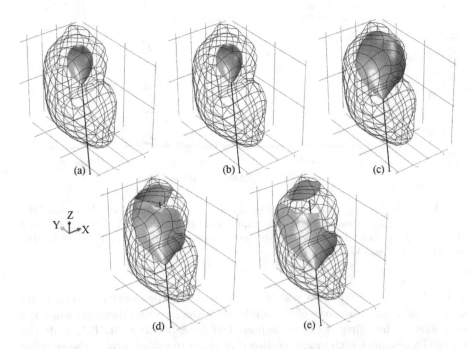

Fig. 6. Temperature distribution at 60 °C (T60) in the 3D IHCT model, which is simulated by inserting MA at 80% depth rate along the long axis of the ellipsoid tissue, with five different microwave powers: (a) 30 W, (b) 90 W, (c) 180 W, (d) 450 W and (e) 900 W.

3.2   Thermal Lesion Zone Under Different Powers

As described in the above thermal lesion estimation method, we chose the temperature T60 as the critical value of thermal lesion. The IHCT model inserting MA at 80% depth rate along the long axis of the ellipsoid tissue was applied to estimate thermal lesion zone under five powers. T60 contour planes were drawn by the equivalent surface of temperature 60 °C from the numerical results of the models. Figure 6 shows that T60 contour planes in the model expand as power increase from 30 W to 900 W. The volume surrounded by T60 contour plane of the models under lower power in the range of 30 W to 180 W display the entire ellipsoid shape. But for the large power of 450 W and 900 W, irregular shape of hepatic cancerous tissue model seemed to break the integrity of the ellipsoid of T60 volume. In fact, these areas that are also the boundaries of the tissue had been defined to constraint heat exposure outside the tissue and keep it inside.

4   Discussion

Three MA inserting directions, five MA inserting depths and five input microwave powers were simulated to analyze the heating performance, bioheat transfer and thermal lesion in the IHCT microwave ablation model. In terms of regular cylinder tissue model, there were widely deterministic FEM models for predicting coagulation zone dimensions during microwave ablation, especially under different powers [5–7, 15]. However, the influence of MA inserting direction and depth on the heating performance and thermal lesion need to be studied in the case of the IHCT model under different powers.

For this matter, the SAR distribution of the models with three MA inserting directions were simulated. It can be found that the inserting direction length along the MA axis is longer than the vertical length in the ellipsoid zone of the SAR distribution as shown in Fig. 3. Therefore, in the case of the long axis of the tissue model, the relatively small number of tissues in the vertical direction of the MA axis can be involved in the SAR distribution when power enlarges. The other tissues in the axial direction of the MA axis can be heating by adjusting the MA inserting depth during the microwave ablation. Correspondingly in other two models with inserting direction along the short axis and axis of the middle transverse plane, a greater number of tissues in the vertical direction of the MA axis had not been heating outside of the SAR distribution. The MA inserting direction along the long axial of irregular tissue could be the better treatment planning for the heating performance on the majority of the cancerous tissue.

The microwave power is transferred to send the energy into the cancerous tissue through the slot of the MA, so the SAR value near the slot is maximal along the line parallel to the MA axis as shown in Fig. 4. The relationship between the microwave power and the maximum SAR is linear, but the SAR values were not affected by the MA inserting depth. Similarly, total power dissipation, which is the product of the SAR and the density of tissue, are the same no matter what the MA inserting depth is. On the other hand, the power absorption rate of total power dissipation at input power change with the MA inserting depth as shown in Fig. 5. There is some energy wasted in reason of the restriction from the irregular tissue boundary when the tip of the MA is inserted close to the boundary. In the vertical direction of the MA axis under large power, energy will readily reach the irregular tissue boundary in the model with inserting direction along the long axis of the ellipsoid tissue. Therefore, the power absorption rate in the model with inserting direction along the long axis of the ellipsoid tissue declined the fastest than those in the other models. It could be concluded that the MA tip should better own a little distance such as 80%–90% MA inserting depth rate.

In this study, T60 is used to analyze the thermal lesion zone during microwave ablation simulation experiment. There were some reports that the volume of thermal lesion defined by T60 was clearly underestimated with a comparison of the ablation results in the in-vivo animal trial [16]. Our FEM simulated results also supported each other by this conclusion. In Fig. 6, the distribution field of the T60 expanded as power gave rise on.

5   Conclusion

This study has investigated the ability of microwave ablation treatment planning, which included the MA inserting direction, inserting depth rate and power, to create thermal lesion zones of clinical interest on the IHCT. To transfer the energy into more cancerous tissue in the vertical direction of the MA axis, the MA inserting direction along the long axis of the IHCT could be the better choice for the microwave ablation treatment planning. Despite incommodity of the MA insertion in the clinical manual application, we believe that our results could aid surgery more effective in case-specific situations. When the technology of clinical image-guided surgical navigation and surgical robot are introduced, the MA inserting methods might be more diversified and feasible. On the other hand, the MA inserting depth rate would influence the thermal lesion zone of the IHCT with the change of the ablated forward distance from the MA tip in the thermal lesion ellipsoid zone under different powers.

Further work on model simulation of two or more times ablation along the long axis of the irregular tissue should be done to help the treatment planning work more perfect. More than 100 W power loaded in our large hepatic cancerous tissue models could go beyond the clinical application, while multiple MAs with small power was used for large tumor microwave ablation in actual operation. Therefore, our work will keep on to study the microwave ablation treatment planning with multiple MAs on basis of the model simulation in this study.

References

1. Yang, D., Converse, M.C., Mahvi, D.M., Webster, J.G.: Measurement and analysis of tissue temperature during microwave liver ablation. IEEE Trans. Biomed. Eng. **54**, 150–155 (2007)
2. Phasukkit, P., Tungjitkusolmun, S., Sangworasil, M.: Finite-element analysis and in vitro experiments of placement configurations using triple antennas in microwave hepatic ablation. IEEE Trans. Biomed. Eng. **56**, 2564–2572 (2009)

3. Livraghi, T., et al.: Hepatocellular carcinoma: radio-frequency ablation of medium and large lesions. Radiology **214**, 761–768 (2000)
4. Lopresto, V., Pinto, R., Farina, L., Cavagnaro, M.: Microwave thermal ablation: effects of tissue properties variations on predictive models for treatment planning. Med. Eng. Phys. **46**, 63–70 (2017)
5. Cavagnaro, M., Pinto, R., Lopresto, V.: Numerical models to evaluate the temperature increase induced by ex vivo microwave thermal ablation. Phys. Med. Biol. **60**, 3287–3311 (2015)
6. Karampatzakis, A., Kuhn, S., Tsanidis, G., Neufeld, E., Samaras, T., Kuster, N.: Antenna design and tissue parameters considerations for an improved modelling of microwave ablation in the liver. Phys. Med. Biol. **58**, 3191–3206 (2013)
7. Keangin, P., Rattanadecho, P., Wessapan, T.: An analysis of heat transfer in liver tissue during microwave ablation using single and double slot antenna. Int. Commun. Heat Mass **38**, 757–766 (2011)
8. Prakash, P.: Theoretical modeling for hepatic microwave ablation. Open Biomed. Eng. J. **4**, 27–38 (2010)
9. Labonte, S., Blais, A., Legault, S.R., Ali, H.O., Roy, L.: Monopole antennas for microwave catheter ablation. IEEE Trans. Microwave Theory Tech. **44**, 1832–1840 (1996)
10. Karampatzakis, A., Kuhn, S., Tsanidis, G., Neufeld, E., Samaras, T., Kuster, N.: Heating characteristics of antenna arrays used in microwave ablation: a theoretical parametric study. Comput. Biol. Med. **43**, 1321–1327 (2013)
11. Pennes, H.H.: Analysis of tissue and arterial blood temperatures in the resting human forearm. J. Appl. Physiol. **85**, 5–34 (1998)
12. Liu, Z., et al.: Radiofrequency tumor ablation: insight into improved efficacy using computer modeling. Am. J. Roentgenol. **184**, 1347–1352 (2005)
13. Johansson, J.D., Eriksson, O., Wren, J., Loyd, D., Wardell, K.: Radio-frequency lesioning in brain tissue with coagulation-dependent thermal conductivity: modelling, simulation and analysis of parameter influence and interaction. Med. Biol. Eng. Comput. **44**, 757–766 (2006)
14. Haase, S., Sss, P., Schwientek, J., Teichert, K., Preusser, T.: Radiofrequency ablation planning: an application of semi-infinite modelling techniques. Eur. J. Oper. Res. **218**, 856–864 (2012)
15. Saito, K., Hayashi, Y., Yoshimura, H., Ito, K.: Heating characteristics of array applicator composed of two coaxial-slot antennas for microwave coagulation therapy. IEEE Trans. Microwave Theory Tech. **48**, 1800–1806 (2000)
16. Varghese, T., et al.: Ultrasound monitoring of temperature change during radiofrequency ablation: preliminary in-vivo results. Ultrasound Med. Biol. **28**, 321–329 (2002)

A Two-Stage Overlapping Community Detection Based on Structure and Node Attributes in Online Social Networks

Xinmeng Zhang[1,2,3(✉)], Xinguang Li[1], Shengyi Jiang[2,3], Xia Li[2,3],
and Bolin Xie[2,3]

[1] Laboratory of Language Engineering and Computing,
Guangdong University of Foreign Studies, Guangzhou 510006,
Guangdong, China
544750945@qq.com
[2] Non-universal Language Intelligent Processing Laboratory,
Guangdong University of Foreign Studies, Guangzhou 510006,
Guangdong, China
[3] School of Information Science and Technology,
Guangdong University of Foreign Studies, Guangzhou 510006,
Guangdong, China

Abstract. Traditional community detection algorithms are mainly based on network structure, while ignoring a large number of node attributes. In this paper, we propose a two-stage overlapping community detection method which combines structure and attributes(tsocd-SA). First, a set of non-overlapping communities are identified by using existing community detection methods, and community attribute summaries which represents high degree homogeneous attribute value of a community are constructed according to the attributes of the special nodes in the community. Then, we propose a similarity measure between node and community based on network structure and community attribute summary. For connector nodes which connect more than one communities, each node is divided into one or more communities based on the similarity and a specific threshold r. Experimental results in online social network datasets show that our proposed method is more effective than solely focus on structural information.

Keywords: Overlapping community detection · Online social network ·
Community attributes summary · Similarity

1 Introduction

Users in online social network with the same interests are closely related and form a social circle, online social networks present obvious community structural characteristics. Community detection is one of the important aspects of online social network research. Traditional community detection mainly depends on network structure [1]. Researchers have proposed a large number of community detection algorithms, including optimization of modularity [2], probability-based method [3], Label propagation

© Springer Nature Singapore Pte Ltd. 2019
A. Zeng et al. (Eds.): HBAI 2019, CCIS 1072, pp. 310–320, 2019.
https://doi.org/10.1007/978-981-15-1398-5_23

algorithm [4], and many more. But these algorithms are usually used to discover non-overlapping communities.

In real networks, different communities overlap heavily, some nodes may belong to multiple communities simultaneously, and form overlapping community structures. Overlapping community detection includes clique percolation methods [5], link partitions [6, 7], label propagation [8–10], LM-NV(Louvain Method with Neighbor Voting) [11], Mathematical [12], and many more. Each algorithm has its advantages and disadvantages, for example, clique method has high time complexity, Link method is prone to excessive overlap, Label propagation method has high risk of error and is easy to fall into local maximum.

In online social network, users usually have a variety of interests and belong to multiple circles. There are many kinds of circles in online social network, which overlap with each other. At the same time, online social network nodes have abundant attributes information, and the nodes in same community have highly similar attributes, which is important for identifying the community to which the node belongs. Some studies [13, 14] have proposed community detection algorithms based on structure and node attributes. However, few community detection algorithms combining links and attributes are available for overlapping community identification. Traditional relational data clustering measures distance between two nodes mainly based on node's attribute similarity. Nodes with highly similar attributes are grouped together, but there may not be any relationship between them. Community detection measures node closeness mainly based on connectivity, the nodes in same community have closer relationship, but it is difficult for some nodes to determine which communities they belong to. Figure 1 shows an illustrating example of friendships network where nodes represent the users and edges represent the mutual friendships, node attributes contain the 'gender' and 'genres' preferences of users. Traditional community detection algorithms only rely on structure, and node g should obviously only be divided into the community 1. But if the attribute 'genres' of the node is taken into account, node g has a homogenization attribute value 'dance' with the nodes in community 2, so the node g should also belong to community 2.

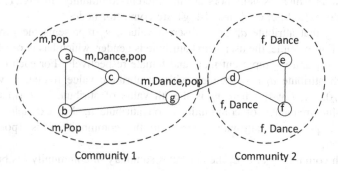

Fig. 1. A friendships network example with attribute 'genres' and 'gender'

The main problem of traditional community detection algorithms is the division of connector nodes. It is difficult to determine which communities the connector nodes belong to if only based on structure. These nodes that form edges across the borders of the communities are called connector nodes, and other nodes are called isolated nodes which only possess links with nodes of the same community [12]. In online social networks, users with similar attributes are more closely connected and easier to form circles. Therefore, it is more accurate to judge the community to which the nodes belong by considering the attribute information of nodes.

In this paper, First, we use existing community detection algorithms to get non-overlapping community partitions, and divide the nodes in the community into isolated nodes and connector nodes according to the results of non-overlapping community partitioning [12]. Isolated nodes have their community membership fixed, whereas connector nodes are free to be assigned to one or more communities. Further, community attributes summary is constructed according to the attributes of isolated nodes in a community which represent the homogeneous attribute values of community nodes. Finally, we assign each connector node to one or more communities according to the structure and attributes similarity between it and community.

2 Problem Definition

In this section we give the basic definitions needed in this paper. An undirected graph with attribute is denoted as $G = (E, V, A)$, where V represents the set of n nodes, and E represents the set of m edges, and $A = \{a_1, ..., a_k\}$ is the set of k attributes associated with nodes in V for describing node properties. Each node $v_i \in V$ is associated with an attribute vector $\{v_{i1}, v_{i2}, ..., v_{ij}\}$ where v_{ij} is the attribute value of node v_i on attribute a_j.

For overlapping community detection, the set of overlapping communities found is denoted as $C = \{c_1, c_2, \cdots, c_L\}$, in which a node may belong to more than one community.

Given a partition of non-overlapping communities, If a node and all its neighbors are in the same community, it is called an isolated node, and other nodes are called connector node which its neighbors are in different community. In Fig. 1, the list of isolated nodes is{a, b, c, e, f}, and {d, g} are connector nodes.

Assuming that attribute a_i has k discrete values, v_{ij} represents the j-th value of attribute a_i. For example, the user's first attribute is gender, which has two values, male and female, v_{11} and v_{12} represent male and female respectively. For each community $c_l \in C$, each attribute a_i is associated with an attribute value frequency vector $f_l = \{f_l(v_{i1}), f_l(v_{i2}), ..., f_l(v_{ij})\}$ where v_{ij} is the jth value of attribute a_i, $f_l(v_{ij})$ is the j-th attribute value frequency of community c_l on attribute a_i. For example, in Fig. 1, the value frequency of attribute 'genres' in the community 1 is {pop = 100%, dance = 50%}.

For each community $c_l \in C$, the attributes summary of community l is built by the top k attribute value frequency vector, it is denoted as

$$s_l = \left\{ \left(f_l(v_{ij}), w_i \right), \ldots, \left(f_l(v_{i'j'}), w_k \right) \right\} \tag{1}$$

where s_l is the attributes summary of community l, $f_l(v_{ij})$ is the jth value of attribute a_i, w_i is the weight of attribute a_i, w_i defined as

$$w_i = \left(\frac{n_i}{\sum n_i} \right)^r \tag{2}$$

Where n_i is the number of values for attribute a_i, $\sum n_i$ is the number of values for all attributes, the parameter r is used to adjust the weight of each attribute. The less the number of values for an attribute, the smaller the weight of this attribute. For example, the attribute 'genre' has 84 values and the attribute 'gender' has only 2 values, If 50% of users are male, it is not helpful for community identification, and if 50% of users' attribute 'genre' is 'pop', it can be a prominent homogeneous attribute feature of community.

For community l and node i, the attribute similarity between them is denoted as

$$s_{il} = \frac{\sum_{j=1}^{k'} f_l(v_{ij}) \cdot w_j}{k'} \tag{3}$$

Where k' is the number of attribute values that simultaneously appear in the attribute value of node i and the attributes summary of community l. According to the community attribute summary construction method, the attribute value contributes to the similarity only when the node attribute value is one of the community high frequency attribute values.

Belonging coefficient of Node i to community l is denoted as

$$b_{il} = \frac{\sum_{j \in N(i)} s_{jl}}{\sum_{j \in N(i)} \sum_{c \in C} s_{jc}} \tag{4}$$

Where $N(i)$ is the neighbors of node i. The numerator represents the sum of the similarities between the neighbors of node i and the community l, and the denominator represents the sum of the similarities between the neighbors of node i and all communities. Therefore, the method includes the structural relationship and attribute similarity between the node and the community. The more the number of neighbors in a community, the more similar the attributes of neighbors and communities are, the greater the belonging coefficient of the node to the corresponding communities is.

3 Overlapping Community Detection Based on Link and Node Attributes

Our proposed two-stage overlapping community detection algorithm is shown in Fig. 1. The procedure can be described as follow.

Input: $G = (E, V, A)$, parameter r for judging a node whether it belongs to a community.

Output: $C = \{c_1, c_2, \cdots, c_L\}$, in which a node may belong to more than one community.

1. Getting a partition of non-overlapping communities by using existing community detection method, and each node is marked as isolated node or connector node according to the location of the node in the community. For each community, it's community attributes summary was built according to the attributes of isolated nodes in the community based on Formula 1.
2. For each connector node, Calculating the belonging coefficients of the node to other connected communities according to the Formula 4. If the belonging coefficients of the node to a community is higher than threshold r, the node will be marked to belong to the community.

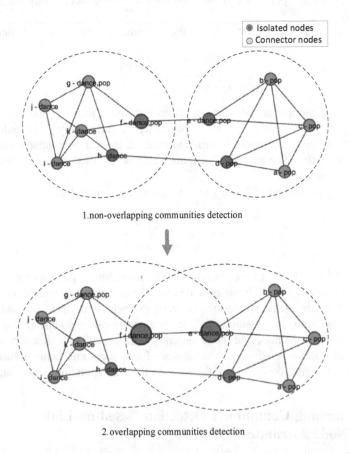

Fig. 2. Outline of two-stage overlapping community detection. Community membership of yellow isolated nodes is fixed, whereas red connector nodes can be assigned to one or more communities based on the coefficients belonging to the community. Large-sized red nodes belong two communities at the same time. (Color figure online)

In the first step, we select the existing community detection algorithm according to the characteristics of network. For big network, the main consideration is efficiency rather than precision.

The time complexity of the algorithm consists of four parts, including non-overlapping community partition, node classification, community attribute summary construction, overlapping community identification. But each part of the algorithm is independent of each other, so the time complexity is simply added by the time complexity of the four parts.

Time complexity of many efficient non-overlapping community detection algorithms can achieve $O(nd)$, where d is the average degree of all nodes. Marking isolated nodes and connector nodes requires traversing each node and its neighbors, therefore the time complexity for marking isolated nodes and connector nodes is $O(nd)$. The step 2 takes time $O(n_1 k)$, where k is the number of values per node attribute, The k value of most data sets is usually very small, n_1 is the number of isolated nodes which is smaller than n. The time complexity last step is $O(n_2 d)$, n_2 is the number of connector nodes which is far small than n. Therefore, The time complexity of the tsocd-SA method is $O(nd)$.

4 Experiments

In this section, we performed extensive experiments to evaluate the performance of our algorithms on online social network datasets.

4.1 Experimental Datasets

We use two real online social networks for evaluation in our experiments. The two data sets are described below.

ego-Facebook [15]: This dataset includes survey participants from facebook and their circle of friends. Facebook data has been anonymized by replacing each user's facebook ids with a new value. The dataset includes the edges in the ego network, the set of circles for the ego node, the features for each of the nodes and the ego user, the names of each of the feature dimensions.

gemsec-Deezer [16]: This dataset is a user relationship network from the music streaming service Deezer, and these users of this dataset are all from Romania. Each node is a user and edge indicates that the two users have a friend relationship. In this dataset, user could like 84 distinct genres, and their favourite genre lists were produced according to their favourite song lists. Figure 2 shows a small community, which almost all members have music genre 'pop' tag.

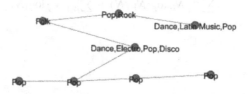

Fig. 3. A small community with common music genre 'pop'.

Table 1 shows the characteristics of the two network datasets used in this experiment.

Table 1. Details of the datasets used in this experiment.

Network	Ego-Facebook	Gemsec-Deezer (Romania)
Nodes	4039	41773
Edges	88234	125,826
Number of triangles	1612010	31791
Average clustering coefficient	0.6055	0.105
Average degree	43.691	6.024

4.2 Comparison Methods and Evaluation

We evaluate our algorithm experimentally on these two data sets with modularity, mni, and overlap index.

Modularity. Modularity is used to evaluate the effectiveness of community detection method. It measures the fraction of intra-community edges minus its expected value in a null model, which is based on the assumption that a community structure isn't found in random networks. The modularity Q can be described as:

$$Q = \sum_{s=1}^{m} \left[\frac{l_s}{|E|} - \left(\frac{d_s}{2|E|} \right)^2 \right] \tag{5}$$

Where l_s is the number of edges between nodes belonging to the s-th community, d_s is the sum of the degree of these nodes in the s-th community, $|E|$ is the number of edges. High values of $Q \in [0, 1]$ represents a evident community structure, the values usually are between 0.3 and 0.7 in most real networks.

NMI. Normalized mutual information (NMI) is another commonly adopted measure to assess the quality of community detection by comparing real communities to the found communities. It is based on a confusion matrix N, where the rows correspond to the real communities, and the columns correspond to the found.

$$I(A,B) = \frac{-2 \sum_{i=1}^{CA} \sum_{j=1}^{CB} N_{ij} \log(N_{ij}N/N_{i.}N_{.j})}{\sum_{i=1}^{CA} N_{i.} \log(N_{i.}/N) + \sum_{j=1}^{CB} N_{.j} \log(N_{.j}/N)} \tag{6}$$

Where $ÇA$ is the number of real communities, and CB is the number of found communities. The sum over row i of matrix N_{ij} is denoted N_i, and the sum over column j is denoted $N_{.j}$.

Overlap. The number of overlapping nodes determines the value of overlapping degree. The formula is as follows.

$$Overlap = \frac{1}{m} \sum_{c \in C} |c| \tag{7}$$

Where $|c|$ is the number of nodes in community c, m is the number of nodes in network.

In the first step, we use the fast community detection algorithm [17] to divide non-overlapping communities. Figure 3 shows the result of community partition of Facebook network datasets. Obviously, the facebook network presents a clear community structure, but there are many bridge nodes between these communities. Although these bridge nodes are divided into a certain community, in fact these nodes may belong to multiple communities.

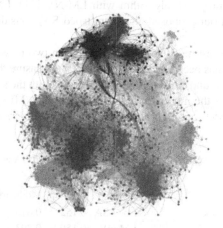

Fig. 4. The result of community detection of Facebook network datasets, nodes of different communities are represented by different colors.

Figure 4 shows an example of overlapping community detection results. According to the community detection results of the first step, the large-sized nodes in the middle belong to only one community, but also have high homogenization attribute values with another community, so they belong to the both communities (Fig. 5).

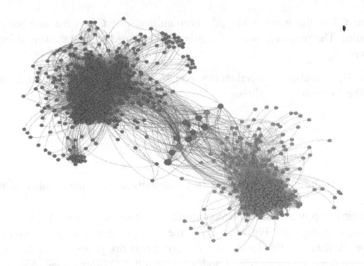

Fig. 5. An example of overlapping community identification results, the large-sized nodes in the middle of two communities belong to two communities at the same time.

We compare our proposed algorithm with LM-NV [11]. LM-NV only considers network structure, but our proposed algorithm(tsocd-SA) considers both structure and node attributes.

Table 2 shows the result of overlap, modularity on two networks by two methods. ego-Facebook dataset has been labeled real circles. We measure the NMI score between the real circles and the found circles. On ego-facebook, With the same degree of overlap, our algorithm increases the modularity by 2.78% and the NMI by 1.69%. On gemsec-Deezer(Romania) dataset, our algorithm increases the modularity by 1.83%.

Table 2. Comparison of overlap, modularity and NMI for tsocd-SA and LM-NV on two social networks

Networks	Methods	Overlap	Modularity	NMI
ego-Facebook	tsocd-SA	0.152	0.816	0.678
	LM-NV	0.150	0.793	0.666
gemsec-Deezer (Romania)	tsocd-SA	0.151	0.723	
	LM-NV	0.143	0.710	

5   Conclusions

In this paper, we discuss a two-stage overlapping community detection method that combines link and node attributes. First, we use existing community detection algorithm to quickly divide non-overlapping communities. According to the position of the node in the community, the node is divided into two types: isolated node and connector node. The frequency of occurrence of attribute values of isolated nodes in the community is used as to build community attribute summary. The second stage determines the membership degree of the node to community according to the similarity between the neighbors and the community, and compares with a threshold r to determine whether the node belongs to the corresponding community.

Our algorithms have low time complexity and are suitable for large-scale online social networks. However, some thresholds need to be determined in our algorithm, and the thresholds of different networks may be different. The selection of the threshold may related to the characteristics of the network structure. In the future, the potential relationship between the selection of the threshold and the network characteristics will be discussed.

Acknowledgments. This research is supported by the National Natural Science Foundation of China (No. 62877013, 61402119).

References

1. Girvan, M., Newman, M.E.J.: Community structure in social and biological networks. Proc. Natl. Acad. Sci. **99**(12), 7821–7826 (2002)
2. Newman, M.E.J.: Equivalence between modularity optimization and maximum likelihood methods for community detection. Phys. Rev. E **94**(5), 052315 (2016)
3. Geng, J., Bhattacharya, A., Pati, D.: Probabilistic community detection with unknown number of communities. J. Am. Stat. Assoc. 1–13 (2018)
4. Zhang, X., et al.: Efficient community detection based on label propagation with belonging coefficient and edge probability. In: Li, Y., Xiang, G., Lin, H., Wang, M. (eds.) SMP 2016. CCIS, vol. 669, pp. 54–72. Springer, Singapore (2016). https://doi.org/10.1007/978-981-10-2993-6_5
5. Wen, X., Chen, W.N., Lin, Y.: A maximal clique based multiobjective evolutionary algorithm for overlapping community detection. IEEE Trans. Evol. Comput. **21**(3), 363–377 (2016)
6. Deng, X., Li, G., Dong, M.: Finding overlapping communities based on Markov chain and link clustering. Peer-to-Peer Netw. Appl. **10**(2), 411–420 (2017)
7. Lancichinetti, A., Fortunato, S., Kertész, J.: Detecting the overlapping and hierarchical community structure in complex networks. New J. Phys. **11**(3), 033015 (2009)
8. Wu, Z.H., Lin, Y.F., Gregory, S.: Balanced multi-label propagation for overlapping community detection in social networks. J. Comput. Sci. Technol. **27**(3), 468–479 (2012)
9. Lu, M., Zhang, Z., Qu, Z., et al.: LPANNI: overlapping community detection using label propagation in large-scale complex networks. IEEE Trans. Knowl. Data Eng. (2018)
10. Xie, J., Szymanski, B.K.: Towards linear time overlapping community detection in social networks. In: Tan, P.-N., Chawla, S., Ho, C.K., Bailey, J. (eds.) PAKDD 2012. LNCS (LNAI), vol. 7302, pp. 25–36. Springer, Heidelberg (2012). https://doi.org/10.1007/978-3-642-30220-6_3
11. Jun-yu, C., Gang, Z., Xiao-bing, X.: Detecting over-lapping community structure with neighbor voting. J. Chin. Comput. Syst. **35**(10), 2272–2277 (2014)
12. Bennett, L., Kittas, A., Liu, S., et al.: Community structure detection for overlapping modules through mathematical programming in protein interaction networks. PLoS ONE **9** (11), e112821 (2014)

13. Cheng, H., Zhou, Y., Jeffrey, X.Y.: Clustering large attributed graphs: a balance between structural and attribute similarities. ACM Trans. Knowl. Discov. Data **5**(2), 12 (2011)
14. Ruan, Y.Y., Fuchry, D., Parthasarathy, S.: Efficient community detection in large networks using content and links. In: Proceedings of the 22nd International Conference on World Wide Web. Seoul, Korea, pp. 1089–1098 (2013)
15. Mcauley, J.J., Leskovec, J.: Learning to discover social circles in ego networks. In: International Conference on Neural Information Processing Systems. Curran Associates Inc. (2012)
16. Rozemberczki, B., Davies, R., Sarkar, R., et al.: Gemsec: graph embedding with self clustering. arXiv preprint arXiv:1802.03997 (2018)
17. Blondel, V.D., Guillaume, J.L., Lambiotte, R., Lefebvre, E.: Fast unfolding of communities in large networks. J. Stat. Mech.: Theory Exp. **2008**(10), P1000 (2008)

Balance Rule in Artificial Intelligence

Wenwei Li[1(✉)], Guangsheng Luo[1(✉)], Fei Dai[2(✉)], and Rong Li[3(✉)]

[1] Fudan University, Shanghai, China
{wwli16,gsluo16}@fudan.edu.cn
[2] Wuhan University, Wuhan, China
2018202110026@whu.edu.cn
[3] Hubei University of Medicine, Shiyan, China
liray89@163.com

Abstract. Deep learning embodied some essence of artificial intelligence, but it relied on data set and lacked migration learning ability. We should build general theorem to explain artificial intelligence from nature or human. We can treat each static data as a variable like wave-particle duality, then we can adopt idea from convolutional neural network or other machine learning algorithms to extract features from little data. This method can open up a new theory to accomplish migration learning and artificial intelligence. The theory will be supported by balance rule: everything has a gradient and tends to remain a zero gradient state, and we can connect different feature spaces by gradients.

Keywords: Artificial intelligence · Wave-particle duality · Balance rule

1 Introduction

Many machine learning algorithms tend to handle data set in limited feature spaces such as decision tree, linear or nonlinear regression, SVM, naive bayes classifier and so on. Decision trees [26] were difficult to link different feature spaces. The kernel function limited the application scope of the SVM [25]. Linear regression like [24] was to classify multiple problems with demarcation lines. Bayes classifier like [27] provided a good idea for the study of uncertainty, but lackd migration learning ability. Many machine learning algorithms dealt with classification problems in the same feature space. We should jump out of the same feature space and stand in a higher dimension to make decisions and classification. Deep learning tended to divide data into different feature spaces and can extract low-to-high-level features by increasing the number of hidden layers. But we lack a theory to explain what happens to each hidden layer. Meanwhile, current deep learning relies on a large data set to act well. Human can process things through a little data and we should find a better way to analyze data.

Although the sensor captures a piece of pixels and converts them into one RGB value for processing by the computer, our brain will have many neurons to

© Springer Nature Singapore Pte Ltd. 2019
A. Zeng et al. (Eds.): HBAI 2019, CCIS 1072, pp. 321–337, 2019.
https://doi.org/10.1007/978-981-15-1398-5_24

be active for these pixels. That's to say, data 1 is not just 1, but in some cases represents more data. We can introduce wave-particle duality into data analysis. When we listen or see some things, our brain will form a whole impression about this thing, even this thing is only related to a little data. Meanwhile, we should make data have attenuating properties which will make AI system filter much useless or old features by itself. Above process can solve the problem of too little data in some scenarios. The convolution process in deep learning is equivalent to the process of data filtering, but here we make a small data set become larger.

How can we connect different feature spaces to accomplish humanized AI? The answer is balance rule. We know gradient plays an important role in deep learning or other machine learning algorithms, but when we analyze gradient deeply we can find the generation of gradient is depended on balance rule. Everything tends to be an balance state like static or uniform linear motion as Newton said in physics, and then the state gradient similar to [23] is equal to zero. But actually too many influencing factors will break this balance state and make the gradient is not zero. We should build relationship between different feature spaces through gradient or balance rule. We can create a large feature space involved many feature subspace, and each subspace is related by balance rule. Current deep learning or other machine learning algorithms can recognize dog through a large data set, but when the data set is small or the identifying object is a cat, they will have poor performance. We need to increase the data dimension, which is equivalent to fluctuating static data. At the same time, the balance rule can connect discrete feature spaces through a larger space to realize migration learning. We need to refine the essence from deep learning, especially in the field of images [17].

This paper proposed a new theory to analyze deep learning or artificial intelligence. [5] proposed M-P model can also be used in this theory. [7] inspired us consider how to make this theory simulate every function in computer science. Data has multiple features in different scenarios, which is similar to wave-particle duality. Balance rule can explain the essence of AI. We can not evaluate our theory through current platform such as TensorFlow, Caffe, Keras and so on, but we can do some physics experimentation to testify our theory and analyze the implementation possibility through computer science. This paper will bring a deeper theoretical foundation to AI.

2   Theoretical Analysis

2.1   Data Properties

All outer things will be transferred into data in computer, so how to treat data is a priority in AI system. Traditional way treat data as a static or constant value. This paper treat data both a constant value and a fluctuating value, which means data have wave-particle duality. In some scenarios, data mainly behaves as a constant value, and that is particle properties; in other scenarios, data need to be treat as attenuated wave, and that is wave properties. When does the data appear as particle or wave properties is depended on feature space. Constant data is similar to step function in signals and systems. Fourier transform has told us step function is not a constant amplitude value in the frequency domain. Convolution can filter a large amount of change data, which is equivalent to reducing a large amount of data to a constant value. In summary, we can assign each data to both static and dynamic attributes. Static attributes are values in the traditional sense, while dynamic attributes are wave-like attenuation values as shown in Fig. 1. Suppose data a stands for particle property and $f(a)$ stands for wave property, then we can get:

Particle property: $a = a$
Wave property: $a = f(a)$

a   f(a)

Fig. 1. Data particle and wave property

How can we get $f(a)$? The answer is from nature. Lots of things in nature behaves like a wave such as water wave, things in our eyes, electromagnetic wave and so on. So we'd better find a function that can simulate these features: sine function or Gauss function, or other functions that have similar varying trend. The trend should generally satisfy the following graphic form which is very close to nature phenomenon and many mathematical laws.

One data can be expanded to many data according to balance rule. For example, suppose there is a RGB value 1, we can fill some useless pixels around 1 as shown in Fig. 2, and then 1 can be a dependent feature space which can be trained by deep learning or similar algorithms. We should treat each data as a attenuated function similar to sine wave in one cycle. We just need to seize the most important features in one thing, and this is particle property; but we cannot ignore detailed features in that thing, and this is wave particle. When do we treat data as particle or wave feature is depended on reference space which will be discussed later in this paper.

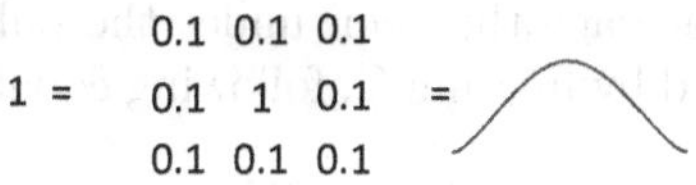

$$1 = \begin{matrix} 0.1 & 0.1 & 0.1 \\ 0.1 & 1 & 0.1 \\ 0.1 & 0.1 & 0.1 \end{matrix} =$$

Fig. 2. Particle property transferred into wave property

The conversion between particle property and wave property of a data is a continuous process. At some point the data is more particle-like, when we treat it as a traditional static data; at other times the data is fluctuating, we use it as a self-attenuating wave. Time and space frequency can influence the data property. The longer the time or the higher the space frequency, the more obvious the wave property; the shorter the time or the lower the space frequency, the more obvious the particle property. Take time for example: if we store RGB value 1 in hard disk in a long time, then 1 itself will attenuate according to $f(1)$; one day when we read this RGB value, the read value may be 0.1 or other attenuated value; The other example is about space frequency: when we join a new team to do something, team members are too many and we don't know each other; as long as we have more contact and understanding, there will always be a small number of people who can become representatives of the team, everyone's ability will be ranked by volatility similar to a wave. As the time or spatial frequency continues to increase, this conversion will occur periodically. We can use a ratio g to represent wave-particle duality extent: $g = \frac{w}{p}$ where w stands for wave property and p stands for particle property.

2.2   Balance Rule

Though we can introduce wave-particle duality into data analysis, we must figure out why we can do this, otherwise, we will not create effective AI system. We must find the answer in nature. In physics, every object can maintain a uniform linear motion or a stationary state, and only force can change this state. Balance state is everything's property, and everything tends to keep balance state. Force is similar to gradient or pivot. Actually, everything follows balance rule. Balance rule can support the conversation between particle property and wave property of every data. The bunch of data we see at this time may become only one data at other time. How to decide this transform process will be depended on balance rule described below.

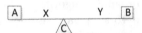

Fig. 3. Balance rule framework

The simplest is the best. We utilize physics to describe balance rule as shown in Fig. 3. According to leverage theorem, under the pull of gravity, if object A and B want to be balanced by fulcrum C, following equation need to be satisfied:

$$AX = BY \tag{1}$$

A, B, X, Y is data and have wave-particle duality. Calculus may be multidimensional and there may be more than two variables, and expressions may be discrete, but they all satisfy the simplest form. All variables have wave-particle duality, but for the convenience of expression, the particle property is mostly used to represent the balance rule in this paper, and the wave property represents the balance rule will be as shown in Fig. 4.

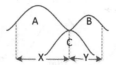

Fig. 4. Utilize wave property to represent balance rule

In fact, the expression is not necessarily an equal sign, but a certain range. Assuming that C represents a certain range, the following relationship will be satisfied:

$$|AX - BY| \leq C \tag{2}$$

Similar to the mechanical vibration of the mass, the balance rule has a relationship with the generation of waves, as shown in Fig. 5. $A = (a_1, a_2, ..., a_n)$, $B = (b_1, b_2, ..., b_n)$, $X = (x_1, x_2, ..., x_n)$, $Y = (y_1, y_2, ..., y_n)$, $C = (c_1, c_2, ..., c_n)$. A is equivalent to gravity and B is equivalent to external force, according to the rule of balance rule we can get:

$$a_n x_n = b_n y_n \tag{3}$$

Actually $|a_n x_n - b_n y_n| \leq c_n$. Everything tends to keep equivalent state. When g reaches the maximum point, the data will represent particle property obviously, and then we can have the data wave property $f(g_{\max})$. Data has multiple manifestations, and the balance rule is the root cause of these manifestations. C is similar to the threshold in deep learning.

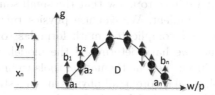

Fig. 5. Balance rule and wave property of data

$f(g)$ can have many multiple manifestations but not only the normal sine wave or Gauss function. Wavelength can represent the attributes of things and does not change. When the AI system collects the feature space about "yellow", the AI system will form a wavelength about yellow according to the balance rule. Other pale yellow or deep yellow wavelengths are similar to this wavelength. The colors are different like $f(G(g))$, and their waveform shapes may be different but the wavelength is the same as shown in Fig. 6.

In fact, the equilibrium state is in a dynamic range, that is, $AX \approx BY$. There may also be more than one fulcrum. Innovation is the process of breaking the balance. In general, all the equilibrium states can be simplified into the simplest form in the Fig. 7. The establishment of a balanced state is divided into three situations that will described below.

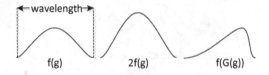

Fig. 6. Multiple manifestations of $f(g)$

Fig. 7. Equivalent model

2.3 Balance State

In order to accomplish humanized AI or advanced deep learning, we must find a theory that can describe everything but not just the data in computer science, and the balance rule proposed above can do it. The model or analysis this paper provided should be transferred into computable problems based on turing model, or they will not be accomplished based on current computer science. Utilize wave property to analyze things will generate too many waveform overlay behavior which is similar to wave interference and superposition in nature, which will make us hard to understand. So we simplify the model and use small black squares to represent the data, but we have to know that the small squares are also waves. Gravity is similar to a gradient. We can use physics rule or phenomenon to analyze AI system but not complicated math formulas to explain AI essence in a abstract way. Once we have determined the model, we can find existed mathematical tools or invent new mathematical tools to implement it.

According to the physical theorem, all physics are in a static or uniform equilibrium until the outside forces break it. In fact, human emotions and behavior are similar. As shown in Fig. 8, when the inside or outside forces come and then $AX > BY$, the lever will be tilted to the left. Human behavior and emotion are just like a system in the figure. When push (inner or outer influence) exerts pressure on the system, the system will be tilted. We can analyze them by the simplest equivalent model. Each black square may contain more black squares. These black squares are A, B, X, Y or C, which are similar to hidden layer in CNN.

Our data, emotions and behaviors are ever-changing. C corresponds to the threshold in CNN or the fulcrum in a lever system. Any data may be the fulcrum of other data. The fulcrum is also a wave with amplitude and attenuation characteristics. How can we quantify them? No matter how complex our brains are, we always follow the balance rule when dealing with problems. These balance states can be attributed to the following three conditions in Fig. 9.

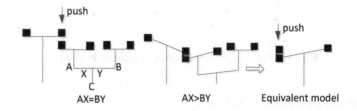

Fig. 8. Balance rule reaction process to things

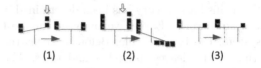

Fig. 9. Balance states

(1) Moving the fulcrum is unnecessary. In this case, in order to maintain the equivalence, it is necessary to adjust the weight of one side. This is also the most common state. The behaviors of learning, cognition, decision and emotion in our everyday life basically fall into this category. In this case, $x < X$ or $y < Y$ indicates that there is room for A or B to move so that the balance can maintain and no need to move the fulcrum.

(2) Fulcrum collapses. In this case, $A + B > C$. A+B exceeds the maximum pressure that C can withstand and the fulcrum collapses. It's like that people may get out of control when they are under tremendous pressure. The essential reason for this situation is that the growth or decline of the gradient is not infinite but limited to some value. This tells us that there are limit values for the AI system. Once the AI system wavelength determined the AI system will have a limited lifetime, and we cannot create a robot with an infinite life.

(3) Moving the fulcrum is necessary. When $x = X$ or $y = Y$, A or B needs to move to maintain balance, but there is no space left. At this point, in order to maintain a balance state, it is necessary to move the fulcrum. Mobile fulcrums are an innovative process that needs to change the state of the original memory. The fulcrum is just like a person's character. It is very difficult to change the character. Therefore, the fulcrum is rarely changed unless there is no other solution.

All our human emotions, behaviors, and actions can be determined in the above three states. In addition, a fulcrum is necessary to maintain the equilibrium. The pursuit of a happy and beautiful life is the fulcrum of human struggle. The fulcrum can promote the balance system to develop in a balanced direction. In Fig. 10, Only under the influence of gravity, these equilibrium states have a unified direction. We must find similar gradients between different feature spaces, and then we can accomplish humanized AI or immigrated learning abilities.

Fig. 10. Gravity as a fulcrum or gradient in nature

2.4   Leaves, Branches and Trees

The balance rule is similar to $1 + 1 = 2$ that constitutes the basis of mathematics and the PN junction in a chip manufacturing. The balance rule is the brick of the AI building. When this basic theory has been determined, we must begin to analyze how the AI system works. Earlier we analyzed the most basic rules that make up the AI system: the balance rule. Below we construct more abstract models based on these rules: leaves, branches and trees. These models make it easier for us to understand the AI system. But it's important to note that all models are based on the wave-particle duality and balance rule of the data collected by various kinds of sensors when we apply these models to current computer science.

All our human emotions and behaviors are like a tree. Our own human thinking and emotional experience is similar to the role of nutrition (inner influence) in the soil on the roots; our response to external events is similar to the effects of wind and rain (outer influence) on branches and leaves. Our final decision is similar to where leaves or branches are tilted. Our memories are like leaves turning into trunks. Our study is like the trunk getting thicker and longer. Our forgetfulness is like leaves and branches withering and falling. Our small movements and emotions only cause the leaves to shake, and our large emotions and actions cause the branches and leaves to shake. When leaves and roots absorb nutrients, they filter out a lot of unwanted stuff. This process is very efficient, and there is no full training of the data set as deep learning. The human brain and tree are also similar. Finding ways to solve artificial intelligence problems from nature is fundamental. The essence of artificial intelligence is the balance rule. The following analysis will be conducted.

As shown in Fig. 11, the formation of leaves, branches and trees represents the human emotion and behavior process. The analysis of artificial intelligence systems can be divided into three processes. This process of data features extraction is much like image processing such as [14–16].

(1) The formation of leaves. Leaves are flexible, easily changeable, and affected. Under the balance rule, as long as it does not exceed the bearing capacity of the fulcrum, the leaves will continue to grow. Our emotions, behaviors and movements are just like the leaves. Only when the amplitude of shaking leaves is large enough can they be alerted to the branches. It is like we only wake up when we have enough stimulus.

(2) The formation of branches. The formation of branches is similar to the leaves. Branches come from leaves, but not every leaf becomes a branch. Only those leaves that have sufficient value will become branches, otherwise they will fade. Judging whether leaves are valuable or not depends on the balance

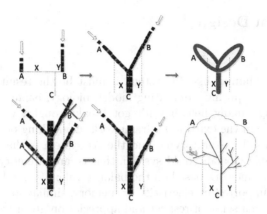

Fig. 11. The formation of leaves, branches and trees

rule. After the leaves become branches, because the fulcrum is difficult to move, the growth of the branches depends mainly on learning rather than innovation. This is like learning mathematics. It may be hard to learn at first, because it is a process of innovation and establishment of branches. It may be easier to learn later because the branches are established. At this time, learning math is a monotonous accumulation of knowledge. Growing new leaves and branches is equivalent to innovation, while the growth of leaves and branches is equivalent to learning and accumulation. Branches are the result of the accumulation of the value of the leaves.

(3) The formation of trees. The growth of the leaves provides nutrients to the branches, and the roots will also give nutrients to the branches from the soil. Under the outer and inner influences, the branches will grow thicker and longer, gradually forming trunks. As the main fulcrum of the entire tree, the trunk will support the growth of the entire tree. Humans, or accurately, the human brain, is like a tree. Our thoughts, actions and feelings are like leaves and branches. An artificial intelligence system is a tree. We analyze how trees deal with information and we know how artificial intelligence systems work.

When we think about something, we don't just rely on the information we collect. We also think of an illusion in our minds to predict or correct the consequences of our choice. In other words, we have something in our mind that guides us based on past experience. This is the dreaming tree. The formation of a dreaming tree is not only related to the individual's initial state, which is the embryo, but also the constant learning and evolution in life. The dreaming tree is the perfect state that we long for. When we fail to achieve this state in reality, we will strive to achieve it. The dreaming tree and the actual tree are another embodiment of the balance rule. The actual tree represents real feature spaces.

3   AI System Design

3.1   Embryo

To achieve a truly human-like AI system, it must be the result of the integration of quantum computing, computing model, biology, balance rule and other disciplines. Though many field haven't got breakthroughs, we can still make use of balance rule in the existing IT framework. Everything doesn't come from scratch, there must be a prototype, and the AI system is the same. We must first design a simplest balanced AI system, that is, an AI embryo. This embryo has the simplest framework based on the balance rule: life, food, sleep, etc. The life here can be supported by electricity or memory, similar to gravity proposed above. Food can be a sense of respect and appreciation given by humans to the AI system. Sleep is the process in which the AI system repairs itself and forms a dreaming tree. It is also a process of self-enjoyment and relaxation.

This embryo is a minimal software system, similar to Linux but more complicated and have stronger concurrency performance than current operating system. It has the basic abilities of collecting or processing external and internal information. According to my understanding, this embryo is the initial dreaming tree and can be formed as Fig. 12.

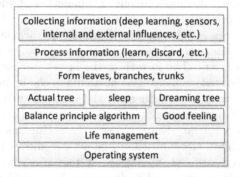

Fig. 12. AI embryo

Embryos grow like animals and plants. We must train him, give him information and nutrition, and let him learn and grow. The rule is the formation of leaves, branches and trunks mentioned above. How do we make the embryo grow to the way we want it? If there is no supervision and punishment for the growth of the embryo, the embryo will eventually become a bad person and even attack humans. This is why AI is likely to destroy humans if not trained well. For this reason, training the embryos can be shown as Fig. 13.

This process is similar to the system function in the signal and system course: In the case of a known system function, the output signal can be obtained from the input signal. For example, if the input is the first time you eat an apple, then

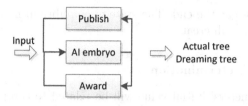

Fig. 13. The process of an embryo growing

the AI embryo will deal with this information and get a initial feeling that may be good or not. If it is a good feeling, it is equivalent to a reward, and this feeling will be preserved in the actual tree and the dreaming tree. The next time you see the apple, you will think of the good impression firstly. If it is a bad feeling, for example, the apple is bad, it is equivalent to punishment, and this feeling will be stored in the actual tree. The next time you see the apple, you may hate it, unless you break the rules to re-attempt to correct the previous impression.

3.2 AI Adult

Just as an adult's personality is difficult to change, AI adults can hardly change his nature. The main reason is that when the lever is under too much pressure, his fulcrum will be difficult to move. Leaves can float with the wind, but the trunk is difficult to move unless the external force is too much powerful. So training the embryos at the right way is very important. We must train the embryos to be what we want. When we reach his adult stage, we can use AI adults to do things like moving bricks in construction site, programming, designing art, etc.

The process of letting AI adults do things for us is very simple. We can tell him what to do by language, words, images and even personally taught. At this time, we should not regard him as a machine, but as a living life. All things are always developing towards a trend that is conducive to itself and stability. This trend may be a static equilibrium, or it may be a balanced state of uniform motion. AI adults will eventually be our ideal, because he will understand us and do what we think. These are governed by the rules of balance. What can AI adults do for us? In theory, everything, he has human behavior and emotional ability.

3.3 Death Stage

Just like people, AI Adult has a longevity and it also goes to age and death. This is also determined by the balance rule that the gradient will be zero one day. The fulcrum C is the trunk or leaves formed through learning and will attenuate with the time going or space frequency grow. The pressure on C is limited, and there will always be branches falling. We also set the upper limit pressure that this dynamic fulcrum C can withstand in the program. With the passage of time or external factors, this value will gradually become smaller and smaller, the fulcrum will collapse at the end. The state of equilibrium no longer exists, and AI Adult will die like all creatures.

3.4   Parameter Determination

Determining parameters' initial value will be related to computation problems in computer science. Tradition information collected by sensors must be transferred into uniform feature space for processing by AI system. BP algorithms [6] can also be introduced to determine gradient here. Inner or outer influence is essentially collected information. This information also needs to be converted before it can be processed by the AI system. The AI system and the real world are two reference systems that can be explained by Einstein's theory of relativity. The AI system is similar to the quantum world. Its time and space follow its own laws, and these laws also use the physical laws we discovered. It's like we see an apple. This process is equivalent to information. Our brain will associate everything with Apple, but how this information is processed by the brain will be another world. According to wave-particle duality, all objects can be described by the two states of particle and wave. After the information is received by the AI system, it will be transmitted by electronic or quantum objects, which all follow wave-particle duality. According to Einstein's theory of relativity, when the macro-world entered the microcosmic world, this wave-particle duality was reflected most vividly, and AI system was in the microscopic world. Therefore, information is both wave and particle, and they can all be described using the balance rule. For example, the number 1, it is information, its particle and wave features can be expressed as follows:

Particle feature: $1 = 1$, we can ignore x, y or fulcrum

Wave feature: $1 = X + 1 - X \Rightarrow AX = BY = B(1 - X)$ wavelength $\lambda = X + Y = 1$.

4   Experimentation and Evaluation

We can introduce ideas from current image recognition algorithms to balance rule but not current tools such as TensorFlow [18], Caffe [19], etc. In essence, the balance rule should belong to the natural sciences, but it can better explain artificial intelligence. Computer science is based on the Turing model. Applying the balance rule to computer science requires a lot of computational theory research. The mathematical model such as leaves, actual tree and dreaming tree created in this paper paves the way for these theoretical studies, and lays the foundation for further in-depth mathematical and algorithm development. The wave-particle duality of data means that each data has an attenuating change characteristic, which is different from the data stored in a conventional computer hard disk or memory. If we use the program to simulate this wave-particle duality, it will press too much pressure to CPU, cache or software performance. An AI system has countless data at all times, and there are countless waveform superpositions and balances. It is difficult for traditional computers and Turing models to handle this behavior. But it does not mean that the theory proposed in this paper is ready for the future but not current, and it only means that it is difficult to verify based on current computer, mathematics or programming techniques. Therefore, unlike traditional machine learning algorithms, we need to find the phenomenon from nature to verify the theory of this article proposed, and then think about how to use current science and technology to achieve this natural phenomenon, and then testify and utilize the theory.

Time and spatial frequencies affect the wave-particle duality and balance rule, and this effect is reflected in the gradient. When the gradient is constant, it indicates that it is in a relatively balanced state; when the gradient changes, it indicates that the wave-particle duality is transforming. We can do two experiments to verify this theoretical speculation, and then illustrate that abstract things have wave-particle duality and the balance rule plays a fundamental role. The wave-particle duality of the data corresponds to the time domain and the frequency domain in the Fourier transform.

4.1 Large Frequencies Can Generate Wave Property

Spatial frequency refers to how often things happen. We first observe the wave property from the spatial frequency, that is, the gradient g. We can observe this gradient from anything, so we chose the easiest way: accumulate small black blocks. As shown in Fig. 14, assuming a wooden board, we accumulate small black blocks that equivalent to data at a constant rate, and the total black block height has an angle with the board, which is similar to the gradient g. We observe the relationship between g and frequency.

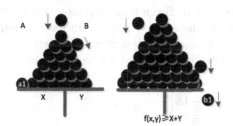

Fig. 14. Accumulating small black blocks to testify wave property

At the beginning, as the black block increased, g gradually increased, but the rate of increase became slower and slower; when all black blocks accumulated to a certain height, the black block gravity and friction among black blocks reached equilibrium. At this time, it was impossible to add black blocks upwards and the gradient g reached the maximum. The quantitative change caused the qualitative change, and the process of the quantitative change was equivalent to the process of wave formation. When the qualitative change was reached, all the black blocks were equivalent to the particle state. The measured data was shown in Fig. 15.

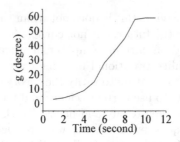

Fig. 15. g varies with black block numbers

We didn't take the black squares, so we only got half of the wave map. It can be observed from the figure that, limited by the length of the board, that is, the wavelength, the black square will be balanced at an angle under the gradient of gravity. "Accumulating black squares on a wooden board" is equivalent to one thing, and we have observed from this matter that the gradient satisfies a similar wave function. The number of squares is equivalent to the spatial frequency.

4.2   Large Time Span Can Generate Wave Property

A sufficient time span can also make us observe the wave properties of things. When a thing does not happen frequently enough, it does not mean that its wave properties can not be observed, but it takes time. We explain the wave property from the thing "listening to the experience of songs". Suppose we first heard a nice song, we like it very much, so this is a very good experience, we record the degree of experience as happiness. As time goes on, we will always have a tired day and don't want to hear it. But a long time later, I will listen it again, and it will bring me a happy feeling again. Each person has a different test curve, but the results are almost the same. My test curve is shown in Fig. 16. The ordinate value 0 is completely unsatisfactory and 1 is very satisfied.

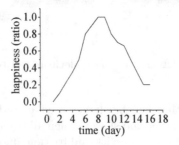

Fig. 16. Time span influence the happiness of listening to songs

As time goes by, everything will never remain their original state. These two experiments are simple, but you can see the abstract thing's wave and particle properties. The wave-particle duality of data is the theoretical basis of this paper. The balance rule is the root cause of the wave-particle duality. We don't even need to use computer programs to validate our theory, because the theory for AI should be applicable to everything.

5 Related Work

Algorithms such as reinforcement learning [28] are not perfect enough. Clustering algorithm like [29] is not systematic enough. Traditional machine learning algorithms lacks a basic computational learning theory that can explain all problems. PAC theory like [30] is difficult to explain the fuzzy cognitive problems similar to human brain. Deep learning relies on large data sets and specific scenarios, and cannot adapt to complex and different things. We should change the traditional concept and let the data itself have wave attenuation characteristics so that we can make a small amount of data generate feature spaces. At the same time, we should find a theory to explain or design a general AI system. The AI system should be able to maintain a large amount of feature spaces to survive and adapt to the uncertainty of the outside world. Just as babies haven't grown up, but have the most basic features to keep survived, we should let the AI system have the simplest feature spaces. The formation of these feature spaces is inseparable from the wave-particle duality and balance rule. Leaves, branches, and trees are equivalent to different learners and work together to accomplish one thing like AdaBoost [31], Random Forest [32].

6 Conclusion and Future Work

Traditional machine learning algorithms lack a basic theory that can act on everything like human. We need to understand how everything works with others from the perspective of nature or the human brain. Starting from the wave-particle duality of matter, this paper explained the wave-particle duality of the data and further reveals the supporting role of the balance rule. Balance rule can explain everything in the world and is a natural phenomenon that cannot be verified by current computer science, but we can analyze its rationality from other phenomena. This paper provides a new foundation for the development of deep learning or artificial intelligence.

Current computational theories are difficult to solve the problem of ambiguity that can be described by balance rule. The wave-particle duality of data means that all feature spaces can vary like a attenuated sine wave or Gauss function on their own. Computer science simulates this phenomenon should require more innovation in mathematics. The future work is to combine balance rule and wave-particle duality with current deep learning so that current deep learning can be applied to less data and more scenarios, thus further validating the theory this paper proposed.

References

1. Abelson, H., Sussman, G.J., Sussman, J.: Structure and Interpretation of Computer Programs. MIT Press, Cambridge (1985)
2. Baumgartner, R., Gottlob, G., Flesca, S.: Visual information extraction with Lixto. In: Proceedings of the 27th International Conference on Very Large Databases, pp. 119–128. Morgan Kaufmann, Rome (2001)
3. Brachman, R.J., Schmolze, J.G.: An overview of the KL-ONE knowledge representation system. Cogn. Sci. **9**(2), 171–216 (1985)
4. Hock, M., Bless, R., Zitterbart, M.: IEEE International Conference on Network Protocols, pp. 1–10 (2017)
5. McCulloch, W.S., Pitts, W.: A logical calculus of the ideas immanent in nervous activity. Bull. Math. Biophys. **5**(4), 115–133 (1943)
6. Pineda, F.J.: Generalization of back-propagation to recurrent neural networks. Phys. Rev. Lett. **59**(19), 2229 (1987)
7. Hornik, K., Stinchcombe, M., White, H.: Multilayer feedforward networks are universal approximators. Neural Netw. **2**(5), 359–366 (1989)
8. Broomhead, D.S., Lowe, D.: Multivariate functional interpolation and adaptive network Complex system (1988)
9. Carpenter, G.A., Grossberg, S.: A massively parallel architecture for a self-organizing neural pattern recognition machine. Comput. Vis. Graph. Image Process. **37**(1), 54–115 (1987)
10. Kohonen, T.: Self-organized formation of topologically correct feature maps. Biol. Cybern. **43**(1), 59–69 (1982)
11. Fahlman, S.E., Lebiere, C.: The cascade-correlation learning architecture. In: Advances in Neural Information Processing Systems, pp. 524–532 (1999)
12. Elman, J.L.: Finding structure in time. Cogn. Sci. **14**(2), 179–211 (1990)
13. Ackley, D.H., Hinton, G.E., Sejnowski, T.J.: A learning algorithm for Boltzmann machines. Comput. Vis. **9**(1), 147–169 (1985)
14. Krizhevsky, A., Sutskever, I., Hinton, G.E.: ImageNet classification with deep convolutional neural networks. In: Advances in Neural Information Processing Systems, pp. 1097–1105 (2012)
15. Szegedy, C., et al.: Going deeper with convolutions. In: Proceedings of the IEEE Conference on Computer Vision and Pattern Recognition, pp. 1–9 (2015)
16. He, K., Zhang, X., Ren, S., Sun, J.: Deep residual learning for image recognition. In: Proceedings of the IEEE Conference on Computer Vision and Pattern Recognition, pp. 770–778 (2016)
17. LeCun, Y., Bengio, Y., Hinton, G.: Deep learning. Nature **521**(7553), 436 (2015)
18. Abadi, P., et al.: TensorFlow: a system for large-scale machine learning, pp. 265–283 (2016)
19. Jia, Y., et al.: Caffe: convolutional architecture for fast feature embedding. In: Proceedings of the 22nd ACM International Conference on Multimedia, pp. 675–678 (2014)
20. Radford, A., Metz, L., Chintala, S.: Unsupervised representation learning with deep convolutional generative adversarial networks. arXiv preprint arXiv:1511.06434 (2015)
21. LeCun, Y., Bengio, Y., et al.: Caffe: convolutional networks for images, speech, and time series. Handb. Brain Theory Neural Netw. **3361**(10), 1995 (1995)
22. Hinton, G.E., Osindero, S., Teh, Y.-W.: A fast learning algorithm for deep belief nets. Neural Comput. **18**(7), 1527–1554 (2006)

23. LeCun, Y., Bottou, L., Bengio, Y., Haffner, P., et al.: Gradient-based learning applied to document recognition. Proc. IEEE **86**(11), 2278–2324 (1998)
24. Dietterich, T.G., Bakiri, G.: Solving multiclass learning problems via error-correcting output codes. J. Artif. Intell. Res. **2**, 263–286 (1994)
25. Cortes, C., Vapnik, V.: Support-vector networks. Mach. Learn. **20**(3), 273–297 (1995)
26. Quinlan, J.R.: Induction of decision trees. Mach. Learn. **1**(1), 81–106 (1986)
27. Domingos, P., Pazzani, M.: On the optimality of the simple Bayesian classifier under zero-one loss. Mach. Learn. **29**(2), 103–130 (1997)
28. Mnih, V., et al.: Human-level control through deep reinforcement learning. Nature **518**(7540), 529 (2015)
29. Jain, A.K.: 50 years beyond K-means. Pattern Recogn. Lett. **31**(8), 651–666 (2010)
30. Valiant, L.G.: A theory of the learnable. In: Proceedings of the Sixteenth Annual ACM Symposium on Theory of Computing, pp. 436–445 (1984)
31. Freund, Y., Schapire, R.E.: A decision-theoretic generalization of on-line learning and an application to boosting. J. Comput. Syst. Sci. **55**(1), 119–139 (1997)
32. Breiman, L.: Random forests. Mach. Learn. **45**(1), 5–32 (2001)

Author Index

Printed in the United States
By Bookmasters